Early Native Americans

World Anthropology

General Editor

SOL TAX

Patrons

CLAUDE LÉVI-STRAUSS
MARGARET MEAD†
LAILA SHUKRY EL HAMAMSY
M. N. SRINIVAS

MOUTON PUBLISHERS · THE HAGUE · PARIS · NEW YORK

Early Native Americans

Prehistoric Demography, Economy, and Technology

Edited by

DAVID L. BROWMAN

MOUTON PUBLISHERS · THE HAGUE · PARIS · NEW YORK

General Editor's Preface

Fossil evidence now permits anthropologists to trace the evolutionary history of the genus *Homo* through some three million years. Almost all of it took place on the Eurasian-African land mass. Not until modern man appeared in relatively recent times is there any evidence of the peopling of North America. We picture small groups of *Homo sapiens* as finally discovering America across the narrow Northeast passage and then quickly opening the New World for exploration and settlement. In the present volume the editor brilliantly weaves together current knowledge about these prehistoric peoples; in different modes their descendants have always remembered and honored them as sacred first ancestors. Their later accomplishments are described in four other volumes by the same editor, all from papers presented to an unusual world Congress.

Like most contemporary sciences, anthropology is a product of the European tradition. Some argue that it is a product of colonialism with one small and self-interested part of the species dominating the study of the whole. If we are to understand the species, our science needs substantial input from scholars who represent a variety of the world's cultures. It was a deliberate purpose of the IXth International Congress of Anthropological and Ethnological Sciences to provide impetus in this direction. The *World Anthropology* volumes, therefore, offer a first glimpse of a human science in which members from all societies have played an active role. Each of the books is designed to be self-contained; each is an attempt to update its particular sector of scientific knowledge and is written by specialists from all parts of the world. Each volume should be read and reviewed individually as a separate volume on its own given subject. The set as a whole will indicate what changes are in store for anthropology as scholars from the developing countries join in studying the species of which we are all a part.

The IXth Congress was planned from the beginning not only to include as many of the scholars from every part of the world as possible, but also with a view toward the eventual publication of the papers in high-quality volumes. At previous Congresses scholars were invited to bring papers which were then read out loud. They were necessarily limited in length; many were only summarized; there was little time for discussion; and the sparse discussion could only be in one language. The IXth Congress was an experiment aimed at changing this. Papers were written with the intention of exchanging them before the Congress, particularly in extensive pre-Congress sessions; they were not intended to be read aloud at the Congress, that time being devoted to discussions — discussions which were simultaneously and professionally translated into five languages. The method for eliciting the papers was structured to make as representative a sample as was allowable when scholarly creativity — hence self-selection — was critically important. Scholars were asked both to propose papers of their own and to suggest topics for sessions of the Congress which they might edit into volumes. All were then informed of the suggestions and encouraged to rethink their own papers and the topics. The process, therefore, was a continuous one of feedback and exchange and it has continued to be so even after the Congress. The some two thousand papers comprising *World Anthropology* certainly then offer a substantial sample of world anthropology. It has been said that anthropology is at a turning point; if this is so, these volumes will be the historical direction-markers.

As might have been foreseen in the first post-colonial generation, the large majority of the Congress papers (82 percent) are the work of scholars identified with the industrialized world which fathered our traditional discipline and the institution of the Congress itself: Eastern Europe (15 percent); Western Europe (16 percent); North America (47 percent); Japan, South Africa, Australia, and New Zealand (4 percent). Only 18 percent of the papers are from developing areas: Africa (4 percent); Asia-Oceania (9 percent); Latin America (5 percent). Aside from the substantial representation from the U.S.S.R. and the nations of Eastern Europe, a significant difference between this corpus of written material and that of other Congresses is the addition of the large proportion of contributions from Africa, Asia, and Latin America. "Only 18 percent" is two to four times as great a proportion as that of other Congresses; moreover, 18 percent of 2,000 papers is 360 papers, 10 times the number of "Third World" papers presented at previous Congresses. In fact, these 360 papers are more than the total of *all* papers published after the last International Congress of Anthropological and Ethnological Sciences which was held in the United States (Philadelphia, 1956).

The significance of the increase is not simply quantitative. The input of scholars from areas which have until recently been no more than subject matter for anthropology represents both feedback and also long-awaited theoretical contributions from the perspectives of very different cultural, social, and historical traditions. Many who attended the IXth Congress were convinced that anthropology would not be the same in the future. The fact that the Xth Congress (India, 1978) was our first in the "Third World" may be symbolic of the change. Meanwhile, sober consideration of the present set of books will show how much, and just where and how, our discipline is being revolutionized.

Readers of this volume will be especially interested in others in the series which deal with native American peoples from early times to the present. Volumes dealing with other continents and peoples provide comparisons and contrasts, and still others present problems of theory and of ethics encountered in their study.

Chicago, Illinois   SOL TAX
September 29, 1979

Preface

The concept of this volume was to transcend traditionally preconceived boundaries thought appropriate for investigation, and to attempt to breed hybrid vigor by mixing a variety of approaches and directions of research together, drawing from regional areas circumscribing the Pacific. As the Congress drew near, it became apparent that the directions being taken in a number of different sessions were beginning to identify the same common theme crosscutting the field. The sessions organized by Dr. William Fitzhugh, Dr. George Quimby and Dr. Richard Casteel, Dr. William Irving, Dr. Richard Morlan, and Dr. Edward Rogers became increasingly intertwined with the theme of this volume. The papers in this volume thus represent not the original formulation of any one of us, but rather the result of redividing and reordering the intellectual contributions. Thus most of the papers on circumpolar adaptation and maritime adaptations were fissioned off and will be found in the volume of Fitzhugh and that of Quimby and Casteel.

I would like to thank Dr. Sol Tax, president of the Congress, and Ms. Karen Tkach, Mouton Publishers editor, for helping to sort this problem out, and for making this volume possible. I would also like to thank Dr. James Adovasio, who on short notice picked up and served as cochairman of part of the sessions, in what was certainly a very trying and confusing situation.

DAVID L. BROWMAN

Table of Contents

SECTION ONE

Pleistocene Man in North America

Introduction

The last decade has seen a three- or four-fold increase in the documented length of time for man on the American continents, from an estimate of only some 10,000 years a decade ago, to estimates of 30,000 to 40,000 years today. Some of the following papers strive to push that time line back to at least 70,000 to 100,000 years ago. Ten years ago, Alex Krieger's paper (1964) on pre-projectile-point cultures in the New World stirred great controversy; now it is well accepted that the earliest groups in the New World were not fabricating stone projectile points. Data summarized by Bryan (1969) and Shutler (1971) indicate that man was in the New World considerably earlier than 10,000 years ago. Recent finds, such as the dates on human occupations in the Yukon of more than 27,000 years ago (Irving and Harington 1973), and the dates on materials in Mexico (Irwin-Williams 1978) and Peru (MacNeish 1971) of approximately 20,000 to 25,000 years ago, have suggested that we must look for the first entry of man into the New World at some time earlier than 25,000 to 30,000 years ago to allow for adequate time to provide for man's dispersal into Mesoamerica and South America.

The information summarized by the articles of Simpson, Stagg *et al.*, Carter, and Dragoo is bound to receive widely divergent reactions — from gleeful acceptance to outright rejection. Simpson's update on the Calico Mountains site contains some new information to bolster the claims made for evidence of human occupation, dated at either 70,000 years or 200,000 years or more, depending on the geological interpretation. Dr. Simpson now believes that more than 600 artifacts have been recovered, consisting of bifacially flaked hand axes, chopping tools, various types of scrapers, anvil stones, and hammerstones. Though Dr. Simpson and her colleagues believe these to be artifacts, the majority of the archaeological community appears to concur with Haynes's review (1973) of the site. Haynes's position is that since the majority of materials are jaspers and chalcedonies naturally occurring in the deposits, the "artifacts" are in fact geofacts. To counter these objections, Dr. Simpson notes that (1) seven of the artifacts are made of stone not naturally occurring in the deposits; (2) one cluster of 1,100 pieces of debitage indicates that the locale is indeed a quarry site; and (3) there is evidence for circles of rocks which may be postholes and fire-hearths. Analysis of the "artifacts" by the methods utilized by Reeves in his paper in this section still needs to be done. Until these more rigorous technical studies are made, it will be impossible to assess the meaning of the Calico Mountains site.

The data discussed by Dragoo and by Stagg, Vernon, and Raemsch also detail information concerning artifact complexes of ages assumed to be greater than 50,000 years. Dragoo compares a number of pebble-tool complexes from the Americas and argues that they are basically similar to Old World pebble-tool complexes some 40,000 to 50,000 years ago. Dragoo's argument is well based on actual complexes, and though one might quibble with the reputed age of some of the assemblages, he has isolated an important component of the lithic technology of late Pleistocene man in North America. The discussion of the complexes in New York State by Stagg, Vernon, and Raemsch makes use of typological comparisons to Europe and utilize such terminology as "Levallois" and "Acheulean" (with inadequate justification) in guessing a date of approximately 70,000 years for the artifacts under discussion. Substantially more work must be done here before we can accept the date of 70,000 years posited for these artifacts.

Carter suggests a major modification in our extant theories concerning the origins of vegetal-food-processing industries, in proposing that the mano and metate may have an antiquity of 80,000 to 100,000 years in North America. Since most cultural reconstructions suggest that manos and metates are technological developments dating to a shift in emphasis from earlier hunting economies to more generalized gathering economies in the last 5,000 to 10,000 years, such a proposition would require a major shift in our views of the lifeways of the earliest inhabitants of the New World. Carter points to artifacts which he views as possible grinding implements at Crown Point near San Diego and also in the Santa Barbara area of California with a possible age of 80,000 years. Though this particular hypothesis requires difficult modification of other evidence, the recent dates by Bada, Schroeder, and Carter (1974), suggesting an antiquity of at least 50,000 years for man in California, support its serious review.

The data in the papers by Reeves and Johnson are much more rigorously presented, and hypotheses much more cautiously conceived; these are the kinds of papers which should serve as guides for future research. Reeves's investigation of the beds of Medicine Hat, Alberta, is as important as the Calico Mountains site. Here Churcher and Stalker earlier reported finds of numerous poorly worked and flaked stones, which they believed to be contemporaneous with the Taber Child, dated geologically to a bed ranging in age from 35,000 to 60,000 years ago. The situation appears to be nearly identical to that of the Calico Mountains site. Reeves's investigation of the cherts suggests that they are most likely geofacts or pseudotools: that is, they are naturally pressure-flaked cherts, the flaking caused by natural processes instead of man — natural processes such as thermofracture and fracture due to compressional and rotational forces operative in the colluvium and tills. Medicine Hat is thus not the possible early-man site it had been hoped it would be, and, because the geological situation is so similar to that of the Calico Mountains till, it points to the desperate need for a similar analysis of the Calico Mountains materials.

The study of California as a possible refuge area during the late Pleistocene is the type of study needed in archaeology to test the validity of our environmental hypotheses. Johnson's reconstruction of the California region as an area with Mediterranean-like climate even during full glacial conditions is particularly applicable for suggesting reasons for the numbers of early finds in the California coastal region. His new evidence strengthens the theory that in the California region, at least, man has been the principal agent responsible for the extinction of the Rancholabrean fauna between 20,000 and 12,000 B.C., and indirectly strengthens the applicability of the hypothesis to the Americas in general.

REFERENCES

BADA, J. L., R. A. SCHROEDER, G. F. CARTER
    1974   New evidence for the antiquity of man in North America deduced from aspartic acid racemization. *Science* 184 (4,138):791–793.

BRYAN, A. L.
    1969   Early man in America and the late Pleistocene chronology of western Canada and Alaska. *Current Anthropology* 10 (4):339–365.

HAYNES, V.
    1973   The Calico site: artifacts or geofacts. *Science* 181 (4,097):305–310.

IRVING, W. N., C. R. HARINGTON
    1973   Upper Pleistocene radiocarbon-dated artifacts from the northern Yukon. *Science* 179 (4,071):335–340.

IRWIN-WILLIAMS, C.
    1978   "Summary of archaeological evidence from the Valsequillo region, Puebla, Mexico," in *Cultural continuity in Mesoamerica.* Edited by D. L. Browman, 7–22. The Hague: Mouton.

KRIEGER, A. D.
    1964   "Early man in the New World," in *Prehistoric man in the New World.* Edited by J. D. Jennings and E. Norbeck, 23–81. Chicago: University of Chicago Press.

MacNEISH, R. S.
   1971   Early man in the Andes. *Scientific American* 224 (4):36–46.
SHUTLER, JR., R., *editor*
   1971   Papers from a symposium on Early Man in North America, New Developments: 1960–1970. *Arctic Anthropology* 8 (2):1–91.

The Calico Mountains Site: Pleistocene Archaeology in the Mojave Desert, California

RUTH DEE SIMPSON

The Calico Mountains Archaeological Project, whose site is shown in Map 1, is an outgrowth of an archaeological survey which encompassed the basin of Pleistocene Lake Manix. That survey began in 1954, under the auspices of the San Bernardino County Museum, as the result of sites reported to the museum and because of the location of the lake basin at the southern end of the Great Basin, close to the Transverse Range.

Manix Basin was supplied with water primarily by the Mojave River, which carried a considerable volume of water from the Transverse Range. There were several fillings of Lake Manix. Ultimately the lake was destroyed by the downcutting of Afton Canyon at the east end of the basin. Subsequently, the Mojave River flowed eastward into Lake Mojave and then northward into Lake Manly (Death Valley), where its waters mingled with those from Owens Valley, Panamint Valley, etc. During the late Pleistocene, at least, Death Valley was a basin of internal drainage.

The last major filling of Lake Manix left beaches and other shore features which are startlingly fresh. Tufa from this 1,780-foot shoreline has been assigned a C-14 date of 19,750 ± 250 years B.P. There are higher, older shore features representing earlier pluvial periods of the Wisconsin, or last glacial, period.

There were no glaciers in the Lake Manix region, but glacial advances farther north and in the mountains were reflected by pluvial periods in the Mojave Desert of today, and elsewhere in the American deserts.

The archaeological survey of Lake Manix Basin, which began in 1954, started with the present course of the Mojave River and the playas of ephemeral lakes, which even today are occasionally covered with shallow water as the result of heavy rains and runoff. Between 1954 and 1963, more than 120 surface sites were recorded. These included recent sites

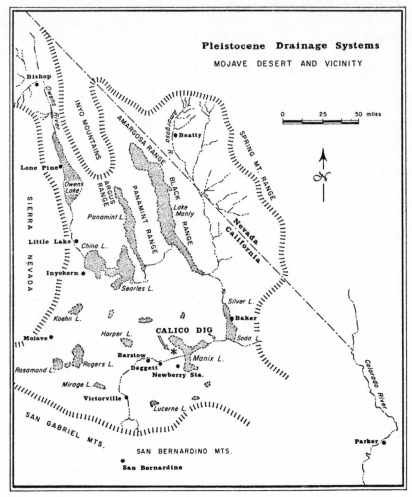

Map. 1.   Site of the Calico Mountains Archaeological Project

along the river, in river-associated dunes and around the playas; slightly older Amargosa (desert basketmaker) material on beaches around the playas; western Paleo-Indian material on the recessive shorelines of Lake Manix below the 1,780-foot level; and the markedly different artifactual material found on sites above that shoreline. No projectile points were part of this latter assemblage. It consisted of choppers and chopping tools, hand-ax-like implements, large scrapers, etc.

So different was this material that it was shown to scientists from various countries. In 1958, Dr. L. S. B. Leakey saw a sample of the specimens; in 1963 he visited the area and saw specimens *in situ* in a commercial excavation of secondary deposited gravels. In an adjacent area, a bulldozer cut showed a primary deposit with potential geological and archaeological significance. This was selected as the location for a test excavation. Subsequently, this first pit became known as Master Pit I, Calico Mountains Archaeological Project, shown in Plate 1.

Plate 1. San Bernardino County Museum site 1500A, the Calico Mountains archaeological site. Master Pits I and II (Master Pit I, beneath roof, 25 × 25 feet) with entrance trenches; piles of rocks from the pits; screening areas in foreground; Calico Mountains in background

The area selected for the Calico Mountains excavation is on a large alluvial fan, shown in Plate 2, which formed below the mouth of Mule Canyon at the east end of the Calico Mountains. This alluvial fan is known as the Yermo Formation. It is of Pleistocene age. As yet, the precise age has not been determined. This is the major problem still facing those concerned with the Calico Project.

The Yermo Formation consists of varied material washed down from the Calico Mountains, including andesite, dacite, volcanic porphyries, and tuffs of Miocene age. Chalcedony deposits are exposed in Mule Canyon in Miocene lake beds. These lake beds and volcanics are known as the Barstow Formation. The chalcedony formed through silicification within the Miocene lake beds or as silica gel in the lake. Uplift and distortion of the beds resulted in fracturing of the rocks. The material was ultimately carried out on the fan and deposited.

Today the fan is separated from the Calico Mountains as the result of

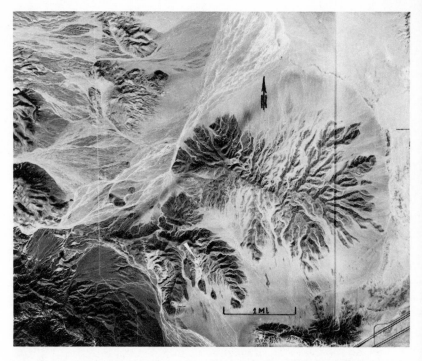

Plate 2.   Aerial photograph of the Calico Mountains archaeological site (arrow) and the associated Pleistocene alluvial fan, which built eastward out of Mule Canyon (upper left)

faulting. This faulting changed the drainage pattern, causing material transported out of Mule Canyon to be washed down arroyos to the north and south. The alluvial fan is currently affected only by erosion, which has been active over a long period. Aerial views reveal an intricate erosional dissection pattern. Four prominent erosional river terraces have developed on the fan during this period.

The project geologist, Dr. Thomas Clements, University of Southern California (retired), assigns these terraces and the erosion they represent to the Wisconsin glacial period and to the subsequent Little Pluvial and related period of mountain glaciation (Hilgard). He therefore suggests that the third (Sangamon) interglacial was the time of the formation of the Yermo alluvial fan. This would imply an age of circa 70,000 years for the fan.

That portion of the alluvial fan which Dr. Leakey selected for the test excavation lies in the north half of Section 22, Township 10 North, Range 2 East, at an elevation of 2,200 feet. The land is owned by the federal government. Excavation was undertaken by the San Bernardino County Museum under permit from the Department of the Interior. Museum Director Dr. Gerald A. Smith is the project administrator; Dr. Clements is the project geologist; as county archaeologist, I am the project archaeologist.

Excavation of Master Pit I, shown in Plate 3, began in November, 1964, with funding from the National Geographic Society. Excavation continued each winter with a crew of ten to fifteen, funded by various institutions, until 1970, when lack of funds caused work to be suspended except for weekend volunteer assistance. During the seven seasons, all excavation was done with awls, dental picks, and other small tools. In the deep levels, in which the fanglomerate is exceedingly compact, a hammer and quarter-inch chisel were also used. The deposit has been and is being

Plate 3.   Master Pit I: excavation and recording in progress. Each worker is assigned to a 5 × 5 foot section. Those in lower left triangulate with tape and line level. Note column in upper right. View is from rim of pit, northwest corner

removed in three-inch levels except in cases in which soil changes require smaller increments. Each increment is literally picked apart. All work is done under tight controls and with close supervision. In this manner, two master pits, five trenches, and twenty-two test pits have been dug.

Thus far, only the two master pits, their entrance trenches, and an adjacent trench have yielded specimens which we believe are man-made artifacts. All rock material removed from the pits is recorded for our statistical and interpretive programs. The unmodified material is stockpiled. All flakes, workshop material, and artifacts are triangulated, plotted, and photographed. All specimens which I believe to be especially significant are left in place to be noted, before removal, by other scientists. Some of these specimens were retained in place for Dr. Leakey.

From the artifacts Dr. Leakey had seen in Master Pits I and II or in the field laboratory, he selected more than 600 which he believed to be definitely man-made. Of these he commented, "The artifacts which have come out of these two pits completely satisfy me that we have at Calico a site with clear evidence that toolmaking man was here over 50,000 years ago."

It is anticipated that in the Museum laboratory, scientists will once more examine the entire collection of modified material retained from the master pits and trenches. This should increase markedly the prime artifact assemblage.

In addition to the 600 most significant lithic specimens, there are other important factors which must be considered. One of these is a series of fragmentary bits of mammoth or mastodon tusk. These tusk fragments were recovered at a depth of thirteen feet in Master Pit I. C-14 tests indicate that this material is too old to date by this method (i.e., more than 45,000 years). A semicircle of rocks in Master Pit II at a depth of twenty-three feet (279 inches) is a vitally important factor, on which I shall comment further.

The fanglomerate matrix in which the specimens are found is varied structurally and petrologically. There are boulder beds, sand lenses, fine silts, and coarse grits. Stratigraphically, the deposits vary from well-sorted to unsorted. There are evidences of mud flows, slow-moving water, and stronger currents. In short, the deposits show the characteristics of a typical alluvial fan.

Preliminary analysis indicates that most specimens are recovered from the contact between the strata — on or close to what were old fan surfaces as the fan was building.

Most of the lithic specimens, both tools and workshop materials, recovered from the excavations were fashioned from chalcedony. More than 80 percent of the specimens already analyzed and accepted are of this material. Virtually all of the other 20 percent are of jasper, which also outcrops in Mule Canyon. However, there are two flakes which have been classified as being of exotic moss agate and three as being of chalcedony not from Mule Canyon exposures, and five quartz crystals which do not have a known local origin. Of the five crystals, one is smoky; three are chipped. The nearest probable origin known is a large pegmatite dike three miles north of the fan and at a lower elevation.

Where the chalcedony outcrops in Mule Canyon it is usually rather brittle and would not lend itself to toolmaking. The movement of this material down the fan broke the larger masses. Blocks of stronger, denser chalcedony were sorted by breakage and movement, with separation occurring along irregular cleavage planes and starch fractures. This fresh, hard material, deposited on the fan, was the source of workshop material for man. Throughout the building period of the fan, there would have been available a supply of fine-grained siliceous material for use in making tools.

Excavation in the various pits and trenches has yielded quantities of chalcedony cobbles and boulders. For example, from Control Pit I (15 × 15 feet), 11,961 chalcedony cobbles and boulders were recorded in the first twenty-eight feet of excavation. In all probability, the presence of this high-quality siliceous material would have been the reason for man's occupation of the locality.

While boulders and cobbles of fine-grained siliceous material and volcanics are recovered throughout the fan deposits, those specimens which have been classified as man-made tools and workshop materials are not evenly distributed. They occur in concentrations of varying intensity. Numerous clusters of flakes and chips have been exposed. These may range in number from ten or twelve to 300 or 500. The largest cluster of such flakes and chips was in an area thirty by eighteen inches and only two inches thick. This cluster encompassed 1,100 pieces of debitage.

Tools — some unfinished, some complete, and some broken — are also unevenly distributed. Distribution charts depicting the position of recorded tools and technically significant flakes exhibit, in addition to several minor peaks and valleys, two major peaks.

These peaks are located six inches and nine inches below the Old Fan surface (this designation refers to the level at which steeply sloping overburden, deposited subsequently on the eroded fanglomerate, is in contact with the underlying, undisturbed, uneroded fanglomerate).

In Master Pit I, only a well-developed A-B-C soil profile averaging twenty-four inches in thickness lies above the Old Fan surface. The overburden mentioned above apparently has been obliterated by erosion over this section of the fan. In contrast, the overburden is twelve feet thick at the west (up-fan) wall of Master Pit II. Thus, the depth of the recovery position on an object from the datum point in Master Pit II might be 300 inches, yet agree rather closely with an object recovered at 156 inches in Master Pit I. For this reason, all final measurements and placement on the distribution charts are from the uniformly positioned Old Fan surface as well as from the datum point.

There is no continuum of archaeological material joining the surface artifact assemblage and that within the fanglomerate. Excavation had reached a depth of forty-five inches in Master Pit I before a significant specimen was recorded.

Archaeological evidence recovered from the excavation may be listed in the following categories:

1. lithic tools, fragmentary and complete;
2. workshop material including flakes, rejects, and markedly modified amorphous objects;
3. technically significant workshop material including flakes with bulb scars, concavo-convex flakes, soft-hammer flakes, flakes with partially or totally obliterated bulbs, flakes and cores with prepared platforms, etc.;
4. features such as apparently artificial arrangements of rocks.

Since analysis of the archaeological material is still in progress, a final typological classification has not yet been made. However, the preliminary analyses show both unifacially and bifacially flaked specimens. There are tools fashioned from cores, one of which is shown in Plate 4, and tools fashioned from flakes. There are numerous specimens with only edge retouch. Thus far, it appears that all flaking was done by percussion.

Complete and broken tools number about 150. This group of prime artifacts includes bifacially flaked hand axes, one of which is shown in Plate 5; chopping and cutting tools, one of which is shown in Plate 6;

Plate 4.   A specimen classified as a core, length 18 cm. (7.2 inches), recovered at a depth of 207 inches

Plate 5.   A specimen classified as a hand ax, length 12.5 cm. (4.9 inches), recovered at a depth of 159 inches

Plate 6.   A specimen classified as a cutting and chopping tool, length 16 cm. (6.25 inches), recovered at a depth of 116 inches

unifacially flaked choppers and scrapers; anvil stones; and hammerstones. By far the largest group is those specimens classified as scrapers. There are multiple scrapers, one of which is shown in Plate 7; convex-edged sidescrapers, hollow scrapers, notched scrapers, and pointed scrapers.

Plate 7.   A specimen classified as a multiple scraper (on a flake with prepared platform), length 10.5 cm., recovered at a depth of 121 inches

Not only are the prime tools fashioned to set and regular patterns, they also have such significant characteristics as prepared platforms, alternate flaking, cones of percussion, wide diffused bulbs, and more than one kind of percussion flaking apparent on a single specimen. Some of the flake tools were developed on side-struck or corner-struck flakes.

All of the prime specimens and a large percentage of the workshop materials are made from good-quality chalcedony and jasper. This is also true of most of the definitive flakes. When one considers the large quantity of poor-grade, weathered chalcedony available on the various fan surfaces as the fan was building, one becomes aware of the high degree of selectivity demonstrated by the persons making the tools and flakes, a selectivity not readily attributable to natural agencies.

Hand axes occur in limited numbers but are one of the most significant tool groups. They are thick-butted, with stout, finely chipped edges and glossy abraded surfaces. The flaking, shape, and thick butt sharply separate these hand axes from the ovate bifaces recovered from sites on the present fan surface.

Technologically, the flakes are the category of greatest significance. The category includes both debitage and tools. It is estimated that at least 30 percent of the flakes were side- or corner-struck. The flakes vary from thin to thick and from small to large; some have very acute edges; many are wedge-shaped. While the majority of flakes have plane platforms, a noteworthy series is characterized by simple platforms displaying some preparation, and about 12 percent have complex platforms. There is an extensive series of concavo-convex or double flakes which bear both a negative and positive bulb. I have made reference to the presence of bulb scars on a sizable series of flakes and to the presence of soft-hammer flakes. There is also a series of hinged flakes. Large bulbs are very characteristic.

Hammerstones are rare — less than a dozen have been recorded thus far — but they are an important aspect of the assemblage. They tend to be round in outline but are naturally faceted. They show intensive use; their shape and battered surfaces resulted from this use.

The entrance trench to Master Pit II is 100 feet long by 5 feet wide. At a depth of 272 to 280 inches below datum, a series of nine rock features was exposed. Two of these, Features 3 and 9, consist of circles of small rocks. The circles average one foot in diameter. In Feature 3, there are three contiguous circles, the central circle backed by upright cobbles. In Feature 9, there are two circles separated by four inches of fine sand. Most of the rocks in all five circles are small, averaging four or five inches in length. The average number of rocks per circle is nine. Feature 1 is shown in Plate 8.

In and around these circles there are no other rocks. This is in marked contrast to the massed surrounding rocks. The other possible features in the trench are not as clearly defined. They consist of larger cobbles and are suggestive of storage areas, fire circles, etc., extending into the north wall of the trench. Their true character has not been determined.

Isolated in the inner section of the trench, but at the same depth below datum (279 inches), is a small circle surrounded by cobbles. It has been suggested that all these small circles surrounded by rocks may have been postholes and that the cluster of features may imply a temporary campsite.

The true significance of the possible rock features in the trench remains to be determined. This would require an extensive widening of the trench both north and south. In view of the depth of the trench, this would be a major project involving funds not available at the present time.

Plate 8.   Feature 1, Section H-11, Master Pit II: this semicircle of rocks lies with its opening to the north (see arrow) at a depth of 279 inches below present ground level. Interior measurements are 41 × 28 cm. As the result of tests conducted on the rock removed by Dr. Rainer Berger, this feature is now described as a fire circle or hearth

The possible features in Master Pit II trench take on added significance when we enter the pit and examine Feature 1, the semicircle of rocks which is now designated as a hearth or fire circle. It also lies 279 inches below datum. This semicircle consists of nine large and eight small rocks. They tilt slightly into the circle and are arranged in groups of three large, two small, three large, etc. Interior measurements of the circle are seventeen inches from east to west and twelve inches from north to south. Chalcedony, limestone, and volcanic rocks were used to form the circle. The cobbles average more than six inches in diameter.

In an effort to determine whether or not this circle of rocks had been used as a fire circle or hearth, Dr. Leakey asked Dr. Rainer Berger to have tests run. Since no carbon was recovered, Dr. Berger removed one of the larger rocks from the circle, one containing iron particles to assist in making magnetic measurements. Half of this rock was sent to Dr. Vaslav Bucha of the Geophysical Institute of the Academy of Science in Czechoslovakia. The following is a quotation from Dr. Berger's report of tests run on the rock from the fire circle:

He [Bucha], in turn, sliced up his half into little cubes, and placed each cube in a highly sensitive spinner-magnetometer of the Jelinek variety, of which the Czechs are building many, and which have a sensitivity that is for these purposes perhaps among the best in the world. When he measured the degree of magnetization in each of these cubes, he found that the ones at the smaller end of the rock —

(toward the center of the feature) were more highly magnetized than the ones at the other end of the rock, which were less magnetized. Now this is commensurate with the heating of a little under 400 degrees Centigrade at one end, and little or very little heating at the other end. In other words, if you assume that there was a fire in the center of the arrangement, these magnetic data would go with it.

In the final analysis, it would appear that in the circular arrangement of stones there must have been a fire.

No such evidence of heating was detected when the same tests were conducted on another chalcedony cobble of similar size and shape from the same stratum forty feet away in the entrance trench.

In 1970, more than 100 scientists from Australia, Europe, Asia, Africa, and North and South America met at the San Bernardino County Museum to examine the specimens. They also visited the excavations and the related geological formations and heard the archaeological and geological summations presented by those in charge of the work.

This meeting did not mark the end of the Calico Archaeological Project; rather, it marked the attainment of a plateau. Much remains to be done, both in the field and in the laboratory. Regarding the opinion of scientific visitors to the site, I believe it would be accurate to say that the general consensus is as follows:

1. The major area of controversy was the age of the site. There were two schools of thought:

a. those who agreed with Dr. Clements that building of the fan occurred about 70,000 years ago, near the beginning of the Wisconsin glacial period. In his presentation, Dr. Clements said, "During the Sangamon interglacial we presumably had an arid climate here, and at that time I believe we had the formation of the Yermo Fan";

b. those who felt that the fan was much older, more in the realm of 250,000 or 500,000 years. Dr. Clements believes that the stage reached in the erosion or geomorphologic cycle does not represent such a great age.

2. In considering the artifacts, some scientists were more interested in the tools, others in the technical flakes. Each category has received support, each has been challenged. The doubts in the minds of those who still question the specimens as being man-made are perhaps best expressed by Dr. Glynn Isaac: "A great many of the objects would arouse no comment if they were found in normal archaeological situations. . . ." In other words, the concern in some minds is that so little is known about alluvial fans.

The feeling of those who are most convinced of the presence of man at the Calico site is well expressed by Dr. Leakey, who said, ". . . I say that some of the Calico specimens are not, and could not be, the work of nature. . . . I say without hesitation, knowing what nature can do, that we are digging in an archaeological site. . . ."

3. There is agreement that the methods of excavation and the controls exercised enable us to derive from the deposits the total story they could tell. It remains now to build the general geological studies and laboratory work to the same level.

At the present time, there are no funds for further work; but we are making a determined effort to preserve the site, to have it set aside by the government (federal, state, or county) as part of our heritage. Meanwhile, what work is being done is predicated on the need to determine more specifically the age of the site.

The Metate: An Early Grain-Grinding Implement in the New World

GEORGE F. CARTER

> Thou shalt not take the nether, nor the upper millstone to pledge; for he hath pledged his life to thee.
>
> *Deuteronomy* 24:6
> (Douet Version).

INTRODUCTION

The biblical reference to the millstone serves to illustrate both the importance of the grain-grinding implements to mankind and the confusion that exists concerning the earliest of these tools. Note this alternate version: "No man shall take a handstone or even an upper millstone in pledge for a debt; for that is to take life itself as a pledge." But the handstone *was* the upper millstone in the Near East in biblical times! What is reflected in this wording is the unfamiliarity of the translator with the milling equipment that preceded the invention of the rotary mill. This ignorance is typical of the reporting on what is one of man's more significant inventions for what it tells us about man's way of life and about his increasing interest in the hard-seeded grasses that were to become his staff of life.

Probably the grain-grinding tools are the first tangible evidence that we will ever have of man's shift of interest toward the hard-seeded grains as an important food supply. While the sickle has had more attention, the grinding tools may be earlier and perhaps even more informative. Clearly there was an immense period of time of specialized seed gathering that preceded the emergence of agriculture based on grass seeds, and we must look to the tools used in the harvesting and preparation of such materials for the first hints of this approaching revolutionary development.

Further, seed grinding along with pottery making led men to work with complex rotary-motion machines and thus foreshadowed the mechanical revolution — the harnessing of animal and then inanimate power. How odd, then, that the basic grinding tools are a center of confusion and lack of reporting.

Nomenclature

Some semblance of order in nomenclature is a first requirement. As an example of the utter confusion that can be found, consider the following statement by Lips (1956:77):

Another important utilization of stone for household implements are the slabs and grinders on which primitive housewives all over the earth chop and mince their grains and vegetables. One large stone serves as a base, with a smaller, round stone as a pestle. From the harvesting tribes of North America to the agriculturists of Africa and the Pacific Islands, such slabs and mortars are common.

It would be difficult to write more confusingly or with greater mixture of descriptive terms for grinding and pounding equipment and processes. Lips' accompanying illustration shows a metate or saddle quern. Responsibility for such rampant confusion can in part be laid at the door of professionals, who have not yet developed a standard terminology.

As an example, without citation of the source (there is no point in singling out one from many), the following terms were used in one recent American publication. For the handstone (identity determined by either usage or illustrations): muller, mealing stone, pitted hammerstone, anvil stone, circular flat milling stone. For the nether stone: flat to slightly concave stone mortar, mortar with a deep concave surface. The last example shows a deeply troughed metate or saddle quern with a mano or muller resting in the depression. When professionals call the nether stone of the seed-grinding apparatus a mortar, confusion is nearing the ultimate. In Table 1 are assembled some of the terms in use. The list could be expanded but should be sufficient to illustrate the difficulty of proceeding without first establishing names for the things that we are to discuss.

The American names for the two parts of the apparatus on which grains were ground on a nether stone by a back-and-forth motion of a smaller stone held in the hand have long been metate and mano respectively. See, for instance, Kroeber's broad and casual usage of the first term: "Grains need threshing and then grinding into flour; this was done on saddle querns — what in Mexico and the southwestern United States are called metates — slabs on which a stone was pushed back and forth" (1948:695), and "The grain was ground in a saddle quern or metate, with back and forth motion" (1948:747).

Table 1. Names for grinding tools

Lower Stone	Upper stone
New World	
metate	mano
milling stone	muller
grinding slab	handstone
mealing stone	pitted hammerstone
shallow mortar	mealing stone
Old World (British Empire)	
quern	muller
saddle quern	rider
dish quern	quern pounder
grindstone	grinder
mealing trough	mealing stone
stone bowls	crushers
plate-shaped mortar	rubber
flat mill	milling stone
dish mortar	pestle rubber

In southern California, men who had Spanish–American backgrounds and firsthand knowledge of the Indians called all such implements metates and manos, adding descriptive adjectives for special shapes of metates such as troughed, basined, three-legged, and so forth. There is no English equivalent for metate except saddle quern, a confusing phrase, and no unequivocal name in English for the handstone, for muller can also mean a pounding implement such as a pestle.

The desire in some American quarters to change from the original term to grinding slab, mealing stone, milling stone, and so forth has caused confusion. Grinding slab is a descriptive but not distinctive name for the handstone. Grinding slab (or milling stone) and handstone are clumsy expressions, and only by definition can we know which word refers to the upper and which to the lower stone. The usual rule in taxonomy is to retain the old, established names. We have only two sets: saddle quern and muller, and metate and mano. As the table shows, saddle quern and muller are not consistently used in British publications, where there is apparently no generally used pair of terms. Further, saddle quern is a clumsy phrase and invites confusion with the rotary mill (quern). Americans once had such a pair of words — mano and metate — but seem now to be adrift in a sea of increasing confusion. I choose to use here these old, established terms: mano and metate. A discussion of the misconception of circular and back-and-forth motion in grinding grain on a metate is reserved for elsewhere. It will be shown that there is neither ethnological nor archaeological evidence for anything except a predominantly back-and-forth motion.

Earliest Use of the Mano and Metate: Seeds or Pigments?

Obviously, any device for grinding could be used to prepare various substances. Mankind has long been fascinated with colors, and pigments often need grinding in the process of preparation. Tough and stringy dried meats are improved by pounding and grinding. Any set of equipment for either pounding or grinding would probably be used for many things. The problem is to determine, if possible, the predominant earliest use, for ethnological studies show that metates are used primarily for preparing vegetable foods and secondarily for all other purposes; this is true among the seed gatherers as well as the agriculturists. If we were to judge the past by the present, we would have to conclude that metates were primarily for grinding seeds.

Currently, great emphasis is placed on the frequent occurrence of color stains on manos and metates from early sites, and the suggestion is advanced that the first use of these implements may have been for grinding pigments. Admittedly, man could have begun by preparing paints and later turned to grinding food, and the very ancient trait of painting the dead with red ocher indicates the great antiquity of the preparation of pigments, with implications of pounding or grinding. However, we should not be overly influenced by these color stains. Traces of pigments last. Traces of food, except under most unusual conditions, could not be expected to do so. Perhaps we should be looking for more subtle evidence of use. Grinding of grain tends to polish the stones. Grinding of clays formed by breakdown of granite scratches the stones because quartz crystals are commonly included in the clay. Pigment grinding should often scratch the stone and also leave a lasting stain. Scratching and staining would make lasting and obvious markings, and, very probably, the minor uses that leave the most obvious evidence are excessively influencing our judgments.

Perhaps the matter can be approached through frequency studies. There would be relatively little need for grinding pigments in comparison with the need for grinding seeds, hence an abundance of well-worn grinding tools would suggest seed grinding more strongly than pigment grinding. Gabel (1963) reports that in the Lochinvar mound in South Africa, manos and metates were found in the bottom levels. Six metates were found and none showed ocher stain; thirty-eight manos were found and two showed ocher stain. Storck and Teague (1952) mention that some of the mortars and "rubbing stones" of the Magdalenian are stained with red ocher, "but many show no trace of color." These citations suggest that a minority of these tools are ocher stained. Because even an incidental use for grinding ocher might leave a lasting stain, while extensive use for grinding food would leave none, the data suggest a predominance of food grinding over ocher grinding. But the need for more data is obvious.

One reason for the belief that grinding tools were used first for pigments and only later for seeds seems to be the assumption that manos and metates cannot precede agriculture. In areas like the American West, this is obviously not true. For example, from at least 10,000 to 2000 B.P., and again after 650 B.P., in the North American Great Basin the metate was primarily used for grinding wild seeds. It is the seed gatherer's preeminent tool, and in that region, as well as in Australia and southernmost Africa, it is totally unrelated to agriculture. Evidence will be presented below for metates in clearly preagricultural positions elsewhere. The whole subject of early grinding tools is filled with explicit or implicit assumptions about their function, age, distribution, and technique of use, and some of the assumptions can be shown to be wrong. I intend here to begin to clarify this situation.

Distribution: Age and Area

The mano and metate have, or had, a nearly worldwide distribution, being used at some time or another on all the continents, including Australia (Farmer 1959, 1960). As always with such a distribution, one is faced with the problem of multiple or single invention, and only extensive distributional studies that focus on space, time, and typology can supply the answer. Because of the lack of these studies, as well as the confused state of our nomenclature, the neglect in reporting these tools, and the assumptions about recency of the tools, at this time only the sketchiest of outlines and most guarded of conclusions can be presented.

The worldwide distribution of the metate suggests antiquity, and diffusion somewhat like that of the atlatl, the dog, or the use of fire. Further, the metate is often used by the simpler cultures of the world, such as the nonagricultural Australians and the nonagricultural tribes of the Great Basin and southern California, suggesting that it is a part of some early way of life. These factors suggest that the mano and metate may have been part of man's early equipment and were carried with him as he spread over the earth. Because they are so important to seed gatherers and continue to be important to seed cultivators, the implication is that the seed-gathering way of life is very early. Very probably, the metate-using seed gatherers evolved into the metate-using agriculturists in the Near East and in Mexico.

Multiple independent invention cannot be ruled out, but it is difficult to see just why the grinding of grains as opposed to other methods of preparing them should be invented early, or repeatedly, or at all. The claim that only three methods are available — pounding, rubbing, or rolling grains to reduce them to finer particles — is false. Grains can be soaked, sprouted, parched, popped, or boiled (especially if pottery is available), and these operations reduce or eliminate the need for mechanical reduction of the hard grains.

If grain is to be reduced mechanically, rolling would seem the least likely method. It involves the principle of the wheel, and for efficient use poses problems of a fixed handle with a free-turning roller. Perhaps significantly, it is rare in the world. Paris (1943) mentioned rollers for grinding grain among the Maya and the Chinese; Prakash (1961) mentioned rollers in use in India. In conversations with people back from Africa, I have learned that cylindrical manos are common in North Africa. They are used with a wrist action that gives at most a three-quarter turn. I know of no published descriptions of the equipment, the process, or the distribution of this complex, which may stretch from Indochina, through India, across North Africa. This deficiency is typical of the present state of knowledge of grinding tools. In Mexico rollers continue in use to this day, and Indian women can be seen buying them in the marketplace in Oaxaca. That this is a transfer to America of a southeastern Asian mano that utilizes the principle of the wheel is a possibility that deserves investigation. The context of the roller mano is interesting: many similar parallels between southern Asia and America can be found (cf. Heine-Geldern's numerous papers) and a compelling case for the trans-Pacific diffusion of a specific tool (a specialized bark beater) from Celebes to Mexico can be made (Tolstoy 1963).

Pounding would seem to be a natural way to reduce a material. This would fit well with primitive man's shaping of stone by striking blows designed to remove flakes, and later by pecking it. Indeed, pounding of some foods on or with stones may antedate striking of stones to make tools. We often assume that earlier men were more impatient, more prone to quick methods than to slow ones (hence flaked stone before ground stone); if this argument were valid, we would expect that the technique of pounding grain might have preceded that of grinding grain. Our present information from studies of both distribution and chronology suggests, however, that for grains, the grinding method is the older throughout the world. With reservations because of the incompleteness of our knowledge, we can say that the choice of the metate suggests a traditional way of doing things, invented somewhere very early and diffused widely prior to the invention and spread of the pounding method. However, we need much more data before this conclusion can be considered as more than highly tentative.

We need to know with what group of lithic industries the metate is usually associated. In southern California the metate is not found with the early bifacially flaked core tools (hand-ax-like) but is characteristic of the unifacially flaked tools (La Jollan culture) similar to the chopper traditions of southeastern Asia. If the associations were the same in Asia, the suggestion would seem to be that a complex of stone flaking and seed grinding was diffused, presumably from Asia to America. The metate is or was widely used in southeastern Asia, from India to China, and metates are found in the Hoabinhian culture, for which age estimates as high as 50,000 years have been made, although no one has specified just how far back the metate extends in this culture. If the metate has very great antiquity in Asia and is associated with unifacial core tools similar to those of the La Jollan culture of America, which also has metates, then this association may prove to be highly significant.

We obviously need much more information on the age of the metate in many areas. I can contribute most to this question by presenting data from the area of my own research.

THE MANO AND THE METATE IN THE NEW WORLD

Age of the Mano and the Metate in the New World

The age of the metate in America is generally thought to be post-Paleo-Indian, or at any rate, not more than 10,000 years. Krieger (1959:31), in an acrimonious exchange with Carter, extended this worldwide:

A considerable amount of controlled and competent archeological work . . . has shown rather definitely that food grinding tools first appeared between 9,000 and 10,000 years ago. This estimate applies to the Old World as well.

This assessment of fifteen years ago is far from correct, as data presented below will make clear. Krieger, in this case, simply reflected the general view that the mano and metate appeared in the early Archaic, a view supported by such synthesizers of American archaeology as Gordon Willey (1966, 1971) and James Ford (1969). In his valuable survey of American archaeology, Ford has placed the metate as post-Paleo-Indian and characteristically appearing in the Archaic period. He recognizes the basined metate as an early form and notes the appearance of troughed metates about 6000 B.P. and metates with legs between 3000 and 2500 B.P. A review of the data from California will show that there is considerable reason to expect far older dates.

The metate is known to precede the mortar in much of California. In central California, Powers (cited in Holmes 1902) recorded that the historic tribes stated that in ancient times they had ground their acorns on a slightly hollowed stone "like a Mexican metate," a practice they had learned from Mouse. Later they learned from Coyote (the Uto-Aztecan trickster god) to pound their acorns in mortars. In the region of Santa Barbara, the early Oak Grove culture had the metate, the intermediate Hunting culture had both the metate and the mortar, and late Canalino culture used the mortar either exclusively or almost so. This pattern is also true of southern California and of Baja California, where the replacement was incomplete, for although mortars were well on the way to displacing the metate in southern California, they were still rare in northern Baja California and probably absent in southern Baja California. The data suggest an introduction of the mortar somewhere near central California and its slow gain of dominance over the metate in adjacent areas.

A hint concerning the time of these shifts in the area of San Diego comes from submarine archaeology (Minshall and Moriarty 1964). Small stone mortars have been recovered from beneath the sea, many of them from a drowned site. The amount of rise in sea level suggests an age ranging from about 9,000 years for the deepest to 5,000 years for the greatest accumulation. Metates have been found farther off shore, in still greater depths, suggesting an antiquity of 10,000 years or more. In California the most conservative authorities (Wallace 1962) will grant about 10,000 years for the age of the metate, and an assumption seems to be made that the later shift from the metate to the mortar accompanied either some ecological or some cultural shift from small wild seeds to acorns. No objective proof has been advanced for such a change due to ecological shifts.

Arnold (1957) found a series of occupations associated with an extinct lake (Lake Chapala) in the now-desert Baja California. The present rainfall is between 12.5 and 25 centimeters, and a rainfall of 50 to 75 centimeters would be required to restore a lake in the area. This condition indicates that full glacial–pluvial climatic changes are involved. A sequence of lakes, associated with weathering phenomena, and successive complexes of artifacts allow these conclusions: all of Wisconsin time is involved; metates are absent in the earliest lithic industry but present in the middle and later lithic assemblages (Arnold's conclusions). The lithic assemblage lacking the metate is marked by "ovate bifaces" (hand axes). The lithic assemblage associated with the metates includes scraper planes, flakes, and simple, leaf-shaped, bifacially flaked points (stemmed and notched points are rare). This latter assemblage seems to be a late phase of the ancient lithic industry of southern California that is characterized by a predominance of unifacial flaking and of the metate. That Arnold places this in Wisconsin time is most important.

The San Dieguito culture (Table 2) represents the attenuated influence of the Paleo-Indian hunting cultures on the earliest simple gatherers of southern California. In the 1930's I assisted M. J. Rogers in fieldwork in southern California and spent hundreds of hours collecting artifacts from eroded sites of the San Dieguito culture. We collected quantities of manos and metates and considered food-grinding equipment a normal part of the assemblage. This long-held view was reversed by Rogers when

Table 2. Correlation of chronology and cultural sequences in southern and lower (Baja) California

General time-period	Area of Santa Barbara	Area of San Diego	Area of Lake Chapala, Baja California	Associated human remains
Late Recent (Bow and arrow)	Canalino	Diegueño*		
Mid-Recent Archaic	Hunting*	Late La Jollan*		
Early Recent	Oak Grove*	Late La Jollan*		
Late Wisconsin (Paleo-Indian)	Oak Grove*	San Dieguito*	Period II*	Burial in Imperial Valley
Early Wisconsin		Early La Jollan*	Period I	
Third interglacial (=Riss-Wurm= ?Illinoisan-Wisconsin?)				
Late Third interglacial, circa 80,000 B.P.				Frontal bone from La Jolla
Middle Third interglacial circa 100,000 B.P.		Texas Street		
Early Third interglacial				

Both sequences and times of cultural changes in southern and lower (Baja) California are questioned by various experts; the table above presents my judicious opinion. The general scale suggests the time intervals and the cultural sequences from flake and core tools to stone projectile points to the Archaic way of life, and finally — with the appearance of stone arrow points — to the protohistoric way of life. Asterisks mark cultures in which the metate is prominent.

The burial in the Imperial Valley, tentatively dated at 20,000 years, is being reported by Morlin Childers.

The human fossil frontal, dated at 80,000 years, is preserved in the San Diego Museum of Man and has been referred to previously by Carter (1957: 217). The date is inferred from the recent dating of the lowest terraces along the Pacific Coast by U/Th ratios determined on molluscan shells.

the cutting of a single trench through a deeply buried site produced no manos or metates. A later trench through this site also failed to produce any grinding tools (Warren and True 1961; Krieger 1964; Heizer 1964). Because the site is a quarry where felsite boulders in a stream bed were being worked, metates obviously could not be expected. As Heizer (1964) has aptly pointed out, one can easily draw an incorrect conclusion from the absence of a tool in situations where evidence of seed grinding would be much more expectable than at this site. In passing, we should note that, although this site is dated by radiocarbon at 9000 B.P., it is culturally a late San Dieguito site (Hayden 1966).

In the area of San Diego and elsewhere, the following sequence can be observed: those manos and metates of the protohistoric tribes made of granite are fresh, hard, and usually white in color; La Jollan manos are nearly fresh even when they have an age up to 9,000 years. Yellowed and weathered manos of granite are often found in the area and were frequently found on San Dieguito sites. They are more weathered than the historic and than the La Jollan, defined as post-San Dieguito, as shown in Table 2. If they do not belong with the other lithic material on those sites, to what culture should they be assigned? The details of the weathering show that they do not belong to any post-San Dieguito culture, but as at Lake Chapala, they belong at least to a mid-Wisconsin period (Arnold 1957). It is also noteworthy that mortars found in submarine locations and placeable at 5,000 to 9,000 years of age are never found on these San Dieguito sites and that mortars are later than metates in California.

At Lake Chapala the earlier metates and manos are weathered to such a degree that polished surfaces on both granite and basalt often have been destroyed wholly or in part. As geologists have often demonstrated, such weathering is not characteristic of the late Wisconsin but is normal for early Wisconsin and earlier time; this evidence would seem to indicate the age for the metates at Lake Chapala. Other data, outlined below, suggest much greater antiquity for the metate in southern California.

From Crown Point, a piece of land projecting into Mission Bay at San Diego, shown in Figure 1, I have reported a series of particularly relevant finds (Carter 1957:286–290). Crown Point represents a period of filling of Mission Bay with sand to a level well above the present sea level. Filling of the bays and lagoons along this coast is accepted as a phenomenon associated with high sea level (Shumway et al. 1961; Hubbs et al. 1965). A fill associated with a sea level about ten feet above the present sea level would suggest a late last (third) interglacial age of about 80,000 years ago (Newell 1965). While there have been suggestions of minor sea-stands at slight elevations above the present within Recent time, the data assembled by Hubbs, Bien, and Suess (1965) tend to negate this theory, for they

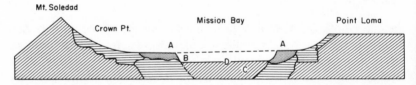

Figure 1.   Cross section from Mount Soledad to Point Loma along Crown Point. Mt. Soledad is a 900-foot-high block elaborately terraced. Point Loma is a 400-foot-high terraced block. The lowland between them is a river valley at times of lowered sea level and an embayment trapping sediments at times of high sea level. At A the Marina sands, a well-known late Pleistocene sand deposit, is shown. This deposit formerly filled the embayment. Beneath it metates were found. Subsequent to the deposit of these sands, the San Diego River excavated the sands to far below present sea level. Subsequent rise of sea level to D in de-glacial time has led to the deposition of recent deposits C. If the sequence of cut and fill on this relatively stable San Diego block is the result of eustatic sea-level fluctuations, as all present evidence suggests, then the age of the buried metates is last interglacial

show a steady rise of sea level with no evidence for sea-stands significantly above the present at any time in the Recent. Furthermore, since the last filling of the area of Mission Bay most of the fill has been cut out far below present sea levels. This erosion clearly must be attributed to the lowered sea levels of last glacial time. Because the fill must precede its own erosion, the fill must date from the late last interglacial, unless we postulate a mid-Wisconsin sea-sand higher than the present one. If the sea-stand was about plus ten feet, which would be the absolute minimum required to create this fill (Carter [1957], for example, considered a twenty-five-foot sea-stand a more likely correlation, although a ten- or fifteen-foot sea-stand was mentioned as possible), then Newell's date of about 80,000 years would seem appropriate. Dates from southern California archaeology, however, are being revolutionized. Bada *et al.* (1974) report a human skeleton at 48,000. This implies man in America before the onset of Wisconsin I at ± 80,000. There are now several unpublished dates for skeletal material in the 50,000-year range. Higher dates can be expected as more material is processed.

The first evidence for man near the base of the latest sand fill was the discovery of a group of large cobbles close together and strongly fire-spalled. This assemblage, typical of temporary hearths commonly found in the area, was completely out of place in these coarse sands in its size, grouping, and evidence of fire. Four hundred yards to the north, a mano of very coarsely crystalline granite was found resting on the shell reef that underlies the sand deposit. The two flat sides of this cobble have been ground so strongly that the quartz crystals are cut off to form a gently curved surface typical of cobble manos in this area. Weathering of the granite since the planation of the quartz crystals leaves these surfaces raised because of the selective etching out of the softer minerals. Late glacial weathering of granites in California is less pronounced than this. The edges of the cobble show no wear. These characteristics identify manos, and such a pattern of wear is not found on stream cobbles.

At a depth of more than six meters in a sewer ditch cutting across Crown Point, engineers found two oval basined metates in a similar position: resting on a Pleistocene shell deposit at the base of the sand stratum that filled Mission Bay at a time when the sea stood about 7.5 meters above the present sea level.

No one has suggested any explanation of these data other than human habitation on the shores of Mission Bay prior to the last high sea-stand in this area. At one time the area was considered to be extremely unstable geologically, and the land–sea relationships were dismissed as attributable to local crustal movements. Detailed local studies by Carter (1957), Shumway, Hubbs, and Moriarty (1961), Hubbs, Bien, and Suess (1965), and others show that the raised beaches that had been assumed to be postglacial are interglacial, that the "Recent" alluvial covers are actually

Wisconsin, and that the alleged evidence for great crustal instability is nonexistent (Allen, Silver, and Stehli 1960: Allen *et al.* 1965).

There is a tendency to lose in the literature findings that at the time of publication were so out of step with the current knowledge as to be unbelievable, and then to fail to recover them when the growth of knowledge shows that they were possible, after all. Such a situation exists for the metate found in the region of Santa Barbara in the same relative position as the Mission Bay artifacts and reported by Rogers (1929); a picture of the locality has been published by Carter (1959). The two metates and the mano at San Diego rested directly on a Pleistocene shell beach and were deeply buried by the alluvial fill of a subsequent high sea-stand. The most recent geochemical dating suggests a minimum age of 80,000 years for such marine transgressions (Mesolella *et al.* 1969; Birkeland 1972). While the region of Santa Barbara is less stable than that of San Diego, Upson (1949) considered it to have been relatively stable since a mid-Pleistocene uplift and believed the lower terraces there to represent the effect of eustatic fluctuations of sea level. At the site where Rogers made his finds, a younger terrace has been truncated by a sea-stand higher than the present sea level, and the terrace cut by that sea-stand was dissected at a time of lower sea level than now, as shown in Figure 2. If the lowest terrace represents the plus-ten-foot sea-stand of last interglacial time or of mid-Wisconsin time at the latest, then the mano and metates buried in a previous deposit must be still earlier and related to a time immediately following a twenty-five-foot sea-stand. If the area of Santa Barbara is regarded as somewhat less stable than that of San Diego, we might possibly fit these events into a somewhat later time, but

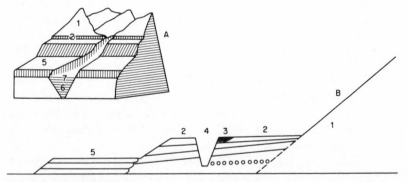

Figure 2.   Metates and geomorphology at Santa Barbara. In A and B, 1 shows the mountainous background, 2 the higher of the two youngest terraces, and 5 the lower one. A surface midden some thousands of years old is at 3, and the highway cut is designated by 4. The circles indicate the location of the marine beach formation. The metates were found on top of this. In A, 6 indicates the dissection of the valley below present sea levels and 7 the current fill up to present sea level. The major criticism of Rogers's finds would be that a landslide might have carried manos and metates down to the beach level, and that even so experienced a field man as D. B. Rogers failed to detect this

one still well back into the last glacial period. The usual correlations with terraces suggest last interglacial time. The deep clay soil profiles on the lowest terrace and the strongly weathered soils on the higher terrace indicate weathering far beyond a 10,000-year scale. As at Crown Point, it seems improbable that these geomorphic features can be accounted for in Recent time; it is more probable that they fit late last interglacial events.

These findings are also supported by recent work on the coast of the area of Malibu, California (Birkeland 1972). Even in this area of obviously active crust, the eustatic analysis of terrace and valley fill is applicable. Evidence at Malibu suggests that the mid-Wisconsin sea level was about nine meters below modern sea levels, and that the last interglacial terrace cut and valley fill along the entire coast (Santa Cruz, Cayucos, Santa Monica Mountains, San Nicolas Island, Palos Verdes Hills) date from about 100,000 years ago. The dates from shell (open-system uranium series) for the lowest terrace range from 70,000 to 140,000, with a clustering about 100,000. Although a sea-stand higher than the present one in mid-Wisconsin time is possible, the weight of the evidence is against it. This study is of particular interest for its support of the work of W. M. Davis (1933) in the same area. My methodology at San Diego was like that of Davis. Birkeland's work with absolute dates confirms our conclusions and links San Diego and Santa Barbara. The drift of the evidence supports late interglacial dating of the metates and manos at Santa Barbara and San Diego.

In the chaotic state of reporting on metates, assumptions should not be allowed to override facts. While the situation at Santa Barbara, San Diego, and Lake Chapala seems out of step with the rest of America, where a 10,000-year limit is generally seen as probable, the finds in California form a coherent set supported by studies of geology, geomorphology, climate, and sea levels. Man in that part of America had specialized tools for grinding hard seeds from mid-Wisconsin time, at the latest, to late interglacial time, at the earliest. In the Great Basin the cultural descendants of these people continued to use these implements with little change and were so focused on their ancient way of life as to be epitomized as the Seed Gatherers. Most interestingly, not only did they fail to initiate agriculture, but also, despite millennia of contact with agriculturists, most of them were not stimulated either to undertake the domestication of their ancient seed plants or to borrow already domesticated plants from their neighbors.

Paleo-Indian Evidence

In the southeastern and midwestern part of the United States, the metate tended to disappear early in the Archaic. At Modoc Rock Shelter in

Illinois (Fowler 1959) the metate appeared only in the lowest levels. If a tool type is fading out toward the opening of a period, the notion that it may be a carry-over from an earlier period would seem worth investigation. The suggestion that the metate might belong in the Paleo-Indian lithic assemblage has both proponents and opponents (cf. Farmer 1960 and Krieger 1959). Actually, the question may be seen incorrectly. May the metate belong to a group earlier than the classic hunting cultures such as Folsom and Clovis? The Lively complex from Alabama (Josselyn 1966) clearly contains both ovate-biface-like materials, with which (on the basis of western American finds) the metate is not expectable, and unifacial tools of La Jollan type, with which the metate is expectable. Because the stratigraphy of the deep cave at Modoc Rock Shelter allows no room in the last 10,000 years or so for any complexes like these, the suggestion seems to be that a pre-Paleo-Indian people with seed-grinding tools preceded the Paleo-Indians in the eastern United States. This idea poses a flood of problems. Are manos in Paleo-Indian sites from a preceding culture? Are they the result of some cultural mixture? Is the Archaic a resurgence of the older foraging way of life enriched by the Paleo-Indian inventory? Just such a sequence seems apparent in southern California (Carter 1957), where a gathering culture emerged after enrichment by a hunting culture (San Dieguito) in the form of the La Jollan culture. The appearance in eastern North America of lithic complexes with pre-projectile points comparable to those of the West is of broad significance for American cultural history, and knowledge of the presence or absence of the metate in these complexes will be of critical importance.

Problems intertwine. The problem of the antiquity of man in America cannot be separated from the question of the metate. Currently, we seem to be leaping from the long-held age estimate of 10,000 years to one of 20,000 or even 40,000. In January, 1973, a presentation at the University of California, Riverside, of Texas Street tools from the controversial interglacial site at San Diego (Carter 1957) resulted in complete acceptance of these disputed items as artifacts.

In the Colorado Desert of California, working with Morlin Childers of El Centro, California, I have seen a burial site at least 20,000 years old. This site is on the west side of the Imperial Valley, on a beach line about forty-six meters above sea level. Dates on the beach line are from shell and travertine; dates on the burial are from soil carbonates and are probably far too young. A more detailed description of the site is to be published by Childers.

Manos and metates of granite on old sites in different parts of the American West (Carter 1957, 1958) uniformly show degrees of weathering in keeping with pre-Wisconsin time on the granite-weathering scales normally used by geologists in this region. Excellent examples of this differential weathering can be seen in Childers's collection in El Centro, California. Many granite manos and metates found at the older sites were in such advanced states of decay that, were there still older sites with manos and metates, no record would exist.

Some years ago, Farmer (1960) reviewed the faint suggestions then available that the metate might be pre-Archaic as follows. Folsom sites east of the front range of the Rockies contain a few manos, and F. H. H. Roberts, Jr., found faceted pieces of sandstone at the Lindenmeir site in northern Colorado and noted that they suggested manos. The absence of metates perhaps has prevented these finds from attracting more attention, but the general assumption of a post-10,000-year dating for the metate is probably a more powerful force. Warnica (1966) reported the finding of a "stone used for grinding" in a stratum that yielded Clovis material and referred to the finding of a small milling stone from a nearby Folsom site. The confusion in terminology is well exemplified by the fact that one must guess that Warnica meant a mano when he wrote "stone for grinding" and a metate when he wrote "milling stone." He did comment quite aptly that the presence of these stones suggested that the Paleo-Indian people were not entirely ignoring the vegetable resources around them.

Everyone recognizes that the Paleo-Indian evidence is very incomplete, for almost all our knowledge comes from butchering sites. That there is as much evidence suggesting seed usage as we actually possess is indeed highly significant.

Manos clearly appear in Paleo-Indian sites. Whether they were used as grinding stones (which seems probable), or were picked up on older sites and brought into camp, or were somehow accidental inclusions (which seems least likely) are problems that future work will solve. The data from San Diego establish the probability of pre-Paleo-Indian dates and should serve as a caution on theorizing that the metate was invented when the big game was exterminated and that under the compulsion of climatic change and the loss of big game as a means of subsistence men suddenly invented seed-grinding equipment and shortly thereafter a seed-based agriculture.

South America

In South America the mano and metate were reported at least as early as 1912 as associated with coastal midden cultures. Fifty years later (Lanning 1963) the metate was reported in early lithic industries in Peru and was associated with large, heavy, thick scrapers, bifacial disk choppers, large unretouched flakes, and rare projectile points. There is also clear evidence of climatic changes toward more humid conditions than now.

Lanning thought that grinding tools were not exceptionally old in America and suggested that their occurrence here goes back only to the late Pleistocene. At El Jobo, Venezuela (Rouse and Cruxent 1957), the mano and metate appeared in early levels, and their presence at other early sites (such as the Ayampitin in Argentina) is reported and cross-dated by the Intihuasi site, which has a carbon-14 determination of 7,970 ± 100 years. Presumably, in South America as in North America, the mano and metate in early levels were certainly present before pottery and agriculture, and perhaps before projectile points. They are often associated with heavy flake-and-core lithic industries suggesting the La Jollan culture of North America, and this association tends to continue even after projectile points and pottery are added to the complex.

Krieger (1964) has presented a masterly summary of our knowledge of early man in America. We disagree on some points, especially concerning the metate (cf. Carter 1959 and Krieger 1959). Krieger (1964) considered the metate to mark the opening of the Proto-Archaic and, at most, to overlap the late Paleo-Indian period. His argument was environmentally deterministic: he viewed the metate as a mark of the shift toward dependence on vegetal foods in postglacial time due to the combination of associated climatic changes and extinctions of large animals. Krieger thought the metate appeared almost simultaneously — about 10,000 years ago — throughout the Americas from Patagonia to Oregon. He tentatively suggested that the spread possibly occurred in 2,000 years. Bird (1965) placed manos (for pigment grinding) in Tierra del Fuego so close to 10,000 years ago as to call for nearly instantaneous spread. The total data would be more easily understood if more time were allowed.

Summary on Age of the Metate in the New World

The metate was nearly universal in America outside the sub-Arctic and surely extended back into the Paleo-Indian level. There is disputed evidence for the metate in sites with fluted points. This conflict pales beside the evidence from California, where several manos and metates have been found at the base of the alluvium overlying the last sea-stand that was significantly higher (ten feet higher) than the Recent level, with a probable minimum age of about 80,000 years. In the archaeological sequence in the United States, metates seem to be associated initially not with bifacially flaked core tools, but with unifacially flaked tools (La Jolla, Early Milling Stone). In many areas metates persisted for long periods thereafter; in some areas they lasted into historic times. With growing recognition of the existence of pre-Paleo-Indian levels, we may be on the way to realization of the real antiquity of the earliest seed-grinding tools. Our progress has been blocked in part by the assumption that nowhere in the world is the metate older than 10,000 years. However, in the Old World, definite metates (grinding slabs) are known from 49,000 years ago at Florisbad, South Africa (see Kraybill 1978), and, when archaeologists become more careful with their reporting, they probably will be found to have existed considerably earlier.

REFERENCES

ALLEN, C. R., LEON T. SILVER, F. G. STEHLI
  1960   Transverse structure of northern Baja California, Mexico. *Geological Society of America Bulletin* 71:457–482.
ALLEN, C. R., S. T. AMAND, C. F. RICHTER, J. M. NORDQUIST
  1965   Relationship between seismicity and geologic structure in the southern California region. *Bulletin of the Seismological Society of America* 55:753–797.
ARNOLD, BRIGHAM A.
  1957   Late Pleistocene and Recent changes in land forms, climate, and archaeology in central Baja California. *University of California Publications in Geography* 10:201–318.
BADA, J. L., R. A. SCHROEDER, G. F. CARTER
  1974   New evidence for the antiquity of man in North America deduced from aspartic acid racemization. *Science* 184:791–793.
BIRD, J. B.
  1965   The concept of a "pre-projectile-point" cultural stage in Chile and Peru. *American Antiquity* 31:262–270.
BIRKELAND, PETER W.
  1972   Late Quaternary eustatic sea-level changes along the Malibu coast, Los Angeles County, California. *Journal of Geology* 80:432–438.
CARTER, G. F.
  1957   *Pleistocene man at San Diego.* Baltimore: Johns Hopkins University Press.
  1958   Archaeology in the Reno area in relation to age of man and the culture sequence in America. *Proceedings of the American Philosophical Society* 102:174–192.
  1959   Man, time and change in the Far West. *Annals of the Association of American Geography* 49 (3):8–33.
DAVIS, W. M.
  1933   Glacial epochs of the Santa Monica Mountains, California. *Bulletin of the Geological Society of America* 44:1,041–1,133.
FARMER, M. F.
  1959   "Some notes concerning grinding implements." Unpublished manuscript.
  1960   A note on the distribution of the metate and muller. *Tebiwa, Journal of the Idaho State College Museum* 3:31–38.
FORD, J. A.
  1969   *A comparison of formative cultures in America.* Smithsonian contributions to Anthropology 11.
FOWLER, M.
  1959   Modoc Rock Shelter: an early Archaic site in southern Illinois. *American Antiquity* 24:257–270.

GABEL, CREIGHTON
1963   Lochinvar Mound: a later Stone Age camp-site in the Kafue Basin. *South African Archaeological Bulletin* 18:40–48.
HANSEN, G. H.
1934   The Utah Lake skull. *American Anthropologist* 36:135–147.
HAYDEN, J.
1966   Restoration of the San Dieguito type site to its proper place in the San Dieguito sequence. *American Antiquity* 31:439
HEIZER, R. F.
1964   "The western coast of North America," in *Prehistoric man in the New World*. Edited by Jesse D. Jennings and Edward Norbeck, 117–148. Chicago: University of Chicago Press.
HOLMES, W. H.
1902   Anthropological studies in California. *Annual Report of the United States National Museum for 1900*:161–187
HRDLIČKA, ALEŠ
1912   Early man in South America. *Bureau of American Ethnology Bulletin* 52. Washington, D.C.
HUBBS, C. L., G. S. BIEN, H. E. SUESS
1965   La Jolla natural radiocarbon measurement, IV. *Radiocarbon* 7:66–117.
JOSSELYN, D. W.
1966   The Lively complex of Alabama. *Anthropological Journal of Canada* 4:24–31.
KRAYBILL, NANCY
1978   "Pre-agricultural tools for the preparation of foods in the Old World," in *Origins of agriculture*. Edited by Charles A. Reed, 485–522. World Anthropology. Mouton: The Hague.
KRIEGER, A. D.
1959   Discussion. *Annals of the Association of American Geographers* 49:31.
1964   "Early man in the New World," in *Prehistoric man in the New World*. Edited by Jesse D. Jennings and Edward Norbeck, 23–81. Chicago: University of Chicago Press.
KROEBER, A. L.
1948   *Anthropology*. New York: Harcourt Brace.
LANNING, E. P.
1963   Pre-agricultural occupation on the central coast of Peru. *American Antiquity* 28:360–371.
LIPS, G. E.
1956   *The origin of things*. Harmondsworth: Penguin.
MESOLELLA, KENNETH J., R. K. MATTHEWS, WALLACE S. BROECKER, DAVID L. THURBER
1969   The astronomical theory of climatic change: Barbados data. *Journal of Geology* 77:250–274.
MINSHALL, N. F., J. R. MORIARTY
1964   Principles of underwater archeology. *Pacific Discovery* 17:17–26.
NEWELL, N. D.
1965   Warm interstadial interval in Wisconsin stage of the Pleistocene. *Science* 148:1,488.
PARIS, P.
1942   L'Amérique précolombienne et l'Asie méridionale, I. *Bulletin de la Société des Études Indochinoises* 17:35–70.
1943   L'Amérique précolombienne et l'Asie méridionale, II. *Bulletin de la Société des Études Indochinoises* 18:45–68.

PRAKASH, O. M.
1961   *Food and drink in ancient India.* Delhi: Munshi Ram Manohar Lal.
ROGERS, D. B.
1929   *Prehistoric man of the Santa Barbara coast.* Santa Barbara: Santa
        Barbara Natural History Museum.
ROUSE, I., J. M. CRUXENT
1957   Further comments on the finds at El Jobo, Venezuela. *American
        Antiquity* 22:412.
SHUMWAY, G., C. L. HUBBS, J. R. MORIARTY
1961   Scripps Estate site, San Diego, California: a La Jolla site dated 5460
        to7370 years before the present. *Annals of the New York Academy of
        Sciences* 93:37–132.
STORCK, J., W. D. TEAGUE
1952   *Flour for man's bread.* Minneapolis: University of Minnesota Press.
TOLSTOY, P.
1963   Cultural parallels between Southeast Asia and Mesoamerica in the
        manufacture of bark cloth. *Transactions, New York Academy of Sciences*
        (series two) 25:646–662.
UPSON, J. E.
1949   Former marine shore lines of the Gaviota Quadrangle, Santa Barbara
        County, California. *Journal of Geology* 59:415–446.
WALLACE, W. J.
1962   Prehistoric cultural development in the southern California deserts.
        American Antiquity 28:172–180.
WARNICA, JAMES M.
1966   New discoveries at the Clovis site. *American Antiquity* 31:345–357.
WARREN, CLAUDE N., D. L. TRUE
1961   The San Dieguito complex and its place in California prehistory.
        *Annual Report of the Archaeological Survey at the University of
        California at Los Angeles, 1960–1961*:264–291.
WILLEY, GORDON
1966   *An introduction to American archaeology,* volume one: *North and
        Middle America.* Englewood Cliffs, N.J.: Prentice-Hall.
1971   *An introduction to American archaeology,* volume two: *South
        America.* Englewood Cliffs, N.J.: Prentice-Hall.

Wisconsin and Pre-Wisconsin Stone Industries of New York State and Related Tools from a Shop Site near Tula, Mexico

RONALD M. STAGG, WILLIAM W. VERNON and
BRUCE E. RAEMSCH

The subject matter of this paper, relating to the relatively great antiquity of man in North America, developed over a period of about eight years of prehistoric studies, principally in New York State, but also in the states of Maine and Wyoming and the country of Mexico.

The study first began as a simple survey of known archaeological sites in central New York with no further intent than to find satisfactory American Indian habitation sites that might serve as areas of field instruction for anthropology students whose study included archaeological field methods and theory.

As the survey continued, it became increasingly apparent that a horizon of cultural material was distributed below the well-known and so-called Paleo-Indian horizon: that is, the material was located within sediments associated with the Wisconsin ice advance, and some, at least, had been deposited as a result of retreating ice, or by meltwater forming kame terraces and deltas. Other material looked as though it had been left by man.

The tools comprising the Wisconsin culture(s) were of pebble, core, and flake types, most produced from cherty materials derived from the Mohawk Valley. Some of the artifacts, collected over a period of three years, are from *in situ* locations in trenches, where they were exposed by backhoes and bulldozers; others were exposed by formal excavation in the course of other work on more recent cultures. All were characterized by the absence of projectile points of stone (those which were easily recognized as such) and the presence of core and flake scrapers and knives, knappers and hammers of chert and metamorphic rock, and

Appreciation for financial aid and encouragement is hereby given to Hartwick College and the Yager Museum and also to benefactors of Dickinson College for the opportunity to carry out the work permitting this study.

bifacially worked chopping core tools very similar to others found in a Mexican site shown in Plate 1, where flake uniface projectile points were discovered with other tools relating to a pre-Paleo-Indian culture. With subsequent developments we began to refer to the Early Man materials when discussing similar stone tools, largely because of previous discoveries and the work of other investigators (Bryan 1969; Haynes 1969; Lee 1957; Munson and Frye 1965; Renaud 1938; Stalker 1969; and others).

Plate 1.   Mexican chopping tools made from felsite. Functional edges face inward in each case, leaving the flattened outside edge to fit into the palm of the hand

Archaeology work continued on better-known and more recent cultures and the early man finds remained peripheral to interests that developed during the excavation of another site known from nineteenth-century activities of amateur investigators. The site, named Adequentaga by the most active researcher of the area, Willard E. Yager, was known to be a stratified Archaic-stage site where more or less sedentary hunting and gathering peoples who had adapted to the Susquehanna River environment from post-Pleistocene times, had lived. Because of the promise offered by amateur recoveries of chert tools and pottery as well as the stratified nature of the site, Adequentaga was chosen by the survey team as the most suitable for initiating students to fieldwork, while at the same time it offered opportunities for productive and original research on cultures already known but incompletely understood in the upper Susquehanna drainage.

After about three years of work at the Adequentaga site, another site was discovered northeast of the one being worked, by another member of the growing research team. The latter, or Timlin site, located about forty miles from the Adequentaga site, also turned out to be a stratified site, but one with cultural and temporal characteristics that were so unusual that it required special attention and absorbed all of the available research funds (which came from an endowment to Hartwick College by Willard E. Yager and his sister Marion for purposes of anthropological research).

The unique aspects of the Timlin site include culture materials found in direct association with ice-contact gravels, clays, and sands; type projectile points of the unifacial flake variety suggestive of Old World paleolithic cultures and regularly referred to as Acheulean (Bordes 1968, 1972; Oakley 1966); absence in the cultural horizons of post-Pleistocene culture materials such as bifacial points and bifacially pitted hammerstones, and the presence of fire-cracked rock. Moreover, core chopping tools and bifacially worked hand axes were found at the Timlin site but not at the Adequentaga site. Furthermore the anvil technique of making large flake tools appeared in association with those tools that were found in the most recent of the two ancient discovered soils in which tools have been found. Lastly, in this site were found lithologies, such as bedded chert and silicified limestone, from which tools were often made but which did not appear in post-Pleistocene cultures.

Finally, during the early excavations on the Timlin site still another site, near Tula, Mexico, was discovered by students who had done work on the Timlin site and who recognized similarities between type tools being found on the Timlin site, such as uniface flake points, uniface scrapers, and knives, and those from the open site in Mexico.

These events have made it quite clear that the antiquity of man in the New World needs to be reappraised in the light of the multiple sources of evidence that permit us to crosscut time and space in prehistoric developments without apparent contradiction in our theory, which, based upon the above findings and the evidence presented below, supposes that man was present in North America as long as 70,000 years ago.

The first indications of the very early appearance of man in the New York area came to us when pebble, core, and flake tools were found lodged in the gravels of kame terraces and deltas of the upper Susquehanna drainage. But the tools that were found almost without exception indicated (through their rolled edges) that they came from sources other than where we found them. Most, if not all, seem to have been transported into the region by water and/or ice. Additional evidence of antiquity was indicated by patinas present on several of the artifacts: one core remnant modified to a simple scraper and a small knife blade both appeared to be made from brownish chert but, when chipped, were found to have been originally made from gray chert that subsequently weathered to its present brown color.

But no real evidence was seen to indicate that the men who made the artifacts had occupied the gravels until, during work on the Adequentaga site, we reached a depth just short of two meters and within fifty centimeters of gravels which are described as being kame terrace gravels (Fairchild 1925). At this particular level (1.9 meters) an entirely different picture than that which we were accustomed to seeing began to develop. Two principal characteristics appeared abruptly, followed by others observed after more of the site was excavated. First was the appearance of a marked weathering of rock, most common in sandstone present at the level just mentioned. Secondly, a single flake uniface point with corner notching, shown in Plate 2(a), was found *in situ*. This point did not show the rolled edges so common to artifacts found in gravels elsewhere.

Plate 2.   Artifacts from within gravel deposits at Adequentaga. Levallois-like point (a) and biface chert points (b) and (c) all come from the same horizon, thought to represent surface of till deposit. Weathered hammerstone (d) with pit (indicated by arrow) shows cortex development

Indeed, the sides of the point were sharp enough to cut flesh as easily as a piece of freshly broken glass. Apparently, the point was made using the characteristic Levallois technique: it is a flake point with a spine on one face and a smooth, somewhat convex surface on the reverse side. The notches were carefully worked into the base of the artifact by pressure flaking and, in so working, the bulb of percussion was removed. The bifacially pitted hammerstone shown in Figure 1(d), though not found in direct relation with the point, showed its antiquity through cortex development (which incorporated the pitting made by man) of the outside part of the stone. It is currently in a marked state of decay and crumbles with each subsequent handling.

No charcoal, wood, or bone was available with which to date the artifacts; the soil was too acid to permit preservation of bone and, moreover, the old land surfaces upon which the culture materials had been left had been severely eroded by water, which periodically washed away any datable charcoal or wood. Two deep fire-hearths, located near the flake point and the hammerstone, were completely free of organic remains or charcoal which might have helped date the artifacts or hearth features. However, a newly discovered Archaic-stage culture phase, heretofore unknown to the region, was found. This culture phase possessed characteristics expected in a long-looked-for early Archaic phase. It revealed a large flake-tool industry, made up of specialized biface scrapers and specialized denticulate tools, all in association with stratified manganese dioxide deposits that enabled us to determine relative ages through geochemical means. Studies by Krauskopf and others in the laboratory suggest the conditions in which MnO_2 is formed under circumstances similar to those that are believed to have prevailed at the Adequentaga site when men occupied the region and left the artifacts behind. Krauskopf writes:

Glacial debris, containing fresh minerals and readily permeable to oxygen-rich meteoric water, is another obvious suggestion [besides lava] for material which could supply manganese in considerable quantity. The ground-water described by Zapffe (1931), containing an average of 0.8 p.p.m. Mn^{++} and only 1 p.p.m. Fe^{++}, is a good example of the sort of solution that might be expected from the water percolating through glacial material. It is perhaps no accident (D. F. Hewett, personal communication) that bog-ores of manganese, both in North America and in Scandinavia, are concentrated, in areas underlain by the latest Pleistocene till (Krauskopf 1957:76–77).

In cases in which the pH is 8.0 and preferably greater, manganese is precipitated instead of iron, which is also present in solution. Iron, however, is found to precipitate best where the pH is less than 7.0 and, indeed, precipitated iron is now found to be common in the soils and gravels in which an acid environment prevails. According to Krauskopf, manganese precipitation is enhanced by bacteria (*Crenothrix* and *Leptothrix*, which utilize bicarbonate as a carbon source), by the catalytic action of MnO_2, and by unusual concentrations of silicate as well as carbonate. And he adds,

If the original concentration of manganese were even slightly greater than normal, the precipitation would of course be aided. Probably the most essential requirement for accumulation of manganese from ordinary surface waters is that the necessary slightly unusual conditions persist for a geologically long time.

From observations such as these it seems to us that events brought man into the upper Susquehanna Valley toward the end of the last glaciation and that these men brought with them a well-established tradition of flake-tool manufacture but a tradition also that probably was in a stage of transition from uniface to biface manufacture, especially where projectile points were concerned. So far as we were able to determine in three years of work at Adequentaga, the tool assemblages were in each case accompanied by clear examples of bifacially pitted hammerstones, the use of fire-cracked rock in cooking, and cutting tools, which were in earlier times unifaces but in more recent times bifaces, with the former suggesting the possible use of the soft hammer and pressure flaking tools. No cultural bottom to the site was ever discovered and continued deep excavation was hindered and then stopped by the rapid accumulation of water fed by springs in the excavation areas.

With the exception of the single uniface dart point cited above, the picture presented by the culture materials, irrespective of the depth of the soils examined, was one of modern prehistoric cultures whose appearances on the scene could logically be explained in terms of post-Pleistocene occupation of the upper Susquehanna region. Yet there was no precedent for the meaning of the presence of the uniface point found there, nor any indication in later cultures concerning its obvious disappearance in them. No hand axes, cleavers, or chopping tools have ever been found on the site, regardless of depth explored.

In the early spring of 1970, Joseph P. Timlin, presently a field assistant in archaeology at Hartwick, made a unique discovery that opened up the whole problem of the temporal position of the flake uniface point as found in the area.

During an examination of the side of West Creek, a tributary of Schoharie Creek, which drains into the Mohawk River and subsequently empties into the Hudson, a variety of flake and core tools were found to have been washed from till deposits that flanked the stream bed. It was noted at this time that the stream, West Creek, flowed over a dark gray clay deposit which contained limestone cobbles and cherts (among other rocks) that were severely striated by movement in ice. Among the artifacts, flake points were repeatedly observed to be characteristic tool types. As several months passed two additional observations were made: first, stream erosion of at least two ancient soils of different ages was contributing to the exposure of the tools, and second, the range of type tools was very similar to that of the well-known Acheulean tools of other parts of the world, especially of Europe.

After several small boxes of tools were collected, it was decided that an excavation should be undertaken in some part of the valley where maximum geological data were available and where tools had been found *in situ*, projecting from the banks of the stream and from the different soils observed, suggesting different ages. Since most of the tools at the time of discovery were found littering the stream bed and only a few were found in place in the ancient soils, our initial plan was to begin a formal excavation with the single purpose of demonstrating the direct relationship of the tools with the soils (glacial gravels, sands, and clays) believed to contain the artifacts. This being done, it was then considered important to be able to demonstrate the presence of horizons within the deposits, if any, in order to eliminate the problem associated with many of the tools, which were clearly derived from other sources.

During three summers of excavation, the positive relationship that existed between the flake and core tools and the glacial sediments was demonstrated time and again. The common point type was the flake uniface, though occasional core biface thrusting-type points were noted. No post-Pleistocene bifacial-type points were found as a part of any assemblage of tools.

It seemed clear by now that some considerable antiquity, beyond that usually ascribed to man in the New World, could be assigned to the still imperfectly understood cultures. The question became one of how much antiquity, and so we began a concerted effort to find an answer to this second question.

The now-common uniface flake point with its suite of flake tools, including sidescrapers and end scrapers, backed flake knives, denticulate tools, and occasional hand axes, constituted good typological evidence suggesting an antiquity of as much as 70,000 years ago; but this evidence would be reliable only if it was supported by other kinds of evidence, derived from other areas of investigation besides culture.

The principal areas of potential investigation, of course, were the geological strata manifest in the character of ice-contact gravels, including striations on limestone and sandstone cobbles, the till-like character of the sediments, and the presence of lithologies unknown to post-Pleistocene sediments, such as bedded chert and silicified limestone. Early in the investigations artifacts had been taken from the clay deposit mentioned above, because this was the deepest of the sediments, and especially because it was overridden by the till sheet, which we call Ancient Soil Number 1, special attention was given to it. Moreover, as we studied the character of the clay deposit, it appeared to present, in specific places, the structure of a weathering-profile (Flint 1949, 1957); but it had an incompletely leached A horizon; and through both the A horizon and the B horizon below it, from the top of the profile to the bottom, the rock sizes increased as the action of weathering processes decreased, and the rock types changed from silica-rich to calcium-rich lithologies. Moreover, where a high exposure along the creek appeared, there was a ferretto zone that strengthened the seemingly weathered character of the clay deposit. It appeared, in short, that an eluviated zone (Hunt 1972:167) of the kind formerly referred to as gumbotil (Kay and Pearce 1920) might have been present at one time and had subsequently been decapitated by movement of the till sheet now lying above the clay.

Several other indicators tended to strengthen this point of view. One was the concretions of carbonate which were found in the clay deposit along the edge of one segment of the creek. They appeared to be associated with the B horizon of the clay. Then, during the summer of 1972, in an excavation at a higher elevation on the site that had been chosen because it offered the maximum opportunity to find the B horizon, which had continually shown evidence of being decapitated, we discovered a thin stratum of leached and oxidized clay underlying Ancient Soil Number 1; the stratum was so thin that we almost missed it. It was 10 to 15.5 centimeters thick and, in addition to being leached, was marked by a characteristic chocolate color and a few pebbles of weather-resistant siliceous material. Below this leached till there was an oxidized zone of lighter brown clay and sand that ran to a depth of 178 centimeters; it then became gray in color and the amount of carbonates, in the form of fine and coarse materials, increased as we dug to the depth of about two meters.

It is interesting to note that where the decapitations of the superficial horizons (i.e. A and B) were noted in other parts of the site, the resulting unconformity was characterized by the presence of a sharp line of demarcation between Ancient Soil Number 1 (A.S.1) and Ancient Soil Number 2 (A.S.2), the latter manifested principally as a dark gray clay. Moreover, the limestone cobbles that projected from the clay at the line of erosion were weathered by the erosion on the exposed sides but unweathered where they stuck into the clay. On the undersides that remained in the clay, numerous striae, which were produced by grinding during glacial transport, were visible. In one particular area the carbonate that precipitated from solution (percolating from above) consolidated the till in the B horizon below so thoroughly that it formed a kind of pavement (Flint 1949), which was almost impossible to penetrate using normal excavation procedures, including heavy hand equipment.

After the formal excavation through the leached, oxidized, and unleached soils that showed the weathering profile cited above, we took samples of the soil covering the whole range of chemical change and submitted them to a laboratory for analysis of mineral content; one soil series is presented in Figure 1. In an excavation performed the year

CHEMICAL ANALYSIS OF WEATHERED SOIL										
Soil Profile	% SiO₂		% Al₂O₃		% Fe₂O₃		% CaO		% MgO	
	Sample		Sample		Sample		Sample		Sample	
	1	2	1	2	1	2	1	2	1	2
Surface										
Topsoil										
	71.84	68.32	8.24	9.45	11.44	12.70	2.24	1.74	1.26	1.19
	64.00	66.36	6.75	7.05	9.04	9.49	9.79	9.65	1.19	1.26
	56.34	60.60	8.24	6.42	10.87	9.04	16.62	12.59	1.79	1.39
	50.02	55.74	11.24	9.54	11.72	11.29	8.33	9.09	1.66	1.66
	54.24	56.94	9.92	7.94	11.01	10.01	8.68	11.05	1.49	1.58

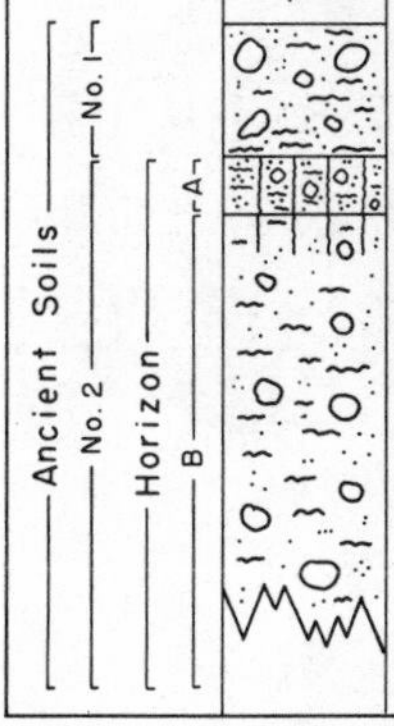

The table is labeled along its left margin: Ancient Soils — No. 1 (Horizon A); No. 2 (Horizon B).

Figure 1. Results of chemical analysis of soil zones of a weathering-profile, beginning at the unconformity produced by a till sheet decapitating the deposits sampled. Artifacts have regularly been taken from the B horizon

before we did these soil studies, artifacts, some of which are shown in Plates 3, 4, 5 and 6, were taken from *in situ* positions in the C horizon, the carbonate and limestone-rich gray component of the soil.

The supposed A.S.2, in superficial examination, stood in marked contrast to A.S.1. The decapitated soil, A.S.2, was an overall gray color that did not appear in the other soil, which was loosely consolidated. When dry, A.S.2 was hard and tenacious and light gray in color except where oxidation along its decapitated surface gave it a light brown color.

A.S.1, on the other hand, was rich in silt, sand, and limestone and sandstone boulders. In one case where it was deeper than in most places familiar to us, we found decaying rock, and often only clay and the outlines of the former stones, from which the clay was derived remained. The clay produced from this decay was thoroughly leached; in some cases it was still firm (but soft) enough to be easily carved with a knife. Some of the larger rocks found in this sediment were argillaceous sandstones that had deep grooves and striations, resulting from ice transport and abrasion. Bedded chert was a common rock type of this deposit, whereas silicified limestone was a common rock type of A.S.2. Artifacts made of chert and limestone were found in each soil, respectively.

Upon discovery of these complex conditions, we decided that deep coring of the regions under excavation would be necessary in order to understand the total picture presented by exposures of these sedimentary

Plate 3.   Chopping tools from the Timlin site. Dark gray silicified limestone tool (a) was found *in situ* in the C horizon of A.S.2. Tool (b) is from A.S.1, one of three similar tools found

deposits. We began this procedure in the summer of 1972. Preliminary results are presented in Figure 2, pending further study of the samples removed down to bedrock.

During these investigations, two students at Hartwick College with field experience on the culture material under discussion left Hartwick to study for one year at Universidad Iberoamericana in Mexico. During their free time there they visited as tourists the outlying areas around Mexico City. One day toward the end of their stay they happened upon an area near the city of Tula and observed great numbers of artifacts strewn over the surface of the ground. According to their account (Aldrich and Binder 1972), most of the artifacts appeared to be late pre-Columbian tools of one kind or another made of obsidian. They also found many milling stones, fragments of balsaltic statues, and pottery sherds in great varieties of design.

Toward the end of a full day of surveying the area, the sun began to set, and as the rays of the sun changed, different kinds of rocks caught their eyes. Now they began to observe the presence of artifacts that remotely resembled those they had seen from the Timlin site in New York.

To shorten the story, they sent a sample box of about a dozen paleoliths to the anthropology department personnel at Hartwick College for inspection and evaluation. As it turned out, most of the objects were flake

Plate 4. Silicified limestone tools, except (f), which is chert. These were found associated with the C layer of A.S.2. All except (d) and (e) were recovered by excavation of the clay. The biface (a) is shown in Plate 6 as it is being excavated by a student. Artifacts (d) and (e) are types of scrapers; (b) an Acheulean-type point; (c) a core end scraper; and (f) a core knife

tools made from felsitic breccia and a white variety of chert. Included among the flake tools were three flake uniface points; they were made of felsitic breccia and were typical of the kind found on the Timlin site. In addition, there were examples of backed knives, transverse end scrapers and sidescrapers, and push-planes. Lastly, there was among the tools a single type tool so specific in design (Plate 7(f) and 7(g)) as to link the culture producing the artifact with one of the cultures represented at the Timlin site. Tools from both sites are shown in Plates 7, 8 and 9.

During the absence of the two students we found this same type artifact, but made of chert instead of breccia, for the first time in the gravel of West Creek, where it had been washed from the bank during the period of high water in spring; it is shown later in Plate 7(g). Moreover, each of the artifacts had been thinned by the removal of a large flake on the worked side of the tool; the manner in which this was done on the artifact from the Timlin site suggested a knowledge of the process of fluting. A quick review of the other artifacts from the Mexican site

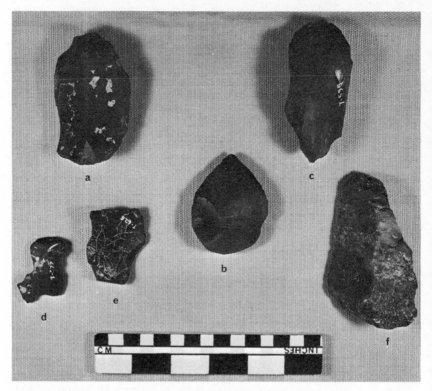

Plate 5.   Reverse sides of artifacts illustrated in Plate 4

demonstrated quite clearly that fluting had been performed on at least three scrapers to remove channel flakes from one side of each tool.

It appeared that the palmar (as we came to call our artifact because of its general similarity to the palm of the human hand) came from some unknown level associated with A.S.1 bordering West Creek in New York, and, indeed, in subsequent months several of these were found *in situ*, beginning at the surface of the upper till deposit (A.S.1).

The projectile points from Mexico also show characteristics similar to many of those found on the Timlin site, as shown in Plate 9. One of the closest relationships is noted between those from Mexico and one shown in Plate 9(c), found in the B horizon of A.S.2, two inches below the unconformity mentioned above, between the two ancient soils. The Timlin point was found *in situ*, is somewhat larger, and was constructed from silicified limestone.

While all the artifacts found in Mexico were surface finds, not buried in soil, some temporal control nevertheless exists as a result of the marked similarities among artifacts from the two sites, which are separated spatially by a distance of more than four thousand kilometers. And because

Plate 6.   Student's trowel points to half the biface (Plates 4 [a] and 5 [a]) so far excavated. She is standing on the surface of the C horizon of A.S.2 at a depth of 1.22 meters. Note gravel of A.S.1 behind the measuring pole (marked in feet)

the palmars, or multipurpose scraping tools, are found in at least one buried soil in New York State, is seems reasonable to expect that, as continued work is carried out, not only will a direct relationship become more apparent; but, what is more important, an enlarged view of man's very early distribution throughout the Western Hemisphere will be more obvious than it is at this time.

At this point it is possible to take two distinct lines of approach and consider the cultures in their temporal relationships separately from their

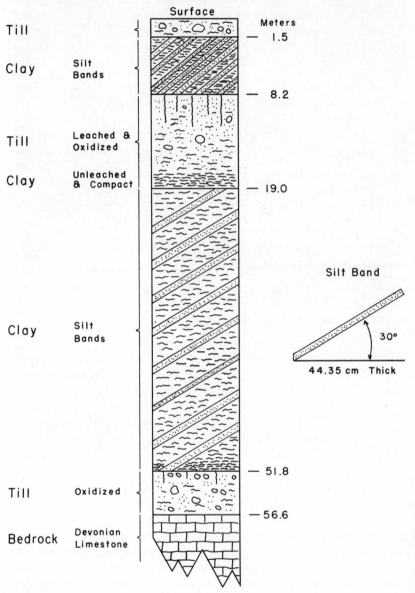

Figure 2.   Preliminary interpretation of the log of a single core taken from the Timlin site near West Creek, next to an earlier excavation at a lower elevation than the terrace worked during the summer of 1972, where an *in situ* assemblage of tools representing an occupation was found

Plate 7. Tools from Mexican and Timlin sites. Mexican: (a), (c), (d), and (f); (a), (b), and (c) are fluted scraping tools; (d) and (e) are flake knives; (f) and (g) are multipurpose scraping tools (type artifacts). Note fluting on (g) from the Timlin site: the object was apparently hafted, and fluting was done to thin as well as to help seat the object firmly in a handle. Both (f) and (g) are flake tools, called palmars

spatial relationships. We propose to combine the two approaches, hoping for the best possible understanding in the shortest possible space. First of all, we would like to describe the nature of the tools found and treat them in broad outline (this applies to all the evidence) with the understanding that much work is yet to be accomplished and many loose ends will, for the time being, remain untied.

In treating the difficult problems associated with interpretation of evidence we will focus our attention on three matters: (1) on a consideration of some tools that are representative of the evidence we have found, localizing ancient cultures in their time–space relationships; (2) on a brief comparative study of tools from Mexico and New York State with respect to a unique spatial distribution of one particular ancient culture; and (3) on a treatment of one particular culture horizon at the Timlin site that seems to shed some unusual light on the time factor controlling our observations concerning the early appearance of man in the New World.

In any treatment of the stone tools the question of dating immediately

Plate 8.   Tools from Mexican and Timlin sites. Mexican: (a), (c), and (e); (a) and (b) are disc cores; (c) and (d) are patinated flake points with concave bases; (e), (f), and (g) are push-planes

arises because morphology and tool-making traditions are so closely interrelated in our case as to imply some time specificity of great length. Materials that could be used for absolute dating of cultures, such as wood and bone, have been lacking, and charcoal is practically nonexistent, except in the topsoils covering the culture-containing gravels. Paleontological evidence such as teeth of extinct animals — horse, bison, and pig, for instance — have not as yet been completely evaluated; even these were random discoveries in pondlike sediments that are also not yet completely understood. Invertebrate fossils are present in sediments, but these have been of species that are nonspecific with respect to relative dating of the Pleistocene. We are also finding plant seeds in the soils, which should ultimately prove helpful. For example, hemp seed has been found scattered throughout the topsoil of one part of the site; this plant is now extinct in the area but was undoubtedly introduced into the region in post-Columbian times. Botanists have not yet identified other seeds we have collected (two species). Pollen studies are planned for the future.

Although it is far from satisfactory, much of the dating is, nevertheless, dependent upon the nature of the lithologies from which the tools were made, traditions involved in their making, the type artifacts themselves,

Plate 9. Mexican and Timlin projectile points. Mexican: (a), (b), and (d). Arrows indicate location of percussion platforms when viewed from the edges of the artifacts

and the geologic contexts in which the tools were found. We are hopeful that the range and kind of evidence bearing upon the antiquity of the tools is sufficient evidence to lend authority to the date assigned the oldest culture.

We have, as is customary, divided the artifacts into core and flake tools, but we are not implying that one type is present in greater number between culture horizons. Flake and core tools are regularly found together. Flake tools predominate and outnumber core tools at least fifteen to one. We feel it is still too early to expect reliable results from statistical studies, so the proportion of flake to core tools is very tentative. One other category, which we will call "miscellaneous," will be treated briefly.

Cores (as flake sources) of specific shapes are not common at the site; when found, they have the character of globular or disc cores. Some artifacts certainly indicate that prepared cores were used as flake sources, and three, possibly four, disc-type cores have been found; but they are never found in great number and the question of their identity as disc cores is somewhat open. A type core chopping tool has been identified. It is usually rudely stemmed and its functional edge is located on one or the other of two sides. It also appears regularly as a very large and roughly worked flake tool, as shown in Plate 3(b). In each case it is patinated gray chert and its weathered faces have taken on a brown color from iron pigmentation. A more specialized core chopping tool, shown in Plate 3(a), was found *in situ* in the other ancient soil, A.S.2. It appears to be a multipurpose chopping and scraping tool and was found associated with other silicified limestone tools: a type point, shown in Plates 4(b) and 5(b), of the same material that compares very closely with one discussed by Bordes (1968:62) as part of an Upper Acheulean tool assemblage from Combe-Grenal, Dordogne, France. Still other tools resemble artifacts found in Middle Pleistocene contexts in Greece (Poulianos 1971).

The chopping tool has at least two functional edges and a notch, perhaps for hafting. A very fine straight edge suggests that a soft hammer was used in part of its manufacture. Other chopping tools found are of ruder manufacture; some are made of gray chert, others of quartzite, but all are marked by having a single edge worked out by percussion flaking from both sides of the stone and a flat back that fits securely into the palm of the hand. Core scrapers and knives are also common, and if anything is characteristic about them as a group, it appears at this time to be their individuality (although there are some exceptions to this).

Plate 10.   Two examples of massive stone tools, often weighing in excess of ten kilograms: (a) is a pointed chopping tool and (b) a possible wood- or bone-shaving tool, with functional concave edge facing the chopping tool. Both are patinated chert

One of the most unusual groups of artifacts found is the one in which the individual tools are large and heavy, shown in Plate 10. They vary from four to eleven kilograms and so suggest that two hands were required to use them. The percussion-flaked edges are often concave, and it is suggested that they might have been used as very large wood- or bone-shavers. Their origin is believed to be the upper till, A.S.1. They are always patinated, as are most of the tools derived from this horizon.

Among the flake tools may be included points, sidescrapers, end scrapers, and transverse scrapers, backed knives, graving tools, and large multipurpose flake unifaces (again, often patinated, even overlain with great weathering). With the exception of the latter, perhaps, these tools are not very different from their corresponding types in toolboxes found in Europe and possibly elsewhere. Because of their size, however, the large uniface flake scrapers shown in Plate 11 appear to be somewhat unusual. Yet this distinction may be more apparent than real. The flake unifaces are quite numerous at the site and suggest the anvil method of manufacture; perhaps this is where our interest in them should end.

Plate 11. Artifacts excavated from the surface of A.S.1 of the Timlin site; (a), (b), (c), and (g) are various flake scraping tools, (d) a possible projectile point of quartz, (e) a knife of chert, (f) a pointed nodular tool (compare Warren 1951:112), and (g) a multipurpose scraper (palmar). Artifacts (a), (b), (e), and (f) are made from bedded chert

The projectile points shown in Plate 12 are represented as flake unifaces with principal retouch performed along the edges from either face by percussion. They come from all horizons examined and differ from one another in terms of the rock source used, the quality of manufacture, and the impact of time upon tradition: it appears that the points made more recently are cruder and were given less attention in their manufacture than earlier ones. Indeed, on the basis of only about six points , it seems that there was a shift from the uniface to the biface. This is evident from the fact that in more recent sediments (sands and gravels near the topsoil) small pebble or core (as opposed to flake) bifaces have been found; with them, however, were also found small, thin uniface points resembling the one illustrated in Bordes (1968:62) and the one illustrated in Plates 4(b) and 5(b). On the other hand, discounting its carefully pressure-flaked and notched base, the single uniface taken from the Adequentaga site, shown in Plate 2(a), shows the usual skill of manufacture associated with the oldest of the points at the Timlin site.

In addition to being flakes, some of the points have faceted platforms, while on others platform remnants are visible. Where platforms are present on either points or other tools, they form angles of 100 to 120 degrees

Plate 12.   Flake projectile points illustrating the range of variation found so far among the flake type. Points (a), (b), (e), and (f) were found *in situ* and (b) and (f) through formal excavation of the site

with the cone faces of the artifacts. Some points have only one shoulder as part of the normal pattern; others have concave bases. There is, in short, a great deal of variation within the limits imposed by the flake structure. There appears, also, within this normal range of variation, no significant difference (except in their material composition) between points from the Timlin site and the half-dozen we have from the site in Mexico.

We have included the so-called hand axes among the miscellaneous category of tools largely because, although they are important tools, they are not as common as chopping tools (or have not been so up to this time). Yet they are present among the artifacts found within the A.S.1 horizon. Because A.S.2 has been difficult to approach and almost impossible to search for artifacts, the lack of a discovery of the hand ax from that horizon may not indicate its real absence.

The hand axes we have seen, some of which are shown in Plate 13, have been poorly made, with one possible exception. They have sometimes been flaked on one end only, and at other times have been carefully worked all around, such as Plate 13(c). They are almost exclusively made of chert, occasionally of quartzite, and the tools themselves show varying

Plate 13. Hand axes. All are chert except (d), which is quartzite. Artifact (a) was excavated from A.S.1 in precisely the same location illustrated in Plate 6, but at a depth of one
meter. All tools are patinated, even the quartzite (d); (b) is yellow with overlay although the
stone when fresh is banded gray and white

degrees of patination, even the one of quartzite illustrated in Plate 13(d), from which a thin flake was accidentally chipped during its recovery, exposing the thin patination.

A number of milling stones have also been discovered. At first thought to be coincidental or fortuitous shapes, they increased in number to such an extent that they could no longer be ignored as cultural in origin. Usually very large and rough stones found in or on A.S.1, they have shallow, concave depressions that are smoother near the regularly used part than on other parts of the stone. They are usually made of sandstone, and their edges are sometimes shaped by having been pounded with another stone. We have been able to predict the presence of a habitation around the very large millstones because, of course, they are not easily moved by either man or nature.

Lastly, one fairly well defined anvil stone weighing between twenty-five and thirty pounds was recovered. It was a large section split from sandstone, apparently in transport, by natural forces. It was then worked to reduce the stone at one end and produce, thereby, a somewhat flat knob that was apparently used to break flakes from large cores.

We cannot proceed without pausing to emphasize two especially significant traits of the artifacts. Of the many characteristics that could be singled out, we think the marked patination of the tools is of special significance because it is found on many tools made from a wide variety of siliceous rocks. A second significant characteristic is that many of the tools are made from lithologies that have not been found by the examination of materials from post-Pleistocene cultures. The sources of these rocks are not presently known, but regular use of them in the materials found suggests either unknown or no longer available rock sources. These characteristics seem to support the estimates of extended antiquity for the cultures.

We have already begun a limited comparative study of the type tools found in a buried soil at the Timlin site and those made of felsitic breccia that were discovered near Tula, Mexico. We indicated that the tools from Mexico could be classified as both core and flake tools although they appear to have come from the same culture. We noted that among the tools indicating this fact were flake uniface points and a type multipurpose scraping tool of rather complex design, shown in Plate 7(f), which could be compared to very similar, if not absolutely identical, tools from the Timlin site in New York State.

In the meantime our attention was called to the appearance of fire-hearths from a site on the Pleistocene beach of Chalco Lake in the Valley of Mexico. A cluster of carbon dates averaging about 20,000 B.C. has been reported (Buckley and Willis 1972). Limited personal communication with the principal investigators of the site (Lorenzo and others) *suggests* possible culture relationships between flake tools from that site and our upper A.S.1 horizon.

Recognizing the nature of the problems associated with the limited materials available at this time and the brief period of time we have known these materials, it is not possible to come to any final conclusions here, a point we have already tried to emphasize. Yet the noted characteristics make it clear that whatever else may be true of the people that produced the tools that have been found, their cultural tradition had a broad spatial distribution.

Besides the palmars and type flake uniface points, marked similarities have been found between core knife blades, push-planes, such as shown in Plate 8(f) and (g), possible line-sinkers, and specialized scraping tools, all of which are core and flake types.

One of the most interesting characteristics, however, is the appearance of uniface fluting on the side-scraping, the transverse-scraping, and the so-called multipurpose scraping tools, such as the palmar. Where fluting is present, relatively long channel flakes have been removed; control has been good in the manufacturing process. Flutes have also been produced on one side only, and then always on the worked face, i.e. the face opposite the one on which the percussion bulb is present. The channel is produced, moreover, by a blow directed onto the platform remnant that was produced originally when the flake was removed from the core. The same technique is apparent in the production of similar tools from the Timlin site (A.S.1).

A high degree of skill is characteristic of the manufacture of many of the Mexican tools that were examined; but both core and flake tools were made by percussion flaking. It is also interesting to note that we have found neither bone nor wood tools at either site although we think that bone tools, at least, must have been used.

Finally, it might be of interest to observe that no recognizable hand axes have been found with the assemblage of tools from Mexico. Disc-shaped chopping tools, however, that are made from rounded nodules of felsite and have flat backs and sinuous edges are common. Two of similar type have been taken from delta gravels in the Susquehanna River drainage.

In order to deal with the difficult problem of dating, it was decided to devote the summer fieldwork of 1972 to searching out and attempting to understand completely (if possible in the brief time allocated) a single culture horizon, which, because it represented an undisturbed occupation, would yield maximum information that would clearly establish its antiquity and which would also become a dependable reference point for placing other cultures in time.

The attempt was made on a part of the site that was elevated and was in the form of a flat; it was higher by about 1.5 meters than the rest of the site and was located along the base of a ridge that bounded the area of occupation to the south. After establishing a twenty-meter trench that varied in depth from 127 to 183 centimeters and penetrated through a topsoil, a till, and finally a clay deposit (where we were stopped from deeper excavation by the presence of ground water), a culture component that seemed to satisfy the requirements described above was identified on the surface of the till. Almost immediately upon reaching the till a worker discovered one of the type multipurpose scrapers that we have described as a palmar. Then, due as much to the fact that the ground water slowed our trench work as to the discovery of a possible culture component on the till, we excavated down to the surface of the till and stopped there in order to extend the work spatially and to expose evidence indicating the occupation of the till by early man.

As the tools began to appear, one of the characteristics of the culture remains that seemed most conspicuous was the mixture of large flake and retouched core tools. The flakes showed signs of being struck from prepared cores, but we found no conclusive evidence, other than the uniformly large size of the flakes themselves and the obtuse angles produced by the percussion platform, that an anvil had been used.

Of all the tools recovered to date, the predominate tool was the scraper, which appeared in a variety of forms. One possible point made of quartz, shown in Plate 11(d), was found. This was a uniface about 5.5 centimeters in length that had been worked on one face only; but it displayed such careless workmanship that if it had been used as a point at all, it must have been used as a thrusting point.

The principal rock used for the flakes was a gray bedded chert; although the source of the rock is presently unknown, the till itself is one possible origin. The waste cores were retouched by percussion and appear to have been used as wood or bone scraping tools, or possibly as chopping tools. A core remnant is shown in Plate 14.

Perhaps the most valuable observation, however, is the recognition of evidence that showed on the one hand, that man had occupied the site and, on the other, that the occupation had been a long time ago. All the tools had been made on this spot, but the tools (with the exception of those made of quartz) were rather heavily patinated also. The processes of weathering had turned the surfaces of each and every tool made of chert brown, to varying degrees.

There was other evidence of occupation. Two large stones, one with a working surface of about one square meter, appear to have been used. The larger was deeply grooved in many places with straight and curved lines and had the appearance of a utilized tabletop. It weighs perhaps somewhat less than one metric ton. The other, a milling stone, was once

Plate 14. Patinated chert core remnant *in situ*, only one of a large number of artifacts found under similar conditions on top of A.S.1. Core was found upon removal to have a curved retouched edge, suggesting its use as a planing tool

considered a questionable artifact; but having found a number of such stones in previous work at the site in clear culture contexts and in every possible culture level, we are inclined to regard the object as what it appears to be.

Finally, the discovery of a palmar (cited above), which are not found in post-Pleistocene cultures, narrows somewhat the temporal range of the people and their occupation of the excavated part of the site. The palmar in Plate 7(g) was of poor (or careless) workmanship and displayed no evidence of fluting. Further investigation will surely make more discreet observations possible.

In the course of digging the trench in this area, the A horizon of A.S.2 was discovered just below the till deposit cited above (i.e. A.S.1). The B horizon (i.e. A.S.2) lies below this.

As excavation of A.S.1 continued it became clear from the fact that the rocks found in it were in varying stages of decay that the till had undergone advanced weathering. Clay minerals were present where rocks had once occupied the same positions as the clay. There were pockets of red, gray, and yellow muds which had previously been rocks.

The outlines of other stones could still be seen and many could be cut through with a trowel or knife. Those stones that showed chemical decomposition but maintained their overall structure were found to be thoroughly leached of soluble salts. Occasionally, before the water problem forced us to abandon this zone we found some artifacts in it. It is also known on the basis of excavations done during 1971 that at least one unconformity is present (at the base of A.S.1).

At the bottom of this stratigraphy in the B horizon of A.S.2 the silicified limestone assemblage of tools was located; this tool assemblage is from the oldest culture horizon found, but it probably does not represent the oldest tools present.

SUMMARY

In an early report resulting from limited excavations on an early man site in New York State it has been suggested, on the basis of cultural and geological evidence acquired under conditions of controlled excavations, that man was present in New York State possibly as early as 70,000 years ago. Further, continued investigations are seen as necessary in order to determine the prehistory of the cultures in cases in which the evidence presented by the appearance of traditions in stone-tool manufacture suggests a long continuity of development. Through evidence of Mexican origin it appears also that there is a spatial as well as a temporal dimension of extended continuity in the prehistory of the New World that precedes the disappearance of the last of the Wisconsin ice.

Description of the early material is made for purposes of acquainting anthropologists with the unique nature of the results of recent research in New York State and of seeking advice with respect to possible future directions the research might take in order to recover maximum data from the sites being worked.

REFERENCES

ALDRICH, STEVEN, JANICE BINDER
     1972   A description of some comparative culture remains of early man from Mexico and New York State. *Yager Museum Publications in Anthropology*, Bulletin 4. Oneonta: Hartwick College.
BORDES, FRANÇOIS
     1968   *The old Stone Age.* New York: McGraw-Hill.
     1972   *A tale of two caves.* New York: Harper and Row.
BRYAN, ALAN L.
     1969   Early man in America and the late Pleistocene chronology of western Canada and Alaska. *Current Anthropology* 10:339–365.

BUCKLEY, JAMES, ERIC H. WILLIS
  1972   Tlapacoya I, Alfa 2, "Isotopes' radiocarbon measurements IX."
         Radiocarbon 14:136.
FAIRCHILD, HERMAN L.
  1925   *The Susquehanna River in New York and evolution of western New York
         drainage.* Bulletin 256. Albany: New York State Museum and Science
         Service.
FLINT, RICHARD FOSTER
  1949   Leaching of carbonates in glacial drift and loess as a basis for age
         correlation. *Journal of Geology* 57:297–303.
  1957   *Glacial and Pleistocene geology.* New York: John Wiley.
HAYNES, JR., C. VANCE
  1969   The earliest Americans. *Science* 166:709–715.
HUNT, CHARLES B.
  1972   *Geology of soils.* San Francisco: W. H. Freeman.
KAY, G. F., J. N. PEARCE
  1920   The origin of gumbotil. *Journal of Geology* 28:89–125.
KRAUSKOPF, KONRAD B.
  1957   Separation of manganese from iron in sedimentary processes.
         Geochimica et Cosmochimica Acta 12:61–84.
LEE, THOMAS E.
  1957   The antiquity of the Sheguiandah site. *Canadian Field-Naturalist*
         71:117–137.
MUNSON, PATRICK J., JOHN C. FRYE
  1965   Artifact from deposits of mid-Wisconsin age in Illinois. *Science*
         150:1,722–1,723.
OAKLEY, KENNETH P.
  1966   *Frameworks for dating fossil man.* Chicago: Aldine.
POULIANOS, ARIS N.
  1971   Petralona, a middle Pleistocene cave in Greece. *Archaeology* 24:6–12.
RAEMSCH, B. E.
  1970   Preliminary report on Adequentaga. *Yager Museum Publications in
         Anthropology,* Bulletin 2. Oneonta: Hartwick College.
RENAUD, E. B.
  1938   The Black's Fork culture of southwest Wyoming. *Archaeological
         Survey of the High Western Plains*, tenth report. Denver: University of
         Denver Press.
STALKER, A. M.
  1969   Geology and age of the early man site at Taber, Alberta. *American
         Antiquity* 34:425–428.
TIMLIN, JOSEPH, B. E. RAEMSCH
  1971   Pleistocene tools from the northeast of North America, the Timlin site.
         Yager Museum Publications in Anthropology, Bulletin 3. Oneonta:
         Hartwick College.
WARREN, S. H.
  1951   The Clacton flint industry: a new interpretation. *Proceedings of the
         Geological Association* 62:107–135.
  1958   The Clacton flint industry: a supplementary note. *Proceedings of the
         Geological Association* 69:123–129.

The Trimmed-Core Tradition
in Asiatic–American Contacts

DON W. DRAGOO

The antiquity and origin of man in the New World has been of concern to many archaeologists for years, but within the past fifteen years interest in this phase of New World prehistory has increased greatly. Many newly discovered early sites have been investigated with the application of new methods and techniques. Increasing emphasis has been placed on the study of tools other than projectile points with a view to understanding the technology employed as well as establishing a typology. Sites have been studied for clues to settlement patterns and subsistence activities of the people who inhabited them. Radiocarbon dates were obtained for several sites and new methods of dating, such as obsidian hydration and archaeomagnetic determination, were applied to early cultural manifestations by some archaeologists. Invaluable insights into the environment affecting man over the past several thousand years have been given to the archaeologists by geologists, paleontologists, and palynologists who have turned their attention increasingly to Pleistocene problems. It has been a period of great advancement, but many questions remain unanswered.

In 1970, a symposium on "Early Man in North America, New Developments: 1960–1970" was held at the American Anthropological Association Annual Meeting in San Diego, California, and the papers resulting from this meeting were published in *Arctic Anthropology* (1971). Their authors presented a survey of the then-current status of knowledge on early cultures of the New World, but the obvious conclusion that can be drawn from these papers is that there is much disagreement as to the age and origin of these cultures. Wormington's comment (1971:88) that "there remain many points to be argued" was an apt summary of the symposium and of the status of our knowledge in general. In this paper it is my intention to discuss some of the major problems confronting students of early man in the New World and to suggest some lines for further research.

One of the crucial questions evading an answer pertains to man's first appearance in the New World and the kind(s) of culture he brought with him. As Wormington (1971:84) has noted, no one really knows when man first came, and all efforts to place certain time limits on the event by some workers are probably incorrect. We do know that man was well established in the New World by 12,000–11,000 B.C., and some radiocarbon dates extend the range to much earlier times. To many workers, however, these early dates are to be seriously questioned on various grounds, and some individuals have discounted them completely.

Some of our arguments and disagreements seem to stem from historical events. The first indisputable evidence of man's association with extinct Pleistocene fauna was found at the Lindenmeier site in Colorado and the Blackwater Draw site in New Mexico, beginning in 1927. Since these early discoveries, several other localities have yielded similar remains in other areas of the southwest United States. The oldest culture found at these sites seems to be the Clovis, which is associated with extinct fauna such as mammoth at "kill sites" where the animal was slain and butchered. The tool assemblages found at such locations tend to be limited to projectile points and occasionally a few knives and scrapers. The distinctive fluted projectile points, however, became the trademark for Early Man and the southwest his center of occupation.

The southwestern homeland bias seems to have been postulated by some workers on the bland assumption that once man crossed the Bering Straits he first made a mad dash for that region with only the briefest of stops in between. Once there, man increased in number and eventually began to push outward to other areas of North America and eventually southward to Mexico and South America. This simple idea of the southwest as the seedbed of New World cultural development has led many workers to view finds in other areas as later than and derived from the southwest. Although this position has recently suffered many blows, it is still maintained by some influential workers.

A prime example of the belief that man arrived in the New World near the end of the last glacial advance, about 12,000 years ago, is a recent article by Martin (1973:969). He presents the thesis that man made his appearance at about that time and that within 1,000 years he had raced to the tip of South America. In this brief period there was a population explosion of sufficient magnitude to exterminate the Pleistocene megafauna. By 11,000 years ago, man had been forced into a major cultural readaptation from big game hunting to a diversified economy in most of the hemisphere. With this change, Martin (1973:973) also thinks there was a sharp drop in human population.

Perhaps there were population declines in some marginal areas such as the southwest, but the evidence for eastern North America indicates quite a contrary situation. The east, and particularly the southeast, was intensively occupied during the early Lithic period as typified by the users of fluted points. More Clovis-type fluted points have been found in such states as Tennessee and Alabama than have been recorded for the entire western United States. In the east there were many subtypes of fluted points developed over a considerable period of time. The work of Coe (1964), Broyles (1966), and others clearly indicates that there was a continuous occupation of the east from the early Lithic period into the succeeding Archaic period. Judging from the size and number of sites and the amount of cultural debris on them, there was also a steady increase in population that began late in the early Lithic period and continued throughout the Archaic period. The southeast was certainly the most densely populated area in North America at the end of the early Lithic period and in the millennia that immediately followed it. Thus, I find it exceedingly difficult to understand how Martin, or anyone else, can reconstruct the early Lithic period and the extinction of the Pleistocene megafauna based only on information from the southwest and with the exclusion of the southeast from any serious consideration as part of the picture.

It is not my intention here to go into the causes of megafauna extinction and to discuss fully the development of early Lithic culture during its later phases, but it has been necessary to draw attention to this southwestern bias, as clearly expressed by Martin, since it has had an enormous influence on the study of New World cultural beginnings. It is a view which I believe to be unfounded in fact and a detriment to enlightened research on the complex problems of the early Lithic period.

All too often the fluted-point complex has been looked upon as the starting point for tracing New World contacts to the Old World. Since the fluted point was considered to be the earliest well-documented and datable artifact, it was assumed that man probably had this tool when he made the crossing from Asia. However, the search for cultures having fluted points, or possible ancestral forms, in northeastern Asia and Alaska has met with little success. Haynes (1964, 1969) and Humphrey (1966) have advocated the thesis that specialized mammoth hunters from Siberia were isolated in Alaska until an ice-free corridor opened, when they became the hunters represented by the early fluted-point horizon of about 10,000 B.C. Wormington (1971) has stated her reluctance to accept this idea on the basis that there are few points in Alaska and none in a firmly datable context. In accord with Wormington, I would agree that "we are not yet in a position to say where, or even when, the tradition of fluting developed." There are no established prototypes for Clovis and other early fluted points, but it is certain that unfluted points must have preceded fluted points somewhere in North America. The transition from unfluted points to fluted points could have occurred in the southeast, where many fluted types were developed, rather than in the west, where only a limited number of forms have been found.

If we consider the fluted point as a New World innovation, then it is necessary to discover and isolate a prior complex, or complexes, from which the fluted point and associated tools could have developed. It seems quite unlikely that man began the making of fluted points soon after his arrival in the New World, and a considerable period of time must have elapsed during their evolution. Wormington (1971:84) has stated her belief that man has been here for a far longer time than the period for which we have absolutely convincing proof, and she has suggested that this time will probably be prior to 25,000 years ago when acceptable evidence is found. I have stated (Dragoo 1968:176) that, on the basis of typological uniqueness, geographic distribution, high degree of patination of tool surfaces, and the similarity of tool types to those of the upper Paleolithic of the Old World, there are complexes that have been found in the New World which possibly date as early as 40,000 years ago. Similar views of the time involved have been presented by Willey (1966:37), Müller-Beck (1966), Krieger (1964), MacNeish (1971), and others who have attacked the problem of early cultures from different perspectives and have worked in various areas of the New World.

In recent years there have been a number of finds for which considerable antiquity has been indicated by radiocarbon dates. Irving (1971:69) has reported a bone scraper found at the Old Crow Flats in the Yukon dated at 27,000 years ago. Bison and mammoth bones, apparently cracked by man, from the same locality were dated 25,750 to 29,100 years ago. Similar finds of mammoth with indications of possible human associations have been found at Santa Rosa Island, California, with dates of 30,000–37,000 years ago (Orr 1968); the Cooperton site in Oklahoma, dated at about 20,000 years ago (Andersen 1962); and several localities in the Valsequillo area near Puebla, Mexico, where a date of 21,800 years ago was obtained at one site, Caulapau, from a stratum containing a simple uniface scraper (Irwin-Williams 1967, 1969). Malde (1967) has studied the stratigraphy of these Mexican sites and suggests that some of the tool-bearing deposits may be as much as 35,000 years old. All of these sites with mammoth and other Pleistocene fauna are of great importance as indicators of man's early presence, but the scarcity of tools at most of them gives us little evidence for the cultures involved.

Several sites for which early dates in excess of 20,000 years have been obtained by radiocarbon analysis, geological placement, or other means have questionable human associations with the dates. Among the more important of these sites that have drawn serious attention in recent years are Lewisville, Texas (Crook and Harris 1957, 1958; Krieger 1964; Willey 1966), Tule Springs, Nevada (Harrington and Simpson 1961;

Shutler 1965), and the Calico Mountains site in California (Leakey, Simpson, *et al.* 1972). At both the Lewisville and Tule Springs sites there has been doubt as to the association of the cultural remains with the materials being dated. In the case of the Calico Mountains site excavated under the direction of Leakey and Simpson, a date of about 70,000 years ago has been suggested by the project geologist Thomas Clements. Wormington (1971:84), with whom I agree, has presented the majority opinion of those of us who have studied the site, which is that the so-called artifacts are doubtful works of man and that they could have been produced by natural forces during the building of the alluvial fan in which they were found. The supposed tools from Calico also lack any patterning to types, and the edges appear to be fractured and crushed rather than deliberately chipped. Some geologists who studied the site would date the alluvial fan deposit from 500,000 to as much as a million years old. Thus, in spite of the tremendous effort, time, and care by the excavators of Calico, the results are still inconclusive and subject to future verification.

Although studies of man's presence in the New World earlier than the bearers of fluted points have met with many difficulties in dating precise associations and in sample size, the evidence for such cultures is now too great to ignore and to sweep under the carpet, even though dating does remain a crucial problem. More than one complex seem to be present among the possible candidates for early honors. We will now take a look at these complexes and their possible connections with the Old World.

In recent years there have been a number of finds of pebble tools in North America (Dragoo 1965; Lively 1965; Borden 1968). The greatest concentrations of these tools have been found in the southeast, but similar tools also occur in the west. In the southeast crude pebble tools were reported from many sites in Alabama by Matthew Lively (1965) working in conjunction with the late Daniel Josselyn (1967) of the Alabama Archaeological Society. The classic tools of this complex consist of chert pebbles that were chipped by percussion. From a simple platform at the end of the pebble, one or more flakes were removed to produce a sharp cutting edge in several variations to form choppers, planes, and scrapers. Several thousand tools have been found at more than seventy sites in northern Alabama. Several distinct and basic tool types seem to be present at all the sites, but there is evidence of change and development in that some tool types, such as pebble drills, seem to be present at some sites and absent at others.

Prior to Josselyn's death in 1971 I had worked with him and Matthew Lively on the collections from many of these classic pebble-tool sites and from several other sites having similar tools fashioned from materials other than chert pebbles. Crude tools of the same types were found to have been made on tabular cherts and quartzites in areas where chert pebbles were not available. Some of the sites where these tools are found seem to be single-component, with only crude tools, while others are multicomponent, with cultures of various time periods represented. The location of these sites varies from isolated hilltops to river terraces and rock shelters. When these crude tools occur on multicomponent sites, the location usually is one that would have been favorable for man at any time or cultural level.

The exact cultural provenience and age of the pebble tools and similar tools in other materials found at the sites in northern Alabama and in adjacent areas of Georgia, Tennessee, and Mississippi are difficult problems to solve. Attempts to assign a specific age to them is not easy since they may span a long period of time. In an attempt to answer the problem of time and context, De Jarnette (1967) excavated the Stutz Bluff shelter site and the Crump site in northern Alabama. At the open-air Crump site, located in an area above a river flood plain, pebble tools were found scattered through a deposit nearly four feet in depth with no noticeable concentration and in association with late early Lithic Dalton points in the lowest levels and early Archaic projectile points in the upper levels. At the Stutz Bluff shelter there was a similar random distribution through the upper levels of the deposit ranging in time from Archaic to Woodland, but in the lower levels, which represented a late early Lithic transition to early Archaic, there was a marked increase in pebble tools, with the lowest level containing mostly pebble tools. Thus, De Jarnette concluded that pebble tools were present from late early Lithic times but that they also persisted through much later cultures.

It has been my observation that nearly all the rock shelters in eastern North America have occupation zones that begin only near the end of the early Lithic period. Prior to that time most rock shelters seem to have been wet and uninhabitable, and there is a layer of water-deposited sand representing this period directly below the late early Lithic deposit. This unfortunate situation has generally precluded the finding of pebble tools with earlier Lithic remains in a datable stratified deposit. However, pebble tools, or crude tools similar in type but of different raw material, have been found at two early Lithic sites assignable to earlier times than the deposit excavated by De Jarnette at the Stutz Bluff site. These sites are the Wells Creek site in Stewart County, Tennessee (Dragoo 1965, 1973), and the Debert site in Nova Scotia (MacDonald 1968), where early to middle eastern Clovis points have been found in association. Thus, pebble tools are at least as old in the eastern United States as the early Lithic Clovis culture. Whether or not they are older is neither proven nor disproven.

Since pebble tools have been found in association with several cultures spanning several thousand years, it has been suggested that they do not represent a complete and distinct industry or cultural complex but that they are a technological tradition employed in certain areas where pebbles provided a convenient source for manufacturing large, crude, disposable tools possibly associated with the exploitation of certain resources. MacDonald (1971:35) has expressed this view in his study of pebble tools in British Columbia, and Wormington (1971:87) has expressed a similar position on the pebble tools reported by Borden (1968) in that same area but apparently of a more recent date than those found in the east. This is a possibility that François Bordes and I also entertained during our extensive study of the Alabama pebble tools in April, 1971. Their apparent association with several cultures through time certainly indicates that pebble tools were a persistent technological tradition, but it is now impossible to answer the question of whether or not they ever represented at an earlier time a separate complex. There is increasing evidence that pebble tools have a wide distribution in the New World, and I believe we are far from having the last word on this intriguing subject.

When we turn to the Old World we find pebble tools as a very important element in the development of man's technology, beginning in Africa with the dawn of man. In Asia, pebble tools were very important in the earliest cultures, and they persisted as an important element in cultures as far north as Siberia, where sites in the Baikal area, such as Mal'ta and Afontova Gora, have produced radiocarbon dates ranging from 21,000 to 12,800 years ago (Cherdyntsev *et al.* 1968). Along with the pebble tools at these sites there are core bifaces, flakes, and blades struck from polyhedral cores. At a site in the Zeya River area, Okladnikov found pebble tools which he believes to be older than other Siberian complexes and which he assigns to a pre-Mousterian complex (Derevianko 1968). Thus it would seem that pebble tools were an old and persistent element in several complexes of both the Old and New Worlds, but, until they can be isolated as a distinct complex in the New World with adequate early dates to indicate their priority over complexes containing core, flake, and blade tools, their relationship culturally and temporally with the Old World will remain obscure. We certainly cannot postulate a pebble-tool stage of cultural development in the New World on the basis of the crude technology involved in their manufacture.

Perhaps a more useful and significant indicator of early Old and New World contacts is the study of those complexes containing trimmed cores of a generally polyhedral form. These cores served not only as primary tools but also often as a source of blades and flakes from which a variety of cutting and scraping tools were fashioned. In the New World there is increasing evidence to indicate that the trimmed core was an important element in the Clovis complex and that there may be some sites where this lithic tradition precedes fluted points by several thousand years.

The most extensive evidence of trimmed polyhedral cores in the Clovis complex comes from the Wells Creek site in Tennessee (Dragoo 1965, 1973). At this site were found many trimmed cores which had been fashioned into denticulates, scrapers, spokeshaves, and planes. In most examples, the core was chipped primarily as a tool and not necessarily as the source for flakes and blades. The total lithic assemblage at Wells Creek is exceedingly rich and varied and contains, in addition to the trimmed polyhedral cores, many unifacially and bifacially chipped tools, such as large hand axes, knives, scrapers, perforators, cleavers, choppers, spokeshaves, picks, and denticulates, in association with typologically early Clovis fluted points in all stages of manufacture.

Of all the known Clovis sites, the tool assemblage at Wells Creek seems to give the most complete and illuminating insight into the cultural foundation upon which the making of fluted points developed. Unlike the western Clovis sites, with their limited tool inventory consisting of a few fluted points and scrapers, Wells Creek and other eastern Clovis sites, on a more limited scale, such as Debert (MacDonald 1968), Williamson (McCary 1951), Shoop (Witthoft 1952), Holcombe (Fitting *et al.* 1966), and several smaller sites, all present a picture of a well-developed tool assemblage with fluted points constituting only one important element in the complete tool kit. If we are to find the complete foundation upon which the fluted-point cultures developed, the best approach would seem to be the study of the core, blade, and flake tools. The large and often crude polyhedral core tools of Wells Creek would seem to be an important clue to the possible antiquity and origin of these early cultures. Because of problems in dating, it is currently impossible to place a date on these tools much earlier than 12,000 years ago in eastern North America; but surface collections made at several high terrace sites in Alabama, Tennessee, and the Ohio Valley indicate that there may be sites containing these crude tools without the association of fluted points. Only the finding of datable, stratified sites will answer this question.

Recent work by MacNeish (1973) in Peru has uncovered an assemblage of crude tools similar to those found at Wells Creek. In the bottom two zones of Flea Cave in the Ayacucho Valley, tool types including sidescrapers, choppers, cleavers, spokeshaves, and denticulates were dated between 19,600 and 14,150 B.C. MacNeish has divided these tools into a lower complex, Paccaicasa, and an upper complex, Ayacucho. No projectile points were found in the lower zone, but bone points were present in the upper or Ayacucho complex. Similar tools have been found recently at several other sites in Peru by James Richardson (of the University of Pittsburgh), who has stated to me their near identity with those found at Wells Creek. Prominent in these assemblages are the same crude polyhedral and bifacial core tools which MacNeish (1973:77) suggests may represent in the Paccaicasa complex the earliest stage of man's appearance in South America between 25,000 and 15,000 years ago. MacNeish (1973:77) has called this earliest complex the "core tool tradition" and the slightly later Ayacucho complex the "flake and bone tool tradition." The "trimmed-core tradition" as used in this paper would encompass both of MacNeish's traditions, since at this point I cannot fully separate the two complexes over a wide range except for MacNeish's evidence at Flea Cave. Such a division may exist at that site, but the evidence for separation of core and flake tools at other sites is not conclusive since the samples are extremely limited in number and kinds of items.

When MacNeish looked for possible origins of his "core tool tradition," he suggested it would be derived from the chopper and chopping-tool tradition of Asia, which is well over 50,000 years old in that area. He (MacNeish 1973:79) further suggests that the "core tool tradition" may possibly have arrived in the New World from 40,000 to as much as 100,000 years ago. Since our discovery of the Wells Creek site in 1963, I have been searching the Asiatic scene for possible clues to the origin of the New World core-tool complexes, with the hope that some hint of the time when contact began could be found. As MacNeish and others have suggested, there are typological similarities between the New World core-tool complexes and those in various areas of east Asia, but since such tools persisted over a very long period of time they are of little use in dating their introduction to the New World. However, I have been impressed with the growing accumulation of evidence for the spread of core tools from the Asiatic mainland to various adjacent island land masses such as Japan, the Philippine Islands, and Australia. The great similarities between the tools that I have examined from these areas and those from Wells Creek, Flea Cave, and other sites in the New World lead me to believe that all these areas were recipients of Asian immigrants possessing a basic core-tool complex at about the same time.

In Japan the Hoshino and Iwajuku complexes seem to be the earliest cultural manifestations (Serizawa 1968; Ikawa 1968). On the basis of radiocarbon-dated geological horizons, the Hoshino complex is at least 30,000 years old and may extend back in time to as much as 50,000 years ago. The Iwajuku complex probably dates to about 25,000 years ago. In 1968 I examined many specimens from the Hoshino and Iwajuku complexes and I agree with Ikawa (1968:198) that the Hoshino complex has rather close affinities with the Ting Ts'un and Chiao-Ch'eng of the Fenho Valley of northern China. Many of these early tools also are similar to those found by MacNeish (1973:79) at Flea Cave in Peru and to the crude core tools at Wells Creek in Tennessee. The later Iwajuku complex contains many more blade tools than the Hoshino, but it is probably a descendant of that culture, just as later flake and blade tools were added to a basic core-tool complex in the New World.

The picture of early complexes now emerging from Australia presents an interesting parallel to that of Japan and the New World (Mulvaney 1969). In 1971 I had the opportunity to visit many of the early sites in

Australia and to study the artifacts found at them. I was impressed with the marked similarity of these early core tools to the trimmed cores at Wells Creek and other New World sites. The radiocarbon dates now available for these earliest sites appear to be about 30,000 years old, with some sites believed to be even older (40,000 years) based upon geological evidence (Thorne, Gallus, and Mulvaney, personal communications).

In the Philippines, radiocarbon dates indicate that man was well established there 30,000 years ago; and on the basis of geological evidence, Fox (1968, personal communication) has suggested that man may have been there as much as 50,000 years ago. Both core and flake tools are present in these early assemblages. Mulvaney (1969:58) has suggested that man may have made his way into Australia from Asia by way of south China, through Taiwan, the Philippines, and Borneo to Celebes, and thence south through New Guinea to Australia, because during the Pleistocene there was more dry land in this direction than on the more direct route by way of Java and Timor. If this is so, we should expect the similarities that seem to exist between the early tools of the Philippines and Australia.

Although there are many gaps in the picture, I find it more than mere coincidence that man seems to have moved outward from the Asiatic mainland at about the same time to the New World, Japan, the Philippines, and Australia. All the present radiocarbon dates indicate that he was well established in all these areas by 30,000 years ago, and we can probably add a few thousand years more for his establishment. However, on the basis of the present evidence, I would not expect this time to be much more than 40,000 years ago. The similarities of the early tool assemblages in all these areas suggest that they were derived from a basic core-tool tradition that was widespread on the Asiatic mainland. This tradition probably had as its foundation a complex like that discovered in the Fenho Valley of northern China. Because flake tools are also prominent in most of these foreign complexes, the outward migrations probably came at a time when the Fenho tradition was being modified and subjected to new influences from western Europe which included the introduction of the Levallois technique and certain tool types reminiscent of the Mousterian. This blending probably occurred between 50,000 and 40,000 years ago. By the time man began his spread to the New World and the outlying areas of Asia, he possessed a basic technology that included a variety of techniques for working stone. Time and isolation eventually saw the differential development of certain techniqes and tool types in each area.

It has not been my intention to suggest that there were any direct contacts between the New World and such distant areas as Australia, the Philippines, or Japan, but I do believe that all these areas were influenced from a common Asiatic source and at about the same time. It is of interest to note that these now unattached and distant areas were at times during the Pleistocene part of an almost continuous land mass that formed the outer margins of Asia and North America. It would have been almost possible to walk on dry land from Australia to the New World during the advance stages of the last glacial period (Würm or Wisconsin).

It is not possible at this time to understand the major factors that may have led to the spread of peoples from the Asiatic mainland to these distant and previously unoccupied areas. However, we may conjecture that during the interstadial period (Gottweig) between 50,000 and 40,000 years ago, man extended his range and increased in number throughout Asia and Europe. It was during this period that European lithic traditions spread into Asia and mixed with the core-tool tradition. As the ice again advanced between 40,000 and 30,000 years ago, large areas of mainland Asia came under its influence; but new lands also became available along the continental shelf because of the drop in sea level, linking it with the New World, Japan, the Philippines, and the large islands leading to Australia. Human groups living in central and north-eastern Asia slowly drifted into these new territories during this time, carrying with them their basic core and flake tool assemblages. By 30,000 years ago the descendants of these wandering hunters had penetrated the most distant of these new lands, and the last major land areas of the world had fallen under the influence of man.

REFERENCES

ANDERSEN, ADRIAN
  1962   The Cooperton mammoth: a preliminary report. *Plains Anthropologist: Journal of the Plains Conference* 7:110.
Arctic Anthropology
  1971   *Arctic Anthropology* 8 (2). Entire issue.
BORDEN, CHARLES E.
  1968   New evidence of early cultural relations between Eurasia and western North America. *Proceedings of the Eighth International Congress of Anthropological and Ethnological Sciences* 3:331–337.
BROYLES, BETTYE J.
  1966   Preliminary report: the St. Albans site (46 Ka 27), Kanawha County, West Virginia. *West Virginia Archaeologist* 19:1–43. Moundsville.
CHERDYNTSEV, V. V., *et al.*
  1968   Geological Institute radiocarbon dates, II. *Radiocarbon* 10 (2):426.
COE, JOFFRE L.
  1964   The formative cultures of the Carolina Piedmont. *American Philosophical Society Transactions,* n.s. 54 (5). Philadelphia.
CROOK, W. W., JR., R. K. HARRIS
  1957   Hearths and artifacts of early man near Lewisville, Texas, and associated fauna material. *Texas Archaeological and Paleontological Society Bulletin* 28:7–97. Abilene.

1958   A Pleistocene campsite near Lewisville, Texas. *American Antiquity* 23:233–246.

DE JARNETTE, DAVID L.
1967   Alabama pebble tools: the Lively complex. *Eastern States Archeological Federation Bulletin* 26:11–12.

DEREVIANKO, A. P.
1968   The history of the ancient settlement of man in the Far East. *Proceedings of the Eighth International Congress of Anthropological and Ethnological Sciences.*

DRAGOO, DON W.
1965   Investigations at a Paleo-Indian site in Stewart County, Tennessee. *Eastern States Archaeological Federation Bulletin* 24:12–13.
1968   Early Lithic cultures of the New World. *Proceedings of the Eighth International Congress of Anthropological and Ethnological Sciences* 3:175–176.
1973   "The Wells Creek site, Stewart County, Tennessee," in *Archaeology of eastern North America.* Eastern States Archeological Federation 1.

FITTING, JAMES E., J. DE VISSCHER, E. WAHLA
1966   *The Paleo-Indian occupation of Holcombe Beach.* Anthropological Papers, Museum of Anthropology, 27. University of Michigan.

HARRINGTON, M. R., R. D. SIMPSON
1961   *Tule Springs, Nevada, with other evidences of Pleistocene man in North America.* Southwest Museum Paper 18. Los Angeles.

HAYNES, C. VANCE
1964   Fluted projectile points: their age and dispersion. *Science* 145:1,408–1,413.
1969   The earliest Americans. *Science* 166:703–715.
1971   Time, environment, and early man. *Arctic Anthropology* 8 (2):3–14. Madison.

HUMPHREY, R. L.
1966   The prehistory of the Utokok River region, arctic Alaska: early fluted point tradition with Old World relationships. *Current Anthropology* 7:586–588.

IKAWA, FUMIKO
1968   The Japanese Palaeolithic in the context of prehistoric cultural relationships between northern Eurasia and the New World. *Proceedings of the Eighth International Congress of Anthropological and Ethnological Sciences* 3:197–199.

IRVING, W. N.
1971   Recent early man research in the north. *Arctic Anthropology* 8 (2):68–82. Madison.

IRWIN-WILLIAMS, CYNTHIA
1967   "Associations of early man with horse, camel, and mastodon at Hueyatlaco, Valsequillo (Puebla, Mexico)," in *Pleistocene extinctions.* Edited by P. S. Martin and H. E. Wright, Jr., 337–350. New Haven: Yale University Press.
1969   Comments on the association of archaeological materials and extinct fauna in the Valsequillo region, Puebla, Mexico. *American Antiquity* 34 (1):82–83.

JOSSELYN, D. W.
1967   The pebble tool explosion in Alabama. *Anthropological Journal of Canada* 5 (3):9–12.

KRIEGER, ALEX D.
1964 "Early man in the New World," in *Prehistoric man in the New World.* Edited by J. D. Jennings and E. Norbeck, 23–81. Chicago: University of Chicago Press.
LEAKEY, L. S. B., RUTH D. SIMPSON, *et al.*
1972 *Pleistocene men at Calico.* San Bernardino County Museum.
LIVELY, MATTHEW
1965 The Lively complex: announcing a pebble tool industry in Alabama. *Journal of Alabama Archaeology* 11 (2):103–122.
MacDONALD, GEORGE F.
1968 Debert: a Paleo-Indian site in central Nova Scotia. *Anthropology Papers, No. 16.* National Museum of Canada.
1971 A review of research on Paleo-Indian in eastern North America, 1960–1970. *Arctic Anthropology* 8 (2):32–41.
MacNEISH, RICHARD S.
1971 Early man in the Andes. *Scientific American* 224 (4):36–46.
1973 "Early man in the Andes," in *Early man in America,* 69–79. Readings from *Scientific American.* San Francisco: W. H. Freeman and Company.
MALDE, HAROLD E.
1967 "Volcanic-ash chronology, with examples from the Valsequillo archaeological sites, Puebla, Mexico." Paper given at Valsequillo Symposium, Arizona State University, Tempe, October 27, 1967.
MARTIN, PAUL S.
1973 The discovery of America. *Science* 179:969–974.
McCARY, BEN C.
1951 A workshop site of early man in Dinwiddie County, Virginia. *American Antiquity* 17 (1):9–17.
MÜLLER-BECK, H.
1966 Paleohunters in America: origins and diffusion. *Science* 152:1,191–1,210.
MULVANEY, D. J.
1969 *The prehistory of Australia.* New York: Frederick A. Praeger.
ORR, PHIL C.
1968 *Prehistory of Santa Rosa Island.* Santa Barbara Museum of Natural History.
SERIZAWA, CHOSUKE
1968 The chronological sequence of the Palaeolithic cultures of Japan and the relationship with mainland Asia. *Proceedings Eighth International Congress of Anthropological and Ethnological Sciences* 3:353–357.
SHUTLER, RICHARD
1965 Tule Springs expedition. *Current Anthropology* 6:110–111.
WILLEY, GORDON R.
1966 *An introduction to American archaeology,* volume one: *North and Middle America.* Englewood Cliffs, New Jersey: Prentice-Hall.
WITTHOFT, JOHN
1952 A Paleo-Indian site in eastern Pennsylvania: an early hunting culture. *Proceedings of the American Philosophical Society* 96:464–495.
WORMINGTON, H. M.
1971 Comments on early man in North America, 1960–1970. *Arctic Anthropology* 8:83–91.

Fractured Cherts from Pleistocene Fossiliferous Beds at Medicine Hat, Alberta

B. O. K. REEVES

In the vicinity of Medicine Hat, Alberta, shown in Map 1, many sections of Pleistocene glacial and nonglacial deposits, Kansan to Wisconsin in age, are exposed along the banks of the south Saskatchewan River. Some sections have been described by Berg (1969), Christiansen (1969), Stalker (1969b), and Westgate (1965), and the faunal assemblages from the nonglacial fluvial deposits have been briefly enumerated by Churcher (1969). More recently a schematic composite stratigraphic and faunal section for Medicine Hat, published by the Geological Survey of Canada (Stalker and Churcher 1970), depicts men manufacturing stone tools in association with faunal assemblages considered to be mid-Wisconsin and Sangamon in age. Man's presence at these locales is inferred solely on the basis of "the occurrence of numerous poorly worked or flaked stones" (Stalker and Churcher 1970; Stalker 1969b:7).

THE SITES

Of the some twelve paleontological locales along the river, the five shown in Map 1 (Mitchell Bluffs, Surprise Bluff, Island Bluff, Reservoir Gulley, and Evil Smelling Band) have yielded fractured cherts. Excavations directed primarily toward the recovery of paleontological specimens

The excavations were carried out in the summers of 1968 to 1970 by archaeological field crews from the University of Calgary under contract to the Geological Survey of Canada. This project was part of an overall study (Stalker 1969a, 1970, 1971) of the Quaternary stratigraphy and vertebrate paleontology of southeastern Alberta. The study was directed by A. MacS. Stalker and C. S. Churcher. The archaeological project was directed by the writer. R. M. Getty, W. J. Elliot, and C. Poole directed the field operations in 1968, 1969, and 1970 respectively. I express my thanks to R. G. Forbis for his helpful criticism on the final draft of this paper.

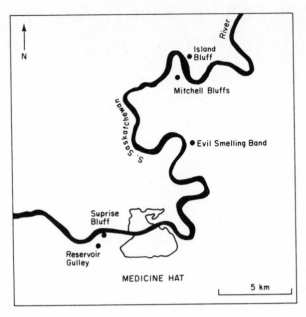

Map. 1   Collection sites, Medicine Hat vicinity, Alberta

were carried out at Mitchell Bluffs in 1968 and 1969 and at Reservoir Gulley in 1970 by the Geological Survey of Canada. Mitchell Bluffs, Plate 1, is located on a promontory some nine kilometers north of Medicine Hat on the south bank of the South Saskatchewan River. Here, the total stratigraphic column consists of 400 meters of preglacial, glacial, and postglacial sediments. The fossiliferous fractured-chert band, known as the "artifact band," is, on the basis of the associated vertebrate fauna, Sangamon in age (Stalker and Churcher 1970). It is buried below ninety-four meters of sands and tills (Stalker 1969b). Overlying sediments were stripped by bulldozer to within two feet of the artifact band prior to initiating excavations.

The band consists of poorly sorted semiconsolidated gravels, sand and silt lenses, and silt blocks deposited in well-developed foreset beds averaging five feet thick. It contains a variety of secondarily deposited vertebrate fossils, including those of mammoth, Mexican ass, horse, camel, deer, caribou, elk, bison, and antelope (Churcher 1969). These deposits were initially excavated by trowel and brush, later by hand pick and shovels. All sediment was passed through a screen of quarter-inch mesh. All cherts and all bones were collected. About 200 cubic meters were eventually removed and screened.

At Reservoir Gulley, Plate 2, located directly west of Medicine Hat, fossiliferous gravels of mid-Wisconsin age were exposed by erosion in a tributary coulee of the South Saskatchewan River. The gravel band is

Plate 1.   Mitchell Bluffs: view west of excavation area from south bank of the South Saskatchewan River

Plate 2.   Reservoir Gulley: view west of excavation area from east side of gulley

overlain by three meters of sands and fifty meters of till. Associated vertebrate fauna include mammoth, dire wolf, Mexican ass, camel, and sabertooth (Stalker and Churcher 1970).

Overlying tills in the area selected for excavation had been removed by erosion. Here the fossiliferous gravels were covered with one meter of fine-grained sandy colluvium. A cultural component consisting of a bison kill/campsite, typologically dating ca. 2500 B.C. lay near the base of the colluvium, which resembled the mid-Wisconsin sands that were exposed by bulldozing in preparing the surface for excavation. The boundary between these two units was exceedingly hard to define; consequently, recent bison bones and projectile points were in places recovered intermixed with extinct Pleistocene fauna and fractured cherts. Some 200 cubic meters were excavated and screened at this site.

THE FRACTURED CHERTS

Description and Analysis

Some 8,000 objects of fractured chert were collected in excavations at the two sites. They were analyzed separately after each field season (Reeves 1969, 1970, 1971). The lithic types, the nonmetric attributes of the cherts, and statistical analyses (one-way analysis of variance and chi square) of the metrics suggest that the samples are identical from the two sites; consequently they are considered here as a single sample.

Visually the cherts exhibit a continuous range of variation from unfractured and unfaceted nodules to fractured forms with "retouched" edges. For descriptive purposes, they are divided into three groups.

GROUP I. Plate 3 (a)–(e) shows some of the 5,732 cherts in this group, or 73 percent of the sample. This group includes both unfractured and faceted chert nodules, which are tabular, irregular, or hemispherical in form. Faceted nodules range from single-faceted specimens that retain some part of the original cortex, to multifaceted specimens with no original cortex remaining. The facets or flaked surfaces are usually very highly polished and exhibit unpatterned macroscopic or microscopic striations suggesting till faceting and striating.

GROUP II. Plate 3 (f)–(m) shows some of the 1,748 cherts in this group, or 21 percent of the sample. Cherts (f) and (m) are flakes; (g)–(k) are tabular and irregular forms with unstriated flake scars or facets. In general, the flakes, which are very rare, lack features such as bulbs of percussion, compression waves, impact scars and lateral fissures such as Plate 3 (m) shows. The surfaces tend to be highly polished and occasion-

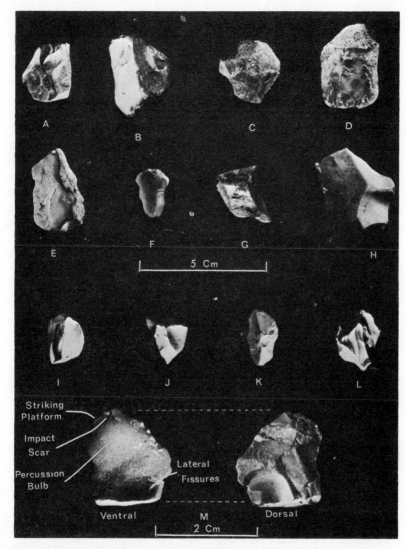

Plate 3. Fractured cherts: (a) – (e) are from Group I, (f) – (m) from Group II

ally patinated. Sometimes adjacent flake scars or facets will exhibit differential patination. Often the more highly patinated surface will exhibit random striations. Edges vary from sharp to rounded and may be crushed or battered. Potlid fracture patterns are common on irregular and angular forms such as Plate 3 (h). On the tabular forms, the flaking of the surfaces may be unidirectional, bidirectional or multidirectional such as Plate 3 (i). Edge angles between adjacent facets range between 80 and 100 degrees. Flake scars and facets are usually heavily glazed.

GROUP III. Plates 4, 5, and 6 show some of the 502 cherts in this group, or 6 percent of the sample. Group III is similar to Group II, but the specimens exhibit retouching of an edge of flaked or faceted surface. Measurements are given in Table 1. Edge angles, shown in Figure 1, range from 39° to 135°, having a mean of 80° with a standard deviation of 15°. The retouching varies from edge nibbling, as in Plate 5 (a) and (b), to well-defined retouch, as in Plate 4 (a) and (c). Retouch is generally confined to one or part of one edge, as in Plate 4 (a). Ocasionally the cherts will have two retouched segments along one edge, as in Plate 6 (d), or two retouched edges, as in Plate 5 (a) and (b). Edge crushing, as in Plate 4 (a) and (c), and step flaking, as in Plate 6 (d), are common, as are small negative impact scars, as in Plate 6 (d), on the retouched edge. Badly obliterated oblique or vertical striations may also be observed by microscope on the retouched edges, which tend to be less highly polished than the adjacent facets. Retouching is usually unidirectional, as in Plate 4 (a), but may be bidirectional. Bidirectional flaking along one edge may result in alternate beveling. Bifacial edge retouching is absent.

Table 1.   Metric measures of Group III fractured cherts

Measurements	n	$\bar{x}$	S	Range
Length in millimeters	493	22.2	3.98	5–50
Width in millimeters	495	14.5	4.75	5–49
Thickness in millimeters	493	8.3	3.15	3–28
Weight in grams	493	3.43	3.75	0.2–46.8

On the basis of formal variation, three varieties of the Group III forms may be distinguished:
1.   Flakes or faceted cherts with straight or slightly convex edges, shown in Plate 4, which form about 60 percent of the sample.
2.   Flakes or faceted cherts with concave edges or notches, shown in Plate 5, which form about 30 percent of the sample.
3.   Flakes or faceted cherts with points or beaks, shown in Plate 6, which form about 10 percent of the sample. Points are produced by retouching two adjacent edges, resulting in a sharp retouched point at the intersection of the two edges, and beaks by either unidirectional or bidirectional double notching of an edge.
   One specimen (from Reservoir Gulley), a thin triangular flake shown in Plate 4 (c), measuring 2.5 × 2.5 × 0.5 centimeters, deserves special mention, as it most resembles a finished tool of all the fractured cherts recovered. Manufactured from a typical cream-colored chert, it combines a concave ventral flake surface, an impact scar, a diffuse bulb of percussion, compression waves, and lateral and bulbar fissures. The dorsal surface is almost completely flaked. The lateral edges and proximal end

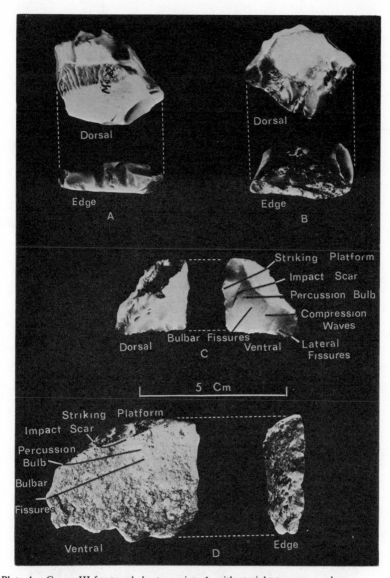

Plate 4.   Group III fractured cherts: variety 1, with straight to convex edges

are retouched to an angle of 60° to 70°. Another specimen, Plate 4 (d), the only quartzite flake recovered in the entire sample from Mitchell Bluffs, exhibits a similar but less well-developed set of attributes.

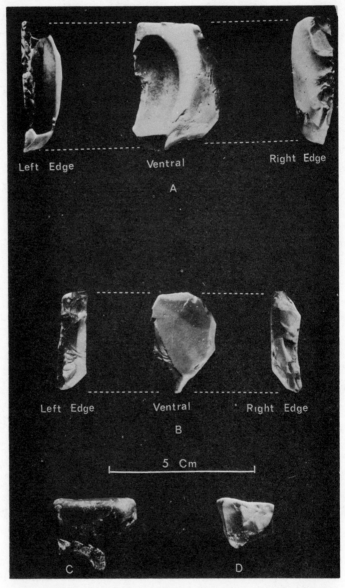

Plate 5. Group III fractured cherts: variety 2, with concave or notched edges

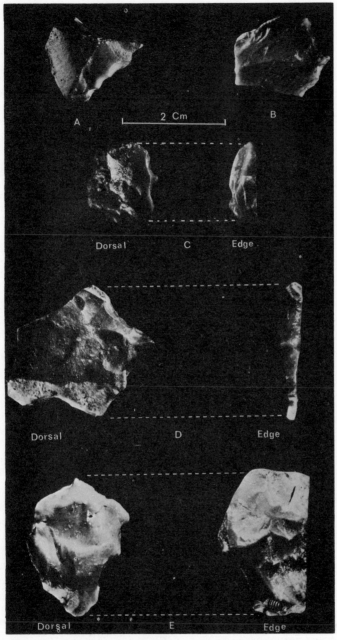

Plate 6.   Group III fractured cherts: variety 3, (a), (b) and (d) are points, (c) and (e) are beaks

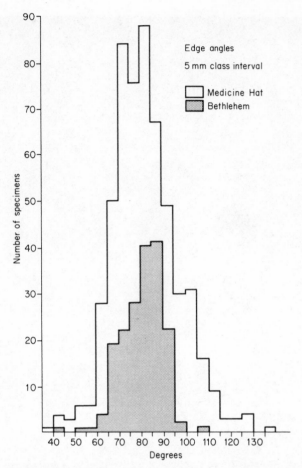

Figure 1. Comparative histogram of Medicine Hat and Bethlehem fractured-chert retouched-edge angles

Interpretation and Comparisons

Petrologically diagnostic limestones and dolomites from the gravels of the artifact band indicate that the fluvial sediments were ultimately derived in part from Laurentide tills (Stalker 1969b). The fractured and unfractured cherts from the artifact band are visually identical in mineralogical type to cherts found in these tills and in large dolomite erratics, suggesting that the fractured cherts were ultimately derived from Laurentide tills. While incorporated in these tills some (Group I) were probably fractured, faceted, and striated by compressional and rotational forces operative in the advancing Laurentide ice.

Since many of the Groups II and III fractured cherts are also thermofractured and highly glazed, they were not incorporated directly from till into the artifact band. Prior to incorporation in the fluvial sediments, the cherts may have lain on a deflation surface. Thermofracture may result from any rapid temperature change (Clark 1961) or from lightning (Laudermilk and Kennard 1938). Thermofracture (Barnes 1939; Jones 1925) produces potlid flakes and angularly fractured cherts with or without the closed ring-and-cup fracture pattern. Chipping and nibbling of fractured cherts may also occur as a result of either sand abrasion or glazing; the latter is produced by the precipitation of silica on the surface of the fractured chert. This process occurs in environments which have high annual rainfall (Phaup 1932).

The retouched edges of the Group III specimens do not generally exhibit a high degree of polishing or patinating when compared to the fractured or flaked facets of Groups II and III, suggesting that the retouching occurred at some time after some of the till-derived cherts were thermofractured and polished. Further, the cherts rarely exhibit the typical abrading and battering patterns which occur in streams, suggesting that the retouching must have occurred prior to their incorporation in the fluvial sediments. However, some of the retouched edges which lack patination or glazing may have been produced by compaction of the gravel band by the pressures of the overlying fluvial and glacial materials at the sites. Notches and concave edges tend to result from this type of flaking (Clark 1961; Warren 1914, 1923).

Barnes, Clark, and Warren, among others, have discussed natural forces which can cause the pressure flaking of cherts and the production of forms identical to those observed in the Medicine Hat sample. In addition to thermofracture and compaction, Barnes (1939:102) lists solifluxion, a process by which the rotation and crushing of cherts in the deposits produces flaked and striated surfaces. Edge crushing is a common result.

Warren (1923) presents a detailed discussion of subsoil pressure flaking methods. He terms the natural process "chip and slide," distinguishing two mechanisms:

1. *Leverage* refers to the effect of pressure on a chert nodule by another stone, resulting in the detaching of a flake. The resultant flake has a fairly straight edge that is retouched at an angle of from 70° to 90°. Striations are not produced.

2. *Friction of one stone against another* produces a variety of retouched edges, varying in form from convex to straight to concave. On tabular pieces, bidirection flaking is common. Striations are usually present on the retouched edges, which may be notched, double notched, or beaked.

Clark (1961) in his study of the Bethlehem, Israel, early Pleistocene fractured cherts, distinguished five varieties: unfractured cherts, tabular cherts, thermally fractured cherts, nodules, and flakes. On the tabular cherts the edge angles cluster around 90°. Steep, often bidirectional, retouch is characteristic, along with notching and nibbling. Clark considers this kind of retouching to have resulted from natural pressure flaking after the cherts were incorporated in the sinkhole at Bethlehem.

A comparison between edge angles of specimens from Medicine Hat and Bethlehem (Clark 1961: Plate 21), shown in Figure 1, is particularly instructive. The Medicine Hat sample (N = 563) has a mean of 80° and a standard deviation of 15°, and the Bethlehem sample (N = 195) has a mean of 79.8° and a standard deviation of 11.8°. Obviously there is no significant statistical difference between these figures.

So the three varieties of the Group III fractured cherts distinguished in the study can all be replicated in Warren's and Clark's series of naturally produced forms. This suggests that the retouched edges and formal variations of the Medicine Hat forms are probably products of natural compressive and rotational forces rather than of human activity.

BONE FRAGMENTS

All identifiable bone specimens were turned over to Churcher in Toronto; I have consequently not had the opportunity to examine the larger bone fragments to look for artifacts among them. I did observe one long bone-shaft fragment, which does have fractures suggestive of green-bone damage by percussion. No human bones are known to be present.

While not the major concern of this paper, over 9,000 bone-unidentifiable fragments consisting of cranial and postcranial skeletal elements were examined. They were initially separated into two groups: (1) rounded, water-rolled fragments characterized by a "pink" earth color; and (2) fragments characterized by a light-yellow cream color often accompanied by relatively heavy mineral staining. Group 1 resembles bone fragments found in the preglacial Saskatchewan gravels and sands. Group 2, far more abundant, varies from fresh forms which show little or no rounding of the edges to fragments which are almost completely rounded. Surfaces of angular or rounded fragments are nearly always highly polished.

These bones were then examined by the naked eye for signs of wear or modification. Those that showed such evidence were then examined under the microscope to determine if any striae possibly indicative of human use have been preserved. But on practically all specimens, the smooth outer cortical tissue sheath had been removed by erosion. Since this surface best preserves striae, they were preserved only if they had been incised deeply enough to penetrate into the adjacent tissue layers. Recognition of the striae was further complicated by the fact that on weathered specimens striae parallel to bone structure can seldom be distinguished from the bone structure. Mineral replacement also complicated recognition of striae.

Over 400 bone fragments that showed shapes or edges possibly indicative of tool use were examined. Thirty-four had microscopic striae preserved on the surfaces, and they were divided into groups based on form and striae directions:

Group I consists of small pieces with pointed to rounded distal ends. Striations run parallel to the longitudinal axis. One complete specimen is made on a split long bone, shown in Plate 7(a).

Group II consists of flat, rectangular pieces of bone with oblique striations. Some fragments in this group are parts of mandibles or scapulae, as shown in Plate 7(d).

Group III consists of flat, rectangular or pointed pieces, characterized by two sets of oblique striae oriented more or less at right angles to each other, as shown in Plate 7(b) and (c).

It should be noted that forms in all groups can be duplicated in the unstriated bone fragments.

The rounded and polished edges and surfaces indicate that many, but not all, of the small bone fragments were subjected to water abrasion. Whether water abrasion can produce some of the forms and striation patterns present on the Mitchell Bluffs specimens is not known.

Wind abrasion by sand apparently produces severe etching and frosting of the surface (Brain 1967; Robinson 1959). There is little to suggest that the bones from Mitchell Bluffs were exposed to any appreciable sand abrasion.

Biologic erosion other than animal gnawing (evident on some of the bone fragments) may occur in the stomachs of carnivores, particularly those of bone-crushing carnivores such as the hyena (Kitching 1963). A number of pseudotool shapes, including bone points, may be produced by this process.

CONCLUSIONS

The fractured cherts from Medicine Hat differ in no essential way from naturally pressure-flaked cherts described by Warren and Clark, and it appears that the Medicine Hat specimens were flaked by similar natural processes: thermofracture, compression, and rotation in colluvium and tills. Even though these fractured cherts are most probably products of nature, man could have been present in the area and utilized if not modified some of the fractured cherts. The Taber site, only some fifty miles away, seems to show evidence of human occupation of the area during the mid-Wisconsin (Stalker 1969c).

Plate 7.   Bone fragments: Group I (a), Group II (d), Group III (b) and (c)

REFERENCES

BARNES, ALFRED S.
1939 The difference between natural and human flaking on prehistoric flint implements. *American Anthropologist*, n.s. 41:99–112.
BERG, T.
1969 "Stratigraphic problems in southeast Alberta." *Nineteenth Midwest Friends of the Pleistocene 1969 Field Conference*. Saskatchewan and Alberta. Mimeographed.
BRAIN, C. K.
1967 Bone weathering and the problem of bone pseudo-tools. *South African Journal of Science* 63:97–99.
CHRISTIANSEN, E. A.
1969 "Pleistocene stratigraphy of the Swift Current Creek, Prelate Ferry, Empress, and Medicine Hat sections." *Nineteenth Midwest Friends of the Pleistocene 1969 Field Conference*. Saskatchewan and Alberta. Mimeographed.
CHURCHER, E. S.
1969 "The vertebrate fauna of Surprise, Mitchell and Island Bluffs, near Medicine Hat, Alberta." *Nineteenth Midwest Friends of the Pleistocene 1969 Field Conference*. Saskatchewan and Alberta. Mimeographed.
CLARK, J. DESMOND
1961 Fractured chert specimens from the lower Pleistocene Bethlehem beds, Israel. *Bulletin of the British Museum (Natural History), Geology Series* 5(4):73–104.
JONES, FREDERIC WOOD
1925 A contribution to the study of eoliths: some observations on the natural forces at work in the production of flaked stones on the central Australian tablelands. *Journal of the Royal Anthropological Institute of Great Britain and Ireland* 55:115–122.
KITCHING, JAMES W.
1963 *Bone, tooth and horn tools of Paleolithic man*. Manchester: Manchester University Press.
LAUDERMILK, J. D., T. G. KENNARD
1938 Concerning lightning spalling. *American Journal of Science* 33(206):104–122.
PHAUP, A. E.
1932 The patina of the stone implements found near the Victoria Falls. *Proceedings of the Rhodesian Science Association* 31:40–44. Salisbury.
REEVES, B. O. K.
1969 "Excavations at Mitchell Bluffs: preliminary report 1968." Manuscript on file, Geological Survey of Canada.
1970 "Excavations at west Mitchell Bluffs: preliminary report 1969." Manuscript on file, Geological Survey of Canada.
1971 "Excavations at Reservoir Gulley: preliminary report 1970." Manuscript on file, Geological Survey of Canada.
ROBINSON, J. T.
1959 A bone implement from Sterkfontein. *Nature* 184 (4,686):583–585.
STALKER, A. M.
1969a Quaternary studies in the southwestern prairies, Alberta. Report of Activities Part A: April to October, 1968. *Geological Survey of Canada Paper* 69–1a:220–221.

1969b   Quaternary stratigraphy in southern Alberta Report II: sections near Medicine Hat. *Geological Survey of Canada Paper* 69–26.

1969c   Geology and age of the early man site at Taber, Alberta. *American Antiquity* 34(4):425–429.

1970   Quaternary studies in the southwestern prairies, Alberta. Report of Activities Part A: April to October 1969. *Geological Survey of Canada Paper* 70–1a:187.

1971   Quaternary studies in the southwestern prairies. Report of Activities Part A: April to October, 1970. *Geological Survey of Canada Paper* 71–1a:180–181.

STALKER, A. M., C. S. CHURCHER
1970   Deposits near Medicine Hat, Alberta, Canada. *Geological Survey of Canada special publication*.

WARREN, S. HAZZLEDINE
1914   The experimental investigations of flint fracture and its application to problems of human implements. *Journal of the Royal Anthropological Institute of Great Britain and Ireland* 45:412–453.

1923   Sub-soil pressure flaking. *Proceedings of the Geologists Association* 34:153–175.

WESTGATE, J. A.
1965   "The Pleistocene stratigraphy of the Foremost–Cypress Hills area," in *Cypress Hills Plateau Guide Book No. 1*. Edited by R. C. Zell, 85–111. Fifteenth Annual Field Conference of the Alberta Society of Petroleum Geologists.

The California Coastal Region: Its Late Pleistocene and Holocene Climate and Function as an Ice Age Refugium

DONALD L. JOHNSON

The climate of California oceanward of the mountains and deserts is distinctive in North America. It is characterized by mild wet winters and warm-to-hot dry summers. Toward the coast at low elevations the air temperatures are ameliorated year-round by the dominating influence of the nearby Pacific Ocean. In wintertime the temperatures are relatively warm, whereas in summer they are relatively cool. With increasing distance from the coast, however, more extreme conditions are met, but even these are mild compared to those in other parts of North America. Only when the interior mountains and deserts are reached does the climate take on a continental cast. This mild climate has made the California coastal region highly attractive to human settlement and has played a major role in California's ranking first in population. Even kings and presidents seek refuge along the equable Pacific shores. It is a climatic refugium.

PURPOSE

A principal purpose of this essay is to review evidence which strongly suggests that the California coastal region[1] has long had a climate that has been basically Mediterranean in character, even when other parts of North America suffered under full-glacial conditions. With a Mediterranean climate, California functioned as a refugium during the Pleistocene. The refugees then, however, were plants and Rancholabrean-type animals.

A secondary but equally important purpose is to point out that a

---

[1] The California coastal region is loosely defined here as that part of the state which experiences a Mediterranean climate.

nonclimatic factor must be invoked to explain the geologically recent extinction of the Rancholabrean mammals in California. The only new, nonindigenous environmental element which appeared during the extinction period of 20,000 to 8,000 years B.P. was cultural man. In California, man, not climate, probably was the principal agent of extinction.

SYNOPTIC SUMMARY OF CALIFORNIA'S MEDITERRANEAN CLIMATE

Most of coastal California experiences a marine or inland (less marine) phase of a Mediterranean type of climate. In the Koeppen system these would be classed respectively as Csb and Csa climates. Winters are wet and cool, characterized by frequent periods of sunny weather interrupted by low-pressure frontal systems arriving from the north Pacific. Most precipitation falls during the low-sun season as rain associated with these transient frontal systems. Rainfall is highest along the northern California coast, in the redwood district, and diminishes to the south, being lowest near the Mexican border where near-desert conditions prevail. This is shown schematically in Figure 1. Rain normally begins between October and December and ends in April or May. As a rule, summer months are rainless and, along the coastal strip, characterized by frequent low-level stratus and fog conditions associated with a persistently cool moist marine layer of onshore-moving air. This layer reduces evaporation and renders the winter rainfall more effective than might otherwise be expected.

Temperatures are mild all year at low elevations along the coast, but inland the summers are warm to hot. However, prolonged cold weather is practically unknown, even during the low-sun season, except in the higher mountains.

The warm dry weather of late summer and early fall is conducive to the occurrence of natural fires. In fact, seasonal fires are as Californian as the chaparral, which is thought to have approximately a thirty-year burn period (Dodge 1970).

REGIONAL CLIMATIC CONTROLS AND MODEL OF A MEDITERRANEAN CLIMATE DURING THE LATE QUATERNARY IN CALIFORNIA

The broad synoptic pattern sketched above is primarily a result of four all-important climatic controls, the Pacific High, the low-sun storm-generating Aleutian Low, the high-sun thermal low of the interior valleys and deserts, and the cool California Current with its associated upwelling.

The Pacific High is a semipermanent anticyclone of dry subsiding air

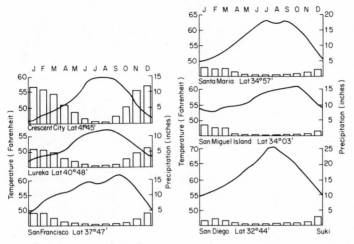

Figure 1. Climographs of six California coastal stations showing annual temperature and precipitation regimes (modified after Cooper 1967)

whose eastern side spills onto the coast of California. During low-sun periods the Pacific High weakens and is displaced equatorward. This allows frontal systems generated in the region of the Aleutian Low, which reinvigorates during the low-sun season, to sweep south of their usual northerly paths, shown in Figure 2(a), bringing California almost all its winter moisture. As the sun rises higher in the early springtime, the Pacific High intensifies and reestablishes its dominance. Concomitantly, a thermal low begins to form over the interior valleys and deserts of the southwestern United States and northwestern Mexico, as shown in Figure 2(b). This dual system of an offshore high and an interior "heat low" generates, in southern California at least, an almost continuous flow of moist but stable onshore-moving surface air during practically all the high-sun season and during much of the winter, as shown in Figure 3. This marine layer of air is commonly from 1,000 to 2,500 feet thick and is defined at its top by a semipermanent inversion produced by dry subsiding air aloft associated with the Pacific High. The moist marine layer is cooled from below and becomes increasingly stabilized as it moves over the cool upwelled surface waters associated with the southward-moving California Current, as shown in Figure 4. Abundant airborne salt particles (condensation nuclei) of wave-spray origin are mixed within the cool moist marine layer, resulting in frequent low-level stratus or fog during the spring, summer, and fall months. This condition also persists for short periods during the winter months.

It is important to note that the four weather-producing factors cited above are all part of the global circulation. The Pacific subtropical anticyclone, the Aleutian Low, and the interior thermal low are major elements in the global atmospheric circulation pattern. The California

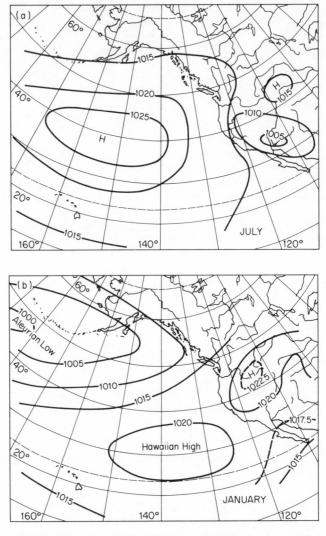

Figure 2.   (a) Normal sea level pressure (mb.) for July; (b) normal sea level pressure for January (modified after DeMarrais *et al.* 1965; Holzworth 1973)

Current likewise is part of the great north Pacific oceanic gyre, as shown in Figure 5. It is reasonable to assume that because all four climatic controls are an integral part of the global circulation, they were operative during most or all of the late Quaternary, although probably at varying intensities. This working model may be tested by consulting the paleoecologic record, which consists of tree-ring, geologic, pedologic, radiometric, and paleobotanic studies.

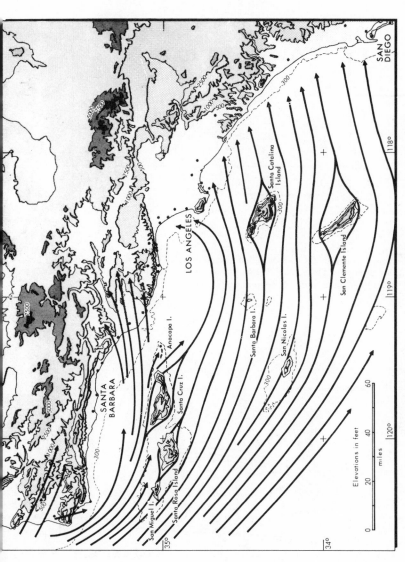

Figure 3. Mean annual wind streamlines, offshore southern California (after de Violini 1976)

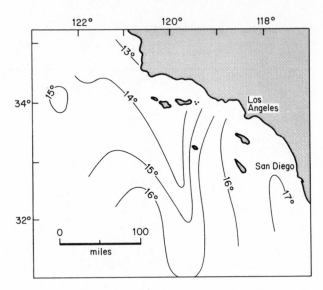

Figure 4.   Offshore southern California showing southward depression of surface isotherms caused by the cool upwelled waters of the southeast-flowing California Current. Information gained from the E. W. Scripps cruise of June 7–16, 1938 (modified after Emery 1960:100). Temperatures in degrees centigrade

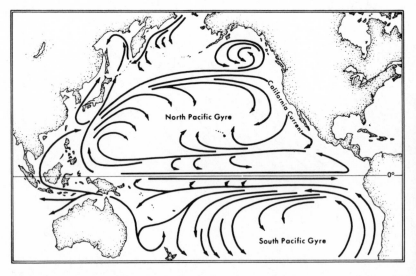

Figure 5.   Diagram showing the California Current as a major component of the north Pacific oceanic gyre

HISTORIC AND PREHISTORIC PRECIPITATION AND TREE-RING RECORDS OF COASTAL CALIFORNIA

In 1954 it was established through weather records that Los Angeles and San Bernardino have recurring trends of wet and dry years that are cyclic in character (Troxell and Hofmann 1954; Troxell *et al.* 1954). The cyclicity was made apparent when precipitation data for Los Angeles covering the period 1878 to 1952 were analyzed; results are shown in Figure 6. The analysis was done by computing the annual departures as a percent from the seventy-five-year mean (using climatological years July 1, 1877, to June 30, 1952) and cumulatively plotting these values to obtain a curve showing total accumulative departure from the mean. The authors point out that:

The upper part of figure [6] gives the observed annual precipitation at Los Angeles for the entire 75-year period from July 1, 1877, to June 30, 1952. In the lower part, the cumulative departures from the 75-year average value are shown for each year since the beginning of the record in 1877. In this type of diagram, an upward trend represents a sequence of years in which the wet years predominate, whereas a downward trend indicates that the dry years predominate. By this

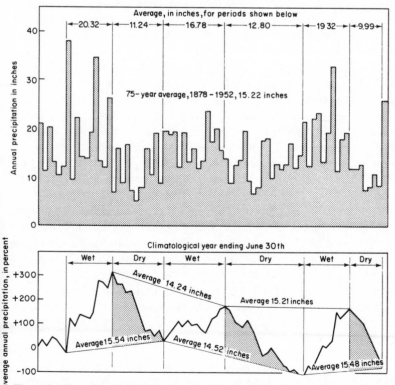

Figure 6. Annual precipitation at Los Angeles, California, for the period 1878 to 1952 (after Troxell and Hofmann 1954)

means it has been possible to divide the annual precipitation record into wet and dry periods. The average annual precipitation for each of these sequences is given across the upper part of figure [6]. These averages range from 9.99 inches for the 7-year sequence of 1945–51 to 20.32 inches for the 10-year sequence of 1884–93 (Troxell and Hofmann 1954).

Troxell and Hofmann then referred to the tree-ring chronology established by Schulman (1947) from big-cone spruce in the mountains of southern California. By plotting the cumulative departure in percent from the average annual tree-ring growth, which reflects past annual precipitation covering a 560-year span from A.D. 1385 to 1944, the same pattern of wet and dry trends shown by the rainfall record was revealed, as shown in Figure 7. A comparison with the Los Angeles precipitation record provided a sixty-eight-year overlap, from 1878 to 1944, and revealed that the wet and dry periods matched. This absolute chronology, which shows well the recurring wet and dry year trends, goes back to about 157 years before Cabrillo, the "discoverer" of California, first arrived in 1542.

In order to find whether Troxell and Hofmann's (and Schulman's) chronology could be extended to other parts of California, precipitation records for San Diego, Los Angeles, Santa Barbara, San Miguel Island, San Luis Obispo, Santa Cruz, and San Francisco were collated and cumulative departure curves drawn for each station. Results are shown in Figure 8. The recurring wet and dry sequences are clearly indicated and a definite correspondence exists between all stations. North of San Francisco the pattern weakens and tends to blur.

The tree-ring record of Figure 7 shows that dry cycles[2] range in length from as much as forty-three years to as little as six years, with a median value of fifteen years. The wet cycles are shorter, ranging from twenty-four to four years, with a median of twelve years. The median for a joint wet and dry cycle would be about twenty-seven years (Troxell and Hofmann 1954).

For almost 600 years coastal California has experienced a precipitation pattern characterized by (1) alternating wet and dry trends of variable duration, on which are superimposed (2) great yearly variations in precipitation. The persistence of these two features over such a long period of time suggests that they are basic elements of California's Mediterranean climate. The remarkable unbroken regularity of the wet–dry sequences, plus other paleoenvironmental evidence cited below, give reason to suspect that the same pattern prevailed in earlier Holocene and late Pleistocene time.

---

[2]   The wet and dry cycles perhaps should, *in sensu stricto*, be called wet and dry *trends* or *sequences*, because for any given dry or wet sequence there invariably are several years of above- or below-normal precipitation respectively. However, because the trends are recurrent they are called cycles in this study.

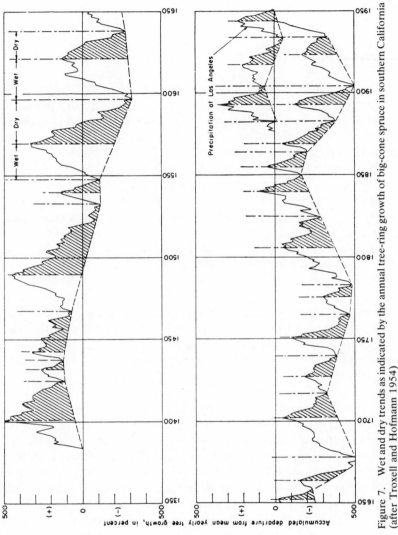

Figure 7.   Wet and dry trends as indicated by the annual tree-ring growth of big-cone spruce in southern California (after Troxell and Hofmann 1954)

PALEOENVIRONMENTAL EVIDENCE OF
A MEDITERRANEAN CLIMATE

Evidence that California has long had a basically Mediterranean type of climate is gained from geologic, pedologic, and paleobotanic studies.

Geological Evidence

Geological evidence comes from the study of Pleistocene sand dunes (eolianites) which blanket the mainland coast and offshore islands of California. But, because eolianites in the area and their paleoecological significance have already been studied (Johnson 1967, 1968, 1972), only a summary statement is necessary here.

The paleoecologic importance of eolianites stems from the fact that they indicate Pleistocene wind directions (McBurney and Hey 1955; Moseley 1965; Butzer 1963; MacKenzie 1964; Johnson 1972). In coastal southern California the present prevailing regional (mesoscale) wind pattern largely reflects the mutual existence and interaction of the semi-permanent Pacific High and interior heat lows (Figures 2 and 3). If studies of eolianites should indicate that the same basic mesoscale wind pattern prevailed during the Pleistocene, the mutual existence of the Pacific High and interior heat lows, as controls of the Mediterranean climate, may thus be inferred. As it turns out, the eolianites do indeed show that the wind pattern of Figures 2 and 3 prevailed during late Pleistocene time. The evidence comes from (1) the location of the dunes and their relationship to present and past prevailing wind direction, and (2) their bedding characteristics.

In the first instance the location of eolianites on the offshore islands of southern California is exactly as would be predicted if the present wind pattern had prevailed during late Pleistocene time. On the five California islands where eolianites occur, their location in each case is on the wind-struck northwest side (Johnson 1972). The winds that emplaced them, therefore, must have prevailed from the northwest, the direction from which they presently blow. Moreover, on certain islands multiple eolianite units occur that are of widely varying ages, as shown in Table 1 (Johnson 1972: 203–215). These multiple eolianites all occur on the northwest, wind-struck sides of the islands and do not reflect emplacement by randomly directional winds. They were emplaced by prevailing northwest winds. The widely varying ages of the eolianites suggest that the present mesoscale wind pattern has persisted for a long time.

In the second instance, the eolianites, regardless of their age, invariably dip downwind (southeast) at high angles (Johnson 1972:202). Conversely, the upwind (northwest) dips are low to moderate. This additional

Table 1. List of radiocarbon dates from San Miguel Island, California

Locality[a]	Laboratory and date	Description of material dated and significance of date
Simonton Cove		
SMI-171[a]	UCLA-1458, 40,000 ry[b]	Charcoal collected two inches below top of lowermost (oldest) soil in that part of Simonton Cove where SMI-171 occurs.
SMI-172	I-4614, 21,480±450 ry	Charcoal randomly collected in Beachrock soil.[a] This date together with Wis-413 and I-4586 shows that probably all but the lowermost of the paleosols are within the range of the radiocarbon method.
SMI-174	I-4587, 6,450±130 ry	Abalone (*Haliotis rufescens*) shell; part of midden debris scattered throughout upper fifteen inches of Abalone Soil; sample collected eight inches below surface.
SMI-178	Wis-413, 20,130±215 ry	Charcoalized stump (probably *Rhus*) of subarboreal vegetation that grew in Simonton Soil immediately prior to time when Yardang Eolianite was emplaced.
SMI-179A	UCLA-1484A, 9,360±200 ry	Charcoal collected immediately below UCLA-1484B in Midden Soil.
SMI-179B	UCLA-1484B, 7,940±80 ry	Mussel (*Mytilus*) and abalone (*Haliotis*) midden debris collected throughout upper twenty inches of Midden Soil.
SMI-180	I-4586, 17,730±300 ry	Charcoalized stump (unidentifiable) collected from the lowermost part of Midden Soil. This date, together with Wis-413, suggests that the eolianite which lies between was emplaced rather rapidly.
SMI-256	I-4852, 7,580±140 ry	Mussel (*Mytilus*) and barnacle (*Balanus*) midden debris in upper four inches of Simonton Soil at Range Pole Canyon, overlain by 140 feet of eolian and fluviatile sediments.
Harris Point		
SMI-86	I-3717, 6,030±106 ry	Abalone (*Haliotis rufescens*) midden shell collected twenty inches below surface of modern soil.
SMI-87	I-4583, 9,750±150 ry	Charcoal, taken twenty inches below surface of modern soil about forty yards west of I-3717.

Table 1. (*continued*)

Locality[a]	Laboratory and date	Description of material dated and significance of date
Otter Harbor SMI-181	UCLA-1457, 40,000 ry	Charcoalized rhizoconcretion, formerly a trunk of subarboreal vegetation which grew in Simonton Soil, the lowermost and oldest paleosol in the Otter Harbor area.
Point Bennett SMI-177	I-4585, 17,370±290 ry	Charcoalized rhizoconcretion of former subarboreal shrub which grew in Point Bennett Soil. Poor preservation of wood structure allowed an identification only at level of "an angiosperm."
Green Mountain area SMI-131-133	I-4584, 14,430±200 ry	Charcoal collected from a truncated paleosol which overlies a buried "fossil forest" of rhizoconcretions which preserve evidence of a former subarboreal shrub type of vegetation.

[a]   Localities and names refer to maps contained in Johnson (1972).
[b]   Radiocarbon years before present.

evidence that the prevailing paleowind direction was from the northwest supports the inferred mutual existence and interaction of the Pacific High and interior heat lows during late Pleistocene time.

Pedological Evidence

The soil evidence which supports the model comes from caliche and charcoal. In the first instance, caliche is a whitish calcium carbonate deposit of pedological origin that commonly occurs in soils in arid and semiarid regions. Caliche does not occur in humid lands because precipitation in such areas is adequate to through-leach soil carbonates. Thus fossil caliche is a paleoclimatic indicator of dry climates. On the California islands the multiple eolianites described earlier are all separated by fossil soils, each of which has an associated fossil-caliche horizon (Johnson 1967, 1972). The soils range from full-glacial to mid-Holocene in age (Table 1). The modern soil also has a caliche horizon. The presence of these caliche horizons shows that a subhumid climate prevailed in coastal California during late Quaternary time.

In the second instance, the paleosols which separate the eolianite units contain great amounts of charcoal (Johnson 1972: 81–82). The charcoal consists of burned fossil vegetation, as for example partially charcoalized trunks, one of which is shown in Plate 1, which have given dates of 17,300 ± 290, 17,730 ± 300, 20,130 ± 215, and greater than 40,000 radiocarbon years. Charcoal in paleosols but not associated with tree trunks in growth position has been dated at 6,450 ± 130, 9,360 ± 200, 9,750 ± 150, 14,430 ± 200, 21,480 ± 450, and greater than 40,000 radiocarbon years (Table 1). This collective charcoal and radiocarbon evidence shows that periodic fires have long been common to coastal California. Charcoal is common in the modern soils, and the present fire regime is intimately tied to California's seasonally dry climate.

Collectively, the presence of caliche horizons and charcoal in almost all the soils intercalated in eolianite, plus the widely varying ages of the soils, provide supportive evidence of a Mediterranean climate during late Quaternary time. The climate is inferred always to have been subhumid or semiarid, although some variations in rainfall and temperature undoubtedly occurred from time to time.

Paleobotanical Evidence

It is well known that the present distinctive vegetation of coastal California strongly reflects the Mediterranean character of the climate. Chaparral, coastal sage scrub, closed-cone pine forest, and oak–grass woodland are among the more common communities reflective of the climate. It would seem that the most critical test of the model would be provided by fossil plants. If a Mediterranean climate prevailed during the Pleistocene, similarly aged fossil plants should verify it, and they do. The Mediterranean character of the vegetation may be judged from the Willow Creek flora of Santa Cruz Island (Chaney and Mason 1930), the San Miguel Island flora (Johnson 1972: 81–83, 88, 261–262, 264, 303–304), the Santa Rosa Island flora (Orr 1967: 320, 1968), the Carpenteria flora (Chaney and Mason 1933), the Rancholabrean flora (Frost 1927; Mason 1927, 1932: 51; Axelrod 1967b: 295–297), the Little Sur flora (Langenheim and Durham 1963), and the fossil floras of Point Sal Ridge and Tomales (Axelrod 1967b). No paleobotanical evidence suggests that coastal California had anything other than a climate that was basically Mediterranean in character in late Quaternary time. What the plant fossil evidence does suggest, however, is that certain elements of the coastal vegetation shifted north and south in response to alternating full-glacial and interglacial conditions elsewhere (Axelrod 1967a, 1967b). Thus, the presence of Douglas fir on Santa Cruz Island and redwood at Carpenteria and La Brea indicates a shift of these species some 200 miles south during full-glacial times. However, evidence of major climatic change from temperate to glacial conditions along the California coast is lacking. The vegetation shifts which did occur are interpreted as reflecting increasing precipitation during full-glacial times, which probably was accompanied by slightly cooler temperatures. On the other hand, recent paleobotanical evidence from the Northern Channel Islands suggests that certain elements of the modern vegetation were present during full-glacial time. Calichified trunks and roots (rhizoconcretions) of a subarboreal type of vegetation occur in great abundance on certain of the California islands, as illustrated in Plate 2. As mentioned, many of the rhizoconcretions are partially charcoalized and four are dated at 17,370 ± 290, 17,730 ± 300, 20,130 ± 215, and 40,000 radiocarbon years (Table 1). These data show that sizeable stands of subarboreal or arboreal vegetation formerly grew on the islands, and periodically burned, during full-glacial time. The general morphology and spatial clustering of the rhizoconcretions hint at a chaparral type of plant community. Microscopic thin-section analyses of the charcoalized rhizoconcretions suggest that several are probably referable to the genus *Rhus* (Johnson 1972). Moreover, the morphologic appearance of the calichified vegetation also strongly suggests *Rhus* or a *Rhus*-like plant. *Rhus integrifolia* presently grows on the islands and is a component of coastal sage scrub and chaparral communities (Munz 1959: 998).

The reconstruction that seems most closely in line with available paleoecologic[3] evidence is that the core Mediterranean climatic unit and certain elements of the vegetation experienced a slight shift southward during full-glacial times and northward during interglacial periods. Beyond this, nothing in the landscape suggests major climatic changes comparable to those which most of North America experienced during the late Pleistocene.

THE CALIFORNIA COASTAL REGION:
A LATE PLEISTOCENE CLIMATIC REFUGIUM

The collective evidence of eolianites, soil caliche and charcoal, Mediterranean-type plant fossils, and radiocarbon dates, plus the historic and prehistoric precipitation data, provide a clear late Pleistocene environmental record. Singly, these lines of evidence may not be conclusive, but collectively they converge and form a solid consensus in support

---

[3] Considerable information on the late Pleistocene marine climate of the near-shore surface waters off California has accumulated in recent years (Valentine 1961; Valentine and Emerson 1961; Valentine and Meade 1961; Valentine and Lipps, 1963; Addicott 1966; and others). However, reference to this literature is omitted because it is not strictly relevant to this essay. The paleomarine interpretations are based on marine invertebrate faunas from emergent marine terraces that are older than 40,000 radiocarbon years, whereas this essay is concerned with the very late Quaternary climate, principally of full-glacial (12,000–20,000 B.P.) and postglacial time.

of the model. If the model is correct, the California coastal region functioned as a full-glacial climatic refugium and the refugees included, besides Mediterranean-type plants, the Rancholabrean fauna. The implications of this apparent fact become clear when set in the context of one of the most intriguing of all questions that environmental scientists are faced with: why did so many large mammals disappear from the North American scene in terminal Pleistocene time? If this question is posed in an area like Illinois, where the observer is literally surrounded by a sea of glacial reminders, the answer may seem obvious. But if the question is asked in California, the answer merits more cautious consideration. Few areas in the world claim such an array of fossil Rancholabrean faunal forms as California. Megafaunal sites such as Rancho La Brea and Carpenteria in southern California, and the Rodeo and other sites in the San Francisco Bay area, plus numerous other sites scattered across the state serve as silent reminders of the great diversity of Rancholabrean mammals that formerly lived in the area.

It may be argued that droughty conditions in postglacial time could be responsible for the disappearance of the Rancholabrean forms in California. That a trend towards droughty conditions occurred during the Holocene is inferred from the discontinuous distribution of coastal and interior plant communities, including ". . . the occurrence of certain arid to semiarid plants in areas well removed from regions of their optimum development" (Axelrod 1967b: 299.) Axelrod (1966, 1967a, 1967b) reviewed other supportive evidence for hotter and drier conditions in southern and central California in the very recent (ca. 8000–3000 B.P.) past. Guilday (1967) has persuasively argued that postglacial droughty conditions were largely responsible for the Pleistocene extinction of the large mammal fauna of North America and other regions. However, this argument cannot be reasonably applied to California because the precipitation has a north–south gradient (Figure 1), and animals would have responded to any variations in this cline. For example, if in the future southern California experiences a trend toward drier conditions, drought-sensitive animals in the area need only expand their ranges north where moisture conditions are ecologically more suitable. Animals and animal ranges are respectively mobile and dynamic, and they respond accordingly to environmental changes. It is well known that east African mammals respond to decreasing moisture and food by migrating or by extending or changing their ranges, and it is reasonable to suppose that the Rancholabrean fauna of California did likewise. The same argument weakens the suggestion by Axelrod (1968) that a trend toward less equability of climate was a major factor in the large-mammal extinctions. If climatic change cannot account for the Rancholabrean extinctions, what can?

Martin (1967) has argued that man was the principal factor responsible for the worldwide wave of megafaunal extinctions in terminal Pleistocene time. According to Martin, the arrival of two-legged superpredators in North America in late Pleistocene times was the major ecological event which distinguished the Wisconsin stage, when major extinctions occurred, from the earlier Illinoisan, Kansan, and Nebraskan stages, when few extinctions occurred. It is inferred that the North American megafauna, being analogous to the dodo birds of Mauritius Island, did not recognize cultural man as a predator and suffered the consequences — extinction. While many have not subscribed to the whole of Martin's views, most researchers close to the problem agree that man probably was *a* factor. The principal argument seems to be, how much a factor?

If it is agreed that cultural man was a factor, among other factors, then it seems reasonable that man must have been a more important factor in some regions than in others. This was almost certainly the case on the Northern Channel Islands, where the pygmy elephants probably became extinct soon after man arrived in late Pleistocene time (Orr 1968; Johnson 1972:267–268). An area like California, where the Wisconsin climate was clement and in which comparatively large human food resources existed, likely attracted and supported greater numbers of humans than did other regions. The fact that California in particular has long been attractive to humans is borne out not only by its present large population but also by the great aboriginal populations and ethnic diversity present in pre-Columbian times (Driver 1961:16). A relationship between human numbers and environmental impact must have existed then as it does now in modern times.

It is suggested that, in the California region at least, man was the principal agent of the late Quaternary extinction of the Rancholabrean fauna. Climate or climatic change was almost certainly not responsible because no significant climatic change occurred. The late Quaternary extinction of Rancholabrean animals marked the beginning of a long history of environmental impact in California by humans.

REFERENCES

ADDICOTT, W.
   1966   Late Pleistocene marine paleoecology and zoogeography in central California. *Geological Survey Professional Paper 523–C*. Washington, D.C.: U.S. Government Printing Office.
AXELROD, D. I.
   1966   The Pleistocene Soboba flora of southern California. *University of California Publications in the Geological Sciences* 60:1–109.
   1967a   "Evolution of the Californian closed-cone pine forest," in *Proceedings of the Symposium on the Biology of the California Islands*. Edited by R. N. Philbrick, 93–149. Santa Barbara: Santa Barbara Botanic Garden.

1967b "Geologic history of the Californian insular flora," in *Proceedings of the Symposium on the Biology of the California Islands.* Edited by R. N. Philbrick, 267–315. Santa Barbara: Santa Barbara Botanic Garden.

1968 The Quaternary extinction of large mammals. *University of California Publications in the Geological Sciences.* Berkeley: University of California Press.

BUTZER, K.
1963 Climatic–geomorphic interpretation of Pleistocene sediments in the Euratrican subtropics. *Viking Fund Publications in Anthropology* 36:1–27.

CHANEY, R. W., H. L. MASON
1930 A Pleistocene flora from Santa Cruz Island, California. *Carnegie Institution of Washington Publication* 415:1–24.

1933 A Pleistocene flora from the asphalt deposits at Carpenteria, California. *Carnegie Institution of Washington Publication* 415:1–24.

COOPER, W. S.
1967 Coastal dunes of California. *Geological Society of America,* Memoir 104.

DE MARRAIS, G. A., G. C. HOLZWORTH, C. R. HOSLER
1965 Meteorological summaries pertinent to atmospheric transport and dispersion over southern California. U.S. Deparment of Commerce, *Weather Bureau Technical Paper* No. 54. Washington: U.S. Government Printing Office.

DE VIOLINI, R.
1967 *Climatic handbook for Point Mugu and San Nicolas Island,* volume 1: *surface data.* Pacific Missile Range Miscellaneous Report PMR–MR–67–2. Point Mugu, California.

DODGE, M.
1970 Fire control of chaparral. *Science* 168:420.

DRIVER, H. E.
1961 *Indians of North America.* Chicago: University of Chicago Press.

EMERY, K. O.
1960 *The sea off southern California.* New York: John Wiley.

FROST, F. H.
1927 The Pleistocene flora of Rancho La Brea. *University of California Publications in Botany* 14:73–98.

GUILDAY, J. E.
1967 "Differential extinction during late-Pleistocene and Recent times," in *Pleistocene extinctions: the search for a cause.* Edited by P. S. Martin and H. E. Wright, 121–140. New Haven: Yale University Press.

HOLZWORTH, G. C.
1973 "Large-scale weather influences on community air pollution potential in the United States," in *Climate in review.* Edited by G. McBoyle, 241–248. Boston: Houghton Mifflin.

JOHNSON, D. L.
1967 Caliche on the Channel Islands. *Mineral Information Services, California Division of Mines and Geology* 20(12):151–158.

1968 "Quaternary coastal eolianites: do they have ancient analogs?" *Programs with Abstracts,* Geological Society of America 1968 Annual Meetings, Mexico City.

1972 *Landscape evolution on San Miguel Island, California.* Unpublished Ph.D. Thesis, University of Kansas.

116 DONALD L. JOHNSON

LANGENHEIM, H. H., J. W. DURHAM
1963 Quaternary closed-cone pine forest from travertine near Little Sur, California. *Madroño* 17:33–51.

MacKENZIE, F. T.
1964 Bermuda Pleistocene eolianites and paleowinds. *Sedimentology* 3:52–64.

McBURNEY, C., R. HEY
1955 *Prehistory and Pleistocene geology in Cyrenaican Libya.* Cambridge: Cambridge University Press.

MARTIN P. S.
1967 "Prehistoric overkill," in *Pleistocene extinctions: the search for a cause.* Edited by P. S. Martin and H. E. Wright, 75–120. New Haven: Yale University Press.

MASON, H. L.
1927 Fossil records of some west American conifers. *Carnegie Institution of Washington Publication* 346:139–158.
1932 A phylogenetic series of the California closed-cone pines suggested by the fossil record. *Madroño* 2:49–55.

MOSELEY, F.
1965 Plateau calcrete, calcreted gravels, cemented dunes, and related deposits of the Maallegh–Bomba region of Libya. *Zeitschrift für Geomorphologie* 9:166–165.

MUNZ, P. A.
1959 *A California flora.* Berkeley: University of California Press.

ORR, P. C.
1967 "Geochronology of Santa Rosa Island, California," in *Proceedings of the Symposium on the Biology of the California Islands.* Edited by R. N. Philbrick, 317–325. Santa Barbara: Santa Barbara Botanic Garden.
1968 *Prehistory of Santa Rosa Island.* Santa Barbara: Santa Barbara Museum of Natural History.

SCHULMAN, E.
1947 Tree-ring hydrology in southern California. Laboratory of Tree-Ring Research Bulletin 4. *University of Arizona Bulletin* 18(3).

TROXELL, H. C., *et al.*
1954 Hydrology of the San Bernardino and eastern San Gabriel mountains, California. *Department of the Interior, U.S. Geologic Survey Hydrologic Investigations Atlas HA-1.*

TROXELL, H. C., W. HOFMANN
1954 "Hydrology of the Los Angeles region," in *Geology of southern California*, Bulletin 170, volume one. Edited by R. H. Jahns, 5–12.

VALENTINE, J. W.
1961 Paleoecologic molluscan geography of the Californian Pleistocene. *University of California Publications in the Geological Sciences* 34(7):309–442.

VALENTINE, J. W., W. K. EMERSON
1961 Environmental interpretation of Pleistocene marine species — a discussion. *Journal of Geology* 69(5):616–618.

VALENTINE, J. W., J. H. LIPPS
1963 Late Cenozoic rocky shore assemblages from Anacapa Island, California. *Journal of Paleontology* 37:1,292–1,302.

VALENTINE, J. W., R. F. MEADE
1961 Californian Pleistocene paleotemperatures. *University of California Publications in the Geological Sciences* 40(1):1–46.

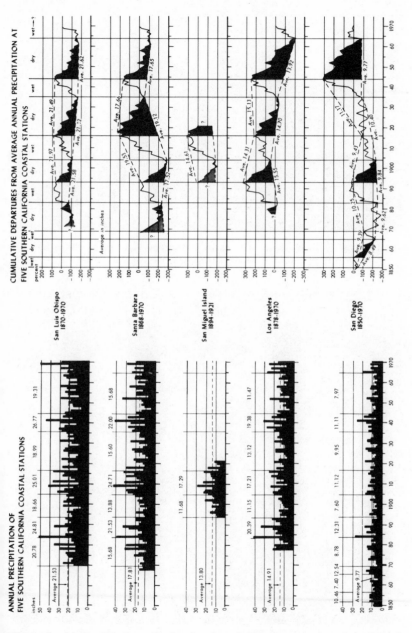

Figure 8. (a) Precipitation records of various Californian coastal stations (calendar years). (b) Cumulative departures from average annual precipitation of stations in (a), in percent

Plate 1. Close-up of charcoalized trunk of pre-existant vegetation exposed by wind erosion on San Miguel Island, California. The radiocarbon age of this plant is 17,370±290 years B.P.

Plate 2. Exhumed calcified trunks of pre-existant subarboreal vegetation on San Miguel Island, California. The soil which overlies these rhizoconcretions at a nearby locality has been given a radiocarbon age of 14,430±200 years B.P.

SECTION TWO

Microblade Traditions and Migrations

Introduction

Unlike the earlier cultures, in which questions of relationship are vague, blade and microblade industries of Alaska and those in Siberia can be correlated on good evidence. The questions now being raised involve just exactly how complete the identity is, and what was the direction of influence — whether concepts diffused in one direction only, from Siberia to Alaska, or whether there was, as one would quite logically suspect, back-diffusion from Alaska to Siberia. Mochanov creates a reconstruction of events in accordance with the views of many North Americanists — an early blade industry, Dyuktai, approximately 35,000 B.C., with descendants crossing into Alaska about 25,000 B.C. and arriving in Mexico about 23,000 B.C. (with a lacuna when the land bridge is submerged between 14,000 and 13,000 B.C.), and then new crossties developing between the Dyuktai of Siberia and the Denali of Alaska about 10,000 B.C.

This is a very comfortable model; however, Abramova argues that the facts do not support it as well as we would like. The Dyuktai people, argued by Mochanov to have arrived in the New World about 25,000 B.C., have good radiocarbon dates only ca. 11,000 B.C., so thus cannot be seen as the antecedents of the Hueyatlaco peoples or the Paccaicasa peoples in the New World with antiquity greater than 20,000 years ago. Abramova is also critical of the concept of a population model in the New World which requires quick nonstop diffusion rather than a long period of gradual cultural radiation.

There appears to be little question that the Denali materials in Alaska, first recognized as a complex by West (1967), and the Dyuktai materials of Siberia are extremely closely related. Portions of interior Alaska and Canada and Siberia were all part of the same larger culture sphere, with prehistoric peoples exploiting the same resources in the same environment using nearly identical material technology. The Denali complex is not the earliest lithic complex in Alaska, but it is extremely important since it documents renewed cultural contacts between America and Asia. The microcore and microblade tradition so diagnostic of the Dyuktai complex and the Denali complex reached southern Alaska by about 8000 B.C., as Ackerman points out in his paper, and diffused southward along the Pacific coast and mountain ranges, reaching Washington state by 5000 B.C. (Browman and Munsell 1972). Whether this diffusion of technology represents movement of ideas or whether it may chronicle movements of a particular people is still hotly debated, but the writers included in this volume lean toward the concept of the tool types actually being tied in with demographic movements.

Dating in the far north is always a problem, and many of our sites are dated on the basis of typological comparisons rather than of physical-chemistry determination techniques. Thus, though there is considerably more data now on the fluted-point tradition in Alaska, the Clarks point out that we still cannot say with certainty whether the first fluted forms were fabricated in Alaska and diffused south, or whether the opposite is true, with Alaska at the northern end of the line of diffusion from the Great Plains and Great Basin. The expanded definition of the Denali complex, based now on sixteen sites as contrasted to the previous sample size of only four sites, plus the numbers of fluted-point finds in Alaska of roughly comparable age to those in the rest of North America, now paint a picture of northern prehistory much more congruent with what we know about the rest of the New World.

REFERENCES

BROWMAN, D. L., D. A. MUNSELL
  1972   Columbia Plateau prehistory: some observations. *American Antiquity* 37(4):546–548.
WEST, F. H.
  1967   The Donnelly Ridge site and the definition of an early core and blade complex in central Alaska. *American Antiquity* 32(3):360–382.

Early Migrations to America in the Light of a Study of the Dyuktai Paleolithic Culture in Northeast Asia

JU. A. MOCHANOV

It is now taken for granted that America knew no early stages of anthropogenesis and that man came to its territory in the Upper Pleistocene from Asia moving across the regions adjoining the Bering Strait. This assumption proceeds from the recognition of great anthropological similarity between the aborigines of the New World and the Mongoloids and from the fact that, at individual stages of the Quaternary period, Chukotka and Alaska were connected by a land bridge.

In dating the early migration to America, scholars, basing their studies upon modern data, attach greatest importance to the following considerations:

1. The age of the Pleistocene sites in the New World. The earliest archaeological sites in America whose ages are firmly established are from 23,000 to 21,000 years old. Radiocarbon dating makes the Tlapacoya site in southern Mexico (20° northern latitude) 23,150 ± 950 years old (Haynes 1969).

The singling out of the pre-point-stage culture, which individual researchers believed to be the earliest in America (Krieger 1964), in the light of recent investigations appears increasingly dubious. Extensive control explorations conducted at one of its basic sites, Tule Springs in Nevada, revealed that man lived there not more than 13,500 to 12,000 years ago — not 28,000 years ago, as was previously believed (Shutler 1965).

Early bifacial stone tools have been discovered, so far, in Idaho, in Wilson Butte cave, 14,500 ± 500 years old (Crabtree 1969), and in Oregon, in Fort Rock cave, 13,300 ± 170 years old (Haynes 1969). The best-studied Pleistocene culture in America is the old Llano (Clovis) culture, which is represented by well-documented sites in the southern

United States and northern Mexico. The sites of this culture are 12,000 to 11,000 years old (Haynes 1970).

Possibly one of the local variants of the old Llano culture is represented by the sites with Sandia points, whose age (15,000–12,000 years) is now open to question.

At least 10,000 years ago man already lived in the far south of America. The lower cultural horizon of the Fell cave, at the Strait of Magellan, is 10,700 ± 30 years of age. Typological analysis has brought out a definite genetic relationship between the Fell cave and Clovis-type points (Lothrop 1961).

2. The existence of the land bridge between Asia and America. In the Upper Pleistocene, the Chukotka–Alaska land bridge, which is traditionally referred to as Beringia, existed twice. The first period of its existence, according to different sources, is dated from circa 70,000–60,000 to 48,000–35,000 years ago, its second period from circa 28,000–25,000 to 11,000–10,000 years ago. During the Vorontsovo transgression, which, as various researchers assume, took place from 48,000–35,000 to 28,000–25,000 years ago, Beringia was completely flooded by the Chukotka and Bering Seas. According to other data, Beringia may have been flooded between 14,500–13,500 and 12,500–11,500 years ago. Finally, the land bridge between the New and Old Worlds ceased to exist about 10,500 years ago. At that time, the coastlines of northest Asia and northwest America acquired their near-present shapes (Hopkins 1967:451–484).

3. The existence of a free passage from Alaska to the south of America. In the Upper Pleistocene, the way from Alaska south was blocked by a solid ice barrier, which stretched from the Atlantic to the Pacific. Its southern border reached about 40° north latitude in the east and 50° north latitude in the west. This barrier formed when the Cordillera and Laurentian glaciers merged during their maximal expansion. It is still to be discovered whether or not the solid ice barrier existed during the early Wisconsin (Altona) glaciation in America. It is believed to be precisely established that it existed during the late Wisconsin (Woodford) glaciation. According to other sources, the late Wisconsin ice barrier existed between 25,000–24,000 and 13,000–10,000 years ago (Hopkins 1967:451–484; Dikov 1969).

Considering the existence of the ice barrier, impenetrable to the Paleolithic hunters, and the dating of the Tlapacoya site and the Old Llano sites, nearly all experts believe that, as he moved from Alaska, man must have reached the south earlier than 25,000–24,000 years ago. Alaska is assumed to have been populated still earlier.

Some researchers maintain that the migration to Alaska must have taken place before the Vorontsovo transgression. This view stems from the assumption that this transgression took place from 35,000 to 25,000 years ago and, when it ended, the way from Alaska south had already been blocked by the glacier (Bryan 1969).

Hopkins (personal communication), citing a vast amount of material, underlines the assumption that the Vorontsovo transgression ended 25,000 years ago, that the ice barrier formed only 24,000 years ago, and that, consequently, man may have reached Alaska at the beginning of the existence of the late Wisconsin Beringia and, within a thousand years (25,000–24,000 years ago), may have crossed Canada to reach what is now the southern United States.

A number of scholars assume that there may have been two waves of migration from Asia to Alaska and further south in the Upper Pleistocene: the first before the Vorontsovo transgression, earlier than 40,000 years ago, and the second between this transgression and the formation of the ice barrier, 28,000–26,000 years ago (Chard 1963, 1969; Muller–Beck 1965, 1966).

There is also the view that during the late Wisconsin glaciation there were warmer periods, when the glaciers receded to form a passage from Alaska south, accessible to animals and man. Some scholars say that one of these periods occurred 15,000–14,000 years ago (Hester 1966). Others think it was 13,000–12,000 years ago (Haynes 1970).

Just as involved as the dating and quantification of man's early migrations to the New World is the elucidation of sources of the ancient American cultures. One explanation is the fragmentariness of the data on New World cultures previous to the Old Llano culture. Another is the fact that until recently no Paleolithic culture which, in time and aspect, could be considered initial for the evolution of Old Llano and the previous American cultures, was known in the Old World. This situation, observes Chard (1969:143), has been puzzling scholars for many years and, on frequent occasions, has led them to sheer speculation.

Suffice it to note here that scholars sought sources of American cultures in sites like Ting-ts'un (Chard 1963; Muller–Beck 1965); in east Asia, in early sites like the Ust-Kansk cave (Wormington 1962); in Siberia; in the Kostyonki–Streltsy culture of the Russian plain (Muller–Beck 1965; Haynes 1970); in the Malta culture in the Transbaikal area (Wilmsen 1964); and in south Siberian sites like Ulalinki and Filimoshek (Laricheva 1971). All these and similar hypotheses are normally based upon remote typological similarity between individual features of the sites compared and, on some occasions, upon mere intuition.

A scientific solution of the problem of migration to the New World calls, above all, for vast amounts of factual material on the Paleolithic in Alaska and northest Asia.

Quite recently, Chard pointed out (1969:142) that the Pleistocene archaeology of these regions was in its infancy. However, the intensive field explorations of the past ten years have been gradually changing the situation both in Alaska, in the singling-out of the Akmak and Donnelly assemblages (Anderson 1970; West 1967), and in northeast Asia (Mochanov 1966, 1969a, 1969b, 1970, 1972a, 1972b; Mochanov and Fedoseeva 1968; Vereshchagin and Mochanov 1972; Dikov 1969). In 1963, the Lena region archaeological expedition of the Yakutian Branch of the U.S.S.R. Academy of Sciences' Siberian section discovered, in the lower reaches of the Aldan at 63° north latitude, Yakutia's first site of prehistoric man, which was related to the Upper Pleistocene deposits. Stone tools lay in the middle part of floodplain Alluvia II of the terrace above the floodplain, together with mammoth, bison, and horse bones. According to geological and archaeological data, this site, Ikhine I, is 20,000–18,000 years old. Next to it, there is a site called Ikhine II, whose cultural stratum forms part of the upper alluvia of the first terrace above the floodplain. The Ikhine II site is about 12,000 years old.

In 1965, on the Aldan, scholars discovered the Paleolithic site Sumnaghi III, about 13,000–12,000 years old.

A major event in the study of the Paleolithic in northeast Asia was the discovery of the Dyuktai cave on the Aldan in 1967. Excavations there, together with mammoth, bison, horse, and musk ox bones, disclosed more than 10,000 man-split flints, among them bifacial willow-leaf and subtriangular spearheads and oval knives. In addition to lying in the cave itself, the Paleolithic finds lay on the ground in front of it, where they were found to form part of the upper mass of the floodplain facies deposits of Alluvia I of the terrace above the floodplain. Three cultural horizons occur there. The researchers say the upper is $12,100 \pm 120$ years old (LE–907) and the middle $12,690 \pm 120$ (LE–860), $13,070 \pm 90$ (LE–784), and $13,110 \pm 90$ years old (LE–908). The lower horizon judging by geological data, is 16,000–14,000 years old.

In 1968, sixty kilometers down the Aldan from the Dyuktai cave, scholars discovered a Paleolithic site, Ust–Mil II. Its cultural remnants are considered to form part of Alluvia III of the terrace above the floodplain, and its horizons with the finds are $35,400 \pm 600$ (LE–954), $33,000 \pm 500$ (LE–100), and $30,000 \pm 500$ years old (LE–1001). Together with mammoth and horse bones, the scholars discovered there flint flakes, a workblank retouched on all sides for a three-faceted wedge-shaped core, a massive pebble core, and a transversally split metacarpal mammoth bone, processed along the split edge. The Ust–Mil finds are of exceptional interest, as they are so far the earliest in Asia north of 53° north latitude. Regrettably, the cultural remnants in the Ust–Mil II site are very few so far.

In 1969, five and ten kilometers up the Aldan from the mouth of the Mai, one of its right tributaries, scholars discovered the Nizhne–Troitskaya and Verkhne–Troitskaya sites. The stone tools and the mammoth, woolly rhinoceros, bison, and horse bones in these sites are considered part of the lower floodplain Alluvia I of the terrace above the floodplain. The cultural remnants there lie both in the deposits, which are dated 18,300 ± 180 (LE–905) and 17,680 ± 250 years old (LE–906), and in the deposits which lie 0.8 to 1 meter below them. The most significant of the tools are bifacial flint spearheads and knives.

In 1970, also on the Aldan, forty-five kilometers below the mouth of the river Mai, scholars discovered the Ezhantsy site. Stone artifacts, together with mammoth and horse bones, were found where the river bed and floodplain Alluvia II of the terrace above the floodplain come into contact. Geologically, they must be 30,000–25,000 years old. Remarkably, among the tools discovered there was a bifacial oval knife, near-identical with those discovered in the Dyuktai cave.

In addition to these sites, Paleolithic discoveries on the Aldan have also been made at sites Ust–Bilir II and Ust–Dyuktai I in the cover deposits III and II of the terraces above the floodplain. The age of the former is not clear. The latter is about 15,000–12,000 years old.

In 1970, Paleolithic sites were discovered on the Kolyma and in the Indigirka basin. The Mayorych site on the Kolyma is at about 63° north latitude. Human artifacts there lay on the exposed surface of the river bed of the first terrace above the floodplain. The exact age of the finds remains to be established but, typologically, they stand closest to the Verkhne–Troitskaya ones. This site may be assumed to have existed between 18,000 and 12,000 years ago.

The Berelekh site, at about 71° north latitude in the Indigirka basin existed on the very borderline between the Pleistocene and the Holocene. Its cultural stratum goes back to the upper mass of Alluvia I of the terrace above the floodplain. It is believed to be 10,600 ± 90 years old (LE–998). On this site, together with mammoth bones, scholars discovered tools which looked much like the Aldan ones. Among them were bifacial points. Other discoveries made there included decorations shaped like biconically drilled little pebbles with edge incision.

The distinction of the archaeological sites discovered in the Pleistocene deposits in Yakutia makes them part of a specific Paleolithic culture, which has been termed Dyuktai — a culture of hunters for mammoths, woolly rhinoceroses, bisons, horses, musk oxen, and, apparently, reindeer. The most indicative elements of the Dyuktai culture are bifacial willow-leaf, lancet-shaped, and subtriangular flint spearheads, as well as oval and semilunar knives. These tools are accompanied by Levalloisian, discoidal, wedge-shaped and massive pebble nodules, end scrapers, median and lateral burins, and large and small blades. There are single examples of choppers, mammoth-tusk spearheads, bone needles, and flint blade points with lateral notches at the bases. A number of these artifacts are shown in Figures 1, 2, and 3.

The latest explorations in Yakutia fail to confirm that between 22,000

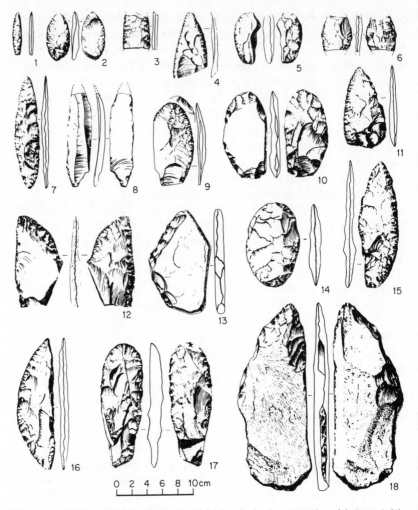

Figure 1.   Artifacts of the stone industry of the Dyuktai culture. Artifacts (1) through (5), (7), (10), (11), (13), (14), and (18) are from the Dyuktai cave; (6) from Berelekh; (8) from Ust–Dyuktai Í; and (9), (12), and (15) through (17) from Verkhne–Troitskaya

and 10,000 years ago a specific Ikhinen culture existed on its territory. The Ikhine I site should apparently be ascribed to one of the local variants of the Dyuktai culture, the final analysis of which remains a job for the future.

The Dyuktai culture must have included some stone tools (bifacial leaf-shaped points and wedge-shaped nodules) discovered by Dikov in 1964–1967 in the Ushki I, II, and IV sites in Kamchatka (Shilo *et al.* 1967; Dikov 1969). In Kamchatka, the Dyuktai remnants are 11,000–10,500 years old.

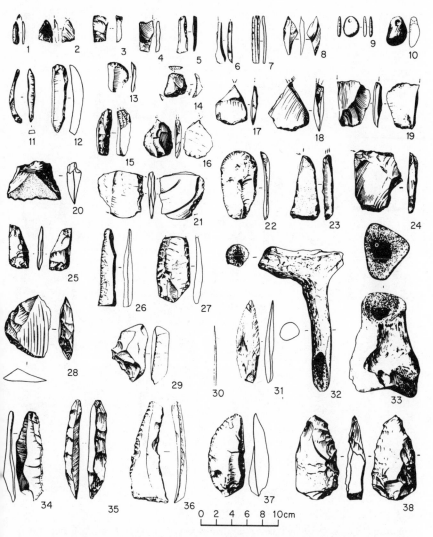

Figure 2. Stone and bone implements of the Dyuktai culture. Artifacts (1), (4), (6), (8), (13), (16) through (19), (21), and (29) are from Ezhantsy; (2), (22), (24), (27), (30), and (36) from Verkhne–Troitskaya; (5), (7), (15), (20), (23), (28), (31), (32), (34), (35), and (37) from the Dyuktai cave; (3) and (14) from Ikhine I; (9), (10), and (25) from Berelekh; (11) from Ust–Bilir II; (12) from Nizhne–Troitskaya; (26) from Mayorych; and (33) and (38) from Ust–Mil II

Judging by radiocarbon data and the mode of occurrence of the Paleolithic finds on the Aldan, the Indigirka, and the Kolyma, and those in Kamchatka, the Dyuktai culture existed in northeast Asia from 35,000–30,000 to 10,500 years ago.

A comparative analysis of the materials from Paleolithic sites east of

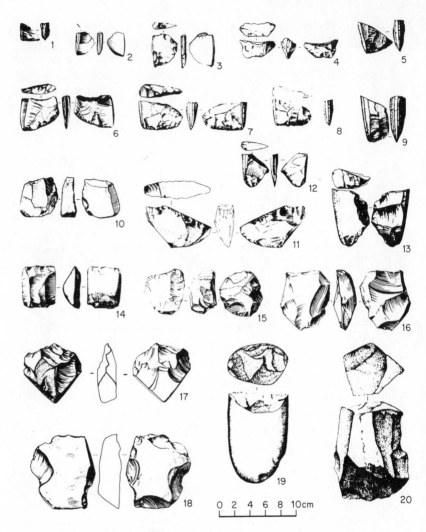

Figure 3.   Cores of the Dyuktai culture. Artifacts (1), (7), (12), (14), (15), and (20) are from Verkhne–Troitskaya; (2), (3), (16), and (19) from Ezhantsy; (4) from Ust–Mil II; (5), (9), (10), (13), (17), and (18) from the Dyuktai cave; (6) and (11) from Ust–Dyuktai I; and (8) from Ikhine I

the Urals allows for a preliminary differentiation in north Asia of two large ethnocultural Upper Paleolithic regions: a western region, which can conventionally be termed Malta–Afontova, and an eastern region, Dyuktai. The different cultures of the western region were dominated by the manufacture of stone tools from blades and flakes by edge processing, while the cultures of the eastern region were characterized by bifacial stone knives and spearheads. The border between these two regions was approximately the Lena–Yenissei watershed. However, in the south — the steppes of the Transbaikal area, Mongolia, and north China — individual Malta–Afontova cultures reached almost to the Sea of Japan. Far west along the southern territory, stretching in the direction of the Altai Mountains, were wedged the Dyuktai-region cultures. The result was the formation of contact regions such as the upper Angara, in which sites with tools processed with edge retouch neighbored sites with elaborate bifaces. The greater part of the pure Dyuktai-type culture area lay east of the Lena and north of the Amur, apparently taking in Sakhalin and a vast part of Hokkaido.

The absence in Asia north of 50° north latitude of well-studied Middle Paleolithic sites makes it very difficult to judge the origin of different cultures of the Malta–Afontova and Dyuktai types. So far, it can only be assumed that the Malta–Afontova region cultures are genetically related to the Levallois-Mousterian cultures of central Asia and Mongolia. Genetically, the Dyuktai region cultures may go back to the culture represented in the Hwang Ho basin by the sites Koho, Lantien, and Ting-ts'un, with their bifacial choppers resembling chopping tools.

The early cultures in America bear no close resemblance either to the Malta–Afontova or to the "pebble-type" cultures that were widespread south of the Hwang Ho and the Kunlun Range.

A different picture can be obtained by comparing the early American cultures with the Dyuktai culture. Early human sites in America south of the ice barrier reveal nonfluted stone spearheads, knives, end scrapers, large blades, discoidal and pebble nodules, and choppers and bone points resembling those of the Dyuktai culture. The two cultures also had an identical economic basis — hunting for mammoths, bison, and horses. Perhaps the only difference between these cultures was the absence of fluted points in the Dyuktai culture and of wedge-shaped nodules in the ancient American culture. True enough, the latter can still be discovered in America's Old Llano and still older sites. One wedge-shaped nodule has been discovered among the materials of the Folsom culture, a genetic derivative of the Old Llano culture (Laricheva 1971:27).

Still closer resemblance is observed between the materials of the latest Dyuktai monuments, 15,000–10,500 years old, and the Akmak and Donnelly assemblages in Alaska, about 12,000–10,000 years old.

The close resemblance between the Dyuktai culture and the early American cultures and paleogeographic data on the Upper Pleistocene in northeast Asia and America lead to the following conclusions concerning early migrations to the New World.

1. It is to be assumed that circa 40,000–35,000 years ago, between the Hwang Ho and the Amur, the still-undiscovered local Neanderthal type finally developed into the physical type of modern man with proto-

Americanoid features. Simultaneously, this area saw the formation of a specific Upper Paleolithic culture — the Dyuktai culture.

2. Circa 35,000 years ago the proto-Americanoids crossed the Stanovoi Range to launch a gradual mastering of the middle Lena basin. In the Middle Paleolithic, earlier than 40,000–35,000 years ago, due to the low level of evolution of Neanderthal man's material culture and the rigorous climate of northeast Asia, the area north of the Stanovoi Range could not be populated. The mean January air temperature there was at least 25 or 30 degrees lower than that in the coldest Neanderthal-populated parts of Eurasia (Sher 1969; Grichuk 1969; Velichko and Gvozdover 1969; Giterman et al. 1968).

3. During the Kargi interglacial in Siberia, circa 35,000–25,000 years ago, the proto-Americanoids slowly mastered Yakutia and Chukotka. The Ust–Mil II and Ezhantsy sites, apparently, represent monuments of this stage. Due to adverse conditions for the mammoth fauna, the Okhotsk seacoast must have held little attraction for the proto-Americanoids. In the Pleistocene this seacoast can hardly have been one of the ways of man's northward migration.

4. Circa 25,000 years ago the land bridge between Asia and America, submerged by the Vorontsovo transgression, resurfaced. According to Paleontological data, at the same time, across the Beringia, north Asian fauna migrated to Alaska (Sher 1970). With it, for the first time, man came to Alaska. Along a free corridor, which still existed between the Laurentian and Cordillera glaciers circa 24,000 years ago, some proportion of the early Dyuktai people migrated south. Circa 23,000 years ago they reached Mexico — the moment marked by the Tlapacoya site.

5. Circa 24,000 years ago America was cut off from Alaska and northeast Asia by a solid glacial shield. The human groups which found themselves south of it evolved in isolation from their relatives who remained in Alaska, Chukotka, and Yakutia. Circa 12,000 years ago they developed different cultures, which, in essence, were local cultures of the Dyuktai region.

6. During the Sartan glaciation in Siberia, 24,000–10,500 years ago, Alaska was part of northeast Asia and part of the Dyuktai-area culture. Alaska's paleoarctic culture, whose early sites, so far, are 12,000 years old, is almost an exact replica of the Dyuktai culture, which is represented by the latest Pleistocene monuments in Yakutia.

7. Circa 10,500 years ago the Dyuktai culture in northeast Asia disappeared, to be replaced by the Sumnaghi culture, which is genetically related to the Malta–Afontova ethnocultural region. The last Dyuktai people must have gone over to Alaska, where they are represented by the Akmak assemblage at the Onion Portage site, 9,875 ± 155 years old. Between 10,500 and 10,000 years ago the land bridge between the New and Old Worlds finally ceased to exist. Alaska again became part of

America. Some proportion of the Alaska Dyuktai people must have moved south across Canada and some proportion of the descendants of Old Llano hunters must have moved north.

8. Archaeological materials collected in northeast Asia so far furnish evidence for only one Upper Pleistocene migration from the Old to the New World. It was part of the northeastern diffusion of the Dyuktai Upper Paleolithic culture 35,000–10,500 years ago.

9. The Holocene appears to have registered two more migrations from northeast Asia to America. The first may have been connected with the diffusion of the Sumnaghi culture from the middle Lena basin northeast, 10,500–6,000 years old (Mochanov 1969b), the second with the Belkachi culture, 4,850–3,750 years old (Mochanov 1967). The last two Holocene migrations remain to be studied.

REFERENCES

ANDERSON, D. D.
  1970 Akmak. An early archeological assemblage from Onion Portage, northwest Alaska. *Acta Arctica* 16.
BRYAN, A. L.
  1969 Early man in America and the late Pleistocene chronology of western Canada and Alaska. *Current Anthropology* 10(1):1–12.
CHARD, C. S.
  1963 The Old World roots: review and speculations. *Anthropological Papers of the University of Alaska* 10(2):115–121.
  1969 *Man in prehistory.* New York: McGraw-Hill.
CRABTREE, D.
  1969 A technological description of artifacts in assemblage Wilson Butte Cave, Idaho. *Current Anthropology* 10(1):1–11.
DIKOV, N. N.
  1969 Verkhnit paleolit Kamchatki [Upper Paleolithic of Kamchatka]. *Sovetskaja Arkheologija* 3:93–109.
GITERMAN, R. E., L. V. GOLUBEVA, *et al.*
  1968 *Osnovnye etapy razvitija rastitel'nosti Severnoi Azii y antropogene* [Basic stages in the development of vegetation in northern Asia in the anthropogene]. Moscow.
GRICHUK, V. P.
  1969 "Rastitel'nost' na Russkoi ravnine v epokhu must'e" [Vegetation on the Russian plain in the Mousterian period], in *Priroda i razvitie pervobytnogo obshchestva na territorii Evropeiskoi chasti SSSR*, 42–52, 58–66. Moscow.
HAYNES, C. V.
  1969 The earliest Americans. *Science* 166 (3,906): 709–715.
  1970 "Geochronology of man–mammoth sites and their bearing on the origin of the Llano complex," in *Pleistocene and recent environments of the central Great Plains.* Edited by W. Dort and Lawrence J. Jones, 77–92.
HESTER, J. J.
  1966 Origins of the Clovis culture. *Thirty-Sixth International Congress of Americanists* 1:129–142.

HOPKINS, D. M., *editor*
1967   *The Bering land bridge*. Stanford: Stanford University Press.
KIND, N. V.
1971   Izmenenie klimata i oledenenija v verkhnem antropogene (absoljutnaja khronologija) [Change in climate and glaciation in the anthropogene (absolute chronology)]. Unpublished doctoral dissertation. Moscow.
KRIEGER, A. D.
1964   "Early man in the New World," in *Prehistoric man in the New World*. Edited by J. D. Jennings and E. Norbeck, 23–81. Chicago: University of Chicago Press.
LARICHEVA, I. P.
1971   Paleolit Severnoi Ameriki i problema svjazi ego s drevnekamennym vekom Sibiri [Paleolithic of North America and its connection with the ancient Stone Age of Siberia]. Unpublished dissertation. Novosibirsk.
LOTHROP, S. K.
1961   Early migrations to Central and South America: an anthropological problem in the light of other science. *The Journal of the Royal Anthropological Institute of Great Britain and Ireland* 91(1):98–120.
MOCHANOV, JU. A.
1966   Paleolit Aldana [Paleolithic of the Aldan]. *Doklady i Soobshchenija Arkheologov SSSR na VII Mezhdunarodnom Kongresse Doistorikov i Protoistorikov*, 68–71. Moscow.
1967   Bel'kachinskaja neoliticheskaja kul'tura na Aldane [The Belkachi Neolithic culture on the Aldan]. *Sovetskaja Arkheologija* 4:164–177.
1969a   Djuktaiskaja verkhnepaleoliticheskaja kul'tura i nekotorye aspekty eë genezisa [The Dyuktai Upper Paleolithic culture and some aspect of its genesis]. *Sovetskaja Arkheologija* 4:235–239.
1969b   Drevneishie etapy zaselenija Severo-Vostochnoi Azii i Aljaski (k voprosu o pervonachal'nykh migratsijakh cheloveka v Ameriku) [Earliest stages in the habitation of northeast Asia and Alaska (on the question of man's earliest migrations to America)]. *Sovetskaja Etnografija* 1:79–86.
1970   Djuktaiskaja peshchera — novyi paleoliticheskii pamjanik Severo-Vostochnoi Azii" [The Dyuktai cave — a new Paleolithic monument of northeast Asia], in *Po sledam drevnikh kul'tur Jakutii*, 40–64. Yakutsk.
1972a   Issledovanie paleolita na Indigirke, Kolyme i Zapadnom poberezh'e Okhotskogo morja [Research on the Paleolithic on the Indigirka, the Kolyma, and the west shore of the Sea of Okhotsk]. *Arkheoligicheskie otkrytija 1971 goda*. Moscow.
1972b   Novye dannye o beringomorskom puti zaselenija Ameriki (stojanka Maiorych — pervyi verkhnepaleoliticheskii pamjatnik v doline Kolymy) [New data on the Bering Sea route of the settling of America (the Mayorych site — the first Upper Paleolithic monument in the Kolyma Valley]. *Sovetskaja Etnografija* 2.
MOCHANOV, JU. A., S. A. FEDOSEEVA
1968   Paleoliticheskaja stojanka Ikhine v Jakutii [The Paleolithic Ikhine site in Yakutia]. *Sovetskaja Arkheologija* 4:244–248.
MÜLLER-BECK, H.
1965   Non-projectile – point stone industries in America and the problem of their Eurasiatic origins (roots). *Abstracts Seventh Congress INQUA, USA*.

1966   Paleohunters in America: origins and diffusion. *Science* 152 (3,726):1,191–1,210.

SHER, A. V.
1969   Mlekopitajushchie i stratigrafija pleistotsena . . . [Mammals and stratigraphy of the Pleistocene . . .]
1970   "Pleistotsenovaja fauna mlekopitajushchikh ravninnykh poberezhii Vostochno-Sibirskogo morja i problema Beringiiskoi sushi" [Pleistocene fauna of mammals of the low-lying east Siberian sea coast and the problem of the Bering land bridge], in *Severnyi Ledovityi okean i ego poberezh'e v kainozoe*, 516–524. Leningrad.

SHILO, N. A., N. N. DIKOV, A. V. LOZHKIN
1967   "Pervye dannye o stratigrafii paleolita Kamchatki" [First data on the stratigraphy of the Paleolithic of Kamchatka], in *Istorija i kul'tura narodov Severa Dal'nego Vostoka*, 32–41. Moscow.

SHUTLER, R.
1965   Tule Springs expedition. *Current Anthropology* 6(1):110–111.

VELICHKO, A. A., M. D. GVOZDOVER
1969   "Rol' prirodnoi sredy v razvitii pervobytnogo obshchestva" [The role of natural surroundings in the development of primitive society], in *Priroda i razvitii . . .*, 227–237.

VERESHCHAGIN, N. K., JU. A. MOCHANOV
1972   Samye severnye v mire sledy verkhnego paleolita (Berelekhskoe mestonakhozhdenie v nizov'jakh r. Indigirki) [The world's northernmost traces of the Upper Paleolithic (the Berelekh location on the lower reaches of the Indigirka)]. *Sovetskaja Arkheologija* 3.

WENDORF, F.
1966   Early man in the New World: problems of migrations. *American Naturalist* 100 (912):253–270.

WEST, FREDERICK HADLEIGH
1967   The Donnelly Ridge site and the definition of an early core and blade complex in central Alaska. *American Antiquity* 32(3):360–382.

WILMSEN, E. N.
1964   Flake tools in the American Arctic: some speculations. *American Antiquity* 29(3):338–344.

WORMINGTON, H. M.
1962   A survey of early American prehistory. *American Scientist* 50:230–242.

Concerning the Cultural Contacts Between Asia and America in the Late Paleolithic

Z. A. ABRAMOVA

Among the many conflicting hypotheses pertaining to the question of migration to America, only one enjoys wide recognition: the migrants came from northern Asia, crossing the land bridge that then existed where the Bering Strait is now. Admitting that man reached the New World sufficiently long ago to have crossed the entire North American continent and to have populated South America toward the fourteenth to twelfth centuries B.C., many scholars seek the initial Lower Paleolithic cultures in central and southeast Asia and even in Europe. They are guided mostly by a technological similarity — by the manufacture of bifacial tools, which may have been the prototype of projectile points, a hallmark of the late American Paleolithic. But because man's emergence in America still defies exact timing, the problem of the origin, the cultural identification, and the cultural standards of the migrants is still more involved. There are two main schools of thought on this point. One is a theory of independent emergence and development of projectile points in what is now the Great Plains. The other is the view that the technique of bifacial processing of points was imported from Asia, and the tribes which settled on the Great Plains had only to invent a flute to make the point base thinner.

Some scholars, such as Chard (1959, 1963), assume that the first to reach America were the bearers of ancient Asian cultures whose technical tradition was related to the comparatively primitive southeast Asian culture of choppers and chopping. This tradition had a long history in America before the emergence of the independent cultural tradition of bifacial points which, far from being related to the Asian influences, on the contrary itself influenced Asian cultures in postglacial times. The scholars single out no Asian complexes as prototypes of the supposedly Middle Paleolithic complexes of America, or mention only the Ting-ts'un location on the Fenho River in northern China as a possible source of the stage that preceded the birth of projectile points, on the basis of a resemblance between the Ting-ts'un material and the complex discovered on the Lake Manix shores in California, which included choppers, chopping tools, and flakes.

Leaving aside the question of whether or not man can have advanced so far north possessing a primitive culture (no Middle Paleolithic sites have been discovered north of Ting-ts'un along the Asian coast, in Kamchatka, or in Chukotka), other archaeologists deny the independent American origin of bifacial points and relate them to Asian or Eurasian elements. This assumption stems from the presence of bifacial points in some Paleolithic complexes of southern Siberia, notably in the Ust–Kansk cave. Wormington puts forward the hypothesis (1961) that the blade technique of the Paleolithic in southern Siberia, as it advanced toward Lake Baikal, met and mixed with the Asian chopper tradition. From Baikal this mixed culture proceeded north toward the mouth of the Lena River, and then turned east toward the Bering Strait. This, Wormington assumes, may have taken place circa 20,000 years ago — early enough for the complex imported to America to provide a basis for the manufacture of bifacial points, which became widespread in the late Wisconsin.

Wilmsen (1964) holds similar views but maintains that the Kogruk and British Mountain complexes in Alaska are marked by the Levallois–Mousterian technique, which he identifies with the Malta–Buret culture on the Angara and the Lena Paleolithic. Wilmsen considers the Malta–Buret age (17,000 to 20,000 years ago) as concurrent with the existence of the land bridge between Asia and America in the interval of from 23,000 to 13,000 years ago.

Still more debatable conclusions have been drawn by Mochanov (1969a, 1969b), who, in an effort to find the source of American Paleolithic cultures, has advanced a hypothesis concerning a colossal belt stretching from Sary-Arka in Kazakhstan to Ting-ts'un in China solely because these two places have been found to be sites of bifacial tools. Mochanov's hypothesis, though at a glance convincing and logical, is to our mind lacking in factual support. We will proceed to consider it in detail. In the Central Asian Middle Paleolithic, Mochanov singles out two cultures, or, which is the same to him, two different techniques of stone-tool manufacture. One is a variation of the Levallois–Mousterian culture with an Acheulian tradition, based upon the Levallois splitting technique and extensive use of bifacial tools, which was widespread from northeast Kazakhstan to northeast China. The other is a Levallois–Mousterian culture which includes most of the ancient sites in Mongolia and is characterized by the absence of bifacial tools and a high level of subprismatic core flaking. Mochanov claims that on the basis of the group I culture, circa 40,000 to 35,000 years ago, Upper Paleolithic cultures developed which carried on the bifacial tool processing tradition.

The Middle Paleolithic group II cultures, according to Mochanov, formed a basis for Aurignacian-type Upper Paleolithic cultures, which are represented by the Malta–Sanny-Mys-type sites. This is true in part only. Indeed, the culture of the lower strata of Sanny Mys, in the Transbaikal region, reveals an influence of Middle Paleolithic Mongolian cultures (Levallois-type cores, blades flaked off such cores, wide-blade knives, and scrapers). But it still remains obscure what there is that is Aurignacian in it, and how Malta and Sanny Mys can be thrown together.

We shall discuss this point later. Now we will proceed to consider Mochanov's idea concerning the destiny of the group I culture whose descendants, as he claims, advanced most rapidly of all in a northeastern direction, toward Chukotka. A long time afterward, these descendants reached the Great Plains and, carrying on the tradition of bifacial tool processing, created original Paleo-Indian cultures of the Sandia–Clovis type.

Mochanov's hypothetical absolute dates reveal that the early Upper Paleolithic tribes, which appeared in the Transbaikal region circa 40,000 to 35,000 years ago, must have reached Alaska circa 35,000 to 30,000 years ago. The only signpost on this way marked by the bifacial processing technique — the Dyuktai cave on the River Aldan — can, even according to Mochanov himself, be timed as coincidental with the closing stage in the evolution of this culture. It can reveal only concurrent development, which, however, failed to lead to the invention of projectile points, but it cannot by any means reveal the "point of departure." The date of the middle stratum of the Dyuktai cave is $13,070 \pm 90$ years ago (LE–784: Mochanov 1969b); that is, it was broadly concurrent with the Clovis culture. They cannot have been one cultural tradition. Nor can the resemblance between individual details be attributed to a common origin from one cultural substratum, for this resemblance is confined to the presence of the bifacial processing technique, which is obviously too little, just as is the fact that this technique cannot be considered an evolution from the Acheulian-type chopping tools.

One important circumstance is left out of account: the migration of the tribes was not a nonstop quick march but an extremely long process. The cultures must have sustained signal changes on their way, as man mastered new geographic zones and adapted himself to new environments. The intermediate landmarks, which will possibly be discovered on the continents, may, more probably, have existed on coastal terraces and the present shelf after the rise in sea level and are irrecoverably lost under the waves of the Bering Strait.

MacNeish (1964) has chosen a different logic, attempting a scrupulous comparison of the typical features of the most ancient complexes in

Alaska and northern Asia. From different signs of resemblance in the flint inventory, he has inferred that the Malta–Buret culture participated in the building of the British Mountain complex. MacNeish was distinctly aware of the difficulties which confronted him, consisting in the scarcity of sources and published material. The present author faces the same difficulties when she undertakes to make judgements about the American Paleolithic. The main danger here is taking subsidiary, insignificant elements as characteristic. MacNeish's error, which is not his fault, is misrepresentation of northern Asian complexes.

To begin with, the Malta–Buret complex bears no signs of the Levallois–Mousterian technique. The main and decisive feature of this complex is not crude pebble choppers (they are few and far between) and not unifacial tools made from flakes removed from discoidal Mousterian-like cores (the discoidal cores are few and differ from Mousterian, and the tools made from big wide flakes are extremely few—they are mostly scrapers) but the many blades flaked off middle-sized prismatic cores. The blades are on the average about 5 cm. long and 1 to 1.5 cm. wide. Many of these blades are retouched along one or both longitudinal edges or have processed ends, sharp or straight. From such blades man manufactured points, gravers, burins, and end scrapers. The gravers are particularly well represented. The burins are of different types: median, angular, lateral, and multifaceted; but there are few of them. Along with the end scrapers made from blades there are scrapers made from flakes: big, rounded, and long, or small and rounded, many of them also sharply retouched. Many of the cores of small flint pebbles, mostly prismatic, are worked off to the limit and retain traces of the chipping of short but wide blade flakes. There are no wedge-shaped cores or corresponding microblades, though the beginnings of this technique are distinctly traceable. There are no inserted microblade tools either. This complex also includes a sophisticated collection of bone and horn tools, decorations, and works of art, which puts it in a unique position in the Siberian Paleolithic and which once enabled researchers to speak of the European origin of this culture. The author shares the view of Gerasimov, who denied the presence of European roots in Malta, which he explored.

As far as the author can judge the British Mountain complex, it differs substantially from that of Malta, above all in tool fashioning: the Malta inventory shows the underlying blade technique, while the British Mountain inventory is based upon the flake technique.

It is also difficult to find analogies to the Flint Creek complex, which came in the wake of that of British Mountain and which MacNeish (1964) classes with the Cordilleran tradition. The basic features of the Afontova Gora complex are other than MacNeish thinks they are. Here there are really many Mousterian-like tools made from large flakes, which, however, did not originate from the previous complex, in which they were almost absent. Above all, there are scrapers, generally oval in shape, sometimes bifacial, with one side convex and the other flattened by many chippings and retouched flakes. Along with these, there is an equal number of scrapers made from flakes, including tiny ones. There are many *pièces esquillées* made from flakes, mostly small, with one working edge slightly concave. Compared with this major series, piercing tools are very few here. They are made from flakes with small symmetrical spears. The sharp and usual points are extremely few and inexpressive. The cores are small and, more often than not, amorphous. There are cores with traces of regularly shaped microblade removal, including wedge-shaped flaking. But the Afontova culture includes no real blades or burins of the type that MacNeish writes about. They are well represented in the Kokorevo (site Kokorevo I) culture singled out in the excavations of recent years on the Yenisei.

The Kokorevo culture cores are mostly large and prismatic, many of them bipolar, made from massive riverside pebbles, with traces of blade flake chipping. Along with these there are typical wedge-shaped cores. Most of the tools are manufactured from large blades. The sharp points form a series which is for the first time well represented in the Yenisei Paleolithic. They are thoroughly retouched along the longitudinal edges and at the ends, and some of them have flaking on the split plane to flatten the impact end. The burins, median and lateral, made from large blades, also represent a new series not only in the Yenisei Paleolithic but all over Siberia. In addition to the blade tools a great number of scrapers have been found there, many of massive flakes and all of them unifacial. The scrapers are manufactured either from quite massive large blades with oval working edges, many of them long, or from middle-sized rounded flakes. The inserted-microblade technique is widely represented. Like the Afontova culture, the Kokorevo culture includes a large number of bone and horn tools as well as decorations. If we were to examine Paleolithic collections rather than old publications we would be able to state with assurance that neither in the Afontova Gora complex nor in any other Paleolithic location on the Yenisei are there any leaf-shaped bifacial points.

The most typical feature of the Paleolithic in the Altai, on the Yenisei, and on the concurrent sites on the Angara and in the Transbaikal region are wedge-shaped cores, thin narrow microblades flaked off such cores, and inserted microblade tools related to this technique, which gained ground particularly at the end of the Paleolithic — precisely the epoch that reveals clearcut contacts between northern Asia and Alaska, where the North Western Microblade industry was developing. It is exactly the Donnelly Akmak complex that brings out with particular clarity interrelations with the Paleolithic of Kamchatka, Hokkaido, and the area stretching as far west as the Angara (West 1967; Anderson 1970).

Biconvex bifacial knives were discovered at Verkholenskaya Gora and the Dyuktai cave. End scrapers, wide blades and blade flakes, wedge-shaped cores, and microblades become widespread everywhere at this time.

If we recognize man's migration to America at a much earlier date than that of the emergence of projectile points — which, the author feels, we have every reason to do — there is no need to seek prototypes of points either on adjacent Asian territory or in the Gravettian or Solutrean cultures of Europe. Incidentally, the comparatively remote resemblance of the Sandia-type point to some Solutrean points has made it possible to advance the assumption, otherwise unconfirmed, that the Sandia-type points were directly related to Solutrean artifacts. The view that projectile-point traditions may have emerged across the southern borders of the fused glacial massifs, the author believes, merits preferential consideration (Bryan 1969). There is no reason to think that the Great Plains hunters were less culturally developed than the Solutreans. There is no reason to believe that they could not have invented and improved the fine bifacial processing technique.

Some points of resemblance between individual elements of the inventory of a number of northern Asian and North American complexes, which may have been broadly concurrent (for instance, Kokorevo I on the Yenisei and Bull Brook in Massachusetts), cannot be attributed to anything except convergence. Undoubtedly, man migrated from Asia to America on many occasions; but incontrovertible evidence of the northern Asian origin of the Donnelly complex — proof that Alaska and Siberia then had one common culture tradition — has been found only for the close of the late Paleolithic.

REFERENCES

ANDERSON, DOUGLAS S.
    1970   Akmak. An early archeological assemblage from Onion Portage, northwest Alaska. *Acta Arctica* 16. Copenhagen.
BRYAN, ALAN L.
    1969   Early man in America and the late Pleistocene chronology of western Canada and Alaska. *Current Anthropology.* 10(1):1–12.
CHARD, CHESTER S.
    1959   New World origins: a reappraisal. *Antiquity* 33(129):44–49.
    1963   The Old World roots: review and speculations. *Anthropological Papers of the University of Alaska* 10(2):115–121.
MacNEISH, RICHARD S.
    1964   Investigations in southwest Yukon. *Papers of the Robert S. Peabody Foundation for Archaeology* 6: 1. Andover, Massachusetts.
MOCHANOV, JU. A.
    1969a   Drevneiishie etapy zaselenija Severo-Vostochnoi Azii i Aljaski (k voprosu o pervonachal'nykh migratsijakh cheloveka v Ameriku)

[The oldest stages of the settling of northeast Asia and Alaska (on the question of man's earliest migrations to America)]. *Sovetskaja Etnografija* 1:79–86. Moscow.

1969b Djuktaiskaja, verkhnepaleoliticheiskaja kul'tura i nekotorye aspekty eë genezisa [The Dyuktai Upper Paleolithic culture and some aspects of its genesis]. *Sovetskaja Arkheologija* 4:235–239.

WEST, FREDERICK HADLEIGH
1967   The Donnelly Ridge site and the definition of an early core and blade complex in central Alaska. *American Antiquity* 32(3):360–382.

WILMSEN, E.
1964   Flake tools in the American Arctic: some speculations. *American Antiquity* 29(3):338–344.

WORMINGTON, H. M.
1961   "Prehistoric cultural stages of Alberta, Canada," in *Homenaje a Pablo Martinez del Rio, 25 Anniversario de la edicion de Los Origines Americanos*, 163–171. Mexico.

Fluted Points at the Batza Téna Obsidian Source, Northwestern Interior Alaska

DONALD W. CLARK and A. McFADYEN CLARK

INTRODUCTION: LOCALITY AND SITES

Among implements recovered from the vicinity of a natural source of obsidian on the Koyukuk River, northwestern interior Alaska, shown in Map 1, is a series of more than sixteen fluted points. The obsidian source, which we have named Batza Téna after a local Athabaskan place-name meaning "Obsidian Trail," was examined by the United States Geological survey in 1967 (Patton and Miller 1970) and by us in 1969, 1970, and 1971, following the lead of information provided by local Koyukon Athabaskan residents and by Patton (personal communications). Fieldwork and analysis have been supported by the National Museum of Man. Our initial archaeologic reconnaissance (Clark 1972a) was undertaken with considerable anticipation, inasmuch as no source for high-quality obsidian had previously been reported for northern Alaska, although obsidian implements had been found at many coastal and interior sites. Aside from native tradition, there was no advance indication of the archaeologic potential of Batza Téna. Fluted points were found during all three field seasons. The present paper is a preliminary report and discusses these Batza Téna finds before preparation of a complete report.

Patton and Miller (1970) describe the primary obsidian source, located between Indian and Little Indian rivers south-east of the village of Hughes, as consisting of mid-Tertiary pearlitic ash beds in which the obsidian occurs as "Apache tears" or small bombs. The ash beds have disintegrated wherever they are exposed. Obsidian pebbles are also distributed secondarily in colluvial and alluvial deposits and archaeological sites of the area. The larger utilized pebbles seldom exceed ten centimeters in their maximum dimension.

The sites that have yielded fluted points can be described in a summary

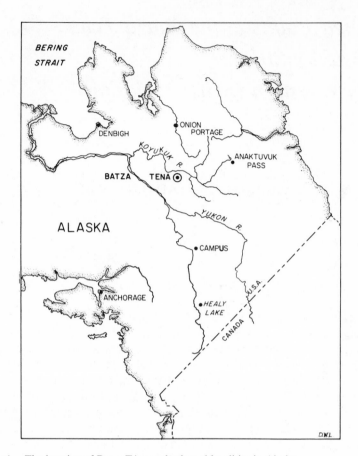

Map 1.   The location of Batza Téna and selected localities in Alaska

fashion. The following remarks also apply to most other sites and flaking stations at Batza Téna. A brief description of each site with specific references to fluted-point provenience is provided in the Appendix. Considerable reliance was placed on surface collecting or on locating surface manifestations for each site. This procedure was more practical at the time of the surveys than it might have been at other times because a considerable part of the region examined had been burned over in 1968.

Most of the fluted-point sites are clustered near the top of a short ridge, elevation 300 to 500 feet, that forms part of the topographic transition between the Koyukuk River flats, with an elevation of about 250 feet, and the upland source area of 800–1,000 feet elevation, located on the southwest flank of yet higher hills of the Kokrines–Hodzana Highlands. One fluted point was found at RkIg–1 on an adjacent ridge, and two additional sites (RlIg–46, RlIg–47) occur on flanking benches farther up

Indian River, where the valley-bottom flats are terminated by constricting hills. The close clustering of fluted-point sites, exclusive of the exceptions noted, is particularly in contrast to the wider distribution of other sites at Batza Téna. This cluster can be regarded as a single area of encampments and flaking stations with semidiscrete topographic segments. These sites offer visual control of the surrounding terrain, although this would be obscured during times of dense forest cover; they also lie along possible access routes to the obsidian source.

At the present time the vegetation consists of a sparse-to-moderate growth of small and scrub trees, primarily aspen, birch, and spruce, as well as smaller plants or bush and the ground cover, in which sphagnum moss and lichens are prominent. Most sites also exhibit some denuded or otherwise partially exposed ground.

The soil is sparse and contains considerable stone derived from local bedrock. Although the area was not covered by late Pleistocene, Wisconsin-stage glaciers (cf. Hamilton 1969: maps), a factor which is acutely pertinent to our discussion, the Batza Téna sites have been subjected to slopewash, solifluction, frost riving, stirring, and sorting. There are no loess deposits. Flakes are often concentrated in the depressed margins between frost hummocks or small polygons in a light-colored clayey matrix, but there are also many striking examples of apparently undisturbed surficial flake concentrations. No hearths or structural features were recognized at the fluted-point sites, all of which are unstratified surface stations.

A site usually consists of several flake clusters located on or close to the surface plus a thinner scatter, either continuous or discontinuous, of flakes not necessarily associated with any cluster. These flake clusters vary in size from approximately two to twelve feet in diameter but, as has been noted, in some cases they may have been disturbed or secondarily concentrated by natural agencies.

FLUTED POINTS, TECHNOLOGY, AND ASSOCIATED ARTIFACTS

Two complete, although damaged, points, many snapped bases, a midsection, and some minor fragments were recovered. Specific information for each specimen is provided in Table 1, and a number of specimens are illustrated in Figure 1 and Plate 1. All fluted points are made of obsidian with the exception of one possibly fluted basalt fragment (RkIg–30: 247) not listed in Table 1. Other projectile types made of both basalt and obsidian, less often of chert, were recovered from some of the fluted-point sites. The complete points are only 29.7 and 53 mm. long, but other fragmentary specimens in the fluted series appear to have been

Table 1.   Batza Téna fluted points

Object[a]	Illustration	Site and number	Base	Ground edge	Ground base	Width (mm.)	Thickness (mm.)	Fluting, flute length (mm.[b])
1. Base	Fig. 1(f)	RkIg-1:49	concave	+	+	25	5.1–6.5	Triple each face, battered condition: 21+–21–25(+?) irregular/18+–32 (+?) –ca. 27.5.
2. Base	Fig. 1(i)	RkIg-10:36	concave	+	+	28	4.4–5.5	Triple each face: 21–28+–12+/9+–24–31 (+?).
3. Base	Fig. 1(g)	RkIg-28:9	concave	–[c]	–[c]	26.3	3.6–4.2	Fluting not seen on short 8 mm. fragment; basal retouch may obscure.
4. Base	Fig. 1(c)	RkIg-29:16	concave	+	+	26.3	3.7–5.9	Triple one face, single other face: 21+–15–16/ca. 19 irregular.
5. Base	Fig. 1(a)	RkIg-30:42	concave	–[c]	–[c]	24.7	3.8–4.8	Two probable each face: 15 irregular-trace/5–15+ irregular. Lopsided appearance, damage.
6. Base (unfinished)	Pl. 1(g)	RkIg-30:220	slightly concave	–	–	23.8	3.5–5.8	Triple each face: 31.4+–30.7+–28/20.5–27.5+ (obscured)–27.4+. Described in text.
7. Base corner	Pl. 1(c)	RkIg-30:254	concave	+	+	NR[d]	4.1–4.9	Double or triple one face only, fragmentation prevents some observations.
8. Base (unfinished)	Pl. 1(b)	RkIg-30:321	concave	–	–	28	3.8–5.0	Triple one face, all 9+–22+; several thinning flakes other face. Described in text.
9. Base (unfinished)	Fig. 1(e)	RkIg-31:15	concave	–[c]	–[c]	22–27	4.6–5.6	Triple one face only, plano-convex cross-section: 21+–17–25+. Described in text.
10. Complete point	Fig. 1(h)	RkIg-31:60	concave	+	+	20.3–23.5	3.5–5.0	Triple, slightly on one face, damaged: 9–21.7 irregular–14/19–18–27; 53 mm. long.

Table 1. (*continued*)

Object[a]	Illustration	Site and number	Base	Ground edge	Ground base	Width (mm.[b])	Thickness (mm.)	Fluting, flute length (mm.[b])
11. Near base (unfinished)	Pl. 1(h)	RkIg–31:119	NR[d]	–	–	27.2	4.0–4.6	Double each face: all 23+. Sides appear unfinished.
12. Base	Pl. 1(f)	RkIg–31:120	concave	+	+	20.6–24.5	3.2–4.3	Triple partly obscured one face, double other but third possibly obscured by overlaying flute. All truncated 17.7+–21.5+.
13. Base	Fig. 1(b)	RkIg–43:1	concave	+	+	23.7	4.2	Double each face, antecedent thinning obscured?: all truncated at 8 mm.
14. Base (unfinished)	Fig. 1(d)	RkIg–44:38	slightly convex	–[c]	–	24.8	5.1	Fluting may have been attempted. Described in text.
15. Near base	Pl. 1(a)	RkIg–44:81	NR[d]	+	NR[d]	24.7	4.4–4.9	Triple one face, double other: 18 partly obscured–17 irregular –20.5+/12+–23.5. Battered condition accounts for NR entries.
16. Base	Pl. 1(i)	RIIg–46:62	slightly concave?	+	+	20–22.2	4.4–6.5	Single wide 18+ off-center with traces 2nd and 3rd each face. Base edge damaged.
17. Complete point	Pl. 1(e)	RIIg–47:13	concave V	+	+	20.0	4.0–4.4	Triple one face only: 18.8 main flute. Point length 29.7.
18. Midsection	Pl. 1(j)	RIIg–47:4	NR[d]	+	NR[d]	28.3	5.1–5.9	Triple one face, off-center double other, all truncated basally and one both basally and terminally between 13 and 30 mm.

[a] All specimens are obsidian. One tip-fragment exception is noted in the text.
[b] A "+" indicates truncation at broken edge with full length being a value in excess of that indicated.
[c] Not obviously ground but lightly crushed.
[d] Not recordable.

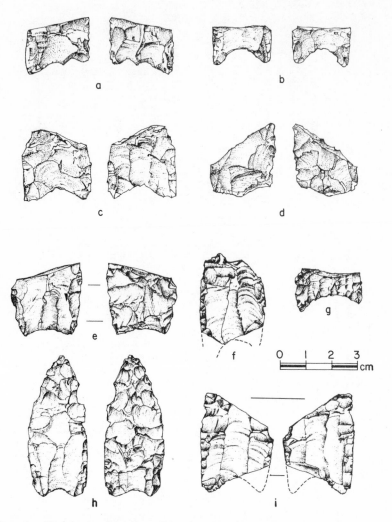

Figure 1.   Fluted points from Batza Téna sites. Identification by letter in Table 1

larger, judging from their greater width and thickness. The widths range from 20 to 28.3 mm. and appear to be, at their maximum, either close to or as much as one-third the distance above the base. The profile above the base ranges from parallel to slightly convex and convergent, as exemplified by the complete specimens. Where considerable convergence is noted, a range of values is recorded in Table 1. Thickness is generally in the order of 4 to 5 mm. The measurements given in Table 1 for thickness are taken approximately 6 mm. above the inside of the basal concavity and at the point of maximum thickness, when different, exclusive of aberrant thick spots. The latter observation may be depressed by the fragmentary condition of the specimens.

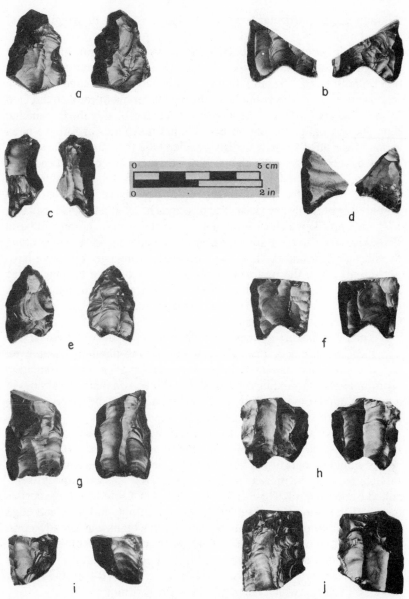

Plate 1. Fluted points from Batza Téna sites, obverse and reverse. Ink opaqued. Identification by letter in Table 1 except (d), an unfluted, flat face fragment (RKIg–30:323)

Fluting usually consists of three shallow vertical thinning flutes on each face, but in some cases only one or two thinning flakes are apparent. The smaller complete specimen is fluted on one side only. Although a flute is often a distinctive narrow channel bounded by parallel adjacent flutes, sometimes it may be obscured or largely removed by a subsequent thinning flake, particularly when the latter is wide or irregular and splayed.

Almost invariably, the medial flute follows the lateral flutes in the flaking sequence, although specimen RkIg–30: 220 presents an exception on both faces. The lateral flutes may be close to the edges and have sometimes been partially removed through subsequent retouch directed from the edges and base. The lateral flutes and probably the first medial flute (occasionally also the obverse medial flute) appear to have been formed from an essentially straight beveled base that has become slightly concave by the stage at which both were thinned. The concave base and ears were then formed through further retouch. The final medial flake on one face was probably not detached until the basal notch had been prepared or partially prepared. The base may have either a U-shaped or a V-shaped profile which varies in depth. No clear-cut dichotomy of basal shapes was seen in the Batza Téna points. Finally, the lower edges along the sides and around the base were blunted through grinding. We have not remarked on the preforming and lateral retouch or shaping of the Batza Téna points inasmuch as these steps are at present inadequately understood. Some shaping and retouch from the edges precedes fluting while further retouch succeeds it.

It is possible that in some cases the blank was a flat flake, the dorsal side of which was thinned, through removal of long parallel flakes, even before elementary shaping of the point was undertaken. This speculation is prompted by our finding of many flakes thinned on their dorsal sides in a manner approximating fluting. In no case, however, did we recover the next step in this conjectured process.

Under opportune circumstances, a thin preform may be shaped into an unfluted piece having the profile of a fluted point. In a broad sense, such points would be part of the fluted-point series if they were made by the same hunters, as the present association suggests. This variation is exemplified by specimen RKIg–30: 323 (not listed in Table 1), a large corner fragment that shows basal notching, ear formation, and base and edge grinding, but is not fluted, probably because the blank was already a thin (4 mm.), flat, smooth-faced flake. There is, in addition to RkIg–30, a very roughly formed and presumably unfinished concave-based point, produced through retouching a relatively planar flake (RkIg–30:178, not listed in Table 1), which measures 38 × 26 × 5 mm.

The base was beveled, probably twice, to form a platform for detaching the thinning flakes. The steps of manufacture are shown in several unfinished specimens. In the case of RkIg–44:38, three or more flakes up to 13 mm. long were struck from the leading edge of a narrow bevel. This, however, did not result in successful fluting. Previous to the beveling, possible flutes or large, broad, thinning flakes had been removed from the obverse side, although this observation is equivocal because of irregularities in this specimen. RkIg–31:15, triply fluted on one face, has a bifacial bevel, but the principal bevel appears to have been formed to serve as a platform for the projected but unconsummated fluting of the face opposite. In its preparation the proximal or bulbar areas of the existing flutes were removed. RkIg–30:220 has been fluted on both sides, but basal preparation has not been carried beyond that stage. Thus, as is seen in RkIg–31:15 noted above, there is a bevel on one face that removes the base of antecedent flutes on the same face, while two subsequent flutes on the obverse face, detached from this bevel as a platform, still have their negative bulbar areas intact. These present conspicuous indentations in the beveled platform. Finally, the basal notch and ears have been formed in RkIg–30:321, which is fluted or thinned on both faces, but the edges along the sides are only roughly flaked and the lower edges have not been ground. This piece might, however, have been functional in its unfinished condition, although this observation is inconclusive because of the fragmentary state of the point base.

Batza Téna comprises a much broader spectrum of culture history than is represented by the material dealt with in the present paper (Clark 1972a; 1972b; Clark and Clark 1972). In addition to the fluted points there are triangular, leaf-shaped, oblanceolate, and lanceolate points, which have a largely unassessed antiquity. Varied microblade and core industries have been found at three sites. Also, a reasonably close approximation of the Tuktu phase (Campbell 1961), but with few microblades, was recovered from a living area. This and other material from Batza Téna may relate to the northern Archaic tradition as defined at Onion Portage (Anderson 1968). Ipiutak-related assemblages were recovered from a group of house pits located south of Batza Téna. Ancestors of the Koyukon Athabaskans are not represented with certainty except through protohistoric houses. A living area characterized by bladelike flakes and other large flakes lightly retouched into points and knives, or more extensively shaped into large end scrapers, is, however, a possible candidate for prehistoric Athabaskan occupation.

Insofar as defining a fluted-point hunter assemblage for Batza Téna is concerned, it is fortunate that most of these cultural expressions do not occur at sites which have yielded fluted points. Nevertheless there is at least one unlikely association — that of fluted points and side-notched points found at three sites. Physical associations on these and other surficial sites are of uncertain validity because the site area may have been used for flaking stations and camps over a period of many millennia. The interference produced by excessive flake accumulations and a preponderance of ubiquitous broken semifinished or roughed-out bifaces, along with amorphous fragments of worked obsidian, hinder our recognition of discrete cultural assemblages. We do appear to be dealing with more than broken and scattered points left by a few hunters who wandered through. This is attested to by the clustering of fluted-point sites and by the presence of both finished and unfinished points on each of two adjacent sites, RkIg–30 and RkIg–31. Possibly groups of hunters stopped to repair their weapons and prepare new obsidian implements after first securing a supply of obsidian cobbles from the source or nearby stream gravels.

The collections from these sites then are our best candidates for assemblages left by the fluted-point hunters. RkIg–31 is suspected of representing more than one component because two side-notched points were found there. Other artifacts, in addition to the four fluted points, consist principally of undistinguished fragments of worked obsidian and biface preforms and a few small biface or point fragments. At the present time this collection can conveniently be excluded from consideration in favor of the somewhat similar but much larger collection from RkIg–30. The latter collection, which as of October 1972 has not been analyzed, consists principally of numerous small and medium-sized bifaces, usually only fragments, ovoid and leaf-shaped in format, often rough or unfinished in appearance. There is also much additional rudimentarily worked material, predominantly obsidian but occasionally basalt. There is one leaf-shaped point, a large basalt lanceolate point, and fragments of at least eight more leaf-shaped or lanceolate points including one square-based fragment. These are in addition to the four fluted-point bases previously noted and six fragments possibly from fluted points. The last include a tip fragment attached to part of a hinged-in flute, four basal ears or corners, and an incomplete basalt tip (RkIg–30:247, measuring 42–plus by 27 by 5.8 mm.) that shows the flutelike terminal traces of three thinning flakes. End scrapers are conspicuously scarce, there being but one good and three questionable specimens. A few retouched flakes or sidescrapers were recovered. No true blade industry is present, although bladelike flakes are not uncommon. If RkIg–30 constitutes a single component, we are confronted with a case in which fluted points are associated with leaf-shaped and probable lanceolate points.

DATING, COMPARISONS, AND DISCUSSION

Fluted points generally similar to those from Batza Téna have been recovered at several other localities in Alaska, located predominantly north of the Yukon River. A list provided earlier (Clark 1972a) need not be repeated here, except that we may note also a possible fluted tip from the northern perimeter of Batza Téna, reported by Reger (1972), and small, apparently fluted, obsidian and basalt bases from one of the tributaries of the south fork of the Koyukuk River (Holmes 1972 and personal communication). Certainly the fragmentary condition of the points described here leaves us open to the inclusion of some relatively recent basally thinned lanceolate points, which are known to occur also in Alaska, but we believe that we have circumscribed a discrete historical type. It thus appears that there is a north Alaskan focal area for the distribution of fluted points. Presently these are considered as a monolithic group, although regionally and temporally differentiated varieties may become recognized. On the Batza Téna points, for instance, the medial flute is usually less prominent than it is on other Alaskan fluted points.

None of the Alaskan fluted points are unequivocally dated. Association of the first discoveries with material of the Denbigh flint complex (Arctic Small-Tool tradition; cf. Hall 1969) appears to be misleading and is probably not indicative of the age of these points. No Arctic Small-Tool-tradition material was recovered at Batza Téna but obsidian, probably from Batza Téna, was used by Denbigh flint-complex people. At Healy Lake near the Tanana River a thinned base — possibly fluted, but this cannot be ascertained with certainty — and a relatively thick, basally thinned lanceolate point were recovered from levels dated by radiocarbon at approximately 9,000 and 10,500 or 11,000 years ago (Cook *et al.* 1970:25, 115; J. P. Cook and R. McKennan, various mimeographed reports and personal communications). Healy Lake indicates that points having the general profile of Batza Téna points were being made in Alaska as early as 10,500 years ago. The fluted obsidian specimens could be in the same age range, or they could differ by several centuries in either direction. We are disinclined to accept the younger possible dating, inasmuch as no fluted points have been found in the few Alaskan sites exclusive of Healy Lake that have been dated by radiocarbon to the 9,000–11,000 year range. Obsidian hydration dating is being applied to Batza Téna by Leslie Davis of Montana State University, but at the present we are not in a position to offer any definitive results from this program.

We have assumed that the Alaskan fluted points are related to fluted points found elsewhere in North America. Considering that the outstanding significance of the former lies in this relationship, the assumption stated should be critically examined. Basally thinned, concave-based lanceolate points do not in themselves consist of a sufficiently definitive set of attributes to indicate membership in a Paleo-Indian point group, but when one adds to these the specific technology of beveling and fluting, the preparation of the basal concavity and ears, and edge grinding, as well as an age estimated in excess of 10,000 years, we then consider that there is a reasonable basis for postulating a close relationship between the Batza Téna points and other North American fluted points of the Paleo-Indian period.

Any further remarks are of necessity vague because of the preliminary state of our comparative research. The weak expression of fluting, perhaps more appropriately called basal thinning, in some of the Batza Téna and other Alaskan fluted points is analogous to the basally thinned Plainview points or Plainview–Clovis intergrades (cf. Irwin 1971; Leonhardy 1966). As long as the Batza Téna points are considered as a single group, however, they should be defined, and relationships sought, on the basis of the more distinctive attributes. Furthermore, the parallel with the Clovis–Plainview intergrade may be due more to technological and functional factors than to historic relationships. The fluting sequence for the Batza Téna points is in most cases the same as that reported for Enterline points: triple fluting with the medial flute last (Witthoft 1952, 1962). Many points from the eastern United States and Canada showing this fluting sequence have been called Enterline points, but we would hesitate to use this designation for the Alaskan points on the basis of the fluting sequence alone.

Among the Clovis points there is a different fluting sequence, in which the medial flute was detached first and the small laterals last, although the lateral-first–medial-last sequence sometimes also is found on Clovis points (Witthoft 1962). An earlier statement in which one of us failed to point out this difference between Clovis and Enterline stands amended (Clark 1972a:6). We would not be surprised to find that the fluting sequence is an attribute of historic significance, of value in determining the relationships of various fluted-point styles in North America.

This leads to the question of the origin of fluted points and their significance in the wider context of early-man studies.

To state an opinion about the origin of fluted points, we will first outline what is known at present and then offer one possible explanation.

1. Fluted points have a wide distribution in the Americas but are unknown to date in Asia.

2. Within the distribution there is little known time slope and no established place of origin.

3. There is increasing evidence for nonstone-projectile-point cultures earlier than Clovis and related types and also evidence for contemporary complexes widespread in North and South America that have nonfluted points. By 11,000 years ago there was considerable diversity of stone industries in the New World.

4. If we disregard the single fluted point in the Denbigh flint complex, no direct dating is available for the Alaskan points; there is, however, reason to expect the Alaskan fluted points to be of an age equal to, if not greater than, those to the south.

5. The timing and nature of events in the ice corridor between Alberta, the District of Mackenzie, and the Yukon Territory may be of paramount importance. However, the history of the corridor is poorly known and the events there, as currently understood, do not present any specifically

definable and datable limitations to hypotheses one might construct (Hughes 1970; Reeves 1971).

6. Alaskan artifacts associated with fluted points show some crossties with their more southerly counterparts, but some implement types, particularly spurs and spurred end scrapers (Irwin and Wormington 1970), which are common in early southern complexes, are lacking in Alaska except in later contexts, among them probable Denbigh flint-complex sites.

7. The principal theoretical choices for origin are (a) a combination of local and independent origins; (b) a development on the High Plains or elsewhere in the main area of distribution, with diffusion or transmission by migration to other areas (this position is taken by a substantial number of archaeologists); and (c) development or origin in Alaska with diffusion or transmission by migration to all other areas (cf. Haynes 1964, 1966; Humphrey 1966, 1970). It is unlikely that the North American points have separate origins, but this might be the case for those of South America.

Most of the hypotheses require a time slope, but we would hesitate to say whether it is one of several centuries or several millennia. If the dated Healy Lake points are considered to be contemporaneous with Alaskan fluted points, the time slope between that area and the older Plains area would be between 200 years and 1,000 years, but the Alaskan fluted points may be older than the Healy Lake lanceolates; this could reverse the time slope. From the Plains to the Debert site (MacDonald 1968) the time slope is also in the order of 300 to 1,000 years, but we cannot be certain that some fluted-point complexes in eastern North America are not considerably older than either Debert or Clovis.

Several migration models have been presented (cf. Haynes 1966), but here we would like to look at the trial fit of a functional model developed for small hunting bands, in which we assume that the group as a whole is not migrating but is expanding or shifting its territory of exploitation. It is based on generational linkage and assumes that younger hunters might move out at the rate of fifty miles per each generation of twenty-five years. At this pace the net rate of migration would be two miles per year, or 500 years per 1,000 miles. To account for the North American distribution of fluted points, a time slope of approximately 700 years would then be required for dispersal from a locality on the southern High Plains throughout the northern United States; dispersal to the east coast and northeast would require up to 1,100 years and to Debert, Nova Scotia, even more. It would take about 1,700 years, or 2,000 years allowing for a slightly circuitous route, to reach the southern High Plains from northwestern Alaska.

Perhaps the fluted points did not spread to Siberia because Alaska was the end of the line and the land bridge may have all but disappeared, or because new arrivals into eastern Siberia, possibly with a more sophisticated technology, were not receptive to fluted points. If fluted points developed in Alaska, they would have been present there at a time when the land bridge might have offered a better connection with Asia, unless they developed and passed through most of their Alaskan temporal span at the time between 14,000 and 13,000 years ago when the bridge may have been closed (Hopkins 1967:464). It is of interest to note that the value derived through adding the postulated time slope from Alaska to the age of Clovis points is 13,000 to 13,500 years. A partial explanation of the negative Siberian distribution may also lie in the fact that diffusion or migration is not likely to proceed evenly in all directions.

The present situation would appear to present an impasse that could be broken through the provision of a very small amount of new information. One hypothesis requires a shift from the classic Clovis fluting sequence to the Enterline technique, and diffusion or migration to Alaska. En route to Alaska, spurred end scrapers and spurred gravers were dropped from the tool kit. As a variation of this hypothesis, to break the time-slope impasse, it could be suggested that the Enterline fluting sequence is representative of the most generalized and widespread of fluted points and that the classic Clovis type is a more specialized later derivative. Enterline-related fluting would have developed 12,000 years ago or probably earlier and diffused northward to Alaska by 11,000 years ago. In Alaska these points underwent relatively little stylistic variation, while there was a proliferation of fluted-point types farther south.

The alternative hypothesis is that triple-fluted points were developed in Alaska. They, and possibly also burins and blades, were carried southward by a spreading or shifting population through a newly opened corridor between 13,000 and 12,000 years ago. South of the corridor various other styles of fluted points were developed, and certain additional implements were also added. In contrast, in Alaska these points were not elaborated into various styles, and they ceased to be made before such elaboration would be likely to have taken place and before they had the opportunity for diffusion into Asia.

Presumably the questions posed above could be answered on the basis of relative age — the younger originated from the older. Prehistorians have waited more than twenty years for an acceptable date on Alaskan fluted points, but there is no guarantee that such dating, when it is obtained, will provide any kind of breakthrough. As has been noted, present indications are that the Alaskan fluted points may be only a few centuries younger than Clovis points, and this certainly will lead to equivocation. A further undetermined factor that cannot be ignored is the age of fluted points from the eastern United States. Even in the case of a simple historical problem, other approaches in addition to dating are required. While an attribute analysis of points presents no difficulty, the delineation of validly associated assemblages, particularly at Batza Téna, which is a prerequisite to the integrity of any analysis, is another matter. At this stage conceptual assumptions about the meaning of fluted points in cultural terms come to the fore. What factors or types of diffusion, including population spread, are responsible for the distribution of fluting? What assumptions can be made about the technology of any people who adopted fluting from other peoples, if that was the case; and what historical and functional associations necessarily exist between fluted points and the other tool types in a Paleo-Indian complex? The Alaska–central North America distribution of fluted points indicates at least that there was communication, probably by stages, between the two areas at a relatively early date. This statement may appear as a regression from our foregoing propositions, model, and discussions, but at a reduced level of assumptions it represents the present state of our knowledge. The archaeological potential of Alaska and the northern Yukon is, we believe, sufficiently great to provide a sharper delineation of reformulated problems and a contribution to their eventual resolution.

APPENDIX: FLUTED-POINT SITES AT BATZA TÉNA

1. RkIg–1 is located toward the high eastern end of the ridge adjacent to the one with the cluster of fluted-point sites. Hereafter "ridge" will refer to the latter. Flakes were collected from eight loci on the seventy-five-foot diameter site. All loci represent flake clusters partially exposed at the surface, but it is possible to trowel out flakes from a shallow depth almost anyplace on the site. These clusters range from concentrated groups of flakes piled on top of each other in an area one to two feet in diameter, to less intensive and sometimes poorly delimited concentrations many feet in diameter.

The battered fluted point, a biface fragment, and an end scraper were found in one of these clusters. At another locus eleven scrapers, mostly end scrapers, and a variant side-notched point were recovered. Few additional implements were recovered. Some of the flake concentrations may be secondary products of frost and soil processes, and it is not certain that the fluted point is validly associated with any other artifacts from the site.

2. RkIg–10 extends along the southern rim of the ridge for approximately 375 feet and provides a good view of the valley below. The several flake loci collected will not be described here; it will suffice to say that some of them appear to be secondary concentrations extending well into the ground along the margins of frost hummocks or small poorly defined polygons. A fluted point was found approximately two inches deep in brown soil adjacent to one of these concentrations. Nine kilograms of flakes and several artifacts were recovered from that cluster. Although this and any other material from the site are not necessarily validly associated with the fluted point, an end scraper and some flakes have yielded encouragingly high obsidian hydration values.

3. RkIg–28 comprises several flake clusters, scattered flakes, and artifacts occurring in an area 270 feet long and 80 to 145 feet wide. The site is situated on a sparsely vegetated flat area of stony soil near the upland apex of the ridge. The lateral margins of the site are largely cove-like with dips about three feet deep into

slightly depressed zones covered with tundra vegetation and soil. At its eastern end the site narrows and is contiguous with RkIg–30 across a slightly elevated topographic neck.

An isolated concave-based point fragment recovered through surface collecting, RkIg–28:9, is too short to be included in the fluted-point class with certainty. Adjacent parts of the site in which flake concentrations were observed were tested. Localized areas produced various leaf-shaped and pentagonal points or fragments, but intensive flake concentrations were generally found to be devoid of implements. A fluted-point fragment, RkIg–30:42, from the surface of the necked area has been grouped with the RkIg–30 collections although it was found closest to the main area of RkIg–28.

4. RkIg–29 occupies a moderately relieved strip of ground running adjacent to and essentially parallel with RkIg–28 and RkIg–30 for approximately 435 feet. Flake distribution over this distance is discontinuous. The site is relatively well vegetated and only a small surface collection was made. The base of a fluted point, RkIg–29:16, was found on the surface 100 feet inside the eastern end of the site among flakes distributed over an area approximately ten feet in diameter. A 1.2-kilogram flake sample physically associated with the point fragment came from a depth of less than one inch.

5. RkIg–30 consists of a constricted area between RkIg–28 and RkIg–29 where base RkIg–30:42 was found on the surface, without noteworthy associations; the site is 290 feet long, its main part approximately 300 feet in diameter. It occupies a slightly elevated, openly forested area of small trees. Several spectacular surface concentrations of obsidian flakes were examined and partially collected, but, as at most Batza Téna sites, such concentrations of flaking debris contained few implements. The center of the site area was, however, more productive. Approximately forty shallow six-foot-square sections were excavated there. These produced a relatively homogeneous-appearing assemblage, including the bases of four fluted points plus additional minor point fragments. This collection is described in more detail in the text.

6. RkIg–31 at its west end almost imperceptibly merges through a forested area with the east end of RkIg–30; like the latter, it is on terrain slightly elevated from its surroundings. Exclusive of poorly discerned outlying flake clusters in areas largely obscured by vegetation, the site occupies a denuded zone approximately 120 feet long and half that in width. With the exception of two fluted points, one of them complete although damaged (RkIg–31:60), two side-notched points, and some rough biface fragments, few distinctive artifacts were found on the surface during the initial reconnaissances. No part of the site appeared to be propitious for test pitting, but two additional fluted bases and several biface fragments were nevertheless recovered through the excavation of 5½ six-foot-square sections. They came from the surface and immediate subsurface in a bouldery soil, in the area in which the other points had been found.

7. RkIg–43 is essentially an arm or offshoot of RkIg–44, which is described next. It consists of one flake cluster and scattered flakes found on the surface of a slight knoll measuring five feet high, thirty feet wide, and fifty feet long. Surface collection produced only a small fluted-point base (RkIg–43:1) found adjacent to the flake cluster, plus a small fragment of a biface and a thick flake bifacially prepared along one edge.

8. RkIg–44, like RkIg–43, is located across the tundra, approximately 100 yards east of RkIg–31, on slightly elevated rocky ground (disintegrated bedrock or colluvial mounds). Although the site is located slightly off the crest of the ridge on the north flank, it provides a good perspective of the middle reaches of the small Indian River valley. It is approximately 160 feet long and occupies most of

the elevated terrain upon which it is situated. The front, or eastern, area of the site is completely denuded of vegetation and soil and apparently also of most flaking debris that may once have been present. Several flake concentrations were found on the better vegetated and forested area of the site; these were sampled, in part through a discontinuously excavated six-by-seventy-two foot trench. Implement recovery was limited principally to biface and biface preform fragments. Among surface finds not from the trench sample are the base of a point showing apparent attempted fluting (RkIg–44:38) and an incomplete, badly battered fluted point (RkIg–44:81), which was not recognized at the time it was first recovered. The flake concentrations appear, at least in part, to be secondary or reworked through natural agencies, and the two points noted do not have any recognized or necessarily valid association with other material from RkIg–44.

9. RlIg–46 is located on a large knoll on the south side of Indian River several miles east of the ridge site cluster. A denuded area about 300 feet in diameter is extensively littered with obsidian flakes, which extend onto vegetated areas of the knoll; but very few artifacts were found during a careful inspection of the surface. Hardly any two implements were closely associated. The principal distinctive artifacts recovered are a fluted-point base, a lanceolate point, and a keeled obsidian microcore.

10. RlIg–47 is situated on a topographic bench on the north side of Indian River across from RlIg–46. Minor flake clusters were observed on the surface in a zone 125 feet long in a semidenuded area. The only distinctive artifacts found with the flake clusters were an end scraper and a side-notched-point base; in addition, a small, nearly complete fluted point and the midsection of a relatively large fluted point occurred as isolated surface finds, spaced thirty feet apart, within the site area.

REFERENCES

ANDERSON, DOUGLAS D.
  1968 A Stone Age campsite at the gateway to America. *Scientific American* 218(16):24–33.
CAMPBELL, JOHN M.
  1961 The Tuktu complex of Anaktuvuk Pass. *Anthropological Papers of the University of Alaska* 9(2):61–80.
CLARK, ANNETTE McFADYEN, DONALD W. CLARK
  1972 "Koyukuk Indian–Kobuk Eskimo interaction." Paper presented at the symposium on The Late Prehistoric/Historic Eskimos of Interior North Alaska, at the Thirty-Seventh Annual Meeting of the Society for American Archaeology, Miami, Florida.
CLARK, DONALD W.
  1972a Archaeology of the Batza Téna obsidian source, west-central Alaska. *Anthropological Papers of the University of Alaska* 15(2):1–21.
  1972b "Filaments of prehistory on the Koyukuk River, northwestern interior Alaska." Paper prepared for the International Conference on the Prehistory and Paleoecology of the Western North American Arctic and Subarctic. University of Calgary.
COOK, JOHN P., *et al.*
  1970 "Report of archaeological survey and excavations along the Alyeska Pipeline Service Company haulroad and pipeline alignments." Mimeographed. University of Alaska, Department of Anthropology.

HALL, EDWIN S., JR.
  1969   Comments to A. L. Bryan, 1969: Early man in America and the late
          Pleistocene chronology of western Canada and Alaska. *Current
          Anthropology* 10(4):339–365.
HAMILTON, THOMAS D.
  1969   "Glacial geology of the lower Atlatna valley, Brooks Range, Alaska,"
          in *INOUA Volume*, 181–223. Geological Society of America Special
          Paper 123.
HAYNES, C. VANCE, JR.
  1964   Fluted projectile points, their age and dispersion. *Science*
          145:1,408–1,412.
  1966   Elephant hunting in North America. *Scientific American* 214(6):104–
          112.
HOLMES, C. E.
  1972   "Archaeological materials from the upper Koyukuk River region,
          Alaska: the problems of affinities and dating." Paper presented at
          the Thirty-Seventh Annual Meeting of the Society for American
          Archaeology, Miami, Florida.
HOPKINS, DAVID M.
  1967   "The Cenozoic history of Beringia — a synthesis," in *The Bering land
          bridge*. Edited by D. M. Hopkins, 451–484. Stanford: Stanford Univer-
          sity Press.
HUGHES, OWEN L.
  1970   "Quaternary geology, Yukon Territory and western District of Mac-
          kenzie," in *Early man and environments in northwest North America*.
          Edited by R. A. Smith and J. W. Smith, 9–11. Calgary: University of
          Calgary Archaeological Association.
HUMPHREY, ROBERT L.
  1966   The prehistory of the Utukok River region, arctic Alaska: early fluted
          point tradition with Old World relationships. *Current Anthropology*
          7(5):586–588.
  1970   "The prehistory of the arctic slope of Alaska: Pleistocene cultural
          relationships between Eurasia and North America." Unpublished
          Ph.D. dissertation, University of New Mexico.
IRWIN, HENRY T.
  1971   Developments in early man studies in western North America,
          1960–1970. *Arctic Anthropology* 8(2):42–67.
IRWIN, HENRY T., H. M. WORMINGTON
  1970   Paleo-Indian tool types in the Great Plains. *American Antiquity*
          35(1):24–34.
LEONHARDY, FRANK C.
  1966   *Domebo: a Paleo-Indian mammoth kill in the prairie-plains*. Contribu-
          tions of the Museum of the Great Plains. Contributions of the Museum
          of the Great Plains No. 1. Lawton, Oklahoma.
MacDONALD, GEORGE F.
  1968   *Debert: A Paleo-Indian site in central Nova Scotia*. Anthropological
          Papers no. 16. Ottawa: National Museums of Canada.
PATTON, WILLIAM W., JR., THOMAS P. MILLER
  1970   A possible bedrock source for obsidian found in archaeological sites in
          northwestern Alaska. *Science* 169:760–761.
REEVES, B. O. K.
  1971   "On the coalescence of the Laurentide and Cordilleran ice sheets in the
          western interior of North America with particular reference to the

southern Alberta area," in *Aboriginal man and environments on the plateau of northwest America.* Edited by A. H. Stryde and R. A. Smith, 205–228. Calgary: The Students' Press, University of Calgary.

REGER, DOUGLAS R.
1972   An archaeological survey in the Utopia area, Alaska. *Anthropological Papers of the University of Alaska* 15(2):23–38.

WITTHOFT, JOHN
1952   A Paleo-Indian site in eastern Pennsylvania: an early hunting culture. *Proceedings of the American Philosophical Society* 96:464–495.
1962   Comment to Ronald J. Mason, 1962: The Paleo-Indian tradition in eastern North America. *Current Anthropology* 3(3):227–278.

Late Paleolithic Cultures in Alaska

FREDERICK HADLEIGH WEST

This discussion of certain archaeological assemblages from Alaska is perhaps more than normally to be hedged about with qualifications, because the data upon which it is based are, for the most part, newly gathered and not as yet detailed in the public record. Lest this last observation be read as adversely critical of the industry of northern researchers, let me say, first, that in no way is any such criticism intended, and, second, that one of the chief beneficiaries of the forbearance I urge is myself.

Although one is inclined to think of interior Alaska as being one of the last great voids in American archaeological research, there has, in fact, been a great deal of field research carried out over the past ten years. I venture to suggest that eventually, when all this is boiled down and digested, the major outlines of interior Alaskan prehistory will have been well established.

The discussion that follows is limited by several factors. To begin with, although in Alaska we are astride the entryway into the New World, and it is thus obvious that the earliest American remains must lie in Alaska, one must bear clearly in mind that earliest Alaskan prehistory need not be directly sequential with that of any other early materials in the New World. It is possible, at least in theory, that there could exist in Alaska archaeological remains which would predate by a large factor the earliest materials recorded elsewhere in the Americas. There could very well be in Alaska — perhaps should be in Alaska — a record of human occupation that would conform to that from Northeastern Siberia and be unlike any known to the south. Thus, direct typological continuity from earliest

I wish to record here my thanks to the several agencies that have supported my research and continue to do so, particularly the National Science Foundation and the L. S. B. Leakey Foundation. My deepest gratitude goes to my wife and coresearcher, Constance.

Alaskan prehistory to earliest (other) American prehistory might simply not exist outside Alaska. Attempts at bridging that gap with reconstructions may be futile. This possibility of a significantly longer sequence of occupation in Alaska than elsewhere in the hemisphere needs to be kept in the forefront of such discussions. It is not necessarily sufficient to posit simply as much more time as logic dictates is necessary to accommodate movement from Alaska to points south. The possibility of an affinal hiatus of some consequence between the earliest prehistoric sequences of these two parts of the hemisphere carries with it an obvious and rather unfortunate corollary: solutions to problems of early Alaskan prehistory will not necessarily solve those problems which concern most Americanists.

A second important caution centers on the nature of the cultures that entered Alaska from the Old World. No matter what the cultural or temporal level under consideration, it must always be realized that any primitive people entering Alaska at any time must have done so fully adapted to the Arctic. To suppose otherwise, or to imply that somehow the movement through the north was accomplished by shivering southern Asians bound at express speeds for more equable climes in the New World, is naïve. Moreover, since it is clear that the early and perhaps only major migrations into Alaska occurred during the Pleistocene, let it be borne in mind that available evidence uniformly attests to Alaska's having had a considerably more rigorous climate then than now (Guthrie 1968; Hopkins 1959; Matthews 1970; Péwé 1969; Péwé and Reger 1972; Schweger 1973). Casual discussions of climatic rigor most frequently have recourse to compiled data such as monthly temperature averages and the like. It is possible, however, that the true requirements of northern climatic adaptation are better suggested by temperature extremes than by average values. It is worth recording in this connection that the winter of 1971 saw a new low temperature record set in central Alaska — minus 80°F (−63.3°C) in the interior foothills of the Brooks Range. One may wonder then what it might have been like when the winters were cold.

For the sake of convenience, we speak of these movements of people as "migrations." In fact, the likelihood of their having represented anything of that sort is nil. As others have been at some pains to point out, these movements were territorial and populational expansions by hunters (cf. Bordes 1968). That the earliest of such movements may nevertheless have been accomplished quickly, after the fashion of Martin's excellent model (1973), appears virtually certain considering the very peculiar and highly favorable circumstances that then obtained. Perhaps, in fact, it was the recall of those days that fostered the American variant of the Golden Age — the "happy hunting ground."

The present paper is not concerned with those several assemblages that purport to represent these earliest expansions into Alaska. The difficulties that presently beshroud those collections are such as to discourage protracted interpretive comment. (While saying this I must at the same time admit to being a proponent of the validity of at least some of these materials [West 1974].) Our interest here is in a long series of sites which seem to me to bear a resemblance to one another and which can be interpreted on much firmer ground. For the moment, these sites will be simply categorized as "core and blade." This survey will not deal with the Denbigh flint complex or the Arctic Small-Tool tradition (Giddings 1964; Irving 1957, 1962).

RECENT DISCOVERIES IN ALASKA

At a series of widely separated points in mainland Alaska there are sites that have produced materials of core-and-blade tradition. My discussion of these will necessarily concentrate more fully on those sites for which I am myself responsible. This, of course, does not imply that I consider these of greater importance than other sites but results simply from the fact that my own data are more familiar to me.

Sites North of the Yukon

The first major grouping of sites to be considered are those discovered by Ralph Solecki in his surveys of 1949 and 1950. In what was later to become recognized as a commonplace in interior Alaskan prehistory, most of the sites found by Solecki were small and entirely surficial (Solecki 1950, 1951). The sites of immediate concern, Site 121 and Site 65, yielded wedge-shaped microblade and blade cores respectively. Associated materials, though sparse, included a small triangular point at the latter, but their significance remains unclear. These materials, nevertheless, have unusual interest in the light of more recent discoveries. Wedge-shaped microblade cores similar to those described by Solecki had been found earlier in a recent Eskimo house at Onion Portage (Giddings 1952), but the significance of that find was not to be learned until Giddings and his associates returned to that site in 1961. The work at this site was assumed by Douglas D. Anderson following Gidding's untimely death in 1964. The deepest levels at Onion Portage, Band 8, have produced limited quantities of a core-and-blade industry resembling that found by Solecki (Giddings 1962; Anderson 1968, 1970). This material has been given the name "Kobuk complex" by Anderson. A still earlier assemblage, Akmak, reveals the same wedge-shaped microblade core forms, but associated with them are also true blades, bifaces, burins made on flakes, and blade scrapers (Anderson 1970).

In surveys conducted in the upper Noatak River drainage between 1961 and 1965, Anderson also located a number of small sites which resemble in general character those found by Solecki and which show the presence of microblade cores, burins, and other materials, which Anderson relates to the appropriate Onion Portage levels (Anderson 1972).

John M. Campbell's Tuktu site in Anaktuvuk Pass also reveals the presence of core-and-blade technology but associated with notched projectile points (Campbell 1961). The Tuktu microblade cores, of which there are but five complete specimens, are not of the wedge form previously discussed.

In the valley of the Atigun River on the north slope of the Brooks Range, Herbert W. Alexander has located a series of sites of which some are candidates for consideration here. At least one of these sites, that called Putu, not only contains core-and-blade material but is also stratified (Alexander 1974). The Putu site appears to contain an association of blade technology with fluted projectile points and thus potentially holds a great deal of interest for studies of early man in the New World.

Two former students and associates of Campbell's have been responsible for the discovery of sites on which microblade cores and other evidences of core-and-blade technology have been found. R. L. Humphrey has provided a brief account of his findings, which include wedge-shaped microblade cores (Humphrey 1966); the same have been found by Dennis Stanford who, in addition, has located large discoidal bifaces or core-bifaces resembling those of Anderson's Akmak at the Kahroak site near Barrow (Stanford 1971).

A number of important sites were discovered north of the Yukon River in conjunction with the archaeological surveys along the proposed route of the trans-Alaska oil pipeline. These surveys, under the direction of John P. Cook, have resulted in the discovery of at least two core-and-blade sites of great interest. One of these, the Gallagher flint station (Dixon 1971), contains an interesting array of core-and-blade materials with core forms ranging from a small, wedge-shaped microblade core to larger rotated microblade-size to blade-size cores. From the Island site in the Koyukuk River drainage, Charles E. Holmes has an assemblage which includes a quite long series of rather crude biconvex bifacial knives, together with small blade cores that are perhaps on the order of those from the Gallagher site (Holmes 1971, 1972).

Among the materials reported by Schlesier (1967) are some examples of microblades recovered from sites along the south slope of the Brooks Range.

Sites South of the Yukon

In this region, which may be said to comprise the largest part of central Alaska, the first "purely" core-and-blade assemblage ever discovered in North America was found. This was the famous Campus site, found on the campus of the then Alaska School of Mines in the early 1930's, reported upon by Nelson (1937) and Rainey (1939, 1940), and subsequently subjected to various degrees of interpretive comment by a great many other investigators. The Campus site is one of the four originally proposed by this writer as a constituent of the Denali complex (West 1967a). This assemblage includes a long series of wedge-shaped microblade cores, multifaceted burins made on flakes (Donnelly burins), and lanceolate points of both the bipointed and the straight-based variety. E. W. Hosley conducted further excavations at the Campus site in the mid-1960's (Hosley 1968), one result of which was to further expand this already large collection. Two side-notched projectile points found in, respectively, the excavations of the 1930's and Hosley's excavation of thirty years later may or may not be contemporaneous with the rest of this assemblage. Certain other elements lend some support to the thought that this assemblage is somewhat mixed, albeit predominantly core and blade and specifically of the Denali complex. The original collection was subjected to a detailed restudy by H.-G. Bandi, but the results of that analysis have not yet been published.

Two other sites that have yielded core-and-blade material have likewise been known for rather a long time. Both lie south of Fairbanks just off the Richardson Highway. The first is at Moose Creek Bluff, the second at Birch Lake (Skarland and Giddings 1948). Both collections are quite small and neither contains wedge-shaped cores. Rather, that from Moose Creek Bluff might be described as blocky or even nondescript (possibly a function of the poor material used) and, in size, either a large microblade core or a small blade core. The one specimen from Birch Lake (illustrated in Skarland and Giddings 1948) is conical and quite well made and is, at approximately five centimeters, about twice the height of most of the small wedge-shaped microblade cores.

The site of Dixthada near Tanacross, excavated by Froelich Rainey in 1937, produced two wedge-shaped microblade cores and other assorted elements that had somehow become incorporated in the recent debris constituting the bulk of the material produced by the site (Rainey 1939). Rainey correctly suggested that these elements were intrusive but was unable to locate their source. Cook and McKennan revisited Dixthada in 1971 and succeeded in determining that the source for the microblade material lay stratigraphically below the recent midden deposits (Cook and McKennan, personal communication).

Irving's Site 9, found in the course of his survey of the Lake

Louise–Lake Tyone region on the south side of the Alaska Range, has also produced evidence of core-and-blade technology in the form of the several microblades that constitute part of the identifiable portions of this very small assemblage (Irving 1957).

The recent excavations carried out by Robert A. McKennan and John P. Cook at Healy Lake have produced abundant evidence of core-and-blade technology. The Garden site and the Village site may both be said to partake of this greater tradition and evidently cover a very long span of time (McKennan and Cook 1968; Cook 1969).

Holmes has recently reported on the discovery of the Minchumina site situated on the lake of that name (Holmes 1972, 1974). Only microblades have been found there thus far; the cores from which they are derived remain unknown.

There is no doubt that some of the materials included in R. S. Mac-Neish's surveys (1964) in the Yukon Territory should be fitted into this discussion. The same observation holds for the material currently being analyzed by W. B. Workman from Chimi and the Canyon site (Workman 1973) and Millar's material from Fisherman Lake, Northwest Territories (Millar 1968), but too little of this material is known to me in proper detail, and it is, besides, technically beyond the purview of a paper dealing with Alaska.

In 1967 the Denali complex was proposed by this writer (West 1967a). At the time of its formulation four sites were considered as constituents, two sites on the Teklanika River in Mount McKinley National Park, the Campus site, and the Donnelly Ridge site on the Delta River, just on the north side of the Alaska Range. In these sites both blades and microblades occur, predominantly the latter. Wedge-shaped microblade cores are abundant, as are the multifaceted Donnelly burins. As with the microblade cores, the latter are demonstrably technologically highly complex and thus have a high degree of characterization (Mauger 1970; Morlan 1970). Additional elements of the Denali complex include boulder-chip scrapers (tci-tho) and biconvex bifacial knives.

One of the results of the intensive investigations in the Tangle Lakes region, begun in 1966, has been the discovery of twelve new Denali complex sites, all of which conform in content with the original four (West 1967a, 1974). In all these sites the very large percentages of burins render it a virtual certainty that an antler industry of considerable importance existed. As yet no site has been found in which there is any indication of the requisite organic preservation.

Several other assemblages have been found in the Tangle Lakes in which the dominant elements are core-and-blade technology, but thus far demonstrable relationships with the Denali complex are difficult to perceive. Of these sites, which thus occupy a somewhat equivocal status, that catalogued as Mount Hayes 122 probably shows its affinities with Denali most clearly. Plates 1 through 12 are intended to convey some notion of the range of the Tangle Lakes core-and-blade assemblages including MH 122. This small assemblage is characterized by four large blade cores of which one is conical and one clearly wedge-shaped. Several blades derived from those specimens, a possible burin, and a number of platform preparation flakes constitute the remaining identifiable elements of the collection. Except for their large size these specimens could be handily accommodated in the Denali complex, and it is perhaps there that Mount Hayes 122 belongs.

The site catalogued as Mount Hayes 72, discovered by my former student and coworker Douglas R. Reger, is another matter. Here, along with a few wedge-shaped cores and microblades derived from them, are conical cores of medium size and their distinctive associated by-products. In addition there are a great many bifaces ranging from a rather small amygdaloid, through straight-based lanceolate, to biconvex forms (the most frequent). There are many scrapers and a very low frequency of burins, especially considering the bulk of this very large assemblage. The microblade core most clearly resembling the conical specimens at Mount Hayes 72 is that recorded by Skarland and Giddings (1948) from Birch Lake. Two more sites, catalogued as Mount Hayes 150 and 152, also give evidence of core-and-blade technology, but as yet their relationships with the other assemblages remain unclear since they are as yet essentially unstudied. Several of the core specimens involved are large enough to suggest that they not be termed microblade cores. Some appear to be rotated, and a couple of specimens show relatively acute platform angles. It must be noted that despite the use of the terms "most" and "some" there are really very few blade cores distributed among these sites, where they will eventually be placed is problematical. At the moment one possible interpretation is that three subtraditions of blade users occupied the Tangle Lakes district. It is most unlikely that they were there contemporaneously.

Recently, as a result of the activities of Mr. and Mrs. Gene Chapman, former private collectors, several localities have been found in the upper Matanuska Valley near Anchorage at which abundant core-and-blade materials occur. These sites, at Ravine Lake, Long Lake, and Bonnie Lake, show a wide range of blade sizes — from those which would be called microblades to full-sized blades. The use of a very poor local material, a very soft carbonaceous siltstone, gives the technology displayed in the manufacture of the various artifacts at these sites an unwontedly crude aspect. If some allowance is made for that condition, the cores, the *lames à crêtes*, the biconvex bifaces, the burins, and the other elements seem morphologically closer to collections previously discussed than might otherwise superficially appear. Test excavations have been carried out at several of these sites by the present writer and his wife and by other workers under the direction of my colleague W. B. Workman. (The latter tests were carried out in state camping areas at Bonnie Lake and Long Lake under a contract with the State Division of Parks.) We hope that our future investigations at these localities will permit their firmer cultural and temporal placement.

Coastal Alaska

Apart from the Denbigh flint complex sites, very few core-and-blade sites have been found in the coastal regions of Alaska. Those which have been found, however, are of considerable importance.

The first of these, the Trail Creek caves on the Seward Peninsula, were excavated by Helge Larsen in 1949–1950. The dominant core-and-blade elements of both caves were Denbigh, but the basal levels yielded core-and-blade material of a different character, as well as producing some evidence of what the putative antler industry of the sites discussed above may have been like. Although the microblade cores which produced them are not present, Larsen (1968) concludes, for several reasons, that the lowest level in Cave 2 represents the leavings of people possessing an industry similar to that of the Akmak site on the Kobuk River.

Far removed from the last locality, the site of Anangula on the coast of Umnak Island in the Aleutians has yielded a very large and very distinctive core-and-blade industry (Laughlin 1951; Laughlin and Aigner 1966). The microblade cores tend generally to be blocky and rotated; there are many burins on blades and other burin-faceted implements. Bifacial elements seem to be totally lacking in the Anangula assemblage.

A recent discovery of considerable importance is that of the Ground Hog Bay site on Icy Strait in southeastern Alaska (Ackerman 1974). Microblade cores from this site are wedge-shaped and appear to be generally similar to those wedge-shaped cores described from Onion Portage, Band 8, Akmak, Denali complex, and others previously discussed. The location of this site makes its ultimate cultural affiliations especially interesting.

Finally, the existence of a core-and-blade site near Egiagig on the Kvichak River in southwestern Alaska has recently come to light (Workman and Hamilton, personal communication). The small assemblage presently available from this site contains several microblade cores that, upon superficial examination at least, appear identical with these other wedge-shaped cores.

Distribution and Age of the Sites

At the present time it would appear that nothing very profound can be said about the distribution of these sites unless it be the impression that in most parts of Alaska in which some archaeological research has been done and in which early material exists, core-and-blade sites will be found. One is tempted to suggest, further, that the distribution of all these sites is such that virtually all were beyond the reach of glacial ice — if indeed, all, or any, were even occupied at such times.

On the question of dating, radiocarbon assays, if all are to be believed, indicate that these sites were occupied in a range of time from 12,000 years ago (the 11,090 ± 170 B.P. date from the Village site on Healy Lake [McKennan and Cook 1968]) until approximately the time of contact, at least in some parts of Alaska. Without becoming involved too deeply in this particular problem, I will venture that the preponderance of believable evidence favors the earlier dating for these sites. Although my coworkers and I, having been involved in more than twenty such sites, appear virtually to have cornered the market on cores and blades in interior Alaska, the only radiocarbon dates we have been able to secure thus far which pertain directly to these sites are "stopdates," *viz.* 3820 ± 115 B.P. (UGA–527), from an organic zone overlying the occupation at the site Teklanika West (Denali complex), and two assays of 5480 ± 300 B.P. (UGA–530) and 4160 ± 175 B.P. (UGA–531) from organic material overlying the cultural horizon at Mount Hayes 72 in the Tangle Lakes. Other evidence on time placement, however, indicates that these are indeed stopdates and the occupations were earlier (West 1967b). As far as I know, radiocarbon dates, which in some way relate to particular occupations, have been run on about fifteen of the sites discussed above. For present purposes I shall say that radiocarbon dates in the range of 6,000 to 12,000 years ago are "early" and all others "late." On this basis, ten sites have early radiocarbon dates. This is not to say that the situation is clear-cut in all cases pertaining to those individual sites: far from it. For example, several of these sites that have early dates also support later ones, in a manner that does not seem to lend itself to ready explanation. In the Tangle Lakes, during the span from 2500 B.C. until just before the contact period, none of the occupations are core and blade (notched-point sites and others). Exactly when (and why) the core-and-blade occupations (principally Denali complex) terminated here is not known. It is clear, however, that by some 4,500 years ago they were gone, with no vestige of their lithic traditions remaining.

In any event, the dating of these sites is really not the major issue in this discussion. No matter how the chronology of all these sites ultimately works out, there can be little doubt of the derivation of most of them virtually intact from neighboring Siberia. To put this another way, there can be little doubt that interior Alaska (construed broadly as that portion of interior Alaska and adjacent Canada which was ice-free) was, in the early phases of its prehistory, part of a vastly larger Siberian culture sphere. This, in my view, is the essential nature of the material under consideration here. The question is, then, how shall it be interpreted?

The Epi-Gravettian or Aurignacoid Penetration of Alaska

Although others, such as Nelson (1937) and Rainey (1939), had left no doubt that Old World affinities were to be seen in the Campus site collection, to my knowledge the first extended, systematic treatment accorded that and other similar materials turned up in the north since World War II was that of Bandi (1964, 1969). Müller-Beck (1966) presented essentially the same idea as part of a general and provocative scheme relating to all early movements of people into the New World. Instead of Bandi's "Epi-Gravettian," Müller-Beck chose the term "Aurignacoid" as being a more apt overall term for this late Würm movement of Upper Paleolithic peoples into the New World. Neither term is intended to describe closely the materials concerned. If there can exist legitimate controversy over whether a site such as Malta should be termed "Aurignacian" or "Aurignacian-like," then one may immediately see objections to the use of that term half as far again to the east. In like manner, recourse to "Gravettian" may give one pause, recognizing the problems which are associated with that term in Europe. Overriding either of these negative observations, however, is one of surpassing importance: either of the two terms serves to call attention to a fact which otherwise may be too easily overlooked: namely, that the assemblages in question are of an Upper Paleolithic character. For this reason alone I would advocate at the present time the continued use of either, or both, of these terms (actually their usages are slightly different, so that one could use both if he so chose) until such time as a better term may be found. In my mind, a better term will have as its prime requisite that it impart the same sense as that conveyed by "Epi-Gravettian" or "Aurignacoid."

I have chosen here to employ the oblique phrase "late Paleolithic cultures," but my aim has been the same as that of Bandi and Müller-Beck. It must be stressed that reference is made in this casual and not-too-tidy enumeration to a fair amount of information concerning early Alaskan prehistory. Some fifty sites have been referred to, practically any one or all of which, found in a more likely part of the world, would immediately be termed Upper Paleolithic or late Paleolithic. To take the position that all such sites and assemblages must be considered in American terms is, to my view, to miss by a very wide mark all that these assemblages have to tell us about prehistory. With possibly one or two exceptions, the materials discussed here are *specifically* Upper Paleolithic in character and bear little resemblance to the "early man" assemblages familiar elsewhere in the Americas. They are, moreover, precisely what one would expect to find at this nexus between two worlds. If anything, my own effort here in using "late Paleolithic" instead of "Upper Paleolithic" represents an uncalled-for compromise. This probably resulted from an intuitive shying away from the latter term as being a bit too typologically and temporally restrictive. My term has, I think, no more logic than that; for present purposes I would consider the two essentially synonyms.

It may be suggested now that, as with other parts of the world in late Pleistocene times, there was a period of some duration in Alaska when core-and-blade technology was the only lithic tradition present. Exactly how this shall be interpreted to aid our understanding of American prehistory at large remains to be determined. Borden's recent suggestions (1969) for the southward movement of these ideas certainly seem pertinent.

It is, of course, unfortunate that to date there has been so little comparable material found in northeastern Russia, but the recognition of the true nature of assemblages discussed in this paper should not be made to await discoveries "close in" in eastern Siberia, nor should that recognition be contingent upon such discoveries. We all know the large part that chance plays in the discovery of archaeological sites; thus, to be blindly insistent upon a virtually unbroken distribution from one region to another is, I submit, to be profoundly unscientific. Such materials may never be found and for all the same reasons that there will never be a complete prehistory of man.

Plate 1. Mount Hayes 150: unassigned fragments of cores and blades. At upper left a platform renewal spall, the facets of which face down

Plate 2. Mount Hayes 152: unassigned. Top tier, cores with acute platform angles; lower right, a chopperlike flake core; the rest are fragments of blades and cores

Plate 3.   Mount Hayes 72: unassigned. All bifaces except specimen at upper left

Plate 4.   Mount Hayes 72: unassigned. Top row: at left two microblades, blade end scraper, double-ended scraper, burin at extreme right; second row: end scraper; third row: unifacial convex scraper, unifacial point straight-edged scraper; bottom row: reeled scraper (?) or core

Plate 5. Mount Hayes 72: unassigned. Top row: left, a blade, three wedge-shaped cores; second row: two blades, two cores; bottom row: left and right, conical cores; center, a core top removal

Plate 6. Mount Hayes 122: unassigned. Upper left, a blade fragment; just below it a unifacial pointed object. Remaining are three blade cores, that at lower left corresponding to Denali wedge-shaped variety except for size

Plate 7.   Teklanika West: Denali complex. Three objects in upper corner are microblade cores; next over (center top), a burin with articulated spall; below it, a Donnelly burin. Upper right, an end scraper. Third row: left, a "pillar" core; center, two triangular projectile points; right, a large biface. Bottom, a straight-edged scraper; at right a large biface

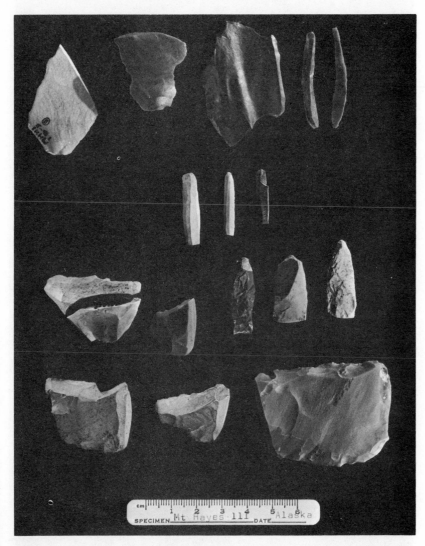

Plate 8.   Mount Hayes 111: Denali complex. Donnelly burins and spalls in top tier; second row: three microblades; third row; at left, two microblade cores (one with entire top removal rearticulated), at right, three platform preparation spalls (facets up); bottom row: three microblade cores; that at extreme right carries a burin facet at edge opposite blade-faceted end

Plate 9.   Long Lake: unassigned. Upper left and at bottom, bifaces; center top, a large retouched blade; right top, rectangular biface

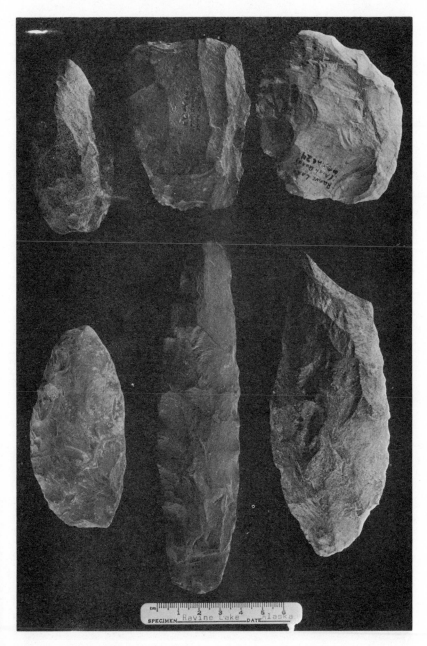

Plate 10.   Ravine Lake: unassigned. Bifaces except top right. Center top specimen may be a blade core

Plate 11. Ravine Lake: unassigned. Top row, two bifaces; bottom, two unifaces: at left, a keeled end scraper; at right, a possible core blank

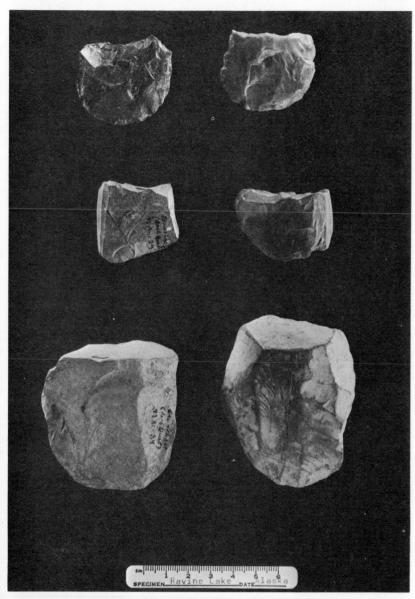

Plate 12. Ravine Lake: unassigned. Top row, two wedge-shaped microblade-core pre-forms: middle, two microblade cores; bottom, possible blade-core blanks (or preforms)

REFERENCES

ACKERMAN, ROBERT E.
1974   "Post-Pleistocene cultural adaptations on the northern northwest coast," in *Proceedings of the International Conference on the Prehistory and Palaeoecology of the Western Arctic Sub-Arctic*, November 1972. Calgary: University of Calgary Press.

ALEXANDER, HERBERT L.
1974   "The association of Aurignacoid elements with fluted point complexes in North America," in *Proceedings of the International Conference on the Prehistory and Palaeoecology of the Western Arctic and Sub-Arctic*, November 1972. Calgary: University of Calgary Press.

ANDERSON, DOUGLAS D.
1968   A Stone Age campsite at the gateway to America. *Scientific American* 218:(6):24–33.
1970   *Akmak, an early archaeological assemblage from Onion Portage, northwest Alaska.* Copenhagen: Fasc. XVI, Arktisk Institut.
1972   An archaelogical survey of the Noatak drainage, Alaska. *Arctic Anthropology* 9(1):66–117.

BANDI, HANS-GEORG
1964   *Urgeschichte der Eskimo.* Stuttgart: Gustav Fischer.
1969   *Eskimo prehistory.* Calgary: University of Alaska Press (distributed by University of Washington Press).

BORDEN, CHARLES E.
1969   Early population movements from Asia into western North America. *Syesis* 2(1, 2):1–13.

BORDES, FRANÇOIS
1968   *The old Stone Age.* New York: McGraw-Hill.

CAMPBELL, JOHN M.
1961   The Tuktu complex of Anaktuvuk Pass. *Anthropological Papers of the University of Alaska* 9(2):61–80.

COOK, JOHN P.
1969   "The early prehistory of Healy Lake, Alaska." Unpublished Ph.D. dissertation, University of Wisconsin.

DIXON, E. J.
1971   "The Gallagher flint station and other sites along the Saga Navirktok River," in *Final report of the archaelogical survey and excavations along the Alyeska Pipeline Service Company pipeline route.* Edited by J. P. Cook. Calgary: University of Alaska Press.

GIDDINGS, J. L.
1952   The arctic Woodland culture of the Kobuk River. *Museum Monographs, The University Museum.* Philadelphia: University of Pennsylvania.
1962   Onion Portage and other flint sites of the Kobuk River. *Arctic Anthropology* 1(1):6–27.
1964   *The archaeology of Cape Denbigh.* Providence, R.I.: Brown University Press.

GUTHRIE, R. D.
1968   Paleoecology of the large-mammal community in interior Alaska during the late Pleistocene. *The American Midland Naturalist* 79(2):346–363.

HOLMES, CHARLES E.
1971   "The prehistory of the upper Koyukuk River region in north-central

Alaska," in *Final report of the archaeological survey and excavations along the Alyeska Pipeline Service Company pipeline route.* Edited by J. P. Cook. Calgary: University of Alaska Press.

1972   "Archaeological materials from the upper Koyukuk River region, Alaska." Paper presented at the Thirty-Seventh Annual Meeting of the Society for American Archaeology, Miami.

1974   "Preliminary testing of a microblade site at Lake Minchumina, Alaska," in *Proceedings of the International Conference on the Prehistory and Palaeoecology of the Western Arctic and Sub-Arctic.* Calgary: University of Calgary Press.

HOPKINS, DAVID M.
1959   Cenozoic history of the Bering land bridge. *Science* 129:1,519–1,528.

HOSLEY, EDWARD H.
1968   "Grant 4083: the McGrath Ingalik Indian, central Alaska (the Birches site)," in *American Philosophical Society yearbook*, 544–547.

HUMPHREY, ROBERT L.
1966   The prehistory of the Utukok River region, arctic Alaska: early fluted point tradition with Old World relationships. *Current Anthropology* 7:586–588.

IRVING, WILLIAM N.
1957   An archaeological survey of the Susitna Valley. *Anthropological Papers of the University of Alaska* 6(1):37–52.

1962   A provisional comparison of some Alaskan and Asian stone industries. *Arctic Institute of North America, Technical Papers* 11:55–68.

LARSEN, HELGE
1968   Trail Creek. *Acta Arctica* (Copenhagen) 15.

LAUGHLIN, WILLIAM S.
1951   Notes on an Aleutian core and blade industry. *American Antiquity* 17(1):52–55.

LAUGHLIN, WILLIAM S., JEAN S. AIGNER
1966   Preliminary analysis of the Anangula unifacial core and blade industry. *Arctic Anthropology* 3(2):41–56.

MacNEISH, RICHARD S.
1964   *Investigations in the southwest Yukon.* Papers of the Robert S. Peabody Foundation for Archaeology 6. Andover, Massachusetts.

MARTIN, PAUL S.
1973   The discovery of America. *Science* 179 (4,077):969–974.

MATTHEWS, JOHN V., JR.
1970   Quaternary environmental history of interior Alaska: pollen samples from organic colluvium and peats. *Arctic and Alpine Research* 2(4):241–251.

MAUGER, JEFFREY E.
1970   "A study of Donnelly burins in the Campus archaeological collection. Unpublished M.A. thesis, Washington State University, Pullman, Washington.

McKENNAN, ROBERT A., JOHN P. COOK
1968   "Prehistory of Healy Lake, Alaska." Paper presented at the VIIIth International Congress of Anthropological and Ethnological Sciences, Tokyo–Kyoto, Japan.

MILLAR, J. F. V.
1968   "Fisherman Lake." Unpublished PhD. dissertation, University of Calgary.

MORLAN, RICHARD E.
1970   Wedge-shaped core technology in northern North America. *Arctic Anthropology* 7(2):17–37.

MÜLLER-BECK, HANSJÜRGEN
1966   Paleohunters in America: origins and diffusions. *Science* 152 (3,726):1,191–1,210.

NELSON, N. C.
1937   Notes on cultural relations between Asia and America. *American Antiquity* 2(4):267–272.

PÉWÉ, TROY L.
1969   "The periglacial environment," in *The periglacial environment, past and present*, 1–9. Arctic Institute of North America. Montreal: McGill University Press.

PÉWÉ, TROY L., R. D. REGER
1972   Modern and Wisconsinan snowlines in Alaska. Proceedings of the 24th International, pp. 187–195.

RAINEY, FROELICH
1939   Archaeology in central Alaska. *Anthropological Papers of the American Museum of Natural History* 36(4):355–405.
1940   Archaeological investigations in central Alaska. *American Antiquity* 5(4):299–308.

SCHLESIER, KARL H.
1967   Sedna Creek: report on an archaeological survey on the arctic slope of the Brooks range. *American Antiquity* 32(2):210–222.

SCHWEGER, CHARLES E.
1968   "Notes on the paleoecology of the northern Archaic tradition." Paper prepared for Session 48, Annual Meeting of the American Anthropological Association, Seattle.
1973   "Late-Quaternary history of the Tangle Lakes region, Alaska: a progress report." Department of Anthropology, University of Alberta, Edmonton (mimeographed).

SKARLAND, IVAR, J. L. GIDDINGS, JR.
1948   Flint stations in central Alaska. *American Antiquity* 14(2):116–120.

SOLECKI, RALPH S.
1950   A preliminary report on an archaeological reconnaissance of Kukpouruk and Koholik rivers in northwest Alaska. *American Antiquity* 16(1):66–69.
1951   Archaeology and ecology of the arctic slope of Alaska. *Smithsonian Institution Annual Report for 1950*: 469–495. Washington.

STANFORD, DENNIS
1971   "Evidence of Paleo-Eskimos on the north coast of Alaska." Paper presented at the Thirty-Sixth Annual Meeting of the Society for American Archaeology, Norman, Oklahoma.

WEST, FREDERICK HADLEIGH
1967a The Donnelly Ridge site and the definition of an early core and blade complex in central Alaska. *American Antiquity* 32(3):360–382.
1967b "New evidence on the time placement and affinities of the Denali complex in central Alaska." Paper presented at the Thirty-Second Annual Meeting of the Society for American Archaelogy, Ann Arbor.
1974   "Amphitheatre Mountain complex," in *Proceedings of the International Conference on the Prehistory and Palaeoecology of the Western Arctic and Sub-Arctic*, November 1972. Calgary: University of Calgary Press.

WORKMAN, WILLIAM B.
  1973 "Dated traces of early Holocene man in southwest Yukon, Canada."
        Paper presented at the Thirty-Eighth Annual Meeting of the Society for
        American Archaeology, San Francisco.

Microblades and Prehistory: Technological and Cultural Considerations for the North Pacific Coast

ROBERT E. ACKERMAN

The hypothesized prehistoric pattern of aboriginal settlement and coastal adaptation along the northern reaches of the north Pacific shores was until 1965 an extension of the familiar historic northwest-coast culture complex. In southeastern Alaska, specifically in the area claimed by the northern Tlingit Indians, prehistoric studies were advanced by the pioneering research investigations of Frederica de Laguna (de Laguna 1960, 1972; de Laguna et al. 1964). This research, through the use of an ethnohistorical–ethnoarchaeological model, focused on the continuity of the historic-to-late-prehistoric Tlingit utilization of coastal and riverine resources (cf. de Laguna 1960: 1–16). This projection of the historical lifeway into the past via late prehistoric archaeological site data was temporally brief, on the order of 200 to 300 years. A more ancient occupation was inferred, but the necessary sites had yet to be discovered.

In 1965, an archaeological survey team from Washington State University found and tested a site with the requisite antiquity.[1] The site is located on a marine terrace now overlooking a small embayment (Ground Hog Bay) of Icy Strait in southeastern Alaska. The site is adjacent to the historic Tlingit village of Kaxnuwu (Grouse Fort), which was occupied during the late nineteenth and early twentieth centuries. Materials in the upper component of the older site (Ground Hog Bay site 2, hereafter referred to as GHB 2) equate to the oldest cultural remains at Kaxnuwu, indicating a local continuum from historic to late prehistoric times. A single radiocarbon date of 10,180 ± 800 B.P. (WSU–412) from the bottom of the GHB 2 site clearly indicated its antiquity (Ackerman 1968).

Further investigations of GHB 2 were conducted in 1971 and 1973

[1] Archaeological survey for the National Park Service in the Glacier Bay National Monument 1963–1965.

under the auspices of the National Science Foundation (GS–29–168). These more extensive investigations have yielded detailed information relative to the site stratigraphy and associated cultural components. Data on site stratigraphy, terrace sediments, and local geomorphology have been provided by Dr. Thomas Hamilton, Department of Geology, University of Alaska.

The GHB 2 site extends over the surface of a flat-topped marine terrace, now fourteen to fifteen meters above mean sea level, and on a horizontal plane fifty-six meters inland. Going from the modern beach to the terrace the sequence is (a) modern inclined beach where cobbles and boulders lie on a sandy-gravel to platy-pebble beach beside abraded bedrock formations; (b) modern storm beach covered with platy pebbles, cobbles, shells, and drift wood, which is carried forward into the edge of the bordering rye grass; (c) beach ridges that front against the terrace slope with an edge cover of alder and an interior stand of Sitka spruce and western hemlock. These beaches have been radiocarbon dated to 540 ± 65 B.P. (SI–1556) and represent the latest series of beach strands to abut against the erosional face of the terrace (Hamilton 1972:3). The terrace itself consists of introduced gravels over a zone of forest loam, underlain by beach sediments resting upon an erosional surface of till and isolated sections of bedrock (Hamilton 1972:5). A more detailed statement is available in an earlier paper (Ackerman 1974).

THE CULTURAL SEQUENCE

Following the glacial retreat of late Wisconsin ice about 11,000 B.P., a marine transgression of fifteen meters or more covered the area. The land was then uplifted, probably through a combination of isostasy and tectonic movement. As the land rose, layers of beach sands and gravels were left lying over the eroded surface of till and bedrock. This bottom unit (soil unit V) is overlain by a layer of clay in which flakes and charcoal have been found (10,180 ± 800 B.P. [WSU–412]; 9130 ± 130 B.P. [I–6304]). At this writing our total recovery from this lowest stratum (cultural component III) consists of two obsidian bifacial fragments with percussion-flaked surfaces, a water-rolled chert scraper, and five flakes of argillite.

Above the clay band is another beach deposit of coarse pebbles and small cobbles as a lag concentrate, with finer sediments (sand, gravels) lower in the stratum. This level (soil unit IV) contains an assemblage (cultural component II) characterized by lithic detritus with few finished pieces. Two basic industries were noted, one based on microcores and blades, the other on macrocores and flakes. Four bifacial fragments with well-executed pressure flaking along the edges have been found within this level. All the bifaces are preforms and were broken in manufacture. Other tool forms are scrapers, choppers, hammerstones, abrading stones, utilized flakes, and irregular tabular pieces. The material utilized is obsidian, chert, fillite, andesite, greywacke, and altered argillite. Charcoal from within the zone dated 7545 ± 185 B.P. (I–7058), 8230 ± 130 B.P. (I–6395), and 8880 ± 125 B.P. (I–7057). Dates from charcoal collected on the surface of stratum are 4155 ± 95 B.P. (I–7056), 3750 ± 100 B.P. (I–6393), and 2970 ± 90 B.P. (I–7054). The extensive span of time indicated for soil unit IV (component II) was not reasonable in the given stratigraphy. Further excavation in 1973 resulted in the discovery of a new component intermediate between components I and II. The new component lies near the bottom of soil unit III with overlying and underlying bands of charcoal in the forest loam. Radiocarbon dates based on samples from these bands will probably indicate that the charcoal collected from the surface of soil unit IV (component II) in other squares in the site has filtered down from the occupation immediately above. The cultural inventory from the component in soil unit III is quite similar to that of soil unit IV (component II) with microblades, microcores, large flake cores, and abrading stones. For the moment it will be considered a cultural descendant of component II and labeled component IIb, with the lower component redesignated IIa. The remainder of soil unit III is a sterile forest loam, with radiocarbon dates of 2240 ± 450 B.P. (WSU–421), 2300 ± 445 B.P. (WSU–422), and 1525 ± 85 B.P. (I–7055).

Component I in soil unit II (gravels intermixed with forest loam) represents a major break in the cultural sequence. The lithic flaking tradition is still present although more in a relic category. Most stone tools are pecked and ground. Decorative items such as beads of amber, jet, or copper are now present. From this level, large post holes (often filled with gravel) have been cut through the previous layers down to till. Split planks with nearby hammerstones and an occasional adze head further indicate the large plank house of the historic period. Barbed and toggling harpoon heads, incised stones, stone bowls (some with zoomorphic designs), bird-bone tubes, copper awls, bear-tooth pendants, bone needles, stone mauls, and miscellaneous bone fragments complete the inventory of component I. A single radiocarbon date of 345 ± 85 B.P. (I–6394) indicates a late prehistoric occupation. The terrace was apparently unoccupied between the period of roughly 2500 to 400 B.P. (neoglacial stage or Little Ice Age). A lower terrace may have been occupied and subsequently destroyed by an encroaching sea. The thick forest-loam layer is suggestive of cool moist conditions, indicating that perhaps better-drained areas were preferable at this time. Another prehistoric site discovered in 1973 with somewhat more emphasis on bifacial production may fall within the cultural hiatus.

THE GHB 2 MICROBLADE INDUSTRY

Microcores and blades in the GHB 2 site[2] are a horizon marker for component II. A macrocore and flake industry is associated with the microblades; but, in addition to the size-range difference, it is the exotic materials utilized and the treatment of the microcore that set this industry apart from the other lithic productions. Microcores have been made from obsidian, chert, quartz crystal, and altered argillite (the latter a local base rock). Most of the microblades recovered are obsidian, although argillite cores are more numerous. The highly acid forest soils are undoubtedly responsible for the low yield of argillite blades, as many of the flakes and larger cores are frequently altered almost beyond recognition. Many of the obsidian microblade segments show side or end use retouch, indicating that microblades were the desired tool form, not trimming flakes produced in the sharpening of a corelike scraper, as some authors have suggested. Proximal segments (bulbar end) are more numerous than other segments. Whole microblades are relatively rare, poorly formed, and obviously rejects.

The preparation of the microcore for detaching blades varies according to the material utilized. Obsidian, for example, is brittle, crushes easily, and requires a special platform preparation to insure successful blade production. Chert and the metamorphosed argillite are much tougher and require less platform preparation. Microcores of the latter, for example, have platforms based on a natural cleavage plane or a single flake surface. The microcores of quartz crystal were apparently more difficult to flake and the efforts seem to have been directed toward driving flakes along the faces of the crystal.

The obsidian microcores are thus the most elaborate in core preparation techniques and as such afford a number of diagnostic attributes that can be correlated with similar attributes on other microcores in northwestern North America. The obsidian microcores were fashioned from small cobbles of obsidian. The cobble was split into two or more sections, each of which could form the basis for a microcore if the break were successful. The cores were fashioned into a rough wedge shape with a rather truncated keel. The platform was formed and rejuvenated by the removal of flakes from the flute surface and lateral margins onto the platform. Edge grinding and/or chipping to remove the overhang on the flute surface is a common feature. On several specimens the platform is at an acute angle to the flute surface with one high lateral edge. Often this edge will be crushed. This appears to be an effort to shape the platform as Mauger has suggested (1971) rather than the use retouch that Cook has implied for the Otter Creek and Healy Lake Campus-type cores (Cook 1968:124–125). The keel frequently has a well-defined notch on one of

[2]   For a more detailed discussion, see Ackerman 1974.

the lateral margins which apparently served as a support point just back of the flute surface. West has suggested (1967:368) that crushing on the lateral margins of microcores is a result of supporting the core in a clamplike device. In the rejuvenation of its platform there is no instance of core tablet removal (platform reformed by the removal of a single flake), as is the case in Campus- or Denali-type cores. Core rotation is common. Grinding on the flake ridges of one core suggests some use of the microcore flute surface for scraping.

In terms of the technological attributes of microcore production, the GHB 2 obsidian microcores show affinity to Campus cores from the Campus site (Mauger 1971), the Donnelly Ridge and Teklanika River sites (West 1967), the Healy Lake and Other Greek sites (Cook 1968), and the Onion Portage site (Anderson 1970). Johnson and Raup (1964) and MacNeish (1964) report polyhedral microcores from the southwestern Yukon, but it is difficult to discern from the illustrations or descriptions if attributes exist which can be related to the GHB 2 forms. The area is central to the proposed spread of peoples (from Alaska southward to British Columbia and Washington) who utilized microcores and blades (Borden 1962, 1968; Dumond 1969). In terms of southeastern Alaska, available evidence indicates that the Chilkat Pass region in southwestern Yukon was open starting about 12,500–9780 B.P. and perhaps became less desirable as an area and a route southward around 2640 B.P. (Denton and Stuiver 1967). The time period during which the southwestern region of the Yukon was open for occupation, the date for microblades at GHB 2 (roughly 9000–7000 B.P.), and the marked correspondence in several microcore attributes between those at GHB 2 and those at sites in interior Alaska argue rather strongly for a dispersal of peoples with a microcore and blade tradition out of central Alaska and into southeastern Alaska beginning 9,000 to 10,000 years ago.

Not included in this distribution were the microcores and blades from the Telegraph Creek locality in north-central British Columbia (Smith 1971). Here microcores were apparently made on split bifaces in a technique somewhat analogous to the Shirataki technique of northern Japan. The location of the sites near large supplies of obsidian may have occasioned the different stages of microcore preparation, but as such it is quite a departure from the microcore types at GHB 2.

Turning to microcores made of materials other than obsidian, we found that microcores of chert embodied attributes shared by those of obsidian. One particular core was made on a flake with the lateral surfaces having once been the dorsal and ventral surfaces of a flake. The platform was prepared on one of the flake edges by steep flaking. Microblades were then driven off along the edge of the flake (parallel to the flake surface). The technique is somewhat reminiscent of that employed by artisans who produced the Donnelly burin (scraper) (West 1967: Figures 8a and 8b). A somewhat analogous technique of utilizing flakes for microcores has been noted by Fladmark on the Queen Charlotte Islands (1970, 1972).

Microblades of quartz crystal have been available from the 1965 and 1971 excavations, but the microcores were not recovered until the summer of 1973. These cores are not yet available for analysis and will not be discussed here.

The remaining microcores, and the most numerous, are those of argillite. This material has been altered by being subjected to intense heat and pressure as the beds were cut by andesite dikes. The material is tough and requires considerable flaking force. The platform is a single flake surface or a natural cleavage plane. The flute surfaces are marked by single to multiple flake scars. Hinge fractures are common on the flute surfaces of the argillite microcores, indicating the toughness of the material. The argillite microcores are more massive, with fairly wide flake scars on the flute surface. There is little evidence of removal of the platform-edge overhang, perhaps indicating that rather thick blades were commonly detached. Core rotation is a usual feature of these cores. The general shape of the argillite microcores ranges from a somewhat wedge shape to a blocky cuboid form with a flat base often as broad as the striking platform. Single microblade scars have been found on an odd assortment of tabular pieces of argillite. These either were rejected core preforms or were utilized for the production of a single ridge flake.

In seeking comparable microcore types, the closest analogies lie to the south and at the extreme of the hypothesized spread of peoples into a forest-adapted economy utilizing microblades (Borden 1968; Dumond 1969). The microcores collected by Fladmark from several localities in the Queen Charlotte Islands have a striking platform based on a single flake scar resulting from the splitting of pebbles of argillaceous slate, chert, and basalt (Fladmark 1972:6). Fladmark also found that the platforms of the split-pebble microcores do not show any evidence of core platform rejuvenation nor platform-edge preparation (1972:6). The core shape tends toward the cuboid. Sanger, in a study of core-and-blade traditions in the Pacific northwest (1968), has noted that the basalt microcores from the Lehman site have platforms based upon a single flake scar but, unlike the microcores of argillite from GHB 2, are characterized by battering, crushing, or grinding of the core edge to remove the overhang on the flute face (Sanger 1968:97). Microcores with unfaceted platforms occur at Ryegrass Coulee near Vantage, Washington, but again with extensive core-edge preparation (Sanger 1968:100). The microcores from Lehman and Ryegrass Coulee have wedge-shaped keels. The attribute similarity for platform preparation is high between interior Plateau microcores and GHB 2 argillite microcores, but when core-edge preparation or core shape is considered, the forms are divergent. Greater overall similarities are then seen with the Queen Charlotte microcores. In the Gulf of Georgia region, microcores of cuboid form with or without platform preparation are found at Whalen Farm, Marpole, San Juan Islands, Cadboro Bay, Fraser Canyon (Milliken site), and others (Sanger 1968; Borden 1968). Interestingly, it is in this area that microcores of quartz crystal are found. Sanger has proposed (1968:111) that the quartz-crystal microcore preparation as dictated by the structure of the quartz crystal was by extension applied to other materials. He does not state that quartz crystal served as the earliest medium for microblade production in the area, but this is perhaps the implication. At GHB 2, the quartz-crystal microcores are contemporaneous with the obsidian, chert, and argillite microcores, and it is not possible to discern any prior usage of one material as against another in the site. The Georgia coast microcores are parallel-sided to somewhat expanding at the base (Sanger 1968:111) and thus are comparable in form to the argillite microcores from GHB 2. They depart in terms of a modified striking platform.

The first impression, then, is that the attribute similarity of the GHB 2 microcores to microcores from other regions is a result of the lithic materials utilized, i.e. the particular manufacturing modes associated with working a specific lithic substance. The question then arises, are the manufacturing techniques material-specific? The answer seems to be, at this writing, perhaps in part, but certainly not totally. Obsidian and quartz crystal do require core platform modification. Chert may, but argillite or basalt certainly do not. The obsidian cores at GHB 2 are most like the Campus-type cores of central Alaska, which were mainly made of chert. The parallel-sided, cuboid-shaped argillite cores are derived from tabular or blocky pieces of argillite marked by well-defined bedding planes (analogous to the structural dictates of prismatic crystals?). But then there are the somewhat wedge-shaped argillite cores. Other factors than material or tightly circumscribed lithic traditions seem to be involved. The length, width, strength, etc., of microblades are dynamics that need to be explored for each of the various lithic materials by resorting to experimental reduplication and usage.

The technological attributes we note may not be simply material-specific within a given manufacturing mode but may reflect a greater dimension of the knapper's world. The evidence from GHB 2 appears to indicate that the occupants knew several different procedures for manufacturing different types of cores and how to adapt these microcore types to different lithic materials. By varying core style and materials they were able to produce microblades that may have served different purposes.

Microcores and microblades are tundra to boreal-forest adaptations that have extensive distributions in both time and space. Their appearance on the northwestern coast of North America is interpreted as movement of interior, riverine peoples to an estuarine or lacustrine context. As such, microblades are tool forms that may chronicle the movements of peoples, as has been suggested by several authors (Anderson 1970; Borden 1968; Dumond 1969; Sanger 1968). The GHB 2 microcores and microblades have temporally and spatially added to this chronicle and have perhaps, through the diversity of core types and lithic materials used, suggested a broader dimension of the knapper's art to investigators.

REFERENCES

ACKERMAN, R. E.
  1968   The archeology of the Glacier Bay region, southeastern Alaska. *Report of Investigations 44.* Laboratory of Anthropology, Washington State University.
  1974   "Post-Pleistocene cultural adaptations on the northern northwest coast," in *Proceedings of the International Conference on the Prehistory and Palaeoecology of the Western Arctic and Sub-Arctic,* 1–20. Calgary.
ANDERSON, D. D.
  1970   Microblade traditions in northwestern Alaska. *Arctic Anthropology* 7(2):2–16.
BORDEN, C.
  1962   "West coast crossties with Alaska," in *Prehistoric cultural relations between the arctic and temperate zones of North America.* Edited by J. M. Campbell, 9–19. Arctic Institute of North America Technical Paper 11. Montreal.
  1968   New evidence of early cultural relations between Eurasia and western North America. *Proceedings of the VIIIth International Congress of Anthropological and Ethnological Sciences* 3:331–337.
COOK, J.
  1968   Some microcores from the western boreal forest. *Arctic Anthropology* 5(1):121–127.
DE LAGUNA, F.
  1960   *The story of a Tlingit community: a problem in the relationship between archeological, ethnological and historical methods.* Bureau of American Ethnology Bulletin 172. Washington, D.C.
  1972   Under Mount Saint Elias: The history and culture of the Yakutat Tlingit. *Smithsonian Contributions to Anthropology* 7, parts 1–3. Washington, D.C.
DE LAGUNA, F., F. A. RIDDELL, D. F. McGEEIN, D. S. LANE, J. A. FREED, C. OSBORNE
  1964   *Archeology of the Yakutat Bay area, Alaska.* Bureau of American Ethnology Bulletin 192. Washington, D.C.
DENTON, G. H., M. STUIVER
  1967   Late Pleistocene glacial stratigraphy and chronology, northeastern St. Elias mountains, Yukon Territory, Canada. *Geological Society of America Bulletin* 78:485–510.
DUMOND, D.
  1969   Towards a prehistory of Na-Dene with a general comment on population movements among nomadic hunters. *American Anthropologist* 71:857–863.

FLADMARK, K.
   1970   Preliminary report on the archaeology of the Queen Charlotte Islands: 1969 field season. *B.C. Studies* 6 and 7:18–45.
   1972   "Early microblade industries on the Queen Charlotte Islands, British Columbia." Paper presented at the Fourth Annual Meeting of the Canadian Archaeological Association, Calgary.

HAMILTON, T.
   1972   "Geological investigations, Ground Hog Bay, Alaska." Unpublished manuscript.

JOHNSON, F., H. M. RAUP
   1964   Investigations in southwestern Yukon: geobotanical and archeological reconnaissance. *Papers of the Robert S. Peabody Foundation for Archaeology* 6:1–198.

MacNEISH, R.
   1964   Investigations in southwest Yukon: archaeological excavations, comparisons, and speculations. *Papers of the Robert S. Peabody Foundation for Archaeology* 6:201–471.

MAUGER, J.
   1971   "The manufacture of Campus site microcores." Unpublished manuscript.

SANGER, D.
   1968   Prepared core and blade traditions in the Pacific northwest. *Arctic Anthropology* 5(1):92–120.

SMITH, J. W.
   1971   The Ice Mountain microblade and core industry. Cassiar district, northern British Columbia, Canada. *Arctic and Alpine Research* 3(3):199–213.

WEST, F. HADLEIGH
   1967   The Donnelly Ridge site and the definition of an early core and blade complex in central Alaska. *American Antiquity* 32:360–382.

SECTION THREE

Paleodemography

Introduction

Human osteological remains have traditionally been dealt with by metrical analysis. There is an increasing trend to look for nonmetrical features as being more sensitive indicators of small population differences or of differential interaction of biology and culture. The papers in this section deal with some more traditional methods for determining mortality curves and paleopathological indications of general population health, in addition to some new variants of studies that provide us with finer control of population interaction at the village level and of population differentiation based on shifts between more nomadic hunters and gatherers and more sedentary agriculturalists.

The fragmentary and incomplete nature of the remains that archaeologists recover is often a major problem. Sometimes this incomplete record is due to decay and other natural processes leading to destruction of the bones, and at other times it is due to cultural processes associated with burials. Thus methods must be devised to extract the greatest possible amount of information from such fragmentary specimens. Ericksen's study of microstructural remodeling among Amerindian populations reaffirms the fact that such systems are age-dependent. While the results clearly demonstrated age dependency for the patterns of osteons and haversian canals, sexual dimorphism could not be observed at this level. However, differences between populations studied showed that there were apparently cultural factors, not yet isolated, which affected rates of remodeling. These factors were most evident in females and thus may be related to dietary patterns during pregnancy and lactation. Such microstructural studies are important in relating biology to culture.

The paper by Lallo, Rose, and Armelagos projects other hypotheses for the interaction of cultural patterns of local populations and their nutritional state as recorded osteologically. For the populations studied (from late Woodland cultures in Illinois, ca. A.D. 800–1500), they suggest that increased reliance upon agriculture, increased population density and sedentarism, and increased extent and intensity of trade will lead to a generally less adequate diet (due to heavy reliance on only one or two food resources produced agriculturally), increased levels of malnutrition (due both to poorer diet and to higher population densities), and increased infectious disease (due to increased contact through trade and to increased susceptibility resulting from poorer health). This should be reflected in increased mortality in both subadult and adult populations and also in higher rates of malnutrition and infectious disease pathologies being recorded for the populations. The studies undertaken indicate that ecological changes, such as shifts to full-time agriculture, are apparently reflected in biological parameters such as retardation in growth, increase in infectious disease pathologies, and increase in the rate of mortality.

Buikstra, focusing on a slightly earlier population in Illinois (middle Woodland culture, ca. 300 B.C. to A.D. 800), is concerned with the development of a methodology for studying relationships between local populations by epigenetic distance in terms of a series of nonmetric traits. Such traits are particularly useful because they can be used advantageously on fragmentary remains when it is not possible to employ more traditional metric measures. The populations of this study had clusters of traits not wholly explicable in terms of biological parameters such as geographic distance and associated genetic drift and isolation. Buikstra calls upon added factors in terms of social distance and concomitant cultural adjuncts to provide the total explanation. The proposed methodology has potential in providing some insights into both prehistoric sociology and demography.

Casteel's paper centers on yet another aspect of archaeological demography. In northwestern North America, about 4000 B.C., there was a major shift in settlement pattern and resource use, marked by a florescence of sea-mammal hunting, fishing, and marine exploitation at the expense of the previous emphasis upon caribou and inland hunting patterns. Casteel points out that, while terrestrial game may have been a limiting factor during earlier time periods, with the adoption of marine exploitation, much greater population densities are possible. Thus there are new limiting factors with this new subsistence technology in terms of the carrying capacity of fish resources, factors which hold in general for all coastal populations above 60° north latitude.

An Ecological Interpretation of Variation in Mortality Within Three Prehistoric American Indian Populations From Dickson Mounds

JOHN LALLO, JEROME CARL ROSE, and
GEORGE J. ARMELAGOS

Death is the ultimate response an organism is capable of making to any given stressful situation. If viewed as such, mortality patterns may reflect the levels of intensity of stress to which an organism is exposed. Cook (1971:16) has suggested that malnutrition, disease, and mortality form an interactive system the effects of which are to increase the sources and/or intensity of stress to which organisms in a given population are exposed. In this context stress is defined as "the state manifested by a specific syndrome which consists of all the nonspecifically induced changes in a biological system" (Selye 1956:3).

Bengoa (1949:716), in referring to the inflated childhood mortality due to episodes of protein–calorie deficiency and the interaction of this deficiency and disease, states; "Early childhood mortality is much increased in such situations. This effect is so marked in the age group 1–4 years that mortality has been proposed as a useful measure of malnutrition and disease where more direct measures cannot be carried out." Bengoa illustrated that during the subadult age intervals (0–15 years) mortality due to malnutrition and disease can be inflated as much as 30 to 40 percent (for similar examples, see Garn 1966; Flores 1966; Malcolm 1970; Frisancho 1970a, 1970b; and Neel 1970).

In a similar analysis Scrimshaw (1966:63–74), in a study of village agriculturalists from Guatemala, demonstrated the relationship between subsistence patterns, protein–calorie deficiency, disease, and increased subadult mortality. Mortality was inflated by 20 to 40 percent due to deaths resulting from the influence of the interaction of malnutrition and disease (especially infectious disease). He compared these results with a Columbian village in which childhood mortality rates fell by as much as one-half to four-fifths when federal health services introduced medical and nutritional programs. The medical programs treated infectious disease while the nutritional program provided protein-supplemented diets for children.

Furthermore, in the same study Scrimshaw points out that in under-developed countries, especially those practicing single-crop agriculture that yields high-carbohydrate, low-protein produce, infectious disease and malnutrition are "synergistic" (i.e. the effects of the interaction of the two are more severe than the effects of each acting independently).

The effects of synergism are expressed, generally speaking, as malnutrition lowers or inhibits the body's defensive mechanisms while at the same time infectious diseases further tax the body's already lowered resources. At the same time, the infectious disease, by further depleting the body's resources, increases the acuteness and severity of the malnutrition. This, once again, further increases the severity of the disease episode. Thus, a cycle is generated that is broken only by proper treatment of both the malnutrition and the infectious disease, or by death.

This principle is illustrated by Scrimshaw (1966:65) when he states, "Infectious disease, usually precipitated by malnutrition, increases metabolic rate, as do requirements for tissue repair in sepsis and trauma, and gastrointestinal infections hamper the absorption of nutrients. Thus, disease episodes can frequently generate further severe protein malnutrition." In general, antibody production and tissue barriers to infection are reduced or absent in moderate to severe malnutrition, permitting a great increase in both mortality and morbidity resulting from the interaction of disease and malnutrition in childhood (see Dubos 1965:147–169, for a further discussion of the relationship of disease and malnutrition). A study by Woodruff (1966) demonstrated that in children with protein deficiency the gamma globulin level in the blood was much lower than in children with adequate nutritional resources. The implication of this study is that one of the biochemical outcomes of malnutrition is the lowering of the body's systemic ability to combat disease.

One of the most common expressions of the interaction of malnutrition and infectious disease in children is the occurrence of "weaning diarrhea" (Stini 1971; Behar 1968; Scrimshaw 1964). As the name suggests, weaning diarrhea primarily affects infants who are just beginning to utilize sources of food other than mother's milk. In agricultural populations, the weaning diet usually consists of high-carbohydrate, low-protein foods. Examples are weaning diets in which either maize, cassava, sweet potatoes, or plantains predominate (Dubos 1968:60; Stini 1971:417). A common result of such diets is malnutrition, which, in combination with common bacterial infections, can generate weaning diarrhea. In its most severe form, weaning diarrhea causes extreme dehydration, muscle wastage and, in the infants affected, a high rate of mortality.

STATEMENT OF PROBLEM

The implications of the suggestions of Cook (1971:16) and Bengoa (1949) are that malnutrition and/or disease are stress-producing mechanisms whose ultimate expression is an increase in subadult mortality. Scrimshaw (1966:74) has also demonstrated that increased or continued exposure to infectious disease will result in an increase in adult mortality.

Mortality, it would appear, is greatly inflated in both adults and subadults when malnutrition and/or infectious disease are present. The conclusion follows that as malnutrition and/or infectious disease increase within a population, there should be corresponding increase in mortality for both subadults and adults of that population.

If these suggestions are examined within the framework of the cultural/ecological circumstances of Dickson Mounds, some inferences can be made regarding mortality patterns, their variation, and possible causative or influential agents.

Hypothesis

Based upon the suggestions of Cook, Bengoa, and Scrimshaw, our hypothesis predicts that as malnutrition and infectious disease increase in the Dickson Mounds populations there will also be a corresponding increase in both subadult and adult mortality. Put into a specific cultural context, the hypothesis predicts that as malnutrition and infectious disease increase in the Mississippian, relative to the late Woodland and Mississippian acculturated late Woodland, there will also occur a corresponding increase in both subadult and adult mortality rates for the Mississippians.

ARCHAEOLOGY AT DICKSON MOUNDS

In general, the archaeological material has demonstrated that the late Woodland group was characterized as a small semisedentary population (75–125) occupying two seasonal camps. The subsistence base of the late Woodland group was a hunting-and-gathering technology, which, from an analysis of the floral and faunal remains, appears to have supplied them with a mixed and balanced food supply. An analysis of artifactual remains from camp refuse and grave offerings has suggested limited trade contact with surrounding groups of the lower central Illinois Valley.

The Mississippian acculturated late Woodland had a larger population (500–600) and was settled in a permanent village site (Eveland). During the Mississippian acculturated late Woodland period a gradual alteration occurred in the subsistence base; hunting and gathering were being supplemented with the cultivation of maize. Toward the end of this cultural period (A.D. 1200) material items began to appear in village refuse and graves, which suggests the beginning of local trade networks. At first, the trade appears to have been carried on within the lower Illinois Valley, but it later expanded to reach as far north and west as Minnesota and as far south as Florida.

The Mississippian represents the culmination of all these trends. For example, the Mississippian village site, Myer, was a permanently settled community of relatively high population density (950–1,050 individuals). Furthermore, an analysis of artifactual remains from the village refuse and Mississippian grave offerings suggests that the Mississippians were heavily involved in extensive and far-reaching trade networks.

With regard to their subsistence base, the Mississippians relied almost exclusively upon the cultivation of maize. Maize appears abundantly in village refuse, in storage pits and jars, and as the exclusive food employed in grave offerings. Also of importance to note is that as maize cultivation increased, hunting and gathering decreased in intensity and/or productivity. This inference is suggested by the archaeological data which demonstrate a decrease in the frequency of occurrence of the remains of wild flora and fauna in village refuse, and a decrease in the frequency of blades, points, and scrapers with a complementary increase in the appearance of grinding implements and hoes. The suggestion made in this paper is that the Mississippians had low-protein, high-carbohydrate diets based primarily upon the consumption of maize.

MATERIALS AND METHODS

The materials from Dickson Mounds provide a good test situation for the suggestion that mortality increases in response to increases in malnutrition and infectious disease. In the first place, archaeological and cultural data have indicated that malnutrition may have been a serious problem faced by the Mississippians, whereas both the late Woodland and Mississippian acculturated late Woodland may have enjoyed varied and balanced diets. Secondly, the analysis of pathological conditions suggests that infectious disease had a high incidence in the Mississippian but a rather low incidence in the other two populations. Thirdly, a sufficient amount of skeletal material has been recovered to permit the calculation of life tables for the analysis of response of mortality to alterations in cultural/ecological relationships.

Human Material

The demographic data were obtained from the analysis of 595 burials excavated during the 1966–1967 field seasons from the Dickson Mounds site. These burials were aged, sexed, and assigned to their appropriate cultural groups.

The sample distribution consisted of the following: 114 burials were assigned to the late Woodland; of these 42 (37.7 percent) were judged to be between 0 and 15 years and 72 (62.3 percent) were determined to be adults, aged between 15 and 65 years. Of these adults 41 (56.0 percent) were males and 31 (44.0 percent) were females. The Mississippian acculturated late Woodland sample contained 224 burials, of which 102 (45.5 percent) were determined to be between 0 and 15 years of age and 122 54.5 percent) were assigned adult status. Of the adults, 61 (50.0 percent) were males and 61 (50.0 percent) were females. The Mississippian sample had a total of 219 burials, of which 110 (51.0 percent) were classified as subadults (0 to 15 years) and 109 (49.0 percent) were assigned adult status (15 to 65 years). Of the adults, 61 (55.0 percent) were females and 48 (45.0 percent) were males.

The Life Table as a Research Tool in Paleodemography

In the analysis of a skeletal series, mortality, as represented by the actual dead, is the most readily observable phenomenon. The problem for the researcher is to find the best possible method to analyze and interpret these data. Swedlund and Armelagos (1969:3) point out that calculating life tables is probably the most meaningful quantitative technique for dealing with mortality. By utilizing the life-table method, a researcher is able to build a model and draw correlations between age, mortality, and sex. These correlations can then be expressed as a percentage or a graph; once quantified in this manner, the data are easier to handle and comparison among populations is facilitated. More importantly, once the life table has been constructed, it can be used as a means for answering additional questions about the demographic processes of a population, such as length of life, fertility, sex, ratios, size of the population, death rate, and life expectation at each age interval.

As can be seen, the life table permits the researcher to make a broader range of analyses and to achieve a higher level of generalization, thus facilitating comparative studies. Previously the most common presentations of skeletal information revolved around age and sex estimates of the individuals, and from these two survivorship and sex ratio could be derived; however, little beyond this could be achieved with regard to demographic processes. The life table, by noting age and mortality by sex, permits an intensive analysis of demographic processes. One of the major advantages of the life table is that it enables the determination of these processes without a knowledge of the total population size. This is very advantageous because of the multitude of uncontrolled variables when trying to estimate population size from archaeological or skeletal remains. If a large sample is used, it can be expected that the sample will reflect the demographic processes of the population (Ascadi and Nemeskeri 1970:57–58).

With the knowledge provided by the life table and an adequate understanding of the cultural data of an archaeological site, the researcher has a unique body of cultural–ecological evidence that can be reviewed for factors affecting the demographic processes of the population. Likewise, knowledge of the demographic processes may yield evidence to help explain some of the cultural–ecological manifestations. By quantifying demographic and cultural–ecological data in this manner, the researcher is capable of going beyond the interpretive level of some of the usual methods of presentation. The incorporation of graphic representations into the life table may help to clarify demographic processes further, especially in relation to the cultural–ecological data. Thus, for example, fluctuations in the nature of mortality with respect to age may uncover critical age intervals in the lifetime of the individual when he is most or least susceptible to death. This knowledge, coupled with the cultural–ecological data, may help illuminate the nature and severity of the stresses operating on the population. As a result, the researcher may be provided with firsthand knowledge of the processes of biological and cultural adaptation to a given set of environmental conditions.

However, Angel (1969) criticizes the use of the life table in paleodemography and offers several "useful guesses" (1969:432) to be used in reconstructing the demographic processes of skeletal populations. Angel believes that constructing a life table, especially of life expectancy (probably one of the most informative calculations that can be made), is biologically unrealistic and that it rests on three false assumptions (1969:428). These assumptions are (1) "that the cemetery represents a single generation cohort", (2) "that death rates are even at all ages after infancy and hence directly reflected in cemetery age frequencies"; and (3) "that the population is virtually stable biologically and socially over the period of cemetery use."

Swedlund and Armelagos (1969:5) propose the use of the composite life table developed by field ecologists and, in so doing, point out that "use of the life table in paleodemography is not dependent upon the assumption that the cemetery under study represents a single generation cohort." The authors go on to point out that although life tables are based on the *concept* of following a cohort through time, demographers, when constructing a life table, study all age groups within a specific amount of time in a specific area. Consequently, the authors conclude that "to apply the life table to a cemetery population, only two assumptions are necessary, and these two assumptions are given: that the population occupies a specific area, and that the cemetery covers a specific amount of time." Ascadi and Nemeskeri (1970:62) echo this feeling when they state that "we may regard all the dead as if they had been born at the same time and their mortality represented that of one cohort, and with constant conditions the mortality of various cohorts will be the same, whatever the date of birth." However, one point must be kept in mind. Because of variation in the composition of each succeeding birth cohort, life tables constructed from cross-sectional data (a sampling of many birth cohorts at the same point in time, which is exactly what a cemetery sample may give) can reflect reality only when the sample is representative. Howell-Lee (1971:14) indicates that if this condition of large sample size is fulfilled and if it can be assumed that the population has been exposed to a stable stress experience, then the percentage of deaths over a certain age interval derived from a cross-sectional (cemetery) study is as meaningful a measure of mortality as that derived from a single-cohort study. As mentioned earlier, it is imperative to have cultural data on the population. The data should enable the investigator to determine whether the level of stress had remained relatively constant for the period of time during which the site was occupied. If this type of data is not available or if it indicates that the level of stress has fluctuated, then a cross-sectional study may present a picture that does not reflect reality. The crucial variables appear to be large sample size, controlled excavation techniques, and adequate cultural reconstruction. If the research situation can fulfill these conditions, then it can be expected that the resulting picture will represent reality, and under these conditions Angel's first criticism is not valid. However, as a guidline, the criticism should be kept in mind.

Angel's second criticism states that death rates are assumed to be even at all ages after infancy and hence are directly reflected in cemetery age frequencies. Swedlund and Armelagos (1969:2) point out that while it is true that the investigator assumes that cemetery age frequencies reflect the death rate of the various age intervals of the subject population, it is not true that death rates are assumed to be even for all ages after infancy. Ascadi and Nemeskeri (1970:62–65) point out that if a large sample size is used and if adequate cultural data can indicate that cultural processes such as mortuary practices have not skewed the age or sex distribution of the cemetery population, then it is reasonable to assume that death rates in the skeletal population will accurately reflect the death rates of the population.

Once a life table has been calculated it is possible to note fluctuations in mortality for the various age intervals. As pointed out earlier in this paper, such information can then provide insight into the critical age periods during an individual's lifetime, indicating that period when he is most or least susceptible to stress and hence disease or death. Consequently, it can be seen that death rates are not assumed to be even at all ages after infancy.

Angel's third criticism is that it must be assumed that the population is virtually stable biologically and socially over the period of cemetery use. Swedlund and Armelagos (1969:2) point out that this assumption is not necessary in applying the composite life table: "The important distinction in this case is that for any time span covered by the life table, the population must be assumed reasonably stable." The job of the investigator is to define accurately the time span covered by the skeletal population. Once this is accomplished, the use of controlled excavation techniques and available cultural data can indicate fluctuations in population stability. For example, through the use of controlled excavation techniques it may be possible to determine that a given site represents more than one time and/or cultural period (i.e. differences in grave goods, burial position or structure, and mortuary practices may indicate a site stratified according to either time period or culture or both). In such a case, the site may then be divided into several time or cultural levels and a life table (or tables) can be constructed for each (see, for example, Swedlund and Armelagos 1969). By doing this, the investigator will be able to demonstrate any fluctuations in the demographic processes for the different time and/or cultural periods. If the site is not stratified or if the archaeological materials and burial practices indicate that the site represents a single cultural and/or time period (admittedly, some time spans may be rather long), then appropriate cultural data may be utilized to make inferences regarding population stability. For example, evidence may be presented on possible migrations, epidemics, or warfare, any of which may affect population stability.

Ascadi and Nemeskeri (1970:45) express this idea in a rather extreme form when they point out that except for a few times and in a few places, human population numbers have been increasing exceedingly slowly, perhaps not all, and that over periods of hundreds of years population levels were stationary. They also mention that between A.D. 1 and the middle of the seventeenth century the world population doubled. During this time the annual rate of increase was only 0.05–0.10 persons per thousand. For the length of one, two, or even three generations, the population did not grow significantly. One need not accept this rather dubious generalization to accept the idea of a stationary population. Large sample size, adequate cultural data, and controlled excavation techniques will help set the limits within which generalizations can be made about demographic processes in a given population.

Angel has not been alone in criticism of the use of life tables. Howell-Lee (1971) has advanced several criticisms, some of which are similar to

Angel's. The criticisms are as follows (1971:16–17): (1) because the number of infant and childhood deaths are underrepresented in a skeletal population, the researcher is at a loss as how to interpret mortality in age groups over 50; (2) some estimate of the rate of growth of the population during the period of time the skeletons were buried must be made in order to interpret the relative numbers of skeletons of different ages, and in prehistoric populations there is no basis to do this; (3) due to the cohort effect (differential birth-group experience) in a growing or declining population, the age composition of each cohort is determined not only by mortality but also by the size of succeeding cohorts, and consequently, a cross-sectional analysis of various cohorts may not present a picture that reflects reality; (4) if age determinations of skeletal material are made according to a "rubber yardstick," it is not possible to gain anything at all by the use of model stable populations.

In regard to Howell-Lee's first criticism, we would respond that it is true that in most skeletal series the number of infant and childhood deaths are underrepresented as a result of either differential preservation, negligent excavation, or burial practices (in many societies infants are not buried in the same area as adults, or are not buried at all). However, she fails to realize that in the computation of a life table, age-specific life expectancy (e_x^0) is influenced primarily by the succeeding age groups and not the preceding. Consequently, computation and comparison can be made of life expectancy and mortality for ages older than the infant group whose representativeness may be questioned. Ascadi and Nemeskeri (1970:39) point out that:

Concerning the span of human life, one of the most important results can be obtained directly from the distribution of deaths. It is this distribution that tells us the length of life attained by most people, or, more directly, the age at which most people die. Although there is a generally experienced high mortality of infants, really important information on the normal age at death is derived from the number of deaths at more advanced ages.

It should be kept in mind, however, that although infant deaths are underrepresented, they are not completely lacking. Consequently, if controlled excavation techniques are employed, some remains (e.g. dentition) will be recovered and some information can be projected regarding demographic processes. In most cases in which sufficient infant and childhood remains have been recovered, the remains have usually been excluded or, occasionally, whatever material was present was used. In either case, it should be kept in mind that some very important information can be lost. This loss in no way invalidates the computation of the remainder of the life table, but limits imposed by this condition should be kept in mind and generalizations made accordingly.

The second and third criticisms are closely related and can be discussed together. It should be noted that these criticisms are similar to Angel's criticism that states that the researcher must assume the population to be stable biologically and socially over the period of cemetery use. Howell-Lee assumes that the rate of growth of the skeletal population must be estimated for the time period during which the skeletal remains were accumulated. If the conditions (as discussed earlier in this paper in response to Angel) of large sample size, controlled excavation techniques, and adequate cultural data are met by the skeletal series, then the investigator should be in a position to determine whether or not his series meets the criteria of a model stable population. Howell-Lee (1971:17) characterizes a model stable population as a "slowly growing population with moderate to high fertility" and goes on to point out that it is a useful model for primitive societies. We would point out that the life table can have utility in archaeological populations even if it cannot be applied to model stable populations.

Likewise, Howell-Lee's third criticism (that because of the cohort effect a cross-sectional study of a population will not reflect reality) is based on the assumption that the model stable population theory cannot be validated for a skeletal series. Again, we would respond that if conditions permit large sample size, controlled excavation, and adequate cultural data, a researcher can then infer whether or not his series conforms to a stable population. If the answer is affirmative, then a cross-sectional study would produce results as meaningful as those derived from a single-cohort study. Howell-Lee (1971:14) points this out herself. The crucial point is that the investigator be supplied with enough data to determine whether or not his series reflects a stable population. If the series does reflect such a population condition, then the results of a cross-sectional analysis should reflect a true picture of the population. If the series does not or cannot (because of lack of data) conform to a stable population model, then the results of analysis may not reflect reality. This criticism of Howell-Lee in no way invalidates the use of life tables in paleodemography; it does, however, call for more stringent controls in making assumptions and generalizations about prehistoric demographic processes, and this word of caution is justified.

In her final criticism, Howell-Lee directs an attack against the "rubber yardstick" employed by physical anthropologists for making age determinations on skeletal populations. She concludes that nothing meaningful can be gained by using life tables based on such age determinations. Although the idea of the criticism is valid (nothing meaningful can be gained if such age determinations are employed), we would seriously object to the implication that all physical anthropologists employ aging techniques that are no better than a rubber yardstick. With regard to our aging techniques, we would suggest that the best we can do at present is to make age estimates and interpretations from them in accordance with the limits of our current technical ability.

From this brief review of the criticisms of using the life table as a research tool in paleodemography, it is clear that its use has not been invalidated or seriously impaired. However, when one is constructing a life table, these criticisms should be kept in mind because they do illuminate several potential sources of error.

On the positive side, Swedlund and Armelagos (1969) point out that the composite life table is well suited to human archaeological populations. This opinion is based on the following:

(1) Archaeological populations (particularly prehistoric ones) did not experience the rapid nutritional and medical improvements common in present-day human populations; therefore, their environmental relationships, in regard to aging and mortality, can be considered more constant than today, and of less influence on their mortality rates through time. (2) Composite life tables have been satisfactorily constructed for natural animal populations using the same types of techniques available to the physical anthropologist, i.e., skeletal aging techniques. . . . (3) Archaeological sites provide a unique situation in which controls on such things as dating, sampling, and areal considerations are superior to those available for nonhuman populations. This can be very important; for example: by careful stratigraphic excavation of burials we may find that the mortality rates at one level are different from those at another. Thus, the stratigraphic controls may suggest that the two components cannot be treated as one, since the age-specific mortality rates have changed through time. Stratigraphic control may also permit us to identify the cultural–ecological factors which account for the change in mortality rates. (4) The archaeological site, being a microgeographic unit, insures homogeneity of stresses on morbidity and mortality, as well as of genetic factors. (5) The fact that the individual skeletons cannot be aged to the exact year does not invalidate the life table. Age classes, other than exact years, are frequently used in abridged forms of all types of life tables.

Although there are limitations to the use of life tables as a research tool in paleodemography, it has been demonstrated that they can provide useful insights for the analysis of skeletal populations. Their most important characteristic is the depth of analysis that they permit. By constructing composite life tables and graphing survivorship and mortality, a researcher is presented with a clear, concise, and quantified statement about the basic demographic processes of a population. By calculating mortality by sex for different age intervals, the researcher may uncover critical age periods during which one or the other sex, or both, are most or least susceptible to death. Using these data in conjunction with cultural information, the investigator may be able to reach conclusions regarding the nature of the ecological relationship. This, in turn, may provide insight into the basic nature of the biocultural processes involved in the adaptation of an organism to its total environmental context. Furthermore, by quantifying biocultural data, the composite life table permits quick and meaningful comparison of the demographic processes of two or more populations. Consequently, we would suggest that the composite life table is not only valid but also an essential research tool in paleodemography.

Weiss (1973) has reiterated this feeling by demonstrating the utility of life tables in anthropological research, whether this research is carried out on a contemporary or an archaeological population. Weiss has applied concepts of the stationary population theory to anthropological data and has developed a series of model life tables based on those data. The utility of Weiss's life tables lies in their rather comprehensive frame of reference; they incorporate the full range of mortality and fertility data reported in the anthropological literature. Also, in addition to the standard entries for life tables, Weiss has included data on such parameters as crude birth rate, mean family size, generation length, and dependency ratio.

These additional parameters can provide the researcher working with skeletal populations with new sources of information that may permit inferences on aspects of demographic processes not heretofore possible. Weiss's suggestions regarding the construction of life tables and their application under given circumstances provide a useful guideline to any anthropologist interested in utilizing demographic data and/or techniques of analysis.

The Life Table: Method of Computation

Life tables are, according to Ascadi and Nemeskeri (1970:45–50), of two kinds, depending upon the source of data used. The first type is the dynamic or generation life table, corresponding to the methods of Graunt, who used it for the first time in the seventeenth century for studying mortality in London (Graunt 1662). This method is based on the analysis of the complete life cycle of a single cohort, from birth to the death of the last member. As can be seen, this type of life table can be used only when an investigator has complete census data for the entire cohort and its total time span. Obviously this method is ill-suited to a prehistoric skeletal population lacking written records. The second type of life table is the time-specific or current life table. In this type of life table all ages are studied within a given time period in a given area. This type of life table is also not suited to an archaeological population; such variables as exact age, date of birth, or date of death would be lacking for a skeletal series.

However, there is a third type, the one most suited to paleodemographic research, the composite life table, which has been developed by field ecologists and game managers (see, for example, Quick 1960). The composite life table is based on the age of animals at death; this is usually determined through kill records (tagged game) or natural mortality observations. Its major advantage for archaeological use is that it is not based on the exact year of birth or death of the animal (it might be recalled that this property of the composite life table assists in neutralizing the cohort effect and the criticisms of a cross-sectional study). The underlying assumption is that even though the animals may represent several generations (a situation that may be encountered in an archaeological site), the series is assumed not to have undergone, through time, significant changes in the probability of dying with respect to each age interval (Quick 1960). It is clear that this assumption may be easier to validate (by the use of large sample size, controlled excavation, and adequate cultural data) for an archaeological series than for a natural animal population. Consequently, the demographic processes of a sample, at any given time, may be assumed to reflect the nature of the demographic processes of the population.

Quick (1960) provides a concise summary of the construction of a composite life table based on the model used by field ecologists and game managers. The life table consists of a series of vertical columns for calculation of the following: (1) x, the age interval; (2) d'_x, the actual number dead in age class x (in a skeletal population, the number of skeletons, male and female, found for each age interval x); (3) d_x, the d'_x value expressed as a percentage of a cohort of 1,000 individuals; (4) l_x, the number of individuals living at age x; (5) q_x, the probability of dying at age x; (6) L_x, the number of individuals in the life table population alive between age x and $x + 1$; (7) e^0_x, the life expectancy, or mean lifetime remaining to those individuals attaining age x.

Estimation of the above values is as follows: x represents the assigned age value expressed either as a number or as a range; d'_x is the actual observed number of deaths at age x; d_x is the d'_x value represented as a percentage of a cohort of 1,000 individuals; l_x is the survivorship, computed by subtracting the deaths in age interval x from the survivors entering this age interval; q_x, the mortality rate, is computed by dividing the number of individuals dying by the number of individuals living and can be expressed as $q_x = d'_x/l_x$; L_x, the mean number of individuals alive between age x and $x+1$, is calculated as

$$L_x = \frac{l_x + (l_x + 1)}{2}.$$

The final column e^0_x is found by taking the sum T_x of L_x values from the bottom of the L_x column to the age interval being calculated and dividing by the l_x: ($e^0_x = L_{x_1} + L_{x_2} \ldots L_x)l/l_x$, or T_x/l_x. For an application of this method to an archaeological population, see Swedlund and Armelagos (1969). It should be mentioned that the e^0_x value is usually calculated in age intervals and must, therefore, be converted into years.

The Statistical Analysis

The mortality data from Dickson Mounds have been treated in a number of ways. The first procedure was to compare the populational mortality frequency across the three cultural groups. This was accomplished by first determining for each population the age-specific mortality frequency (the d_x value of the life table) for each of the age classes between 0 and 65 years, and expressing these values as the cumulative frequencies of mortality for that population. Next, the cumulative frequencies of the three populations can be statistically tested to determine if a significant difference existed across the three populations. The Kolmogorov–Smirnov test was employed to test for the differences.

In general, the Kolmogorov–Smirnov test (Siegel 1956:127–138) for two samples is a test of whether two independent samples have been drawn from the same population, or from a population with the same distribution. This two-tail test is quite sensitive to any kind of difference in the distribution from which the two samples were drawn. The test is based upon the assumption that if the two samples have, in fact, been drawn from the same population distribution, then the cumulative distributions of both samples may be expected to be fairly close to each other inasmuch as they both show only random deviations from the populational distribution. If, however, the two-sample cumulative distributions are too far apart at any given point, this suggests that the samples come from different populations. Applied to the cumulative distribution of mortality, the Kolmogorov–Smirnov test should indicate if a difference in mortality exists among the three populations.

Once mortality patterns have been examined across the three populations, they will then be analyzed within each population to determine if a sex differential exists in mortality. This can be accomplished by first determining within each population separately the age-specific mortality frequency for males, then for females, for each of the age classes between 0 and 65 years and expressing these values as the cumulative frequencies of mortality for males and females respectively. Next, the cumulative frequencies for males and for females of a population can be statistically tested to determine if there is a sex differential with regard to mortality.

The Kolmogorov–Smirnov one-tail test can be employed to test for sample differences within a single population. Applied to the mortality data, the Kolmogorov–Smirnov one-tail test will demonstrate if there is a difference between male and female mortality within a given population.

The interpretation of results from the analysis of mortality data can then be undertaken within the framework of the cultural/ecological circumstances at Dickson Mounds. Specifically, the interpretation of mortality is based upon the resultant effects of the interaction between malnutrition and infectious disease.

RESULTS AND DISCUSSION

Mortality Frequencies for Ages 0 to 65 Years Compared Across Populations

Mortality data for the late Woodland, shown in Table 1, the Mississippian acculturated late Woodland, shown in Table 2, and the Mississippian, shown in Table 3, are derived from the life tables computed for each of the populations.

A comparison of the life tables reveals some interesting differences. For example, relative to the late Woodland and Mississippian acculturated late Woodland, the d_x value (age-specific mortality) and the q_x value (probability of dying) are consistently higher in all age classes of the Mississippian. Similarly, the l_x value (survivorship) and e_x^0 value (life expectancy) are consistently lower in all age classes of the Mississippian.

Table 1.   Life table for the late Woodland, Dickson Mounds, A.D. 1050–1150 (ages 0–65)

x	d_x'	d_x	l_x	q_x	L_x	e_x^0
0–1	11	96	1,000	105	947.5	5.55
1–2	7	61	895	68	864.5	5.20
2–5	7	61	834	73	803.5	4.50
5–10	10	88	773	114	729.0	4.00
10–15	7	61	685	89	654.5	3.20
15–25	14	123	624	197	562.5	2.50
25–35	12	105	501	210	448.5	2.00
35–45	16	140	396	354	326.0	1.40
45–55	20	175	256	656	172.0	0.84
55–65	10	88	88	1,000	44.0	0.50
Total	114	1,000	0			

Table 2.   Life table for the Mississippian acculturated late Woodland, Dickson Mounds, A.D. 1150–1250 (ages 0–65)

x	d_x'	d_x	l_x	q_x	L_x	e_x^0
0–1	38	143	1,000	143	928.5	5.40
1–2	19	88	857	103	813.0	5.20
2–5	18	50	769	65	744.0	4.70
5–10	18	50	719	70	694.0	4.00
10–15	9	27	669	40	655.5	3.20
15–25	39	149	642	201	567.4	2.40
25–35	19	92	493	187	447.0	2.00
35–45	20	130	401	324	336.0	1.20
45–55	34	244	271	900	149.0	0.60
55–65	10	27	27	1,000	13.5	0.50
Total	224	1,000	0			

Table 3. Life table for the middle Mississippian, Dickson Mounds, A.D. 1250–1350 (ages 0–65)

x	d_x'	d_x	l_x	q_x	L_x	e_x^0
0–1	48	219	1,000	219	890.5	4.10
1–2	19	87	781	111	737.5	4.60
2–5	16	73	694	105	657.5	4.20
5–10	17	78	621	126	582.5	3.60
10–15	10	46	543	185	520.0	3.00
15–25	23	105	497	241	444.5	2.30
25–35	24	110	392	281	337.0	1.74
35–45	27	123	282	436	220.5	1.22
45–55	25	113	159	911	102.5	0.79
55–65	10	46	46	1,000	23.0	0.50
Total	219	1,000	0			

Survivorship and probability of dying are graphically represented in Figures 1 and 2 respectively; life expectancy is summarized in Table 4.

The differences observed appear to outline a general trend of changes that may have occurred in the demographic parameters between the late Woodland and the Mississippian. This trend is consistent throughout all age classes and seems to indicate a general increase in mortality during the Mississippian.

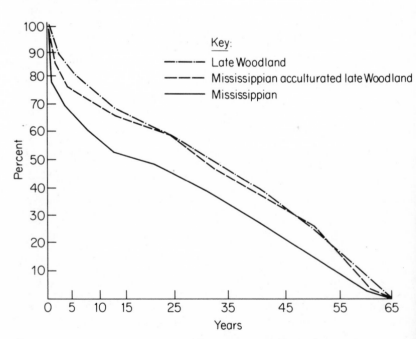

Figure 1.   Survivorship curve for the three populations (ages 0–65)

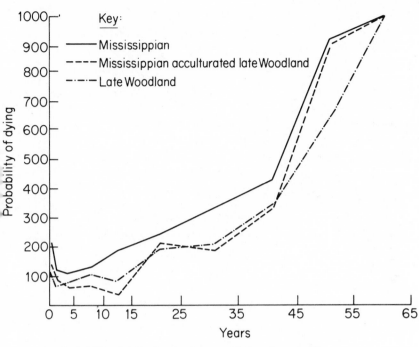

Figure 2. Probability of dying for the three populations (ages 0–65)

Table 4. Summary of life expectancy in years (ages 0–65, sexes combined)

Age	Late Woodland	Mississippian acculturated late Woodland	Mississippian
0–1	21	19	11
1–2	27	27	21
2–5	30	32	27
5–10	35	35	31
10–15	37	37	35
15–25	40	39	38
25–35	45	45	41
35–45	49	47	46
45–55	53	52	52
55–65	60	60	60

When the cumulative frequencies of mortality are graphed, as in Figure 3, and compared for the age classes between 0 and 65 years for the three populations, it becomes evident that overall mortality is consistently relatively higher during the Mississippian than in either of the other two populations. The Kolmogorov–Smirnov two-tail test on the cumulative distributions of mortality for the late Woodland and the Mississippian

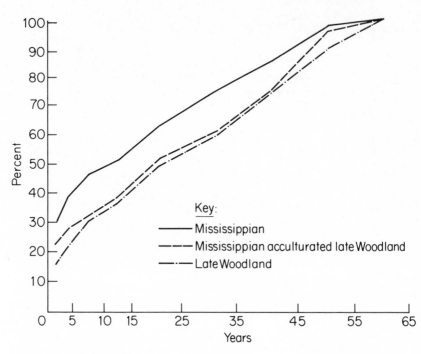

Figure 3.   Cumulative percentages of mortality for the three populations (ages 0–65)

acculturated late Woodland, as seen in Table 5, demonstrates that the difference observed between the two populations is not significant. Consequently, the assumption can be made that there is no difference in mortality between the two populations.

However, the Kolmogorov–Smirnov two-tail test, when applied to the cumulative distributions of mortality for the late Woodland and the Mississippian, indicates that at the 0.05 ($p = 0.95$) level there is a significant difference in the cumulative frequencies of mortality for the two populations, as shown in Table 6. The differences between the cumulative frequencies of mortality of the two populations appear to be greatest in the 0–15 year (subadult) segment of the population; the differences observed between the adults (15–65 years) of the two populations are not quite as high as the differences observed in subadult mortality. In fact, the largest and most significant difference observed in subadult mortality occurs in the 2-to-5-year age class. It is worth mentioning, at this point, that Bengoa (1949:716) has suggested that early childhood mortality, especially in the ages 1–4 years, may be a reflection of malnutrition and disease within a population.

Similarly, the Kolmogorov–Smirnov two-tail test, when applied to the cumulative distributions of mortality for the Mississippian acculturated late Woodland and the Mississippian, demonstrates that at the 0.05

Table 5. Results of Kolmogorov–Smirnov test for late Woodland and Mississippian acculturated late Woodland (ages 0–65, sexes combined)

Age	Cumulative percentage of mortality: late Woodland	Difference	Cumulative percentage of mortality: Mississippian acculturated late Woodland
1–2	15.7	7.4[a]	23.1
2–5	21.8	6.3	28.1
5–10	30.6	2.5	33.1
10–15	36.7	0.9	35.8
15–25	49.0	1.7	50.7
25–35	59.5	0.4	59.9
35–45	73.5	0.6	72.9
45–55	91.2	6.1	97.3
55–65	100.0	0	100.0
Total n	114		224

Values for levels of significance:

one tail: $p = 0.90$ $\quad p = 0.95$ $\quad p = 0.975$ $\quad p = 0.99$ $\quad p = 0.995$

two tail: $p = 0.80$ $\quad p = 0.90$ $\quad p = 0.95$ $\quad p = 0.98$ $\quad p = 0.99$

$$1.07\sqrt{\frac{m+n}{mn}} \quad 1.22\sqrt{\frac{m+n}{mn}} \quad 1.36\sqrt{\frac{m+n}{mn}} \quad 1.52\sqrt{\frac{m+n}{mn}} \quad 1.63\sqrt{\frac{m+n}{mn}}$$

$$1.36\sqrt{\frac{114+224}{25{,}536}} = 0.1561[b]$$

[a] Denotes the largest difference between the two populations.
[b] Denotes the critical value.

Table 6. Results of Kolmogorov–Smirnov test for late Woodland and Mississippian (ages 0–65, sexes combined)

Age	Cumulative percentage of mortality: late Woodland	Difference	Cumulative percentage of mortality: Mississippian
1–2	15.7	14.9	30.6
2–5	21.8	16.1[a]	37.9
5–10	30.6	15.1	45.7
10–15	36.7	13.6	50.3
15–25	49.0	11.8	60.8
25–35	59.5	12.3	71.8
35–45	73.5	10.6	84.1
45–55	91.2	4.2	95.4
55–65	100.0	0	100.0
Total n	114		219

Values for the levels of significance:

one tail: $p = 0.90$ $\quad p = 0.95$ $\quad p = 0.975$ $\quad p = 0.99$ $\quad p = 0.995$

two tail: $p = 0.80$ $\quad p = 0.90$ $\quad p = 0.95$ $\quad p = 0.98$ $\quad p = 0.99$

$$1.07\sqrt{\frac{m+n}{mn}} \quad 1.22\sqrt{\frac{m+n}{mn}} \quad 1.36\sqrt{\frac{m+n}{mn}} \quad 1.52\sqrt{\frac{m+n}{mn}} \quad 1.63\sqrt{\frac{m+n}{mn}}$$

$$1.36\sqrt{\frac{114+219}{24{,}966}} = 0.1573[b]$$

[a] Denotes the largest difference between the two populations.
[b] Denotes the critical value.

($p = 0.95$) level there is a significant difference in the cumulative frequencies of mortality for the two populations, as shown in Table 7. It is also evident that the differences in mortality are greatest in the age classes of the subadult segment (0–15 years) of the population. This trend is similar to the one noted between the late Woodland and the Mississippian; these significant trends will be represented graphically.

When the age-specific mortality frequencies are graphed for the age classes between 0 and 65 years for the three populations, as in Figure 4, it is evident that higher mortality during the Mississippian is reflected in the figures for mean age at death. For example, the mean age at death for the late Woodland population (subadults and adults) is 25.8 years; for the Mississippian acculturated late Woodland it is 25.7 years; while for the Mississippian population it is 18.4 years. The vital statistics for the three populations are summarized in Table 8.

Table 7.   Results of Kolmogorov–Smirnov test for Mississippian acculturated late Woodland and Mississippian (ages 0–65, sexes combined)

Age	Cumulative percentage of mortality: Mississippian acculturated late Woodland	Difference	Cumulative percentage of mortality: Mississippian
1–2	23.1	7.5	30.6
2–5	28.1	9.8	37.9
5–10	33.1	12.6	45.7
10–15	35.8	14.5[a]	50.3
15–25	50.7	10.1	60.8
25–35	59.9	11.9	71.8
35–45	72.9	11.2	84.1
45–55	97.3	1.9	95.4
55–65	100.0	0	100.0
Total n	224		219

Values for levels of significance:

one tail: $p = 0.90$ $p = 0.95$ $p = 0.975$ $p = 0.99$ $p = 0.995$

two tail: $p = 0.80$ $p = 0.90$ $p = 0.95$ $p = 0.98$ $p = 0.99$

$1.07\sqrt{\dfrac{m+n}{mn}}$ $1.22\sqrt{\dfrac{m+n}{mn}}$ $1.36\sqrt{\dfrac{m+n}{mn}}$ $1.52\sqrt{\dfrac{m+n}{mn}}$ $1.63\sqrt{\dfrac{m+n}{mn}}$

$$1.36\sqrt{\dfrac{224+219}{49{,}056}} = 0.1289^{\text{b}}$$

[a] Denotes the largest difference between the two populations.
[b] Denotes the critical value.

Mortality Frequencies for Ages 0 to 15 Years Compared Across Populations

By separating the mortality data and the graphic illustrations into subadult (0–15 years) and adult (15–65 years) segments of the populations,

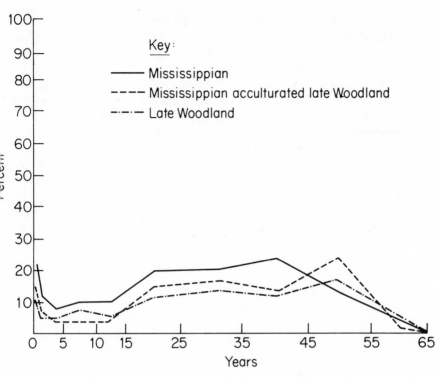

Figure 4. Age-specific mortality rate for the three populations (ages 0–65)

Table 8. Summary of the vital statistics for the three populations (ages 0–65)

Population	Mean age at death (in years)
Late Woodland	
total population	25.8
subadults (age 0–15)	5.8
adults (age 15–65)	38.9
adult males	37.6
adult females	40.3
Mississippian acculturated late Woodland	
total population	25.7
subadults (age 0–15)	4.9
adults (age 15–65)	38.5
adult males	37.4
adult females	39.5
Mississippian	
total population	18.4
subadults (age 0–15)	2.7
adults (age 15–65)	33.5
adult males	35.5
adult females	33.4

the researcher can be supplied with a clearer picture of the processes involved and their pattern and direction. Also, by treating the adult segment of the population separately, the investigator can generate inferences regarding sex differences in mortality.

If the cumulative frequencies of death for the subadults (0–15 years) of the three populations are graphed, as in Figure 5, it is demonstrated that mortality is consistently higher for Mississippians in all age classes between 0 and 15 years. A comparison of mortality frequencies reveals that in the late Woodland 37.7 percent (42) of the population died prior to reaching the age of 15 years; in the Mississippian acculturated late Woodland 37.0 percent (93) died prior to age 15; while in the Mississippian 51.0 percent (110) died prior to the age of 15 years.

Although Blakely (1971) does not provide data on the late Woodland or the Mississippian acculturated late Woodland, his analysis of 479 Mississip-

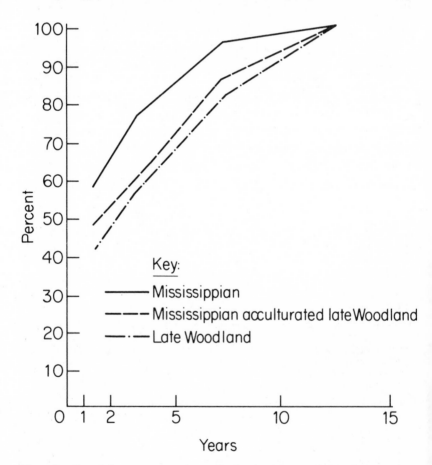

Figure 5.   Cumulative percentage of mortality for the three populations (ages 0–65)

pian burials from Dickson Mounds reports that by age 15 almost 54 percent of the population had died. In a similar analysis, Harn (1971), working with 234 Mississippian burials *in situ* at Dickson Mounds, reports that 50 percent of the population had died prior to the age of 15.

If age-specific mortality is graphed and compared for the age classes between 0 and 15 years for the three populations, as in Figure 6, it becomes evident that the distribution of deaths in the three populations differs somewhat. Mortality is initially high for the first few years following birth with a gradual tapering off in the later years of childhood. In fact, in the late Woodland and the Mississippian acculturated late Woodland, mortality declines in later childhood and adolescence, while remaining consistently high for the Mississippians.

This trend in mortality is reflected in the mean age at death for the subadults of the three populations. For subadults of the late Woodland,

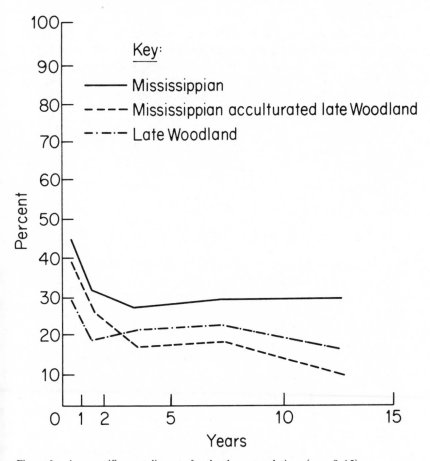

Figure 6.   Age-specific mortality rate for the three populations (ages 0–15)

mean age at death is 5.8 years, for the Mississippian acculturated late Woodland it is 4.9 years, and for the Mississippian it is 2.7 years (see Table 8). Likewise, this mortality trend is also reflected in the life expectancies of the subadults (see Table 4) and the probability of dying. For example, in the age class 0–1 year, life expectancy is 21 years and the probability of dying is 105/1000 for the late Woodland; these figures for the Mississippian acculturated late Woodland are 19 years and 143/1000, respectively; and for the Mississippian 11 years and 219/1000, respectively. These patterns are consistently found for life expectancy and probability of dying in all age classes of subadults and are even carried over into the mortality patterns observed in adults.

Mortality Frequencies for Ages 15 to 65 Years Compared Across Populations

In graphing the cumulative frequencies of mortality for the age classes between 15 and 65 years for males of the three populations, as in Figure 7, it becomes evident that mortality is consistently higher for the Mississippian males. If the age-specific mortality frequencies are likewise graphed for the males of the three populations, as in Figure 8, it is seen

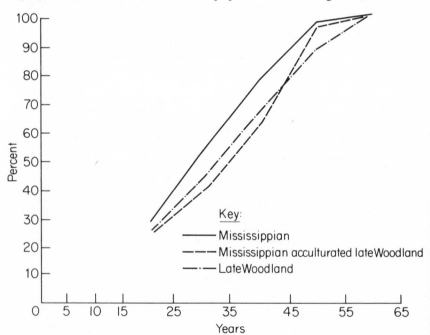

Figure 7.   Cumulative percentage of mortality for males of the three populations (ages 15–65)

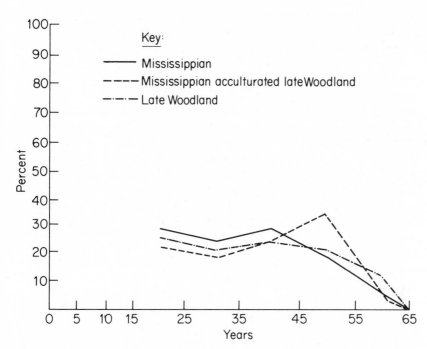

Figure 8. Age-specific mortality rate for males of the three populations (ages 15–65)

that there is a differential distribution of deaths according to age. The data indicate that males of the Mississippian died at somewhat younger ages; their peak death rate occurs between the ages of 35 and 45 years, whereas males of the late Woodland and the Mississippian acculturated late Woodland reach their death peak between the ages of 45 and 55 years.

Graphing the cumulative frequencies of mortality for the age classes between 15 and 65 years for females of the three populations, as in Figure 9, demonstrates a very obvious differential in female mortality. This differential would appear to suggest a somewhat higher mortality rate for female Mississippians. The mortality pattern for females of the late Woodland represents a gradual incremental increase with age, whereas, though females of the Mississippian acculturated late Woodland follow a similar trend, between the ages of 35 and 45 years they experience a sharp increase in mortality, great enough so that in the ages 55–65 years, the females of the Mississippian acculturated late Woodland have a mortality frequency almost as high as Mississippian females, while late Woodland females still display a somewhat lower frequency.

The age-specific mortality frequencies for females of the three populations illustrate the differential distribution of deaths for the age classes between 15 and 65 years, as shown in Figure 10. An examination of this

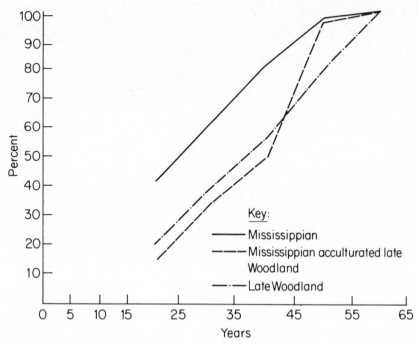

Figure 9.   Cumulative percentage of mortality for females of the three populations (ages 15–65)

figure reveals that not only are mortality frequencies higher for Mississippians but they died at considerably younger ages. The peak death period for Mississippian females is between the ages of 25 and 35 years, while for females of the late Woodland and the Mississippian acculturated late Woodland it is between 45 and 55 years. The trend toward higher mortality in Mississippian females is reflected in the mean age at death. For example, the mean age at death for late Woodland females is 40.3 years and for Mississippian acculturated late Woodland females it is 39.5 years, while for Mississippian females it is 33.4 years. These figures suggest almost a seven-year differential between the mean age at death for late Woodland and Mississippian females.

The data represented in Figure 10 also reveal an interesting trend in the mortality patterns of females in all three populations. The graphs demonstrate a gradual increase in female mortality that begins at about age 20, reaches a peak at about age 30, and then gradually declines to a low at age 40, at which point mortality begins to increase again, reaching a peak between the ages of 45 and 55 years and then declining. This trend is evident in the female mortality graphs of all three populations. An interesting speculation at this point would be that the inflated female mortality between the ages of 20 and 40 years may reflect an increase in female deaths due to difficulties experienced in childbearing.

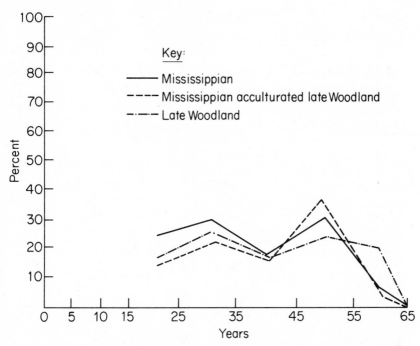

Figure 10. Age-specific mortality rate for females of the three populations (ages 15–65)

A Comparison of Male and Female Mortality Within Each Population

By introducing sex as one of the variables, it is then possible to make comparisons between adult male and female mortality frequencies within any given population. Such a procedure makes it possible to generate inferences on mortality patterns not only between populations but also within a population. Because sex determinations were not made on the subadults, no inferences can be made regarding sex differentials in sub-adult mortality patterns.

In graphing the cumulative frequencies of mortality for adult males and females of the late Woodland, as in Figure 11, it is observed that mortality frequencies are higher for males than for females. This trend begins in early adulthood and continues throughout all the age classes between 15 and 65 years. The graph also illustrates that the differences between male and female mortality frequencies increase somewhat between the ages of 30 and 55 years. The Kolmogorov–Smirnov one-tail test, shown in Table 9, has indicated that the differences observed between male and female mortality are not significant and may therefore be due to random variation.

If the age-specific mortality frequencies are graphed for adult males

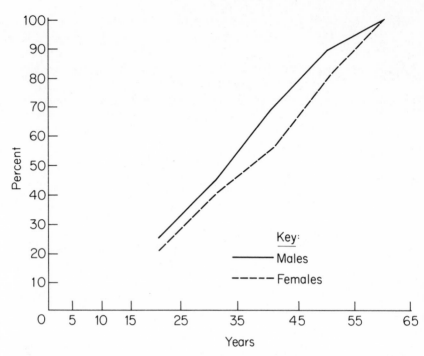

Figure 11.   Cumulative percentage of mortality for males and females of the late Woodland (ages 15–65)

Table 9.   Results of Kolmogorov–Smirnov test for late Woodland males and females (ages 15–65)

Age	Cumulative percentage of mortality: males	Difference	Cumulative percentage of mortality: females
15–25	25.0	5.0	20.0
25–35	45.5	5.5	40.0
35–45	68.2	11.1[a]	57.1
45–55	88.6	8.6	80.0
55–65	100.0	0	100.0
Total n	41		31

Values for levels of significance:

one tail:	$p = 0.90$	$p = 0.95$	$p = 0.975$	$p = 0.99$	$p = 0.995$
two tail:	$p = 0.80$	$p = 0.90$	$p = 0.95$	$p = 0.98$	$p = 0.99$
	$1.07\sqrt{\dfrac{m+n}{mn}}$	$1.22\sqrt{\dfrac{m+n}{mn}}$	$1.36\sqrt{\dfrac{m+n}{mn}}$	$1.52\sqrt{\dfrac{m+n}{mn}}$	$1.63\sqrt{\dfrac{m+n}{mn}}$

$$1.22\sqrt{\frac{41+31}{1,271}} = 0.2902^{b}$$

[a] Denotes the largest difference between the two sexes.
[b] Denotes the critical value for late Woodland males and females.

and females of the late Woodland as in Figure 12, it is observed that there is a somewhat different distribution of mortality. Males appear to be dying at a somewhat younger age. As can be seen by the graph, peak periods of male mortality occur between the ages of 15 and 25 years and again between 35 and 45 years. Female mortality, on the other hand, reaches its first peak between the ages of 25 and 35 years and its second peak between the ages of 45 and 55 years. The graph also illustrates that female mortality frequencies are higher between the ages of 50 and 65 years.

This trend in mortality is reflected in the difference in mean age at death for males and females. The mean age at death for late Woodland males is 37.6 years, while for females it is 40.3 years. The data appear to suggest that males are dying younger; this would account for the higher female mortality found between the ages of 50 and 65 years. The point must be made that the differences observed in the age-specific distribution of mortality may be due only to random variation.

When the cumulative frequencies of mortality are graphed for adult males and females of the Mississippian acculturated late Woodland as in Figure 13, it can be noted that male mortality is higher between the ages of 20 and 45 years, at which time female mortality becomes greater and

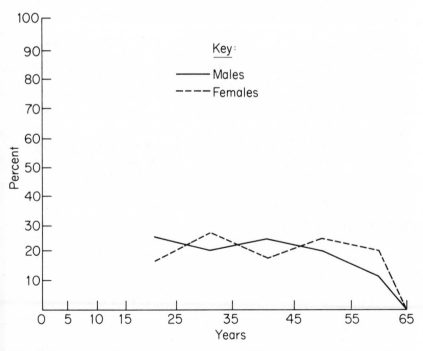

Figure 12.   Age-specific mortality rate for males and females of the late Woodland (ages 15–65)

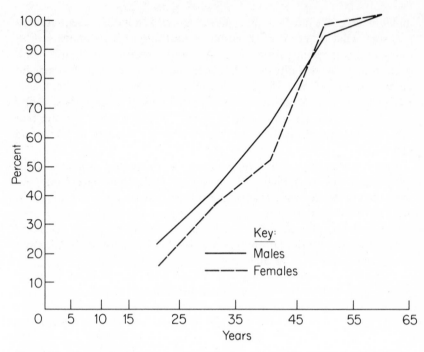

Figure 13.   Cumulative percentage of mortality for males and females of the Mississippian acculturated late Woodland (ages 15–65)

continues so until age 65. The increase in female mortality, it may be noted, begins at about age 40. The results of the Kolmogorov–Smirnov one-tail test, shown in Table 10, indicate that the differences observed between male and female mortality are not statistically significant and may therefore be due only to random variation.

Graphing the age-specific mortality frequencies for adult males and females of the Mississippian acculturated late Woodland, as in Figure 14, indicates a somewhat different distribution in male and female mortality. The results suggest that males may be dying at a younger age than females. For example, male mortality is higher in the 15 to 25 year interval, decreases by age 30, then gradually increases until it reaches a peak between the ages of 45 and 55 years. Female mortality on the other hand is low for the 15-to-25-year interval and gradually increases to a peak between the ages of 25 and 35 years, after which it declines until age 40, at which point it increases sharply to a second peak between the ages 45 and 55 years. It can also be noted that between the ages of 45 and 55 years female mortality is higher than male mortality.

These trends in mortality are reflected in differences in the mean age at death for males and females. For example, the mean age at death for Mississippian acculturated late Woodland males is 37.4 years, while for

Table 10. Results of Kolmogorov–Smirnov test for Mississippian acculturated late Woodland males and females (ages 15–65)

Age	Cumulative percentage of mortality: males	Difference	Cumulative percentage of mortality: females
15–25	22.1	2.9	25.0
25–35	40.0	5.3	34.7
35–45	63.1	11.7[a]	51.4
45–55	95.7	1.5	97.2
55–65	100.0	0	100.0
Total n	61		61

Values for the levels of significance:

one tail:	$p = 0.90$	$p = 0.95$	$p = 0.975$	$p = 0.99$	$p = 0.995$
two tail:	$p = 0.80$	$p = 0.90$	$p = 0.95$	$p = 0.98$	$p = 0.99$
	$1.07\sqrt{\dfrac{m+n}{mn}}$	$1.22\sqrt{\dfrac{m+n}{mn}}$	$1.36\sqrt{\dfrac{m+n}{mn}}$	$1.52\sqrt{\dfrac{m+n}{mn}}$	$1.63\sqrt{\dfrac{m+n}{mn}}$

$$1.22\sqrt{\frac{61+61}{3,721}} = 0.2206^{b}$$

[a] Denotes the largest difference between the two sexes.
[b] Denotes the critical value for Mississippian acculturated late Woodland males and females.

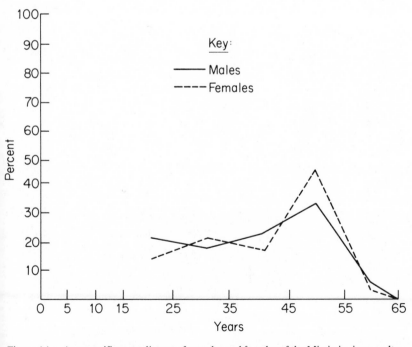

Figure 14. Age-specific mortality rate for males and females of the Mississippian acculturated late Woodland (ages 15–65)

the females it is 39.5 years. However, it must be noted that the differences observed in the age-specific distribution of mortality may be due only to random variations.

The graph for the cumulative frequencies of mortality for adult males and females of the Mississippian in Figure 15 illustrates a trend in mortality somewhat different from that observed in either of the other populations. The results appear to suggest that during the Mississippian female mortality was higher than male mortality. The differences are most noticeable between the ages of 20 and 50 years, at which point the increase in male mortality is sufficient to bring the two frequencies close to each other. The results of the Kolmogorov–Smirnov one-tail test given in Table 11 indicate that the differences observed in the cumulative frequencies of mortality are not significant and may therefore be due to random variations.

The age-specific mortality frequencies for males and females of the Mississippian graphed in Figure 16 suggest that females are dying at a younger age. Female mortality appears to be quite high between the ages of 15 and 25 years, after which it shows a steady decline until age 40, where it levels off and then begins declining again. Male mortality, on the other hand, is high between the ages of 15 and 25 years (though not as

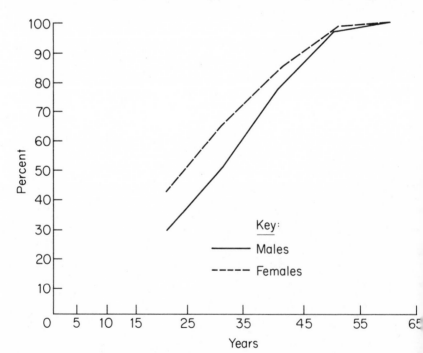

Figure 15.   Cumulative percentage of mortality for males and females of the Mississippian (ages 15–65)

Table 11. Results of Kolmogorov–Smirnov test for Mississippian males and females (ages 15–65)

Age	Cumulative percentage of mortality: males	Difference	Cumulative percentage of mortality: females
15–25	27.3	13.7	41.0
25–35	48.5	13.8[a]	62.3
35–45	75.8	4.6	80.4
45–55	94.9	1.9	96.8
55–65	100.0	0	100.0
Total n	48		61

Values for the levels of significance:

one tail: $p = 0.90$ $p = 0.95$ $p = 0.975$ $p = 0.99$ $p = 0.995$

two tail: $p = 0.80$ $p = 0.90$ $p = 0.95$ $p = 0.98$ $p = 0.99$

$$1.07\sqrt{\frac{m+n}{mn}} \quad 1.22\sqrt{\frac{m+n}{mn}} \quad 1.36\sqrt{\frac{m+n}{mn}} \quad 1.52\sqrt{\frac{m+n}{mn}} \quad 1.63\sqrt{\frac{m+n}{mn}}$$

$$1.22\sqrt{\frac{48+61}{2,928}} = 0.2352^{b}$$

[a] Denotes the largest difference between the two sexes.
[b] Denotes the critical value for Mississippian males and females.

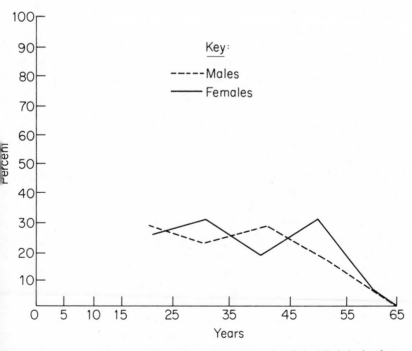

Figure 16. Age-specific mortality rate for males and females of the Mississippian (ages 15–65)

high as for females), after which it declines until age 30, at which point it begins to increase and reaches a peak between the ages of 35 and 45 years, then declines steadily until the age of 65 years. These trends are reflected in the differences in the mean age at death; for Mississippian males it is 35.5 years, while for Mississippian females it is 33.4 years.

An interesting point to note is the depth and scope of analysis that can be derived from the life table, which provides the investigator with several vantage points from which to view the data. For example, by computing and graphing the cumulative frequencies of mortality in a population, it is possible to obtain an overall picture of the nature, direction, and intensity of mortality within that group. Also, computing the cumulative frequencies of mortality facilitates comparison of mortality on a cross-populational basis and provides a means whereby statistical analyses may be undertaken. By graphing age-specific mortality, it is possible to obtain a picture of the distribution of deaths in each age class, thus noting periods of greater or lesser susceptibility to stress and/or periods of greater or lesser levels of stress.

Furthermore, separating the data into subadult and adult segments of the population provides a basis for the comparison of mortality frequencies of infants, children, adolescents, and adults, on both an intrapopulational and an interpopulational basis. Likewise, separating males and females makes it possible to note sex differentials with regard to mortality on both an intra- and an interpopulational basis.

By utilizing these various approaches, the investigator is permitted a more intensive analysis of mortality which may facilitate populational comparisons and generate a broader range of inferences regarding the interrelationships of age, sex, culture, and mortality.

SUMMARY OF DEMOGRAPHIC PARAMETERS

Skeletal material from three prehistoric American Indian populations from Dickson Mounds has been analyzed to test the suggestion that a high incidence of malnutrition and infectious disease will be reflected in correspondingly high frequencies of mortality, especially in the subadult (0–15 years) segment of the population. Put into the specific cultural context of Dickson Mounds, the suggestion was made that there would be a higher relative frequency of mortality for the Mississippian than for either the late Woodland or the Mississippian acculturated late Woodland.

In general, the results suggest that the cumulative frequencies of mortality for the age classes between 0 and 65 years are significantly higher for the Mississippian than for either the late Woodland or the Mississippian acculturated late Woodland. The Kolmogorov–Smirnov two-tail test indicates that these results are significant at the 0.05 ($p = 0.95$) level. The results also demonstrate that the probability of dying is higher for Mississippians between the ages of 0 and 65 years, while mean age at death, life expectancy, and survivorship are lower than for either of the other two populations. As pointed out earlier, probability of dying, mean age at death, life expectancy, and survivorship are direct functions of mortality frequencies. The Kolmogorov–Smirnov two-tail test indicated that there were no differences in mortality between the late Woodland and the Mississippian acculturated late Woodland.

When mortality data are separated into subadults, adult males, and adult females, the results appear to suggest that mortality frequencies were higher in all three of these categories of Mississippian relative to the corresponding categories for either of the other populations. Likewise, the probability of dying is higher, while mean age at death, life expectancy, and survivorship are lower than in the other two populations.

Mortality frequencies for adult males and females were compared with each other on an intrapopulational basis. The results appear to suggest that during both the late Woodland and the Mississippian acculturated late Woodland male mortality frequencies were higher than those of females, while during the Mississippian, female mortality was higher than male mortality. However, the results of the Kolmogorov–Smirnov one-tail test on adult male and female mortality frequencies of each population indicate that these differences are not significant and may therefore be due only to random variation.

REFERENCES

ANGEL, J. L.
  1969   The basis of paleodemography. *American Journal of Physical Anthropology* 30:427–437.
ASCADI, G. Y., J. NEMESKERI
  1970   *History of human life span and mortality.* Budapest: Akademia.
BEHAR, MOISES
  1968   "Food and nutrition among the Maya before the conquest and at the present," in *Biomedical challenges presented by the American Indian.* Pan American Health Organization.
BENGOA, M.
  1949   Some implications for the broad assessment of the magnitude of PCM in children. *American Journal of Clinical Nutrition* 7:714–720.
BLAKELY, ROBERT L.
  1971   Comparison of the mortality profiles of Archaic, middle Woodland and middle Mississippi populations. *American Journal of Physical Anthropology* 34(1):43–53.
COOK, D.
  1971   "Patterns of nutritional stress in some Illinois Woodland populations." Unpublished M.A. thesis, University of Chicago.
DUBOS, R.
  1965   *Mankind adapting.* New Haven: Yale University Press.
  1968   *Man, medicine, and environment.* New York: Mentor.

FLORES, I.
   1966   Food intake of Guatamalan Indian children ages 1 to 10 years. *Journal of the American Dietetic Association* 48:480–487.
FRISANCHO, A. R.
   1970a   Unequal influence of low dietary intakes on skeletal maturation during childhood. *American Journal of Clinical Nutrition* 23:1,220–1,227.
   1970b   Childhood retardation resulting in reduction of adult body size due to lesser adolescent skeletal delay. *American Journal of Physical Anthropology* 33:325–336.
GARN, S. M.
   1966   "Malnutrition and skeletal development in the pre-school child," in *Pre-school child malnutrition*. NAS–NCR. Washington, D.C.
GRAUNT, JOHN
   1662   *Natural and political observations . . . made upon the Bills of Mortality . . . with reference to the government, religion, trade, growth, ayre, and diseases of the said city.* London.
HARN, A.
   1971   *The prehistory of Dickson Mounds: a preliminary report.* Springfield: Illinois State Museum.
HOWELL-LEE, N.
   1971   "The feasibility of demographic studies in small and remote populations." Paper presented at the 1971 Columbia University Ecology Seminar.
MALCOLM, L. A.
   1970   Growth and development of the Bundi child. *Human Biology* 42:293.
NEEL, J. V.
   1970   Lessons from a primitive people. *Science* 170:813–822.
QUICK, H. L.
   1960   "Animal population analysis," in *Manual of game investigational techniques*, 190–228. Edited by H. S. Mosley. Ann Arbor: Wildlife Society.
SCRIMSHAW, N.
   1964   Ecological factors in nutritional disease. *American Journal of Clinical Nutrition* 14:112–122.
   1966   "Effects of the interaction of malnutrition and infectious disease," in *Pre-school child malnutrition*, 63–74. NAS–NCR. Washington, D.C.
SELYE, H.
   1956   *The stress of life.* New York: McGraw-Hill.
SIEGEL, SIDNEY
   1956   *Non-parametric statistics for behavioral sciences.* New York: McGraw-Hill.
STINI, W. A.
   1971   Nutritional stress and growth: sex differences in adaptive response. *American Journal of Physical Anthropology* 31:417–426.
SWEDLUND, A., G. ARMELAGOS
   1969   Une recherche en paleo-démographie: la Nubie soudanaise. *Annales: Economies, Sociétés, Civilisation* 24(6):1,287–1,298.
WEISS, K.
   1973   *Demographic models for anthropology.* Memoir 27, Society for American Archaeology.
WOODRUFF, C. W.
   1966   "An analysis of the ICNND data on the physical growth of the pre-school child," in *Pre-school child malnutrition*. NAS–NCR. Washington, D.C.

Patterns of Microscopic Bone Remodeling in Three Aboriginal American Populations

MARY F. ERICKSEN

Amprino and Bairati (1936) demonstrated the microstructural remodeling that bone undergoes between fetal life and old age. They did not quantify their data, but they did show that bone changes throughout life followed a regular pattern. Jowsey (1960) used microradiography to investigate the changing pattern of cortical bone remodeling and mineralization from youth to old age. Most striking were her observations that in the elderly increasing numbers of new osteons failed to close completely, leaving widened haversian canals, that mineralization of osteons was increasingly variable, and that vascularization was increasingly interrupted by plugging of haversian canals and lacunae by calcified connective tissue.

Currey (1964) used a point-counting method to attempt to measure the changes in ratio of intrahaversian (osteonal) bone to extrahaversian (fragmental or interstitial) bone in the femoral cortex with age. He found that the osteons of older individuals were smaller and of more regular shape than those of the young and that the increase of interstitial bone with age was partly compensated for by the increase in number of haversian systems. However, he suggested that age led to decreased efficiency of the remodeling system, because many of the new, smaller osteons lay completely within the circumference of former osteons, which meant that

I am extremely grateful to the Smithsonian Institution for its hospitality during the course of this study, and specifically I wish to thank the members of the Physical Anthropology Division of the National Museum of Natural History. Dr. J. Lawrence Angel, curator, gave permission to use the collections and facilities of the division. Dr. T. Dale Stewart gave advice and encouragement and allowed me to use his large collection of casts of pubic symphyses of individuals of known age as an aid in aging skeletons. Dr. Donald J. Ortner generously allowed me to use his bone biology laboratory for preparing the thin sections and made possible the use of the Smithsonian's computer facilities. Mr. Robert S. Corruccini, a visiting scholar from the University of California at Los Angeles, gave much-needed advice and aid in the computer programming.

their vascular channels were supporting a smaller amount of bone than before. He also concluded that there was no change in size of haversian canals with age. Jowsey (1966) studied haversian systems in the femoral diaphysis of several species, including man, and directly contradicted Currey on two points. Using a different measuring technique, she concluded that osteon size was species-specific and did not change with age, but that haversian canals did change in diameter, leading to increased cortical porosity.

Kerley (1961) presented the first attempt to quantify the changes in bone microstructure with aging, with the aim of working out a system for estimating age at death, for use in forensic medicine and physical anthropology. He studied complete cross-sections from the mid-diaphysis of femur, tibia, and fibula of United States whites and blacks of known sex and age, from birth to eighty-two. The method was to count the numbers of certain structures in four standardized microscopic fields in the outer zone of the cortex. This zone was chosen because a pilot study showed that it presented the most significant and consistent changes with age. Four microstructural elements were studied; osteon number, osteon fragment number, and pseudo-haversian canal number were totaled for the four fields, and the average percentage of circumferential lamellar bone was estimated for each bone section. Kerley calculated regression formulas for each of these factors upon age and also devised a profile chart method for age estimation (Kerley 1965).

As would be expected, the study showed that osteons and fragments increased in number with age. Also, the increase in fragments is linear, while osteon number increases as a curve, concave downward (Blumberg and Kerley 1966: Figure 25). Again to be expected was the finding that circumferential lamellar bone and the pseudohaversian canals that house its vascular supply decrease with age; here the curves are concave upward. Estimation of age using these four factors was not affected by sex or race. Kerley (1961) also included such factors as osteon and haversian canal diameter in his original analysis but found them too variable to be useful, a fact that may explain the contradictory findings of Jowsey (1966) and Currey (1964).

One factor, which Kerley described but did not attempt to quantify, was the age-related shift in resorptive patterns. Resorption spaces tended to occur evenly throughout the cortex in childhood. In early adolescence they concentrated in the outer periphery. These channels filled in with haversian bone by age twenty, and resorption spaces were rare until around age fifty. At this time resorption spaces began to show up in the inner zone of the cortex, increasing in size through the sixties, until in the seventies the inner third of the cortex had the appearance of cancellous bone. A sex difference did occur in the timing of these resorptive shifts, the onset of both the late adolescent filling-in and the adult resorption in the inner cortex being earlier in females.

During his dissertation study, Kerley (1961) applied his method of histologic aging to a small sample from the Indian Knoll (Kentucky) archaeological collection and got results consistent with his findings on skeletons of modern blacks and whites of known age. By 1965 he had tried his system on other archaeological samples from the Philippines, the Aleutians, Virginia, and Florida, ranging in time depth from 500 to about 5,000 years old. He found that the specimens retained enough clarity and detail for application of his method, although in some cases it was necessary to use polarized light.

Although Kerley found that race and sex had no effect on age-related changes in the microstructures he studied, the work of Ortner (1970) suggests that certain environmental factors affecting health may influence remodeling rates and thus accelerate or retard the "normal" pattern of aging changes. The purpose of the present study is to apply Kerley's methods, with certain modifications, in an investigation of the possible effects of environmental and genetic factors upon intracortical remodeling with age in three archaeological populations.

These are the questions to be answered:

1. Can age changes be demonstrated, and if so, do the three populations differ in the way these changes take place?

2. Are there sex differences, and do the three populations differ in this respect?

3. Are there differences between the populations, and, if so, can they be related to genetic factors or to such environmental factors as life-style and diet?

4. Is it worth it? That is, in spite of the fact that true age and sex can never be determined for archaeological specimens, does such an investigation increase our knowledge of earlier populations enough to be worth the effort?

It is obvious from the outset that, as a "dry bones" physical anthropologist, I am biased toward a positive answer to the last question, or this study would never have been undertaken. We have recently become more and more conscious of the dead-end quality of studying the physical anthropology of ancient populations only from the point of view of the gross dimensions of their bones, and one symposium (Brothwell 1968) included papers ranging from paleodemography to the biochemistry of early skeletons. Thus, I consider it worthwhile to make an effort to find out what three sets of dry bones can tell us about the answers to the first three questions. The reader will have to decide for himself about the fourth.

MATERIALS AND METHODS

Populations

The three archaeological populations chosen for this study are part of the large skeletal collection of the Physical Anthropology Division of the National Museum of Natural History, Smithsonian Institution, Washington, D.C. Theoretically, it was considered desirable to confine the study to a single large racial group, while at the same time the individual populations chosen should differ widely in their environment and their cultural adaptations to the environment. The choice fell upon the Alaskan Eskimo, the Pueblo of the southwestern United States, and the Arikara of South Dakota. The latter group was chosen as representing an environment and, in many ways, a cultural adaptation midway between the other two. Genetically, the Arikara and the Pueblo are much closer to each other than to the Eskimo, who are distinguished from other American native groups by several genetic traits (Oswalt 1967; Layrisse 1968). Spencer (1965) considers the Eskimo a separate subrace of the Mongoloid stock, and Garn (1971) lists them among his "puzzling, isolated, numerically small local races" rather than among the American Indians.

The Alaskan Eskimo population studied consists of fifty-three skeletons from mainland coastal settlements ranging from Point Hope on the Arctic Ocean shore, around the Seward Peninsula, to Pastolik on the south shore of Norton Sound in the Bering Sea. This is an enormous distance and includes several tribal groups, but basically the subsistence pattern was much the same. At Point Hope the emphasis was on hunting whales from open boats, while in the southern part of the area more emphasis was placed on fishing than elsewhere, but all along the coastal stretch the dietary staple was the seal (Nelson 1969). Alaskan coastal Eskimo tended to be semisedentary, settling into permanent sod-house villages in the winter and dispersing to fishing and hunting camps in summer (Oswalt 1967). Although the skeletal material from Point Hope may be precontact, it is probable that the rest of the skeletons date only from the late nineteenth and early twentieth centuries.

The sixty-eight Pueblo Indian skeletons studied were collected in New Mexico during the excavation of Pueblo Bonito, Puye, and Hawikuh. All three sites are on the high, arid Colorado plateau, an area blessed by maximum sunshine but also plagued by the constant threat of drought and killing frosts. The Pueblo were sedentary Indians, living in permanent, elaborately constructed towns and basing their subsistence on the cultivation of corn, beans, and squash. Hunting, mostly for rabbits, was only subsidiary, as was the gathering of wild plants, and fish were considered inedible (Stewart 1965). Pueblo Bonito was abandoned about A.D. 1130 (Judd 1954). The last dendrochronological date for Puye is A.D.

1565 (Seltzer 1944), but it is probable that the site was abandoned before the Spanish reached the area, as the excavators found no trace of Spanish influence (Hewett 1909). Hawikuh continued to be inhabited until long after its conquest by the Spanish in 1540, although the skeletons in the Smithsonian collection are considered to date mainly from the late pre-Spanish and early Spanish periods (Smith *et al.* 1966).

The sixty-eight Arikara skeletons included in this study were excavated from archaeological sites along the upper Missouri River and its tributaries, mostly in a stretch between the modern cities of Pierre and Mobridge, South Dakota. Most of the material is from sites occupied during the eighteenth century before the time of extensive European contact, although a few skeletons are from earlier sites (Jantz 1970; Lehmer and Jones 1968), and another few are from the nineteenth-century Leavenworth site (Bass *et al.* 1971).

Unlike the Siouan Mandan and Hidatsa, near whom they were living at the time of the Lewis and Clark expedition in 1804, the Arikara were a Caddoan people whose closest relatives were the Pawnee of Nebraska and whose roots lay in the south (Holder 1970). They lived in settled riverside villages and in many ways had the best of two worlds. Around their villages they cultivated corn, beans, and squash, enough to supply themselves and often to provide a surplus to be sold to the nomadic "buffalo Indians" around them. But hunting the buffalo was also a basic and important part of their way of life, and the rivers were enthusiastically fished as well. Besides horticulture and hunting, a third important factor in the Arikara economy was their position as middlemen in an extensive trade network, both before and after European contact (Lehmer and Jones 1968).

Sample Size and Composition

Each skeleton was examined in its entirety to determine sex (principally on the basis of innominate bone morphology) and biological age at death, and for bone-affecting pathology that would cause exclusion from the study. Skeletons showing gross pathological changes other than simple osteoarthritis or trauma were excluded. Age determination was based on assessment of the whole skeleton, mainly using the data of McKern and Stewart (1957), including their standard casts of pubic symphysis changes. It is fully realized that the McKern and Stewart criteria, derived from the study of modern American males, cannot be used to determine chronological age in groups like those of the present study. However, it is hoped that they do provide a reasonably accurate estimate of biological age.

Early in the study it was decided not to attempt exact estimation of age at death for skeletons over the age of twenty-five and to divide the collections into three age groups: young (eighteen to twenty-five), middle-aged (thirty to under fifty), and old (fifty and above). A gap was left between the ages of twenty-five and thirty in the hope that any early-developing age changes might thereby become more evident. The obvious scarcity of individuals over forty among the Eskimo, the first population sampled, necessitated lumping of the fourth and fifth decades into a single age category. Later, when it was discovered that the Arikara collection included a relative abundance of males in the fourth and fifth decades, it was decided to make up a double sample of this group. The proposed sample size was ten for each age and sex group, but in some cases this was not obtainable, and the final result is shown in Table 1.

Table 1. Sample size and composition by age group

Group	18–25	30–40	40–50	total 30–50	50+
Eskimo males	10 (22.0)[a]	8	2	10	7
females	8 (22.9)	9	3	12	6
Pueblo males	10 (22.3)	10	2	12	11
females	12 (22.6)	6	4	10	13
Arikara males	10 (21.4)	13	11	24	10
females	12 (20.8)	10	–	10	2

[a] Average age is given in parentheses.

Histologic Study

A $\frac{3}{8}$-inch diamond-core drill bit,[1] mounted in a Black and Decker drill and portable drill press, was used to take half-inch plugs through the anterior cortex of the left femur. The cores were taken directly opposite the linea aspera and just below the measured midshaft point, in order to preserve the latter anthropometric landmark. The cores were then made into undecalcified ground thin sections, using the technique described by Ortner (1970). In two cases the bone was too poorly preserved to be worked directly and had to be infiltrated with Araldite before grinding. These cases were both from Pueblo Bonito, the most ancient population in the study, and in spite of the punky softness of the gross bone, the microstructure was excellently preserved.

Three fields near the periosteal edge of each section, shown schematically in Figure 1, were selected for assessment: (1) the far left, (2) the far right, and (3) the center. Thus, the fields lay in the outer third of the cortex, the zone that Kerley (1961, 1965) found to be most closely correlated with age. Each field was photographed on 35-mm film with a

[1] Supplied by the Arthur J. Robertson Company, Washington, D.C.

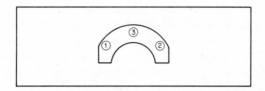

Figure 1.   Sketch of thin section of anterior femoral cortex on glass slide, showing locations of three fields assessed for microstructures (not to scale)

Pentax camera using a Leitz MIKAS attachment for microphotography, mounted on a Leitz petrographic microscope. The MIKAS attachment was fitted with a 10× ocular and an 8× objective, giving a magnification of approximately 80× and a rectangular photographic field 0.58 × 0.84 millimeters with an area of 0.49 square millimeters. The negatives were enlarged and printed as photographs measuring 115 ×165 millimeters. The technique of photographing the microscopic fields to be assessed was adapted from Ortner (1970) and has several advantages over direct assessment through the microscope alone:

1. The field is arbitrarily defined; there is no temptation to lose objectivity by shifting to a more "interesting" area or to enlarge the field.

2. With the photograph the same field can be found repeatedly and assessed in different ways, as was done in this study. Also, the photographs can be filed as a permanent record.

3. Structures can be outlined and labeled on the photographs; there is no danger of losing count.

4. In many cases the photographs supplement direct vision. This is especially true when polarized light is used.

However, I would not recommend use of the photographs alone; there is no substitute for being able to focus up and down on a structure that is evading identification.

In two of the populations, interpretation of the microstructure was hampered in some cases by poor preservation. Quite a few femora of the Pueblo group, grossly in a perfect state of preservation, were riddled with microfractures that tended to cut across the true structures and obscure their outlines. This presented a minor difficulty, overcome by taking extra care and time in assessing the field. A greater difficulty arose in eight Arikara specimens. Some sort of postmortem process, perhaps a fungus, was destroying the microstructure, so that many areas appeared completely amorphous in direct light, both to the camera and to the human eye. However, in polarized light the structures usually appeared dramatically displayed. It was in these cases that the use of photography proved especially valuable. Using all available light and exposure times up to fifty seconds, the photograph could actually be made to show more than the eye could see.

Once the photographs were printed, the fields they defined were assessed as to the numbers of the various types of microscopic structure they contained. The thin sections were assessed in the order of their museum catalog numbers, without knowledge of age or sex of the individual. The fields were viewed directly in the microscope, and the structures were outlined in carbon drawing-ink with a fine-pointed pen and labeled as to type.

OSTEONS. Osteons were basically counted as such when the haversian canal was intact and not breached by a resorption area or impinged upon by the walls of a later osteon. This follows Ortner's practice (1970) and differs somewhat from Kerley's (1965), in that the latter stipulated that not only should the haversian canal be intact but the osteon should also be "easily distinguishable over 80 percent or more of its area." The osteon category includes not only mature osteons and those still being filled in but also, following Kerley (1961), the more transversely running vascular canals lined by circumferential lamellae, termed Volkmann's canals. As Kerley pointed out, these are an essential part of the "osteone tree." Osteons whose entire haversian canals lay outside the photographic field were not counted but were marked with a cross for future reference.

In the cortex of young individuals some osteons are very large, while a few are quite small and can resemble the pseudohaversian systems around larger vessels incorporated during the deposition of periosteal circumferential lamellae. However, the circumferential lamellae can be seen to bend around the pseudohaversian systems, whereas they are always cut across and interrupted by true osteons.

FRAGMENTS. Fragments are remnants of former osteons, and they range from tiny slivers to full-sized "dead" osteons whose haversian canals have been breached by their own blood vessels or vessels from outside. All fragments were counted, even those only partly within the field, as it was felt that any attempt to set up criteria for exclusion of partial fragments was bound to be burdensome at best.

RESORPTION AREAS. Until old age, at least, resorption areas represent the first step in the formation of a new osteon; they are destroying older bone to make space for the laying down of new bone. They range from the first tiny breakthrough of bone walls by a vessel in circumferential lamellar bone or within the haversian canal of an osteon to the grossly visible resorption cavities in the bones of older individuals.

It has been the previous practice (Kerley 1961, 1965; Ortner 1970; Singh and Gunberg 1970) to report and work statistically with the total number of structures counted in a specified number of fields of the same bone section. However, there are obvious disadvantages to this system.

Field size, and thus total counts, will vary from microscope to microscope and according to magnification, and thus the histologic studies to date are not directly comparable, although they do not essentially contradict each other. Similarly, total counts will vary according to the number of fields assessed per section. For these reasons the structure counts derived from this study will be reported as number of structures per square millimeter. That is, the three fields assessed were considered to cover 1.5 square millimeters (actually 1.47 square millimeters), and total counts were simply divided by 1.5 to arrive at the number of structures per square millimeter. Thus, these results should be directly comparable with similarly derived figures from any other study of the anterior femoral cortex, regardless of field number or size.

There is a fourth major component of cortical bone, one which cannot be counted, periosteal circumferential lamellar bone, the bone which the other structures are in the process of replacing throughout an individual's lifetime. (In the following sections, for the sake of brevity, I propose to refer to this simply as "lamellar bone," in the full realization that osteons and fragments are also lamellar bone.) Kerley, in his pioneering studies (1961, 1965) visually estimated the percentage of lamellar bone present. Ahlqvist and Damsten (1969) refined this method by using a 100-square reticle inserted into the eyepiece of a microscope at a level that would cover one square millimeter at the level of the thin section. Thus they were able, by counting the grid squares, to determine the percentage of the area occupied by osteons and fragments as opposed to lamellar bone. For this study their method was modified by drawing on transparent acetate a 100-space grid the same size as the photographs. Because of the shape of the photographic field the "squares" were actually rectangles measuring 11.5 × 16.5 millimeters, but, just as surely as a square, each rectangle delineated one percent of the field. For this count, then, four types of structure could be defined:
1. osteonal bone: this included the peripheral osteons marked with a cross in the earlier count;
2. fragmental bone;
3. resorption areas: this method probably underestimates the amount of resorption activity going on in a field, as newer resorption areas are usually too small to be the predominant structural type in a grid space;
4. lamellar bone.

The grid was laid over the photograph and each space was counted, with the aid of a hematologic counter, according to the structure type predominating in the space. The total count for each type in each field thus represented the percentage of the field occupied by that type. Totals for the three fields were then added up and divided by three, to arrive at the average percentage per individual.

RESULTS

The data derived from the histologic study were processed by the computer center of the Smithsonian Institution, and Table 2 lists the means and the standard errors of the means for each of the age and sex groups in each of the populations. As described in the preceding section, three types of bone microstructure were counted (resorption spaces, osteons, and fragments), and four types of structure (lamellar, osteonal, and fragmental bone, and resorption areas) were assessed as to the average percentage of the field they occupied. It was felt that approaching the structures from the point of view not only of their number per square millimeter but also of the average percentage of the field they occupied would help to compensate for the bias inherent in counting all fragments but only those osteons whose haversian canals could be seen in the photograph. Also, it should help to compensate for differences between individuals in the size of the structures. Osteons, in particular, differ in size, and an attempt was made to estimate osteon size by dividing the number of osteons in a single field per individual by the percentage of the field occupied by osteons. In each case the field chosen was the most remodeled one, that is, the one with the highest percentage of osteonal and fragmental bone. This figure, called "osteon size" in the tables, is really a rough score rather than a true measurement and cannot be taken very seriously.

Table 2. Means and standard errors

Measurement	Mean	Standard error	Mean	Standard error	Mean	Standard error
Eskimo males	young ($n = 10$)		middle-aged ($n = 10$)		old ($n = 7$)	
resorption count/mm²	5.00	0.79	5.13	0.65	5.33	0.70
average percent resorption	1.47	0.41	1.50	0.62	1.81	0.31
osteon count/mm²	11.93	1.59	19.00	0.86	18.00	0.74
average percent osteonal	41.20	6.10	57.57	2.50	49.05	4.63
fragment count/mm²	6.93	2.39	18.80	3.12	26.00	4.34
average percent fragmental	12.27	3.56	24.73	4.22	33.52	5.14
average percent lamellar	45.06	7.14	16.20	4.52	15.62	6.92
osteon size	8.63	1.66	6.77	0.40	4.99	0.52
Eskimo females	young ($n = 8$)		middle-aged ($n = 12$)		old ($n = 6$)	
resorption count/mm²	2.83	0.83	6.44	0.69	6.11	0.72
average percent resorption	0.58	0.19	2.81	0.66	8.94	2.16
osteon count/mm²	17.33	2.46	18.78	1.76	12.89	1.69
average percent osteonal	64.13	6.46	53.58	3.15	37.50	6.42
fragment count/mm²	9.00	2.65	27.11	2.83	42.67	5.08
average percent fragmental	12.25	2.94	35.00	4.09	50.39	4.56
average percent lamellar	23.04	8.81	8.61	2.36	3.17	1.11
osteon size	9.49	2.31	6.01	0.35	6.86	1.41

Table 2. (*continued*)

Measurement	Mean	Standard error	Mean	Standard error	Mean	Standard error
Pueblo males	young (n = 10)		middle-aged (n = 12)		old (n = 11)	
resorption count/mm²	2.60	0.83	5.78	0.90	5.64	0.94
average percent resorption	1.57	0.54	1.83	0.41	2.48	0.94
osteon count/mm²	11.40	1.33	14.72	1.87	17.34	0.90
average percent osteonal	48.90	5.90	45.83	6.08	51.42	4.10
fragment count/mm²	5.53	1.27	15.44	3.33	26.00	4.76
average percent fragmental	10.73	2.65	21.00	4.03	33.46	5.30
average percent lamellar	38.80	6.62	31.33	8.92	12.64	3.98
osteon size	11.12	1.33	8.06	1.31	5.62	0.42
Pueblo females	young (n = 12)		middle-aged (n = 10)		old (n = 13)	
resorption count/mm²	3.72	0.62	3.60	0.65	4.36	0.60
average percent resorption	0.56	0.14	0.80	0.28	2.46	0.55
osteon count/mm²	12.06	1.91	16.27	1.36	16.82	1.13
average percent osteonal	38.86	7.05	54.07	4.78	52.67	2.63
fragment count/mm²	4.28	0.83	11.60	2.69	25.38	1.74
average percent fragmental	6.75	1.82	16.30	2.61	35.46	3.19
average percent lamellar	53.83	8.18	28.84	4.91	9.41	2.31
osteon size	8.49	1.03	7.56	0.70	6.93	0.61
Arikara males	young (n = 10)		middle-aged (n = 24)		old (n = 10)	
resorption count/mm²	3.47	0.81	4.14	0.54	6.33	0.72
average percent resorption	1.47	0.74	1.75	0.35	4.03	1.03
osteon count/mm²	11.33	1.84	18.53	0.98	18.00	1.53
average percent osteonal	47.33	8.24	58.97	3.27	51.53	3.74
fragment count/mm²	6.33	2.49	14.67	1.89	25.73	2.78
average percent fragmental	11.50	4.85	23.44	3.01	32.80	3.79
average percent lamellar	39.70	11.20	15.83	3.22	11.63	3.82
osteon size	7.82	0.79	6.64	0.57	6.00	0.59
Arikara females	young (n = 12)		middle-aged (n = 10)		old (n = 2)	
resorption count/mm²	2.61	0.71	3.80	0.75	8.66	3.77
average percent resorption	0.53	0.19	2.10	0.61	15.00	5.19
osteon count/mm²	10.94	1.49	16.87	1.45	8.67	2.83
average percent osteonal	45.69	7.25	56.20	4.45	25.00	15.66
fragment count/mm²	3.22	0.78	12.93	2.65	35.33	5.66
average percent fragmental	5.53	2.02	17.53	3.26	51.84	6.84
average percent lamellar	48.25	8.24	24.17	6.65	8.17	3.54
osteon size	8.90	0.68	7.46	0.76	9.00	2.83

The computer study tested the differences between the sample means by Student's *t* and the variances by the *F* ratio. Comparisons between groups were analyzed according to three categories: differences between the two sexes (holding population and age constant), between populations (holding sex and age constant), and between age groups (holding sex and population constant). Tables 3, 4, and 5 record the significant differences found and the levels of significance. Differences which are significant according to the t test but whose F ratios are not acceptable are so marked and should be used with caution, if at all.

It can be seen at a glance that by far the most significant differences occur in the third category, that comparing age groups (Table 5). Differences between the sexes (Table 3) are minimal. This is not surprising in view of Kerley's finding (1961) that the only real differences between males and females was in the age of onset of resorption patterns in the cortex, with both the peripheral resorption of adolescence and the medullary resorption after middle age occurring earlier in the female. In his 1965 publication, he notes that structures in the outer zone of the cortex showed only very low correlation with sex, the lowest being $r = 0.022$ for osteons in the femur and the highest $r = 0.391$ for nonhaversian (pseudohaversian) canals in the fibula. The data in Table 3 suggest that in the Eskimo and Arikara there may be some difference in internal remodeling of the anterior cortex in old age, as reflected by the number of osteons relative to fragmental bone in a given area. This is seen in Table 2; old Eskimo and Arikara females show a higher percentage of area occupied by fragmental than by osteonal bone, whereas the percentages are reversed in the males. These females also show considerably more area occupied by resorption spaces, although not at a statistically significant level. On the other hand, Pueblo males and females are very close in all these percentages.

Table 4 gives the significant differences found between populations and presents a clear pattern, although one which is difficult to interpret. Males show no differences at all except for a single dubious measurement, "osteon size," whereas the females differ in quite a few measurements, especially in middle and old age. Young Eskimo females have more osteonal bone and less lamellar bone than do Pueblo and a higher osteon count than do Arikara females. However, this last difference may well be due to the young Eskimo being on average two years older than the Arikara (Table 1). Middle-aged Eskimo females have more resorption spaces and more fragments per square millimeter than both other groups, and they apparently have a higher average percentage of fragmental bone and less lamellar bone. Together with the differences found between the young groups, these findings hint at either a faster rate of remodeling or, more probably, that more remodeling is taking place in Eskimo females. By the time we first meet them at an average age of about twenty-three, they have more osteons replacing primary lamellar bone, and in the fourth and fifth decades a greater number of osteons have been and are being replaced, as seen in the higher fragment and resorption space counts. This

Table 3. Levels of significance of differences between sex group means (age and population held constant)

Sex groups	Resorption count (per mm²)	Percentage resorption	Osteon count (per mm²)	Percentage osteonal	Fragmental count (per mm²)	Percentage fragmental	Percentage lamellar	Osteon size
Eskimo								
young males versus young females	–	–	–	0.05	–	–	–	–
middle-aged males versus middle-aged females	–	–	–	–	–	–	–	–
old males versus old females	–	0.01[a]	0.02[a]	–	0.05	0.05	–	–
Pueblo								
young males versus young females	–	–	–	–	–	–	–	–
middle-aged males versus middle-aged females	–	0.05	–	–	–	–	–	–
old males versus old females	–	–	–	–	–	–	–	–
Arikara								
young males versus young females	–	–	–	–	–	–	–	–
middle-aged males versus middle-aged females	–	–	–	–	–	–	–	–
old males versus old females	–	–	0.02	–	–	0.05	–	–

[a] *F* ratio not acceptable.

Table 4.   Levels of significance of differences between population group means (age and sex held constant)

Population groups	Resorption count (per mm²)	Percentage resorption	Osteon count (per mm²)	Percentage osteonal	Fragmental count (per mm²)	Percentage fragmental	Percentage lamellar	Osteon size
Young males								
Eskimo versus Pueblo	—	—	—	—	—	—	—	—
Eskimo versus Arikara	—	—	—	—	—	—	—	0.05
Pueblo versus Arikara	—	—	—	—	—	—	—	—
Middle-aged males								
Eskimo versus Pueblo	—	—	—	—	—	—	—	—
Eskimo versus Arikara	—	—	—	—	—	—	—	—
Pueblo versus Arikara	—	—	—	—	—	—	—	—
Old males								
Eskimo versus Pueblo	—	—	—	—	—	—	—	—
Eskimo versus Arikara	—	—	—	—	—	—	—	—
Pueblo versus Arikara	—	—	—	—	—	—	—	—
Young females								
Eskimo versus Pueblo	—	—	—	0.02	—	—	0.02	—
Eskimo versus Arikara	—	—	0.05	—	—	—	—	—
Pueblo versus Arikara	—	—	—	—	—	—	—	—
Middle-aged females								
Eskimo versus Pueblo	0.01	0.02ᵃ	—	—	0.01	0.01ᵃ	0.01ᵃ	—
Eskimo versus Arikara	0.02	—	—	—	0.01	0.01	0.05ᵃ	—
Pueblo versus Arikara	—	—	—	—	—	—	—	—
Old females								
Eskimo versus Pueblo	—	0.01ᵃ	—	0.05	0.01ᵃ	0.02	0.05ᵃ	—
Eskimo versus Arikara	—	—	—	—	—	—	—	—
Pueblo versus Arikara	—	0.05ᵃ	0.02	—	—	0.05	—	—

ᵃ F ratio not acceptable

Table 5. Levels of significance of differences between age group means (sex and population held constant)

Age groups	Resorption count (per mm²)	Percentage resorption	Osteon count (per mm²)	Percentage osteonal	Fragmental count (per mm²)	Percentage fragmental	Percentage lamellar	Osteon size
Eskimo males								
young versus middle-aged	–	–	0.01[a]	0.05[a]	0.01	0.05	0.01	–
young versus old	–	–	0.01[a]	–	0.01	0.01	0.01	–
middle-aged versus old	–	–	–	–	–	–	–	0.02
Eskimo females								
young versus middle-aged	0.01	0.01[a]	–	–	0.01	0.01	–	–
young versus old	0.02	0.01[a]	–	0.02	0.01	0.01	0.05[a]	–
middle-aged versus old	–	0.02[a]	0.05	0.05	0.02	0.05	–	–
Pueblo males								
young versus middle-aged	0.02	–	–	–	0.02[a]	0.05	–	0.01[a]
young versus old	0.05	–	0.01	–	0.01[a]	0.01[a]	0.01	–
middle-aged versus old	–	–	–	–	–	–	–	–
Pueblo females								
young versus middle-aged	–	0.01[a]	0.05[a]	–	0.02[a]	0.01	0.02[a]	–
young versus old	–	0.02[a]	–	–	0.01[a]	0.01[a]	0.01[a]	–
middle-aged versus old	–	–	–	–	0.01	0.01	0.01[a]	–
Arikara males								
young versus middle-aged	–	–	0.01	–	0.02	0.05	0.05[a]	–
young versus old	0.02	–	0.02	–	0.01	0.01	0.05[a]	–
middle-aged versus old	0.05	0.05[a]	–	–	0.01	–	–	–
Arikara females								
young versus middle-aged	–	0.05[a]	0.01	–	0.01[a]	0.01	0.05	–
young versus old	–	0.02[a]	–	–	0.01[a]	0.01	0.01[a]	–
middle-aged versus old	–	0.05[a]	0.05	–	0.01	0.01	–	–

[a] *F* ratio not acceptable.

same pattern of differences continues between Eskimo and Pueblo in old age. Pueblo and Arikara females show no significant differences until old age, when the Arikara cease to differ from the Eskimo and seem to be "catching up" with them, having fewer osteons and a larger average percentage of fragmental bone (and perhaps resorption spaces) than the old Pueblo females. This reflects the sexual pattern seen in Table 3; old Eskimo and Arikara females differ from males, whereas old Pueblo females follow the male pattern.

Table 5, which shows the greatest number of statistically significant differences, compares age groups, with sex and population held constant. Four of the eight measurements show simple, more-or-less linear trends with age: fragment count and the complementary fragment percentage, percentage resorption area, and percentage lamellar bone. As would be expected, the first three measurements increase with age, while lamellar bone decreases. These trends are graphed in Figures 3, 6, 7, and 8. (Because of the tiny sample of old Arikara females, individual measurements for these two specimens are noted on all graphs, so that the reader may judge for himself whether the graphed point is meaningful.) As can be seen in Table 5, most numerous significant differences pertain to fragmental bone, especially the areal percentage.

Figures 2, 4, 5, and 9 graph the other four measurements, and it can be seen that "osteon size" and number of resorption spaces also tend toward linearity in most age–sex groups, whereas osteon number and areal percentage tend to rise into middle age and then either drop or level off, except in the Pueblo males. This is in some contrast to Kerley's finding (1961) that femoral osteons increase in number up to age ninety-five, although with some leveling off after late middle age, that is, after fifty, rather than between thirty and fifty as seen here. I am reluctant to attribute this difference to the small size of my samples, as the trend is so consistent, especially in osteon count, except for the Pueblo males. Equally, I hesitate to conclude that the three populations of this study were aging considerably earlier than a modern population, especially as Kerley (1961) found his methods directly applicable to the Indian Knoll skeletons. It is possible that the earlier-noted differences in the definition of an osteon affected the result of osteon counts. But the most likely explanation lies in the fact that, while Kerley totaled structures in four fields around the femur diameter — medial, lateral, anterior, and posterior — this study is confined to the anterior cortex alone. It is quite probable that local cortical areas behave differently at the microscopic level, than at the gross level. Van Gerven et al. (1969) found that the various areas of the femoral cortex differed in their patterns of loss in thickness with age.

RESORPTION SPACE NUMBER PER SQUARE MILLIMETER. This count shows no significant sex differences. Between populations it differs only in middle-aged females, Eskimo having a significantly higher count than the other two groups. As for age trends, most notable is the pattern followed by Eskimo females and Pueblo males, in contrast to that of the other four groups as can be seen in Figure 2. Both show a significant rise between youth and middle age and then a slight decrease in old age, although the count in old age is still significantly higher than in youth. The other groups tend to show a steady rise in count, significant only in the Arikara males between middle-aged and old as well as between young and old.

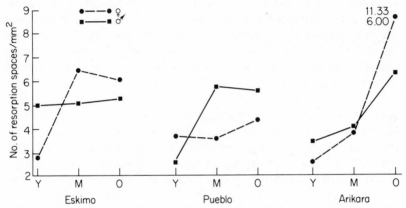

Figure 2. Relation to age of number of resorption spaces per square millimeter (Y = young, M = middle-aged, O = old)

AVERAGE PERCENTAGE OF RESORPTION SPACE. Although the average percentage of area occupied by resorption spaces shows a tendency to increase with age, as seen in Figure 3, there is only a single assuredly significant difference between means: Pueblo males have more resorption area than

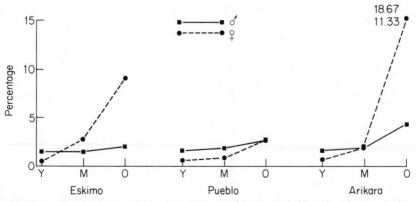

Figure 3. Relation to age of average percentage of area occupied by resorption spaces (Y = young, M = middle-aged, O = old)

females in middle age (see Table 5). Otherwise, the pattern would appear to be one of greater increase of resorption area with age in females than in males and greater in Eskimo and Arikara females than in Pueblo. Arikara males also appear to have an appreciable increase in resorption area after middle age. The fact that, unlike resorption count, quite a few differences between means for resorption area had significant t values but unacceptable F ratios would seem to reflect a high individual variation in the areal extent of resorption spaces in the outer cortex.

The increase in the number of resorption spaces and their areal extent with age should not be interpreted as an increase in resorption *rate*. Sedlin (1964), in discussing resorption spaces in rib cortex, notes that the actual rate of resorption in any individual focus decreases with age. However, the slowed rate of resorption is more than offset by the increase in number of resorptive foci, so that the result is "a net rise in total bone resorption after age 35."

OSTEON NUMBER PER SQUARE MILLIMETER. As mentioned before, significant sex differences in osteon count are confined to old Arikara and, possibly, old Eskimo. Similarly, only two significant population differences occur: young female Eskimo have more osteons than young Arikara females (probably accounted for by the fact that the Arikara sample averages about two years younger than the young Eskimo females), and old Pueblo females have a higher count than old Arikara females. That this may be a true population difference is suggested by Figure 4, which shows that Eskimo and Arikara, especially females, follow similar patterns in change of osteon count with age and differ from the Pueblo. Eskimo and Arikara show a rise between youth and middle age (significant in Eskimo males and in both sexes among the Arikara) and a slight drop for males and a steep, significant one for females between middle and old age. Pueblo, on

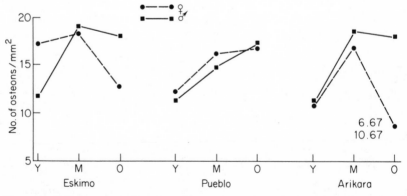

Figure 4.   Relation to age of number of osteons per square millimeter (Y = young, M = middle-aged, O = old)

the other hand, show a steady rise in count, significant only between youth and old age.

AVERAGE PERCENTAGE OF OSTEONAL BONE. Young Eskimo females have a significantly higher percentage of osteonal bone than the young males. Indeed, they have a considerably higher percentage than any other group, as can be seen in Figure 5, although the only significant population difference is with young Pueblo females. In old age the Eskimo females go to the other extreme and have significantly less osteonal bone than Pueblo females; this, of course, reflects the significantly higher fragment count of the old Eskimo females. As for age trends, all groups except Eskimo females and Pueblo males show a rise in percentage of osteonal bone between youth and middle age and a drop thereafter, with no significant differences between any age levels. The apparently aberrant curve followed by Pueblo males is quite probably due to sampling error, and the differences between the means are very slight, as can be seen in Table 2. Unlike all other groups, the Eskimo females show a significant decline in percentage of osteonal bone with age, especially between middle and old age.

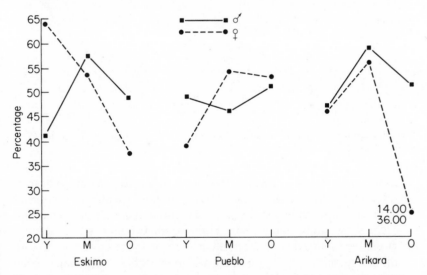

Figure 5.   Relation to age of average percentage of area occupied by osteonal bone (Y = young, M = middle-aged, O = old)

FRAGMENT NUMBER PER SQUARE MILLIMETER. The only significant sex difference in fragment count is between old Eskimo. Also, although all groups increase steadily in fragment count with age, this seems to happen earlier in Eskimo females, who have a significantly higher fragment count than the other female groups in middle age. Eskimo female fragment counts increase significantly between all ages, and while the data in Table 5 suggest that this may be true for the other females, their only assuredly significant rise is between middle and old age. Arikara males show significant differences between all ages, while the major increase in fragment count for Eskimo males is between youth and middle age, the rise after middle age being significant only when compared with the young. Pueblo males do not show assured age differences in fragment count, but they appear to follow much the same pattern as Eskimo males. Indeed, as seen in Figure 6, all three male populations are strikingly parallel.

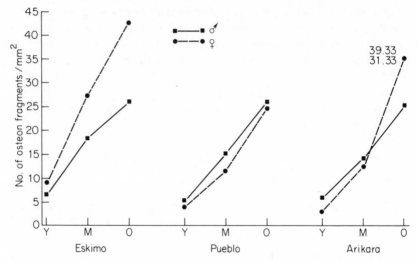

Figure 6.   Relation to age of number of osteon fragments per square millimeter (Y = young, M = middle-aged, O = old)

AVERAGE PERCENTAGE OF FRAGMENTAL BONE. Average percentage of fragmental bone is the measurement with the greatest number of significant differences between age levels. Out of eighteen possible combinations, thirteen show surely significant differences, and two more differences are of probable significance. That is, all groups show a steady trend upward with age, as shown in Figure 7, so it is improbable that young Pueblo males have significantly less fragmental bone than middle-aged males but not less than old males. Similarly, if young Pueblo females have less fragmental bone than middle-aged females and the latter have less than old females, it is probable that the young females really have significantly less fragmental bone than the old females.

Eskimo and Arikara females have significantly more fragmental bone than males in old age. In males the greatest increase in percentage of fragmental bone comes between youth and middle age, while females

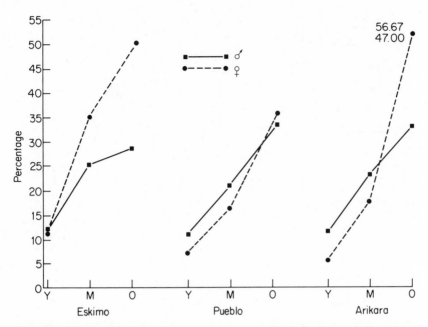

Figure 7.   Relation to age of average percentage of area occupied by fragmental bone (Y =
young, M = middle-aged, O = old)

show significant increases between all ages. However, the Eskimo
females seem to show an earlier increase in fragmental bone. By middle
age they differ certainly from the Arikara and perhaps from the Pueblo.
By old age Eskimo females definitely have a higher percentage of fragmental bone than the Pueblo, while the old Arikara females have caught
up with the Eskimo and now differ significantly from the Pueblo females.

AVERAGE PERCENTAGE OF LAMELLAR BONE. The areal percentage of lamellar
bone shows no significant sex differences, and the only assured population difference is between young Eskimo and Pueblo females. However,
Figure 8 demonstrates that Eskimo females have less lamellar bone than
any of the other five groups at all ages. This finding cannot be ascribed to
a higher average age of the Eskimo females (see Table 1). Is remodeling
really accelerated in Eskimo females? They have already been seen to
have more resorption spaces and osteon fragments than the other females
by middle age.

As for age changes, as seen in Table 5, Eskimo males have a significant
drop in percentage of lamellar bone between youth and middle age, with
little or no decline thereafter; the Arikara males seem to follow a similar
pattern, but without assured statistical significance. Pueblo and Eskimo
females show a steadier pattern of decline between youth and old age, the
only surely significant difference being between young and old Pueblo

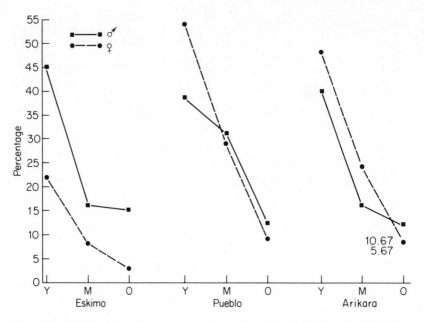

Figure 8.   Relation to age of average percentage of area occupied by lamellar bone (Y = young, M = middle-aged, O = old)

males. The Arikara female pattern of lamellar bone loss is ambiguous; it shows a significant drop between youth and middle age, but it is uncertain whether the apparently smooth drop into old age would be borne out by a larger sample, although the individual data suggest that this would be the case.

OSTEON SIZE. As mentioned before, "osteon size" is really only a rough score and not an actual measurement of osteon diameters. In general, the trend in this score appears to be downward with age, as shown in Figure 9, significant only in Eskimo males and, possibly, in Pueblo males. Several authors, among them Currey (1964), have measured osteon diameters and reported that they decrease with age, and this would appear to be the case in all but the Arikara and Eskimo females in this study. On the other hand, Jowsey (1966) concluded that there was no age trend in size, and Kerley (1961) also found no consistent association between measured osteon size and age. Thus, whether osteons do or do not become smaller with age would appear to be still open to debate.

DISCUSSION AND CONCLUSIONS

We introduced the study described in this paper by enumerating four

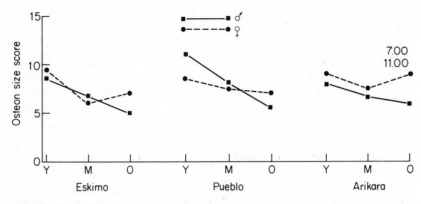

Figure 9. Relation to age of osteon size score (not a measurement) (Y= young, M = middle-aged, O = old)

questions that it might answer. The fourth, on the value of attempting such a study, was left to the reader, and here I shall try to answer the other three.

CAN AGE CHANGES BE DEMONSTRATED, AND IF SO, DO THE THREE POPULATIONS DIFFER IN THE WAY THESE CHANGES TAKE PLACE? It seems clear, from the data in Table 5 and the trends graphed in the figures that age changes in peripheral cortical microstructure can be demonstrated for all three populations, in spite of our ignorance of the chronological age of the individuals. Basically, primary (lamellar) bone decreases as it is remodeled into secondary (osteonal and fragmental) bone. In two of the populations, Eskimo and Arikara, this decrease would appear to trace the same concave-upward curve described by Blumberg and Kerley (1966). As for secondary bone, the fragments of former osteons accumulate steadily, and in most groups this accumulation is at the expense of intact osteons after the age of thirty. Similarly, the number of resorption spaces and the areal extent of such spaces tend to increase with age. Many of these trends, especially the accumulation of fragments, show statistically significant differences between age groups.

It must be noted that the present data do not permit inferences as to the *rates* at which the processes involved occur. That is, the structures seen in the microscope represent a frozen moment in the life of an individual. Some structures will have been present for many years, whereas others may have been in the process of formation at the time of death. Thus, the data presented here record the average *amount* of a given activity or of end-products of activity present in a group of individuals dying within a given age range. We can state — on the basis of differences in relative percentages of lamellar and osteonal bone — that young Eskimo females have undergone a greater amount of cortical remodeling than have young

Pueblo females, but we cannot say that they are remodeling at a faster rate.

With this in mind, then, do the three populations show differences in intracortical remodeling with age? As far as statistically significant differences are concerned, the answer for males would seem to be a resounding *no* (see Table 4). Table 6 shows the means for each age and population group, to enable easier comparison between populations than is possible using Table 2. The male means can be seen to agree remarkably well with each other in most instances, with a couple of exceptions that imply possible differences in *pattern* of remodeling activity with age. Unlike the other two groups, the Pueblo males seem to reach a plateau in areal percentage of osteonal bone in youth and change little thereafter (Figure 5). That this is not due to lack of remodeling can be seen in the steady accumulation of osteon fragments (Figure 6, Figure 7). At the same time Pueblo males retain a high percentage of lamellar bone into middle age, rather than remodeling most of it long before that time, as do the other two groups.

Comparisons between the female groups are hampered by sampling peculiarities in the Arikara. That is, the young Arikara females average somewhat younger than the young females in the other two groups. Similarly, all the Arikara middle-aged females are under forty (see Table 1). And finally, the sample of old Arikara females numbers only two. This situation is unfortunate, if only because a more comparable set of Arikara samples could help to explain the differences between Eskimo and Pueblo.

Briefly, Eskimo females seem "advanced," while Pueblo seem "retarded." For example, young Pueblo females have an average of over 50 percent of lamellar bone, whereas Eskimo females of the same biological age average less than 25 percent and also have a significantly higher percentage of osteonal bone. Further evidence that the Eskimo are ahead in remodeling is seen in the higher fragment count and greater percentage of area occupied by fragments (Table 6), although the latter is quite consistent with the young male values. This state of affairs continues into middle age, accompanied by significantly higher numbers of resorption spaces. Eskimo females are the sole group of either sex that shows a drop in percentage of area occupied by osteons between youth and middle age (Figure 5). This is not simply because of a decrease in size of osteons, as can be seen by the relatively minuscule increase in osteon count in the same interval (Figure 4, Table 6). As previously mentioned, Eskimo females also have consistently less lamellar bone than any other group of either sex at all ages (Figure 8, Table 6), although the differences are not necessarily statistically significant.

The only evidence of "retardation" in young Pueblo females is their closeness to the slightly younger Arikara females (a situation that con-

Table 6. Means arranged to compare population groups (sex and age held constant)

Groups	Resorption count (per mm²)	Percent resorption	Osteon count (per mm²)	Percent osteonal	Fragmental count (per mm²)	Percent fragmental	Percent lamellar	Osteon size
Young males								
Eskimo	5.00	1.47	11.93	41.20	6.93	12.27	45.06	8.63
Pueblo	2.60	1.57	11.40	48.90	5.53	10.73	38.80	11.12
Arikara	3.47	1.47	11.33	47.33	6.33	11.50	39.70	7.82
Middle-aged males								
Eskimo	5.13	1.50	19.00	57.57	18.80	24.73	16.20	6.77
Pueblo	5.78	1.83	14.72	45.83	15.44	21.00	31.33	8.06
Arikara	4.14	1.75	18.53	58.97	14.67	23.44	15.83	6.64
Old males								
Eskimo	5.33	1.81	18.00	49.05	26.00	33.52	15.62	4.99
Pueblo	5.64	2.48	17.34	51.42	26.00	33.46	12.64	5.62
Arikara	6.33	4.03	18.00	51.53	25.73	32.80	11.63	6.00
Young females								
Eskimo	2.83	0.58	17.33	64.13	9.00	12.25	23.04	9.49
Pueblo	3.72	0.56	12.06	38.86	4.28	6.75	53.83	8.49
Arikara	2.61	0.53	10.94	45.69	3.22	5.53	48.25	8.90
Middle-aged females								
Eskimo	6.44	2.81	18.78	53.58	27.11	35.00	8.61	6.01
Pueblo	3.60	0.80	16.27	54.07	11.60	16.30	28.84	7.56
Arikara	3.80	2.10	16.87	56.20	12.93	17.53	24.17	7.46
Old females								
Eskimo	6.11	8.94	12.98	37.50	42.67	50.39	3.17	6.86
Pueblo	4.36	2.46	16.82	52.67	25.38	35.46	9.41	6.93
Arikara	8.66	15.00	8.67	25.00	35.33	51.84	8.17	9.00

tinues into middle age) and their lagging behind the young Pueblo males in the relative percentages of area occupied by lamellar and osteonal bone. They catch up with the males in these values in middle age, but it has already been noted that middle-aged Pueblo males differ from the other males in this respect, especially in the amount of lamellar bone retained. (Of course, it should be noted that none of these differences attains statistical significance.) Final evidence for "retardation" of remodeling in Pueblo females is their differing in old age from the other female groups in having a lower percentage of fragments and a higher percentage (than Arikara) and number (than Eskimo) of intact osteons. It is probable, though not necessarily statistically significant, that they have fewer and smaller resorption spaces in old age.

As for the Arikara females, we feel very much the lack of middle-aged individuals in the fifth decade. The sample chosen for this study was part of a larger group of twenty-six individuals included in a study of aging changes in cortical thickness, but even in that larger group only four of the twenty-six could be considered to be over forty. This and the scarcity of old females may indicate much about life as a female Arikara, but it is a definite hindrance to the study of aging changes. Thus, we can conclude only that the present data suggest that young Arikara females differ from Eskimo in a single value, which could be accounted for by their relative youth; that in middle age they differ from the Eskimo in almost exactly the same way as do Pueblo females; and that in old age they show increased resorption, increased fragmental bone, and decreased osteon count in a pattern more closely resembling that of the Eskimo than that of the Pueblo females.

ARE THERE SEX DIFFERENCES, AND DO THE THREE POPULATIONS DIFFER IN THIS RESPECT? The few statistically significant differences between the sexes found in this study have been discussed in the preceding section, but some remarks can be added on the way the three populations differ in this respect. The "retarded" pattern of cortical remodeling found in Pueblo females is also seen in the males. In many characteristics the Pueblo follow a tighter curve than the other two groups, with fewer differences between the sexes from age to age. This is best seen in Figures 3, 4, 6, and 7. The loosest curves are followed by the Eskimo, although statistically significant differences between the sexes are almost entirely confined to old age (Table 3). The Arikara are intermediate, being quite close in youth and middle age but tending to differ (in two cases significantly) in old age. However, in certain characteristics they have an even tighter pattern than the Pueblo in youth and middle age (Figures 2 and 5), and it is possible that the differences seen in old age would be eliminated if a larger sample of old females were available.

ARE THERE DIFFERENCES BETWEEN THE POPULATIONS, AND IF SO, CAN THEY BE RELATED TO GENETIC FACTORS OR TO SUCH ENVIRONMENTAL FACTORS AS LIFE-STYLE AND DIET? Significant differences were found between the female populations; Eskimo females appear to be "accelerated" and Pueblo females "retarded." This difference is most evident in middle age, and at this age the Pueblo males also appear to fall behind the other males, although not at a statistically significant level.

Perzigian (1971) suggested that genetic factors were more likely than diet to account for differences between Hopewell and Indian Knoll populations in aging loss of bone mineral. Unfortunately, essentially nothing is known about the genetic factors involved in this process or in intracortical remodeling. That remodeling differences exist, at least on the species level, is evident from the fact that there are differences between species in microstructure and composition of adult bone (Enlow 1963; Jowsey 1964, 1966). Further, Detenbeck and Jowsey (1969) demonstrated that there are species differences in remodeling rates. The cortical bone of dogs eleven to eighteen years old had the same sort of microradiographic pattern of increased resorption spaces, occluded haversian canals, and low-density osteons as would be characteristic of humans several times their age. However, because of our ignorance of the processes involved and Kerley's finding no differences (1961, 1965) between modern blacks and whites in intracortical remodeling, the remarks below must be considered purely speculative.

It is difficult to imagine genetic differences between populations that would affect females alone, unless these differences involved pregnancy and/or lactation. In the late nineteenth century Eskimo women as far apart as St. Michael on Norton Sound and Point Barrow on the Arctic Sea were nursing children of four and even five years (P. H. Ray 1885; D. J. Ray 1966), and even today sometimes two successive children are nursed at the same time (Spencer 1959). Hrdlička (1908) noted that Pueblo women nursed children as long as four years, unless another pregnancy came along, and sometimes even while pregnant. We have no direct data for the Arikara, but Lowie (1954) describes "delayed weaning" as a characteristic of the Plains tribes and states that nursing continued as late as the age of four among the Cree.

Garn (1970) has shown that modern white females build up a deposit of endosteal bone during pregnancy. Presumably this same protective process was operating among the females of the present study. And also, presumably, this endosteal deposit would be lost during the prolonged lactation characteristic of aboriginal groups. It may be that among the Eskimo some genetic factor caused the pregnancy buildup mechanism to be less efficient than in the other two groups. Bone mineral and protein needed in lactation, then, would be mobilized not only by resorption of the endosteal buildup of pregnancy but also by increased remodeling farther out in the cortex, reflected in the increased osteonal bone of youth and later increased fragmental bone of middle age. The significantly higher count of resorption spaces in the middle-aged Eskimo females would, then, indicate increase in the number of remodeling focuses as the protein–mineral "debt" accumulated with further pregnancies. (I suspect that mineral would be more important than protein among the Eskimo.) This increase in turnover would be reflected later in the differences between Eskimo and Pueblo females in old age. It is difficult to postulate such a mechanism as the cause for the apparent elevated amounts of remodeling occurring some time after forty in the Arikara females, but data are lacking for the critical period.

We know as little about the effects of environmental factors in stimulating or retarding cortical bone remodeling as we do about possible genetic effects. Although Ortner (1970) found evidence that chronic alcoholism (which could be considered a form of dietary deficiency) retards internal remodeling, I am unaware of any other studies of environmental effects. Again, the answer must be in the form of speculation.

Several authors, including Heller and Scott (1967), have maintained that the Eskimo diet is deficient in calcium, and some have even gone so far as to postulate that the Greenland Eskimo illness known as *pibloktoq* is a form of adaptation to low dietary calcium plus insufficient sunlight for vitamin-D synthesis (Wallace 1961; Katz and Foulks 1970). *Pibloktoq* occurs most commonly in females at the end of winter. It is possible that relatively low dietary calcium and/or vitamin D could, under the stress of pregnancy and lactation, cause a demand for increased cortical remodeling because of the need for greater amounts of labile bone surfaces. However, it is by no means certain that the native Alaskan Eskimo diet is deficient in calcium or vitamin D. Modern dietary surveys tend to concentrate on dairy products and discount other sources of calcium and vitamin D in a diet calling, for instance, for the regular consumption of whole raw fish, including internal organs and bones.

Mazess (1970) made a photon absorptiometry study of bone mineral in modern Eskimo in Wainwright, Alaska, and found that younger Eskimo had about the same amount of bone mineral relative to bone width as United States whites of the same age, but that Eskimo over forty had 11 percent less bone mineral than comparable whites. He suggested that the Eskimo's highly acid diet was the cause of this phenomenon, and later study by nutritionists (Draper, cited by Hanna *et al.* 1972) implicated either high protein or high phosphorus consumption. As bone mineral is lost only by remodeling, the findings of Mazess would appear to imply greater amounts of remodeling with age among the Eskimo than among whites. As far as the present study is concerned, we should have to fall back upon the demands of pregnancy and lactation to account for the fact that possible diet-mediated remodeling effects are significant only among females when Eskimo are compared with the other two populations.

Physical activity is generally acknowledged to be a factor stimulating bone remodeling (Johnson 1966), and it is tempting to relate the even-tempered, sedentary Pueblo life-style (perhaps combined with a "bone economy" effect due to a diet low in high-quality protein) to their relatively even, tight pattern of age changes in remodeling. An individual Pueblo, whether male or female, could probably count on steady but not particularly strenuous work throughout his lifetime. By this reasoning, the comparatively "loose" pattern followed by the Eskimo could be related to a life-style calling for periods of strenuous and sustained activity alternating with period of patient inactivity. However, this sort of explanation strains the imagination, and the strain becomes unbearable in the case of the Arikara. Among the Arikara most of the physical labor (even earth lodge construction) was done by the women, and by the reasoning above they should show greater differences between the sexes than do the Pueblo. On the contrary, in the area for which we have adequate data — up to about the age of forty — they differ as little as or even less than the Pueblo.

On the whole, I would suggest that the findings of this study indicate an interplay between a possible genetic factor, affecting females because of the peculiar demands of pregnancy and lactation, and a dietary peculiarity, high or low protein or phosphorus. Confirmation or refutation of this hypothesis must await further research, not only in the form of studies of this nature, but also in the basic bone biology of various human groups. Although Kerley's work would seem to indicate no racial differences in bone remodeling at the microscopic level, it is possible that modern living conditions — especially the great reduction in length of lactation — are masking genetic or environmental factors. However, we need to make sure that the results of this study are not just due to sampling error as a result of the many biases that can creep into an archaeological collection.

REFERENCES

AHLQVIST, J., O. DAMSTEN
    1969   A modification of Kerley's method for the microscopic deter-mination of age in human bone. *Journal of Forensic Sciences* (14:205–212.

AMPRINO, R., A. BAIRATI
    1936   Processi di recostruzione e di riassorbimento nella sostanza compatta delle ossa dell' uomo. Richerche su centro sogetti dalla nascita sino a tarda eta. *Zeitschrift für Zellforschung und Mikroskopische Anatomie* 24:439–511.

BASS, W. M., D. R. EVANS, R. L. JANTZ
1971   *The Leavenworth site cemetery: archaeology and physical anthropology.*
University of Kansas Publications in Anthropology 2.

BLUMBERG, J., E. R. KERLEY
1966   "Discussion: a critical consideration of roentgenology and microscopy in palaeopathology," in *Human palaeopathology.* Edited by Saul Jarcho, 150–170. New Haven and London: Yale University Press.

BROTHWELL, D. R., *editor*
1968   *The skeletal biology of earlier human populations.* Oxford: Pergamon.

CURREY, J. D.
1964   Some effects of ageing in human Haversian systems. *Journal of Anatomy* 98:69–75.

DETENBECK, L. C., J. JOWSEY
1969   Normal aging in the bone of the adult dog. *Clinical Orthopaedics* 65:76–80.

ENLOW, D. H.
1963   *Principles of bone remodeling.* Springfield: Thomas.

GARN, S. M.
1970   *The earlier gain and the later loss of cortical bone.* Springfield: Thomas.
1971   *Human races* (third edition). Springfield: Thomas.

HANNA, J. M., S. M. FRIEDMAN, P. T. BAKER
1972   The status and future of U.S. human adaptability research in the International Biological Program. *Human Biology* 44:381–398.

HELLER, C. A., E. M. SCOTT
1967   *The Alaska dietary survey.* Public Health Service Publication 999–AH–2. Washington: Government Printing Office.

HEWETT, E. L.
1909   *The Pajaritan culture.* Archaeological Institute of America, Papers of the School of American Archaeology 3.

HOLDER, P.
1970   *The hoe and the horse on the Plains: a study of cultural development among North American Indians.* Lincoln: University of Nebraska Press.

HRDLIČKA, A.
1908   *Physical and medical observations among the Indians of the southwestern United States and northern Mexico.* Bureau of American Ethnology Bulletin 34. Washington: Government Printing Office.

JANTZ, R. L.
1970   "Change and variation in skeletal populations of Arikara Indians." Unpublished Ph.D. dissertation, University of Kansas.

JOHNSON, L. D.
1966   The kinetics of skeletal remodeling. *Birth Defects, Original Article Series* 2:66–142.

JOWSEY, J.
1960   Age changes in human bone. *Clinical Orthopaedics* 17:210–218.
1964   "Variations in bone mineralization with age and disease," in *Bone biodynamics.* Edited by H. M. Frost, 461–479. Boston: Little, Brown.
1966   Studies of Haversian systems in man and some animals. *Journal of Anatomy* 100:857–864.

JUDD, N. M.
1954   *The material culture of Pueblo Bonito.* Smithsonian Institution Miscellaneous Collections 124.

KATZ, S. H., E. F. FOULKS
1970 Mineral metabolism and behavior: abnormalities of calcium homeostasis. *American Journal of Physical Anthropology* 32:299–304.
KERLEY, E. R.
1961 "The microscopic determination of age in human bone." Unpublished Ph.D. dissertation, University of Michigan.
1965 The microscopic determination of age in human bone. *American Journal of Physical Anthropology* 23:149–163.
LAYRISSE, M.
1968 Biological subdivisions of the Indian on the basis of genetic traits. *Pan American Health Organization Scientific Publication* 165:35–39.
LEHMER, D. J., D. T. JONES
1968 *Arikara archaeology: the Bad River phase.* Smithsonian Institution River Basin Surveys: Publications in Salvage Archaeology 7.
LOWIE, R. H.
1954 *Indians of the Plains.* New York: McGraw-Hill.
McKERN, T. W., T. D. STEWART
1957 *Skeletal age changes in young American males.* Natick: Quartermaster Research and Development Center.
MAZESS, R. B.
1970 Bone mineral content in Wainwright Eskimos: preliminary report. *Arctic Anthropology* 7:114–116.
NELSON, R. K.
1969 *Hunters of the northern ice.* Chicago and London: University of Chicago Press.
ORTNER, D. J.
1970 "The effects of aging and disease on the micromorphology of human compact bone." Unpublished Ph.D. dissertation, University of Kansas.
OSWALT, W. H.
1967 *Alaskan Eskimos.* San Francisco: Chandler.
PERZIGIAN, A. J.
1971 "Gerontal osteoporotic bone loss in two prehistoric Indian populations." Unpublished Ph.D. dissertation, Indiana University.
RAY, D. J., *editor*
1966 The Eskimo of St. Michael and vicinity as related by H. M. W. Edmonds. *Anthropological Papers of the University of Alaska* 13.
RAY, P. H.
1885 *Report of the International Polar Expedition to Point Barrow, Alaska.* Executive Documents of the House of Representatives 44.
SEDLIN, E. D.
1964 "Uses of bone as a model system in the study of aging," in *Bone biodynamics.* Edited by H. M. Frost, 655–666. Boston: Little, Brown.
SELTZER, C. C.
1944 *Racial prehistory in the southwest and the Hawikuh Zunis.* Peabody Museum of American Archaeology and Ethnology Papers 23.
SINGH, I. J., D. L. GUNBERG
1970 Estimation of age at death in human males from quantitative histology of bone fragments. *American Journal of Physical Anthropology* 33:373–381.
SMITH, W., R. B. WOODBURY, N. F. S. WOODBURY
1966 *The excavation of Hawikuh by Frederick Webb Hodge.* Contributions from the Museum of the American Indian, Heye Foundation 20.

SPENCER, R. F.
1959   *The north Alaskan Eskimo.* Bureau of American Ethnology Bulletin 171.
1965   "Arctic and sub-arctic in native America," in *The native Americans.* Edited by R. F. Spencer and J. D. Jennings, 119–167. New York: Harper and Row.
STEWART, K. M.
1965   "The southwest," in *The native Americans.* Edited by R. F. Spencer and J. D. Jennings, 283–336. New York: Harper and Row.
VAN GERVEN, D. P., G. J. ARMELAGOS, M. H. BARTLEY
1969   Roentgenographic and direct measurement of femoral cortical involution in a prehistoric Mississippian population. *American Journal of Physical Anthropology* 31:23–38.
WALLACE, A. F. C.
1961   "Mental illness, biology, and culture," in *Psychological anthropology: approaches to culture and personality.* Edited by F. L. K. Hsu, 255–295. Homeward: Dorsey Press.

Epigenetic Distance: A Study of Biological Variability in the Lower Illinois River Region

JANE E. BUIKSTRA

Since the days of Samuel Morton, physical anthropologists have studied the builders of the prehistoric earthworks so common in eastern North America. The physical remains of these "mound builders" have been palpated, measured, and compared in numerous attempts to answer the question, "Who were these people?" For over a century, a diffusionist paradigm has led workers to answer this question in terms of the origins of radical types and to reconstruct the routes of population movement.

As they emphasized interregional comparison and migration, these workers neglected another important source of information: biological variability within and between local populations. An ability to focus upon microevolutionary change should allow us to "flesh out" the image of our mound builder as a cultural individual: one who inherited or acquired wealth and status, who perhaps buried his dead with his mother's people, and whose family may have lived in one village long enough to become biologically distinct from contemporaries up the river.

Such a perspective requires data and procedures beyond those afforded by traditional techniques. The purpose here is to develop and demonstrate a suitable methodology, using materials from the lower Illinois River region — an area long inhabited by the builders of the enigmatic burial mounds.

MATERIALS

The total available skeletal series from the principal components of seven mound groups are included in this study. As indicated in Table 1, six of the mound groups date from the middle Woodland period. In the lower Illinois River region, such affiliation is synonymous with participation in

Table 1.   Cultural and burial associations of mound groups

Name of mound group	Number of mounds (or cemetery areas) from which skeletons were collected	Cultural association	Minimum number of individuals
Bedford	5	middle Woodland	77
Pete Klunk	10	middle Woodland	378
Gibson	7	middle Woodland	161
Peisker	3	middle Woodland	58
Tom Collins	1	middle Woodland	16
L'Orient	3	late middle Woodland	104
Ledders	2	late Woodland	184

the Hopewell interaction sphere. The range of diagnostic artifacts and the spread of available carbon-14 dates (40 B.C. ± 160 to A.D. 400 ± 250) suggest long-term and contemporaneous occupations for Peisker, Bedford, Klunk, Gibson, and perhaps Collins. (For a detailed summary of archaeological information, see Struever [1972].) On the basis of stylistic elements, L'Orient is suggested by the excavator to be contemporaneous only with the more recent middle Woodland sites or perhaps to be slightly later in time (Gregory Perino, personal communication). Diagnostic late Woodland artifacts indicate that Ledders may date as much as four to six hundred years later than the most recent middle Woodland series. The location of the seven mound groups is shown in Map 1. With the exception of Peisker and Collins, all the middle Woodland sites are located on bluff crests overlooking the Illinois River. Peisker and Collins are floodplain sites, also on the Illinois. The Gibson and Pete Klunk sites are clustered approximately fourteen miles north of Peisker–Collins, with L'Orient in an intermediate position. Ledders is located directly west of Gibson–Klunk, on a bluff crest overlooking the Mississippi River. Bedford, the northernmost of these sites, is situated approximately sixteen miles north of the Gibson–Klunk mound groups.

METHODOLOGY

Several critical decisions must be made in a study of biological relationships. First, one must choose a class or classes of morphological attributes that will represent maximally the epigenetic information available from the skeletal series. Next, one must collect data according to techniques that minimize the effect of environmental "noise," such as cranial deformation, asymmetry, age, and sex of the individual. Finally, one must choose statistical procedures appropriate to both the data base and the hypotheses to be tested. Because the decisions made in the course of this study depart somewhat from those traditionally made in mid-

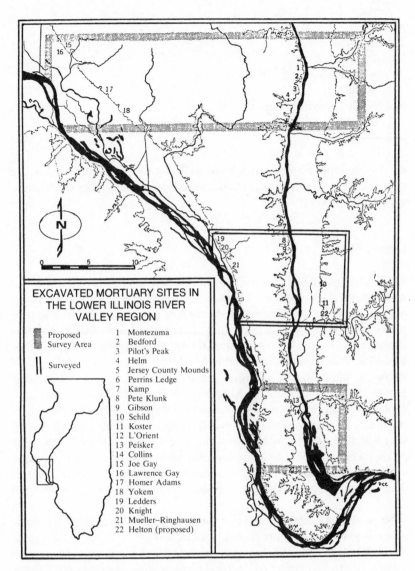

Figure 1.   Map of region under study

western physical anthropology, procedural development will be treated in detail.

KINDS OF MORPHOLOGICAL VARIATION

The classes of morphological variants available as indicators of biological distance can be grouped conveniently under the following headings:

Metric:
  1. skeletal*
    a. cranial
    b. postcranial
  2. dental*
Nonmetric or morphological:
  1. skeletal
  2. dental*

All of the above were considered as potential data sources for the analysis. Those marked by asterisks were rejected according to the arguments that follow.

Cranial Metrics

This is the traditional data source for assessing biological relationship in midwestern skeletal series. Charles Snow and Georg Neumann relied heavily upon the undeformed male skull as a normative representative for skeletal series and cultural unit. It is argued here that population characteristics more representative of total burial groups should be chosen. Male adults constitute roughly one-fourth of most skeletal series if historical and prehistoric cultural practices have not interfered. Among groups such as the Adena — assuming that the deformed versus undeformed distinctions are real — 89 percent (Webb and Snow 1945:251) of the males showed the effects of cradleboarding. This means that discussion was limited to roughly one-fourth of 11 percent, or 2.7 percent of the skeletal series — assuming that all skulls were in an excellent state of preservation and fully measurable. Even the predictive abilities of multivariate statistics are markedly limited in the face of such odds.

Neumann attempted to clarify the situation by adding morphologic observations to the metric observations of undeformed male skulls. However, the fact remains that in Neumann's typology (Neumann 1950:6) up to 70 percent of the (undeformed male) group could deviate significantly from the standard chosen to represent it. Neumann's heavy reliance upon subjective morphologic observations suffers from this and other limitations, including replicative difficulties and uncertain ties to the genetic substrate (cf. Stewart and Newman 1954).

A more recent attempt to employ cranial metrics as biological distance indicators has been made by Wilkinson (1970). Even working with questions of interregional comparisons, he found his work severely limited by the paucity of undeformed, measurable skulls (1970: 145).

Individuals in six of the seven series used here show evidence of artificial cranial deformation. In addition, the highly fragmented Peisker and Collins series together contain only a single measurable (deformed) skull. Likewise, obligatory partitioning of samples by sex would effectively prohibit the use of a L'Orient data set. Clearly, if we are to learn anything at all from fragmented remains of deforming populations, an alternative source of epigenetic information must be employed.

Postcranial Metrics

Long-bone dimensions are heavily affected by environmental factors. Although certain gross measurements may represent the genetic substrate fairly well (Osborne and DeGeorge 1959; Strouhal 1971), indications are that many such aspects are highly plastic (Kaplan 1954; Hulse 1960; Hughes 1968). Fractures, disease, and fragility also limit the number of measurable long bones in a population. Thus, in this study, fragmented series such as Peisker and Collins would effectively be eliminated from analysis.

Dental Morphology and Metrics

Dental parameters, although not affected by cultural practices such as cradleboarding, are severely limited by another environmental effect: attrition. Most individuals over thirty years of age in these middle Woodland series have occlusal surface attrition obscuring surface morphology, obliterating lingual ridges and protostylids, and rendering accurate measurement impossible. Although there is potential here for the resolution of special problems, such as biological relationship between deformed and undeformed individuals and sexual dimorphism in subadults, these are not useful markers for these skeletal series.

Cranial and Postcranial Nonmetric Traits

The use of nonmetric or "discrete" traits overcomes many of the limitations of other genetic markers. The nonmetric traits are readily scorable in fragmentary series, and most traits appear not to be associated with the sex of the individual. This gives them the advantage of representing more of the total skeletal series and a potential for discussion of intrapopulation differences, such as those produced by culturally determined marriage patterns (Lane and Sublett 1972).

Although family studies for most traits are not available, one such study (Selby *et al.* 1955) indicates high sibling concordance in the occurrence of posterior bridging of the first cervical vertebra. Studies using nonhuman mammals also suggest a high inheritance factor in nonmetric traits. For instance, Rees (1969), in a careful study of a white-tailed deer population (*Odocoileus virginianus*), produced comparable results from cranial metric and nonmetric biological distance statistics.

A dissenting opinion has been voiced by Wilkinson (1970:133–137), who concluded that nonmetric traits are not useful discriminators in small paleopopulations. He based this conclusion primarily on the fact that no sensitive distance statistics exist for nonmetric traits and that the general pattern presented by his analysis was inconsistent with the result of his metric analysis (1970:136). These results can, however, be explained by a careful evaluation of his choice of traits. Wilkinson (1970:39) used the following variants:

1. pterion form;
2. epipteric bones;
3. mandibular tori;
4. auditory meatus exostoses;
5. palatine tori;
6. nasal profile;
7. nasal gutter;
8. Wormian bones (suture not indicated);
9. tympanic dehiscenses;
10. superior sagittal sulcus direction;
11. parietal notch bone;
12. dental caries;
13. antemortem tooth loss.

Of the above, mandibular tori, auditory exostoses, and probably palatine tori are strongly associated with sex or age of the individual (Adis-Castro and Neumann 1948; Hrdlička 1935; Mayhall *et al.* 1970; Suzuki and Sakai 1960). Wilkinson has made no correction for unequal age/sex distributions within and between his populations. Nasal guttering and nasal profile are difficult to justify as discontinuous variables. Dental caries and antemortem tooth loss are heavily affected by environmental forces and individual age, and the two characteristics associated with pterion are undoubtedly related (Collins 1930). This leaves five traits, three of which may be associated (Hertzog 1968). It is not surprising that three distinctive measures of biological relationship should be confounded when they are coupled with at least seven other traits whose main effect would be to demonstrate age and sex inequalities in population distribution. A careful evaluation of each variant used is imperative if meaningful results are to be obtained.

Table 2. Nonmetric variants: cranial variants

Trait	Degrees of expression
Epipteric bone	1,2,9
Asterionic bone	1,2,9
Parietal notch bone	1,2,9
Os lambdoid suture	1,2,9
Os coronal suture	1,2,9
Infraorbital suture	1,2,3,9
Supraorbital notch	1,2,3,9
Supraorbital foramina	1,2,9
Accessory supraorbital foramina	1,2,9
Multiple mental foramina	1,2,9
Mylohyoid arch	1,2,3,4,5,9
Tympanic dehiscence	1,2,3,9
Auditory exostoses	1,2,3,4,9
Divided hypoglossal canal	1,2,3,4,5,9
Foramen ovale incomplete	1,2,3,9
Foramen spinosum open to foramen lacerum	1,2,3,9
Multiple zygomatico-facial foramina	1,2,3,4,5,6,7,9
Pterygoalar spurs	1,2,9
Pterygospinous spurs	1,2,9
Metopic suture open	1,2,3,9
Bregmatic bone	1,2,9
Inca bone	1,2,9
Apical bone	1,2,9
Os sagittal suture	1,2,9
Superior sagittal sulcus turns right	1,2,9
Mandibular torus	1,2,3,4,9
Palatine torus	1,2,3,4,9
Obelionic foramina	1,2,9
Atlas: lateral bridging	1,2,3,9
Atlas: posterior bridging	1,2,3,9
C3: accesory foramina	1,2,3,4,5,9
C4: accesory foramina	1,2,3,4,5,9
C5: accesory foramina	1,2,3,4,5,9
C6: accesory foramina	1,2,3,4,5,9
C7: accesory foramina	1,2,3,4,5,9
Humerus: septal aperture	1,2,3,9
Humerus: supracondylar spur	1,2,3,9
L5: spondylysis	1,2,3,4,9

CHOICE OF TRAITS

Several steps were taken in choosing the nonmetric traits used in this study, shown in Table 2. Initially, the question of symmetry was considered and a decision made concerning the method for evaluating bilateral traits. Next, characteristics were eliminated from the list if their frequency of occurrence was significantly associated with the presence of cranial deformation or with sex of the individual. Next, variants were excluded if they showed a low frequency of occurrence or if they were not readily scorable in the smaller series. Finally, traits showing significant association with age of the individual or with occurrence of other traits were removed and a final listing of ten variants generated. The following discussion outlines these factors as they contributed to the development of the final trait list.

Scoring Procedures

In general, the following definitions obtain:
1. absent;
2. present;
9. cannot be evaluated.
The specific definitions for each trait are as follows:

Cranial variants:

   a. Epipteric bone or fronto-temporal contact:
     1. absent;
     2. present.

   b. Infraorbital sutures:
     1. absent;
     2. partial, i.e. not to infraorbital foramen;
     3. complete.

   c. Supraorbital notch:
     1. absent or slight notch without angle;
     2. one-half occluded by spicules;
     3. one-half occluded by spicules, but not complete.

   d. Supraorbital foramina: generally included under primary or secon-
     dary headings; must have apertures on both the orbital and the
     exterior surfaces of the frontal bone.

   e. Mylohyoid arch:
     1. arch absent;
     2. partial arch;
     3. complete arch;
     4. enters from mandibular canal, no further arch;
     5. enters from mandibular canal plus arch.

f. Tympanic dehiscence:
   1. absent;
   2. true failure to ossify;
   3. foramen.

g. Auditory exostoses:
   1. absent;
   2. less than one-third auditory aperture occluded;
   3. between one-third and two-thirds auditory aperture occluded;
   4. more than two-thirds auditory aperture occluded.

h. Divided hypoglossal canal:
   1. absent;
   2. partial on medial surface of canal (near foramen magnum);
   3. complete;
   4. partial internal division;
   5. complete internal division.

Postcranial variants:

a. Bridging in atlas:
   1. absent;
   2. partial;
   3. complete;
   9. cannot be evaluated.

b. Accessory foramen: C3–C7:
   1. absent;
   2. partial small foramen on dorsal aspect of lateral foramina;
   3. complete small foramen on dorsal aspect of lateral foramina;
   4. partial division of lateral foramina into subequal parts;
   5. complete division of lateral foramina into subequal parts;
   9. cannot be evaluated.

c. Septal aperture:
   1. absent;
   2. very small;
   3. present.

Bilateral Symmetry

All bilateral traits listed in Table 2 were tested for significant side-to-side association. The null hypothesis was that there was no association of bilateral traits; that is, that traits occurred independently on right and left sides. With the exception of L'Orient, all middle Woodland series were included in the sample.

With three exceptions, all traits of reasonable sample size (all cells in a 2×2 contingency table equal to three or more) showed a lack of independence significant at the 0.01 probability level. The three exceptions include the divided hypoglossal canal ($X^2 = 6.27$), and the presence of accessory foramina in the fifth ($X^2 = 5.26$) and seventh ($X^2 = -5.60$) cervical vertebrae. These exceptions occur only if traditional scoring techniques are used and partial expressions are scored as an absence of the trait. Even these chi-squares are significant at the 0.05 probability level and could all be accepted as indications of bilaterality. However, it is important to note that in the divided hypoglossal canal and the C5 accessory foramina, a shift in scoring technique to include partially closed foramina with those already closed produces interside association significant at the 0.01 percent level. This means a chi-square of 17.30 for the hypoglossal canal and a change in the phi coefficient from 0.18 to 0.29. For C5 accessory foramina, the second chi-square is 12.59. A similar shift occurs in the sixth cervical vertebra. Here the phi coefficient is doubled from 12.27 to 24.49 with the revision of the scoring technique. The association of partial with complete manifestations of the same trait provides further evidence that a similar genetic substrate is represented in both instances. It also suggests that the most reasonable dichotomous scoring technique should include both partial and complete bridging in the "present" category.

The phenomenon presented by the seventh cervical vertebra is slightly different. A shift to the second scoring technique reduces phi from 0.19 to 0.17 and produces a lower chi-square. A careful evaluation of the various expressions of blood-vessel patterns at the foramen suggests that there are two types of bifurcations present: one in which the transverse foramen is divided into two subequal parts and another which is reflected in a small accessory foramen similar in size to those in C3–C6. The fact that these may not be phenotypic variants of the same genotype is indicated by a high interside correlation if the more common division is treated separately from the subequal bifurcation. The bilateral association for the former is significant at the 0.01 probability level ($X^2 = 11.70$); that for the latter is not ($X^2 = 2.73$). This suggests that the subequal division does not behave in a manner similar to most other traits and should therefore be more carefully studied before its inclusion as a genetic marker is warranted.

In view of the strong bilateral expression of most traits, the decision was made to score trait occurrence by individual, rather than counting each side independently, as most workers have done. This is the same technique suggested by Korey (1970) after he had noted a similar strong tendency for symmetry in bilateral traits. Each individual in whom the trait appeared was scored as having the trait — even though the occurrence was unilateral. A trait scorable on one side only was scored as if both sides were identical. It is recognized that this will produce an underestimation of frequency for traits present, but this is less of a disadvantage than losing *all* information in a fragmented skeleton.

Cranial Deformation

Prior to the work of Ossenberg (1970), most workers (e.g. Sullivan 1922, Comas 1942) concluded that cranial deformation did not affect the occurrence of nonmetric traits. These conclusions had been limited by the fact that comparisons were being made between genetically different populations. Ossenberg (1970), by using individuals from a single Hopewell mound (Klunk Mound 11), hoped to produce distinctions based solely upon the effects of deformation, because population differences would be controlled. She claims, "Neither grave furniture nor mode of burial indicated that the former [the deformed] belonged to a distinct social class or caste" (1970:359). One assumes, therefore, that her sample includes an equal number of deformed individuals from both major components of the mound, as well as equal representation for those within and outside the various areas of mound structure, i.e. the central features, subfloor pits, etc.

As will be demonstrated below, all bilateral traits under consideration show side-to-side correlation significant at the 0.01 probability level. Ossenberg has not corrected for this in her statistics. Counting each side separately has overstated a case already based on low cell counts. For instance, halving the sample size while retaining the same proportions she reports — as one might if treating each side separately — would reduce all individual trait correlations to insignificance.

A more serious problem arises in Ossenberg's attempt to group traits into locational and developmental clusters. She compares frequencies of deformed and undeformed by summing observations as if sample sizes were equal and observations were not correlated. She casts these figures into a 2 × 2 contingency table and tests using chi-square with *one degree of freedom*. The customary technique for testing for significant differences in trait frequencies of n traits between two groups is either (1) to develop an $n \times 2$ contingency table or (2) to sum the chi-square statistics for each trait pair and test the result using n degrees of freedom (d.f.). Both should give comparable results. Reevaluating Ossenberg's data using the second technique, the chi-squares having already been computed, the results shown in Table 3 were obtained.

In other words, only one of Ossenberg's trait clusters really exhibits a

Table 3.   Reevaluation of Ossenberg's data

Trait cluster	χ^2	Probability	Degrees of freedom (d.f.)
1. Supernumerary sutures of the cranial vault			
Posterior	6.50	$0.20>p>0.10$	4
Lateral	5.02	$0.20>p>0.10$	3
2. Sutural variations of the facial skeleton	2.30	$0.50>p>0.30$	2
3. Frontal bone variations	6.91	$0.30>p>0.20$	5
4. Variations of the cranial base and mandible	13.31	$0.30>p>0.20$	11
5. Emissary foramina	11.67	$0.01>p$	3

significant difference in frequency between the deformed and undeformed groups. This is the "emissary foramina" grouping, which is heavily influenced by the presence of the obelionic foramina — the only trait
significantly different between deformed and undeformed at better than
the 0.02 probability level. If the other two traits are considered together,
their probability lies between 0.10 and 0.05 (2 d.f.).

A problem also arises in Ossenberg's explanatory model. She notes:

In the deformed, at the posterior region of the vault where growth had been
inhibited because of the cradleboard and bandages, there is an increased frequency of wormians: *lambic, occipito-mastoid,* and *asterionic.*
In contrast, there is a decreased frequency of wormians in the lateral vault
where the skull was free to expand to meet the growth demands of the brain:
parietal notch bone, epipteric bones, and *coronal (pars complicata)* (1970:363,
365).

However, in bifronto-occipital deformation, pressure was apparently placed *on the lateral vault* as well as the posterior (Neumann 1942),
most notably in the region of pterion. There may be a local effect
here, although the trait frequencies do not differ significantly, but
the simple response to compensatory expansion is not a sufficient explanation.

In an attempt to eliminate those individual traits that correlate significantly with cranial deformation, individuals from the Gibson site
were arranged according to a subjective judgment of degree of
occipital deformation. Attempts were made to standardize this observation between two independent observers and agreement was
reached.

The series was then divided into two subequal groups, one representing
the less deformed individuals and the other those more severely
deformed. A test for significance was then made for association of each

trait, sides considered independently, with these groupings. The only trait to show an association significant at the 0.01 probability level was the obelionic foramen, right side ($X^2 = 6.94$, d.f. $= 1$, $n = 49$). The chi-square for the left side was not significant ($3.63, n = 50$). Although this is not conclusive proof of relationship, the fact that this was the single trait in Ossenberg's study that showed a strong association with deformation suggested that it would be advisable to exclude it from further consideration.

Sex

As mentioned above, auditory exostoses have frequently been cited for their significant association with one of the two sexes. Septal apertures are also subject to sex effect (Tanzer 1960). In order to remove this association as a possible source of bias, these two variants were eliminated from consideration. Given a widespread agreement among other workers (e.g. Berry and Berry 1967; Ossenberg 1970; Korey 1970) on the lack of significant sex association for the remaining traits, it was decided that further confirmation on yet another population would be an unnecessary redundancy.

Variability and Representation

Traits were eliminated if (1) they could not be scored in a consistent manner; (2) they did not exhibit variant forms within these middle Woodland populations; and (3) they were not scorable for nine or more individuals in the smaller series (Peisker–Collins or L'Orient). Adult open metopic sutures and bregmatic bones occurred in one and none, respectively, of the individuals examined. One supracondylar foramen appears and there was a similar low frequency of individuals with ossicles in the coronal and sagittal sutures, inca bones, and open foramina ovale. Accessory foramina in the third and fourth cervical vertebrae were also infrequently observed. The fact that the coronal and sagittal sutures close relatively early in adulthood, coupled with the scoring technique (see below) designed to minimize age correlation, may contribute to the low frequency of positive identifications for the Wormians.

Variants which may otherwise meet the criteria but which have been excluded here because they could not be scored effectively in fragmentary series include epipteric bones, foramen spinosum open, pterygoalar spurs, pterygospinous spurs, C7 accessory foramina, and spondylysis.

Age

The developmental nature of many nonmetric traits is well known. One example of such a trait is the tympanic dehiscence, whose ontogenetic sequence has been thoroughly studied by Anderson (1962). Many other traits involve progressive ossification — the formation of bony spurs, the bridging of canals. However, most studies of biological distance that utilize nonmetric traits have ignored the effect of age on trait frequency (e.g. Wilkinson 1970; Laughlin and Jørgensen 1956). A few others have indicated a recognition of age correlations but have chosen to dismiss these as insignificant differences that could not affect other aspects of the analysis, e.g. Ossenberg (1970:357).

Korey (1970), however, has demonstrated that many, although not all, traits display a significant association with age. Over a quadripartite age division — with a small (28 of 395) infant–child sample — (Korey 1970:25 ff.) found significant (p ≤ 0.95) frequency correlations over the entire range for eight variants: supraorbital foramina, accessory infraorbital foramina, ossicles in the coronal suture, epipteric bone, tympanic dehiscence, divided hypoglossal canal, foramen spinosum open, and mylohyoid arch. Two other traits showed significant frequency changes between adult groups only. These were the parietal notch bone and foramen ovale open. Such widespread correlation of trait frequency with age could easily affect population comparisons in groups whose age profiles are not identical.

Age-regressive traits include two kinds of variation: ossicle frequencies and progressive ossifications. Korey (1970:11ff.) associates ossicle frequencies with progressive suture obliteration. As sutures close, it becomes increasingly difficult to detect ossicles. For this reason, the frequency of ossicles in older individuals will appear lower than it should unless compensatory measures are taken.

Korey (1970:12) has attempted to adjust for progressive sutural obliteration of ossicles by adopting from Hertzog (1968) two standards for exclusion of material from the sample:
1. obliteration of any part of the coronal, lambdoid, or sagittal suture if no accessory bone can be found within it;
2. obliteration of any part of a margin of a tentative accessory bone. In Korey's work, this managed to compensate for accessory bones in or bordering on the sagittal and lambdoidal sutures. However, the epipteric and parietal notch bones and the coronal ossicles remained significantly associated with age. Although coronal sutural bones have already been excluded here, the epipteric and parietal notch bones are under consideration. The standards suggested by Korey were adopted in this study, with special care being taken to observe obliteration patterns at pterion and the parietal notch. No ossicle was counted unless it was observable on

both external and internal surfaces of the cranial vault, and a possibility of sutural closure in either region caused exclusion from the sample.

Korey did not attempt to compensate for the other class of age-correlated variants by modifying his scoring technique. That this might be possible is suggested by Selby, Garn, and Kanareff's observation (1955:131) that if, in their sample, the first cervical vertebra was to develop a posterior bridge, the tendency was apparent by the fourteenth year. This fact, coupled with Korey's observations concerning progressive bilaterality of traits (1970:30–33) as age increases, suggested (1) that only postadolescents should be used to represent a series unless all age grades are equally numerous in both groups; and (2) that partial and complete ossifications, e.g. division of the hypoglossal canal, are really phenotypic expressions of the same or closely similar genotypes.

To test the utility of these technical modifications, the pooled Gibson–Klunk series was tested for significant correlation of traits with age, first in the total population and then in adults only. The following six age categories were used:

1. 0–2.99 years;
2. 3–11.99 years;
3. 12–19.99 years;
4. 20–34.99 years;
5. 35–49.99 years;
6. 50+ years.

All partially completed ossifications were scored as a positive occurrence of the trait.

A test for independence of age and trait frequency was made using the point-biserial r coefficient (r_{pb}) (cf. Walker and Lev 1953:262–267, 271). Table 4 indicates the value of r_{pb}, Student's t, and the degrees of freedom for (1) the total sample, and (2) age groups (4) to (6) only.

As might be predicted from the literature (Suzuki and Sakai 1960; Mayhall and Mayhall 1971), the occurrences of palatine and mandibular tori are significantly correlated with age in both the total series and the adult sample. For this reason, the tori were eliminated from further consideration.

Apparently, the Hertzog scoring technique corrected for age correlation in the presence of most sutural bones. The single exception is the adult occurrence of ossicles in the lambdoid suture, which shows a correlation significant at the 0.05 probability level. Either this is an artifact of the inconsistent application of the scoring technique, or it could indicate that (lambdoid) sutures containing ossicles close less quickly than those without. Whatever the explanation, the significant correlation caused the removal of lambdoid ossicles from the listing of potential epigenetic traits.

Of the remaining eighteen variants, most of which should reflect pro-

Table 4.   Results of test for association of age and trait

Trait	Total series			Adults only		
	r	t	d.f	r	t	d.f.
Asterionic bone	0.05084	0.738	210	0.10676	1.428	177
Parietal notch bone	-0.00100	0.015	223	-0.09505	1.299	185
Os lambdoid suture	-0.00845	0.117	190	-0.17273	2.148[a]	150
Infraorbital suture	-0.34059	5.589[b]	238	-0.07863	1.007	163
Supraorbital notch	-0.03201	0.575	322	-0.03796	0.549	209
Supraorbital foramen	0.21160	3.897[b]	324	-0.04745	0.544	210
Accessory supra-orbital foramen	0.13017	2.345[a]	319	-0.16803	2.452[a]	207
Multiple mental foramen	0.03482	0.610	307	-0.04504	0.644	204
Mylohyoid arch	0.37227	6.783[b]	286	-0.01787	0.253	200
Tympanic dehiscence	-0.44676	9.058[b]	329	-0.08326	1.166	218
Divided hypo-glossal canal	0.14374	2.409[a]	275	-0.06371	0.847	176
Multiple zygomatico-facial foramina	0.03277	0.545	276	0.09713	1.352	192
Pterygoalar spurs[c]	0.26905	4.029[b]	208	0.02621	0.330	158
Pterygospinous spurs[c]	0.19581	2.887[b]	209	0.03127	-0.389	155
Os at lambda	0.11980	1.794	221	0.07847	0.999	161
Superior sagittal sulcus right	0.10817	1.710	247	-0.04139	0.535	167
Mandibular torus	0.53912	1.216[b]	307	0.23450	3.411[b]	200
Palatine torus	0.37196	5.944[b]	220	0.19922	2.705[b]	177
Atlas lateral bridge	0.22176	3.388[b]	222	-0.00326	0.039	141
Atlas posterior bridge	0.21811	3.307[b]	219	0.06531	0.772	139
C5: accessory foramina[c]	0.11998	1.705	199	-0.05951	0.710	142
C6: accessory foramina[c]	0.20269	3.000[b]	210	-0.06016	0.728	146

[a] Significant at 0.05 probability level.
[b] Significant at 0.01 probability level.
[c] Trait subsequently eliminated due to paucity of data in fragmented series.

gressive ossification, eleven show significant age correlation when the total series is considered. Of these, only the presence of accessory supraorbital foramina remains significantly correlated with age (0.05 probability level) when partial ossifications are scored as positive occurrences and only adults are considered. Therefore, with the elimination of this trait, we may assume that our population comparisons will not be affected by differences in age profiles.

Trait Intercorrelation

In order to eliminate the effects of pairwise association between the remaining traits, a series of 2 × 2 contingency tables was developed using all possible trait pairs. The statistics include data from all middle Woodland adults, with the exception of L'Orient. The following traits were eliminated because of significant association (0.1 confidence level;

$X^2 = 6.35$) with one or more other variants:
1. Infraorbital suture: with mylohyoid arch ($X^2 = 12.41$) and tympanic dehiscence ($X^2 = 13.70$).
2. Supraorbital notch: with supraorbital foramen ($X^2 = 69.59$).
3. Tympanic dehiscence: with multiple zygomatico-facial foramina ($X^2 = 8.88$) and infraorbital suture (above).
4. Lateral bridging on atlas: with posterior bridging ($X^2 = 22.62$).

Final Trait List

The final list of traits included the following ten variants:
1. asterionic bone;
2. parietal notch bone;
3. supraorbital foramen;
4. multiple mental foramina;
5. mylohyoid arch;
6. divided hypoglossal canal;
7. multiple zygomatico-facial foramina;
8. ossicle at lambda;
9. superior sagittal sulcus flexes right;
10. posterior bridging on atlas.

STATISTICAL PROCEDURES

Chi-Square

The first test made between all groupings was a test for simple significance used to answer the question, "Are the samples morphologically distinct from each other?" This was done by summing the chi-square values from each of eleven 2 × 2 contingency tables. The X^2 value at 11 degrees of freedom is 18.30 for the 0.05 probability level and 23.21 for the 0.01 level.

Mean Measure of Divergence

There are many ways of measuring biological distance using dichotomous data. Laughlin and Jørgensen (1956) have adapted Penrose's size-and-shape statistic to discontinuous information, while others, such as Grewal (1962), Berry and Berry (1967), Rees (1969), and Cavalli-Sforza and Bodmer (1971), prefer techniques involving angular transformations.

The statistic used here is one of the latter: the mean measure of divergence developed by C.A.B. Smith and used by Grewal, Berry and Berry, and Rees. The formula as given by Berry (1968) is as follows:

$$D_e = [\Sigma \, (\theta_1 - \theta_2) \,^2/_N] - (^1/_{n_1} + ^1/_{n_2}), \text{ where}$$

θ is the angular transformation measured in radians of the percentage incidence of each variant; N is the number of variants used; and n is the number of individuals in each population. Likewise, the variance (V) of D_e is computed as follows:

$$V = 4 \, (^1/_{n_1} + ^1/_{n_2}) \, \Sigma \, [(\theta_1 - \theta_2)^2 - (^1/_{n_1} + ^1/_{n_2})]/ \, N^2.$$

In each of these formulas it is assumed that each characteristic is scorable in each individual and therefore the term used to correct for random sampling ($1/n_1 + 1/n_2$) is considered constant across all variants. Since this was not the case in the archaeological populations considered here, the formulas were modified so that the error term would be computed separately for each variant. The resultant formulas are as follows:

$$D_e = \frac{\Sigma \, [(\theta_1 - \theta_2)^2 - (^1/_{n_1} + ^1/_{n_2})]}{N} \; ;$$

$$V = \frac{\Sigma \, [(^1/_{n_1} + ^1/_{n_2}) \, ((\theta_1 - \theta_2)^2 - (^1/_{n_1} + ^1/_{n_2}))]}{N^2} \; .$$

EPIGENETIC COMPARISONS

Mound Clusters

As noted in the introduction, most physical anthropologists have emphasized questions relating to origins and migrations. In these studies, it has generally been assumed that local groups that share a common cultural tradition show no important or recognizable intergroup biological variability. Distinct morphological types associated with culturally or temporally distinct populations have been emphasized, and no attempt has been made to study variability within and between local series. A corollary to this is the assumption that any cemetery series adequately represents regional variability.

Archaeologists tell us, however, that middle Woodland communities in the lower Illinois River region represent long-term occupancies, and a degree of sedentism is implied (Struever 1968; Struever and Houart 1972). If this is indeed the case, contemporaneous communities during succeeding generations of occupation may have become genetically and hence epigenetically distinct. We may test this using information from three contemporary middle Woodland burial series.

Three 10 × 2 chi-square tables were developed testing the nonmetric variants for significant association with the three geographically distinct mound clusters. A significant X^2 at the 0.05 probability level is equal to 18.3. The results of the comparisons are Peisker–Collins versus Bedford: 17.3; Gibson–Klunk versus Peisker–Collins: 20.79; and Bedford versus Gibson–Klunk: 26.96.

Two of the three statistics are significant at the 0.05 probability level. The third statistic has a probability between 0.05 and 0.10. The weight of the evidence suggests intercluster heterogeneity and a hypothesis of intergroup variability accepted.

Given the linear distribution of these sites along the Illinois River, one might suggest that an explanation of the epigenetic difference should emphasize geographic distance. In other words, the distinctions may be due primarily to sampling error and drift in small populations. If so, we might expect a close correlation between the epigenetic distance (D_e) and the number of linear miles separating the three clusters. The epigenetic distances between the three local groups were computed as Peisker–Collins versus Gibson–Klunk: 0.0403; Gibson–Klunk versus Bedford: 0.2131; and Peisker–Collins versus Bedford: 0.1466.

Geographic distances between the groups are 13.5, 16.5, and 29.75 linear miles, respectively. The Pearson (r) correlation coefficient for this matrix is 0.28, a relatively low figure. It is likely, therefore, that simple geographic separation only partially explains the differences measured by the epigenetic distance statistics. Other factors, perhaps relating to social organization, affect local patterns of biological variability.

Culturally Defined Within-Mound Units

A possible status distinction with associated biological attributes has been noted in certain middle Woodland cemeteries (Buikstra 1972). This distinction was between certain individuals receiving special burial treatment and the remainder of the series at the Gibson site. The "high status" burials were taller individuals, and the single measurable skull from this group was consistently distinguished from other males in the series by showing a large number of female dimensions.

The height of the central-feature, special-status burials could reflect either acquired or achieved status within Hopewell social units. The presence of children within the highly selective contents of the central features and the distinctive nature of the single measurable cranium suggest that the central-feature burials were a distinctive unit in which status was acquired through kinship. Because stature, like other morphological characteristics, has a heritable component, it is possible that the central-feature burials represent a distinctive genetic stock. This could have arisen from special marriage patterns within the middle Woodland community, or from an initially distinctive heritage perpetuated by intraclass endogamy. Although the question of etiology cannot be resolved without comparative materials from other geographic areas, the question of a distinctive hereditary morphology for the central-feature burials can be tested with available data.

Data from the Gibson and Klunk series were cast into the following burial groupings:

1. Central-feature and associated burials: these include bundle or isolated bone burials located on or in the surface of ramps or the original ground surface.

2. Subfloor pits: these include all burials from subfloor pits.

3. Residual intramound burials: these include all other skeletons not associated with intrusive pits or diagnostic late Woodland artifacts.

If the burial groupings are significantly different, an argument for inherited status would be strengthened. However, as may be seen in Table 5, none of the chi-squares developed through two-way comparisons is significant. Although these data may not be sensitive enough to pick up subtle variations, the comparison would not support the argu-

Table 5. X^2 statistics developed in a comparison of epigenetic characteristics for culturally defined burial units

Gibson ____ Klunk	Central feature	Subfloor pits	Other
Central feature	. . . .	3.87	9.55
Subfloor pits	4.75	. . . .	12.77
Other	5.64	6.12	. . . .

Klunk and Gibson Total Series			
Central feature	. . . .	3.46	4.30
Subfloor pits	. . . .	. .	10.46
Other	. .	. .	. .

ment for inherited status determining access to the relatively inaccessible features.

SEX DIFFERENCES IN INTERMOUND VARIATION

As demonstrated by Lane and Sublett (1972), the amount of morphological variation within and among males and females of a skeletal series can be interpreted as a mirror for residence and/or marriage patterns. For instance, using Seneca reservation data, they have defined what they believe to be a residence system based upon male–male bonds. Their results are supported by ethnographic information. The formal propositions tested by Lane and Sublett (1972:9) are as follows:

1. If the resident units of a rural neighborhood-type pattern of localized nuclear family households are based on a male–male genetic relationship, then comparisons of (a) males and females within a single cemetery should be heterogeneous; (b) males and males between cemeteries should be heterogeneous; and (c) females and females between cemeteries should be homogeneous.

2. If the resident units of a rural neighborhood-type pattern of localized nuclear family households are based on a female–female genetic relationship, then comparisons of (a) males and females within a single cemetery should be heterogeneous; (b) males and males between cemeteries should be homogeneous; and (c) females and females between cemeteries should be heterogeneous.

The protohistoric Seneca cemeteries have one important attribute that separates them from prehistoric Hopewell cemeteries: known time depth. The Seneca cemeteries resulted from deaths in contemporaneous social units within a circumscribed length of time (about eighty years). The Hopewell mounds could have been (1) cemeteries of the same or different social units built in quasi-serial order or (2) cemeteries under simultaneous long-term construction by certain subgroups, such as lineages, within the same social unit. In the latter case, the formal propositions would resemble those for Lane and Sublett's Seneca cemeteries; in the former, they would not. The interpretations of social organization will vary according to which set of propositions one accepts.

Only individual mounds within the Klunk cemetery have samples of adequate size to perform the intramound comparison. Discussion will, therefore, consider the Klunk mounds with reasonable sample sizes — 1, 2, 5, and 11 — and will emphasize 1 and 11, whose samples of sexable adults approximate forty individuals each.

Dyadic Relationships Tested

Three types of dyadic relationships must be considered: (1) male–female, (2) female–female, and (3) male–male. The following summarizes the results of the comparisons for each dyad.

MALE–MALE: RELATIVE HOMOGENEITY. Table 6 summarizes the chi-square and epigenetic distant statistics for the Klunk comparisons. None of the chi-squares is significant at the 0.05 level. Five of the six D_e statistics are less than or equal to 0.03 and none is greater than twice its standard deviation.

Table 6.   Male–male intermound comparisons of heritable traits in Klunk series [a]

1	2	5	11
1 . .	11.21	7.52	13.13
. .	0.21	0.009	0.03
2		8.83	7.98
. . . .		0.09	0.004
5		. .	13.91
. . . .		. .	0.08
11		. .	. .

[a] Upper figure is value of chi-squared; lower is epigenetic distance statistic.

FEMALE–FEMALE: RELATIVE HETEROGENEITY. As seen in Table 7, all the epigenetic distance statistics are greater than or equal to 0.06 and two are in excess of twice the value of their standard deviations. Even though none of the chi-squares is significant at the 0.05 probability level, this would seem to indicate an order of magnitude difference between the male–male and female–female comparisons.

MALE–FEMALE: HETEROGENEITY. Table 8 shows that a difference exists in the male–female pairs similar to or greater than that for the female–male comparisons. Four, or one-fourth, of the dyads produced significant chi-squares (0.05 level, 11 d.f.) and an equal number of epigenetic distance statistics exceeded twice the value of their standard deviations. Two pairs shared both significance factors.

Table 7. Female–female intermound comparisons of heritable traits in Klunk series

	1	2	5	11
1	· ·	14.63	17.23	10.23
		0.14	0.14[a]	0.08
2	· ·	· ·	13.72	15.21
			0.12	0.10
5	· ·	· ·	· ·	14.90
				0.06[a]
11	· ·	· ·	· ·	· ·

[a] Indicates D_e equal to more than twice its standard deviation.

Table 8. Male–female intermound comparisons of heritable traits in Klunk series

	1	2	5	11
1	15.11	13.02	18.28	18.76
	0.07	0.06	0.09	0.17[a]
2	20.77[b]	16.40	8.42	14.60
	0.33[a]	0.30	–0.02	0.09
5	18.85	15.16	12.72	25.93[b]
	0.25	0.24	0.08	0.35
11	23.16[b]	14.24	8.77	15.72
	0.31	0.17	0.01	0.09

[a] Indicates D_e equal to more than twice its standard deviation.
[b] Chi-square value significant at 0.05 probability level.

Explanatory Models

MODEL A: CONTEMPORANEOUS MOUND-BUILDING BY SOCIAL SUBUNITS. In this case, the formal propositions suggested by Lane and Sublett pertain. Evidently, despite the special attention given the male in various parts of the burial program, a female–female biological relationship influences membership in the total mortuary unit. This is indicated by the distinctive clusters of females, who are dissimilar from males within their own group, and by the homogeneous nature of the male population.

MODEL B: MOUND-BUILDING IN SERIAL ORDER. In this case, the most reasonable interpretation of the previously presented pattern would be a relatively stable lineage of males with females from other genetic stocks entering the area. The fact that the Klunk females, as a whole, do not differ significantly from the Gibson males, as they do from the males from their mound group (0.05 probability level) suggests that part of the interaction may involve association at this level of proximity. However, this possibility cannot be pursued due to the limited size of the Gibson samples. The Klunk females do, however, differ significantly from both Bedford males and females, indicating that gene flow was at least not consistently from that direction. The possibility of sporadic gene flow from certain areas, such as the Bedford–Bixby regions, could still occur. However, Table 9 indicates that the Klunk females are no more like the Bedford females (or males) than they are like their own females. Given the nature of the Bedford series, which must include all available skeletons from the entire mound group if an adequate sample is to be used, this is not conclusive proof of the point. However, there is no recognizable evidence here for residence or marriage patterns that include interaction with the middle Woodland population represented in the Bedford mounds.

The similarity of the distance statistics for the intermound pairings at Klunk–Gibson (Buikstra 1972) would appear to support model A. If mound-building were serial, it should be possible to order the mounds in decreasing order of similarity. The relative identity of individual mounds

Table 9. Comparison of epigenetic characteristics between Klunk females (by mound) and Bedford males/females

Klunk females	Bedford males	Bedford females
1	19.36	20.99[a]
	0.57[b]	0.37
2	15.61	16.65
	0.52	0.36
5	16.20	15.09
	0.42	0.21
7	17.04	24.28[a]
	0.91[b]	0.77[b]
11	18.71	21.69[a]
	0.34	0.25[b]

[a] Indicates D_e value more than twice its standard deviation.
[b] Indicates chi-square significant at 0.05 probability level.

— in terms of both burial programs and epigenetic traits — with each other suggests relative contemporaneity for their use.

NONCONTEMPORANEOUS SERIES COMPARISONS. Our perspective of intraregional variability may be clarified through a consideration of additional series. For instance, L'Orient may be slightly later than the other middle Woodland series, yet it shares a similar mortuary pattern. Our model of relatively stable middle Woodland communities whose genetic affinities are to some extent explicable in terms of spatial proximity would lead us to predict that L'Orient should most closely resemble nearby Gibson–Clunk and Peisker–Collins. Likewise, a repeated emphasis by other workers (Neumann 1952, 1960; Hunter 1968) on the typologically distinct late Woodland Indian would lead us to predict that all the middle Woodland series should be more closely related to each other than to a local late Woodland series, such as that from the Ledders site.

Epigenetic distances were computed for the remaining two-way comparisons necessary to complete the matrix developed in comparing all five mound clusters. Table 10 summarizes the result of all these comparisons.

Table 10.   Epigenetic distances for all series

	Gibson–Klunk	Ledders	Peisker–Collins	Bedford
L'Orient	0.011	0.041	0.060	0.336
Gibson–Klunk	—	0.093	0.040	0.213
Ledders		—	0.201	0.348
Peisker–Collins			—	0.147

The results of this comparison appear somewhat different from that which was predicted on the basis of previously existing hypotheses concerning biological distance. To be sure, L'Orient's closes affinity is with nearby Gibson–Klunk. However, it is also similar to Ledders. In fact, Ledders is apparently quite closely tied to the middle Woodland series — especially to those geographically closest to it.

One means of ordering these data is by use of the double-link method, as described by Renfrew and Sterud (1969). Briefly, each unit or series is linked with the two other series with which it shares most similarity. Each linkage is marked with an arrow indicating the direction of the linkage. Figure 1 summarizes the results of the double-link ordering of the epigenetic distances.

It is evident both from the distribution of (D_e) scores and from the double-link ordering that the four southernmost mound clusters share a great deal of epigenetic similarity. Late Woodland Ledders is linked to nearby middle Woodland populations, with the double linkage to L'Orient explicable in terms of both temporal and spatial proximity.

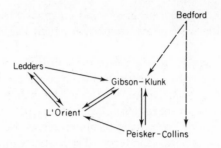

Figure 2.   Double-link ordering of epigenetic distance statistics

Apparently, microevolutionary changes were not marked, and these data would argue for a rather stable gene pool within this area during the marked cultural change from middle to late Woodland.

By contrast, middle Woodland Bedford shows strong association with neither contemporary nor later populations. As noted before, a simple geographic separation is insufficient to explain the differences noted here. Careful consideration should be given to probable social causes as an explanation for this patterning.

SUMMARY AND CONCLUSIONS

Nonmetric traits are a useful source of epigenetic information ideally suited to biological distance. In comparisons of small and poorly pre-served skeletal series, a technique for minimizing factors such as intertrait correlation and age association has been developed, utilizing series of over 300 middle Woodland Indian skeletons. The fact that the expansion of many nonmetric characteristics may vary in other populations due to differences in threshold effects (cf. Berry 1968) will, however, limit the possibility that all studies will show identical trait correlations and that interactions with such factors as age and cranial deformation will be identical. It is suggested that the technique itself should be useful in other studies of unrelated series.

The three contemporaneous middle Woodland sites included in this study have produced skeletal series significantly different from each other in an epigenetic sense. At least part of this difference may be explicable in terms of geographic isolation and drift, but indications are that part of the explanation also involves the complexities of middle Woodland social organization. Other epigenetic comparisons have argued against inherited status in middle Woodland communities and for burial rules based upon genetic relationship. In addition, the small differ-ences between spatially proximal middle and late Woodland populations suggest that in the lower Illinois River region the major cultural shift between A.D. 400 and 600 was not accompanied by marked fluctuation in the (epi)genetic character of local groups.

REFERENCES

ADIS-CASTRO, ELIAS, GEORG K. NEUMANN
  1948   The incidence of ear exostoses in the Hopewell people of the Illinois Valley. *Proceedings of the Indiana Academy of Science* 57:33–36.
ANDERSON, J. E.
  1962   *The development of the tympanic plate.* National Museum of Canada Bulletin 180. Ottawa, Ontario.
BERRY, A. C., R. J. BERRY
  1967   Epigenetic variation in the human cranium. *Journal of Anatomy* 101:361–379.
BERRY, R. J.
  1968   "The biology of non-metrical variation in mice and man," in *The skeletal biology of earlier human populations.* Edited by D. R. Brothwell, 103–133. Oxford: Pergamon.
BUIKSTRA, JANE E.
  1972   "Hopewell in this lower Illinois River valley." Unpublished doctoral dissertation, University of Chicago.
CAVALLI-SFORZA, L. L., W. F. BODMER
  1971   *The genetics of human populations.* San Francisco: W. H. Freeman.
COLLINS, H. B., JR.
  1930   Notes on the pterion. *American Journal of Physical Anthropology* 14:41–44.
COMAS, J.
  1942   *Contribution à l'étude du métopisme.* Geneva: Kundig.
GREWAL, M. S.
  1962   The rate of genetic divergence in the C57BL strain of mice. *Genetics Research* 3:236–237.
HERTZOG, K. P.
  1968   Associations between discontinuous cranial traits. *American Journal of Physical Anthropology* 29:397–404.
HRDLIČKA, ALEŠ
  1935   Ear exostoses. *Smithsonian Miscellaneous Collections* 93:1–100.
HUGHES, DAVID R.
  1968   "Skeletal plasticity and its relevance in the study of earlier populations," in *The skeletal biology of earlier human populations.* Edited by D. R. Brothwell. Oxford: Pergamon.
HULSE, FRED
  1960   "Adaptation, selection and plasticity in ongoing human evolution," in *The process of on-going human evolution.* Edited by G. W. Lasker, 63–79. Detroit: Wayne State University Press.
HUNTER, KING B.
  1968   Preliminary report on the Hopewellian skeletons from the Klunk site, Colhoun County, Illinois. *Illinois Archeological Survey Bulletin* 6:125–128.
KAPLAN, BERNICE A.
  1954   Environment and human plasticity. *American Anthropologist* 56:780–800.

KOREY, KENNETH
1970   "Characteristics of the distributions of non-metric variants." Unpublished master's thesis, University of Chicago.
LANE, REBECCA A., AUDREY SUBLETT
1972   The osteology of social organization: residence pattern. *American Antiquity* 37:186–201.
LAUGHLIN, W. S., J. B. JØRGENSEN
1956   Isolate variation in Greenlandic Eskimo crania. *Acta Genetica et Statistica Medica* 6:3–12.
MAYHALL, JOHN T., A. A. DAHLBERG, DAVID G. OWEN
1970   Torus mandibularis in an Alaskan Eskimo population. *American Journal of Physical Anthropology* 33:57–60.
MAYHALL, JOHN T., MELINDA F. MAYHALL
1971   Torus mandibularis in two Northwest Territories villages. *American Journal of Physical Anthropology* 34:143–148.
NEUMANN, GEORG K.
1942   Types of artificial deformation in the eastern United States. *American Antiquity* 7:306–310.
1950   "Racial differentiation in the American Indian." Unpublished doctoral dissertation, University of Chicago.
1952   "Archeology and race in the American Indian," in *Archeology of the eastern United States*. Edited by James B. Griffin, 13–34. Chicago: University of Chicago Press.
1960   Origins of the Indians of the middle Mississippi area. *Proceedings of the Indiana Academy of Science* 69:66–68.
OSBORNE, R. H., F. V. DEGEORGE
1959   *Genetic basis of morphological variation.* Boston: Harvard University Press.
OSSENBERG, NANCY
1970   The influence of artificial cranial deformation on discontinuous morphological traits. *American Journal of Physical Anthropology* 33:357–372.
REES, JOHN
1969   Morphologic variation in the cranium and mandible of the white-tailed deer (*Odocoileus virginianus*): a comparative study of geographical and four biological distances. *Journal of Morphology* 128:113–130.
RENFREW, COLIN, GENE STERUD
1969   Close-proximity analysis: a rapid method for the ordering of archaeological materials. *American Antiquity* 34:265–277.
SELBY, SAMUEL, STANLEY GARN, VERA KANAREFF
1955   The incidence and familial nature of a bony bridge on the first cervical vertebra. *American Journal of Physical Anthropology* 13:129–141.
STEWART, T. D., MARSHALL T. NEWMAN
1954   Review of *Archaeology and race in the American Indian*. *American Journal of Physical Anthropology* 12:1–5.
STRUEVER, STUART
1968   "A re-examination of Hopewell." Unpublished doctoral dissertation, University of Chicago.
STRUEVER, STUART, GAIL HOUART
1972   "An analysis of the Hopewell interaction sphere," in *Social exchange and interaction*. Edited by Edwin N. Wilmsen, 47–49. Anthropological Papers of the Museum of Anthropology 46. University of Michigan Press.

STROUHAL, EUGEN
1971 Anthropometric and functional evidence of heterosis from Egyptian Nubia. *Human Biology* 43:271–287.

SULLIVAN, L. R.
1922 The frequency and distribution of some anatomical variations in American crania. *Anthropological Papers of the American Museum of Natural History* 23:203–258.

SUZUKI, M., I. SAKAI
1960 A familial study of torus palatinus and torus mandibularis. *American Journal of Physical Anthropology* 18:263–272.

TANZER, H.
1960 Anthropological looks at an anomaly — septal apertures in the humerus. *University of Toronto Medical Journal:* 151–152.

WALKER, HELEN M., JOSEPH LEV
1953 *Statistical inference.* New York: Holt, Rinehart and Winston.

WEBB, WILLIAMS S., CHARLES E. SNOW
1945 *The Adena people.* University of Kentucky Reports in Anthropology and Archeology 6. Lexington, Kentucky.

WILKINSON, RICHARD G.
1970 "Biological relationships among middle and late Woodland populations in the Great Lakes region." Unpublished doctoral dissertation, University of Michigan.

A Sample of Northern North American Hunter–Gatherers and the Malthusian Thesis: An Explicitly Quantified Approach

RICHARD W. CASTEEL

> A conjecture, however improbable on the first view of it, advanced by able and ingenious men, seems at least to deserve investigation.
>
> THOMAS ROBERT MALTHUS, *Population*, p. 87

The works of Malthus, particularly those dealing with questions of human population size, have stirred debate for nearly 200 years. Both advocates and opponents of his views have been eloquent, informed, and enthusiastic. Within anthropology today there still exists a basic dichotomy of views with regard to Malthus's proposals on human population size. Some feel Malthus's views to be inadequate, especially so for dealing with changes in both plants and animals as well as in the technology of agriculture and the increased yields derived therefrom (Boserup 1965; Spooner 1972). Many of these critics often focus upon Malthus's suppositions (1967:8) that while population could increase geometrically, the means of subsistence could do so only arithmetically. As Flew (1970:34) has stated, "it is only fair to remember that Malthus made it [the theoretical maximal limit] in the light of the then available evidence, and with what seemed all reasonable generosity towards the opposition." Since this portion of Malthus's argument is not central to the present work, dealing as it does with hunter–gatherers only, the criticisms likewise need no further explication. It is perhaps characteristic of the state of the art, however, to note that in a recent book of articles (Spooner 1972), which focused upon Boserup's and, hence, Malthus's views, and which contains a number of discussions of Malthus's as well as of "neo-Malthusian"

My sincere thanks to Dr. Gordon H. Orians, Department of Zoology, University of Washington, for his suggestions and comments and to Dr. J. B. Birdsell, Department of Anthropology, University of California, Los Angeles, for his invaluable discussions. My gratitude to the Computer Center, University of Washington, for providing funds for the processing and analysis of data.

views, there is not a single reference to Malthus in the bibliography. One is reminded of the first line of the advertisement for the 1830 "Summary" edition of Malthus's work, which states that "it has been frequently remarked, that no work has been so much talked of by persons who do not seem to have read it as Mr. Malthus's *Essay on Population*" (Malthus 1970:221).

MALTHUS'S THESIS

The concern of the present work is not with Malthus's thesis in its entirety, for the gaps in this have been well documented by able critics. Instead attention is focused upon one portion of his thesis, that which deals with the relationship between human population size and the food available to sustain it. Specifically, concern is focused upon the limiting influence of available food energy upon the maximum potential size of a human population. This part of Malthus's proposals seems to be the most straightforward and unassailable component of his "simple, yet very powerful theoretical scheme" (Flew 1970:17).

Put forth as part of a rebuttal to the utopian views of the Marquis de Condorcet and to the early poor laws of England, Malthus maintained that:

Elevated as man is above all other animals by his intellectual faculties, it is not to be supposed that the physical laws to which he is subjected should be essentially different from those which are observed to prevail in other parts of animated nature. He may increase slower than most other animals; but food is equally necessary to his support; and if his natural capacity of increase be greater than can be permanently supplied with food from a limited territory, his increase must be constantly retarded by the difficulty of procuring the means of subsistence (Malthus 1970:225).

Malthus felt this situation to be due to the fact that "by the laws of nature man cannot live without food" (Malthus 1970:242, 1967:4, 13, 49). Thus, while the human population size could be well below the maximum size that could be sustained over time (although Malthus maintained this gap would quickly be filled by the "passion between the sexes"), the food available would ultimately limit the maximum attainable human population size. This is the ultimate form of Malthus's positive checks to population increase. Under these assumptions the population tends to increase through continued recruitment and is limited only by mortality, the level of which is ultimately set by the available food resources.

Malthus applied these views to his study of the North American Indian. In 1798 he stated, with specific reference to the North American Indian, that "the effort toward population, even in this people, seems to be always greater than the means to support it" (Malthus 1967:14). In 1817 in his "Second essay" Malthus presented a more detailed examination of the North American Indian case utilizing the ethnographic materials then available to him. Here he stated that the North American Indian situation was "merely an exemplification of the obvious truth, that population cannot increase without the food to support it" (Malthus 1817:52). He further stated that:

In a general view of the American continent, as described by historians, the population seems to have been spread over the surface very nearly in proportion to the quantity of food, which the inhabitants of the different parts, in the actual state of their industry and improvement, could obtain: and that, with few exceptions, *it pressed hard against this limit* (Malthus 1817: 80; emphasis added).

It is the last part of the above statement which forms the focus of the present study. Malthus proposed that the aboriginal human population of North America lived at a level at which the population continually pressed against the maximum size attainable given the available food-stuffs and their mode of procurement.

Whatever one may feel for Malthus's views and for his thesis regarding the North American Indian in particular, it must be granted that he was an empiricist. He relied upon evidence to support or refute his contentions. Indeed, he himself stated that he had not "acquired that command over his understanding which would enable him to believe what he wishes, without evidence, or to refuse his assent to what might be unpleasing, when accompanied with evidence" (Malthus 1967:xiv). He also urged that "a theory that will not admit of application cannot possibly be just" (Malthus 1967:63).

RESEARCH STRATEGY

To examine how accurately Malthus's views might reflect the situation of human populations in aboriginal North America, two elements were required. First, a method of estimating how much food energy would be available is necessary. Second, a sample of aboriginal groups is required, along with their subsistence regimes and population sizes, in order to compare their actual population sizes with those predictable under the conditions of Malthus's thesis.

METHODS

In order to solve the first problem a method for estimation of the maximum carrying capacity is required. In an earlier publication (Casteel 1972) a method for the estimation of maximum population density figures for hunter–gatherer groups was proposed. This method was based upon a knowledge of the net primary productivity of terrestrial resources along with estimates of other energy sources. Two models were presented that would allow these population estimates to be made. The first, $P_{max(1)}$, would be amenable to modern ethnographic investigations. The second, $P_{max(2)}$, was presented as a more general version that could be utilized with regard to less detailed ethnographic materials. This latter model, $P_{max(2)}$, will be utilized below to examine the relationships between expected and observed population sizes in a sample of North American hunter–gatherers situated at or above 60° north latitude. Prior to doing so, it is necessary to review the model and add a slight modification in order to increase its applicability and objectivity.

The model is defined as follows:

$$P_{max(2)} = \sum_{i=1}^{n} (Z \cdot N_j) + F + S \tag{1}$$

where
$P_{max(2)}$ = the estimated maximum human population density for a hunter–gatherer group for a single year;
Z = the percent of the annual cycle spent in a given ecosystem$_i$;
n = the number of ecosystems$_i$ utilized;
N = the maximum human population density of a given ecosystem$_i$ at a given trophic level$_j$;

$i = 1, 2, \ldots n$; and
$j = 2, 3, 4.$

The variables F and S are defined as follows:

$$F = \sum_{k=1}^{n'} T_k'' (B E_k) \tag{2}$$

where
F = the estimated maximum human population density based upon the total aquatic and/or migratory terrestrial energy sources, if not already included in P_{max};
T'' = the percent of the annual cycle which a given work group or age or sex class spent exploiting a given aquatic or migratory terrestrial energy source$_k$;
B = the total area habitually utilized by the group;
E = the annual maximum human population density based upon any given aquatic or migratory terrestrial energy source$_k$;

n' = the total number of aquatic or migratory terrestrial energy sources$_k$;
and
$k = 1, 2, \ldots n$;
and:

$$S = \frac{\left(\sum_{q=1}^{n''} \frac{C_q}{D} \right)}{B} \tag{3}$$

where
S = the estimated maximum human population density based upon energy (food items) traded into a given area;
B = the total area habitually utilized by the group;
C = the total caloric value of a given class of traded food$_q$ in kilocalories (such as meat, plant foods, and so forth);
D = the annual individual energy requirement of 8×10^5 kilocalories;
n'' = the total number of traded food items included; and
$q = 1, 2, \ldots n$.

In the data to be examined here, no reliable, objective estimates could be obtained for the values of F and S. For this reason they will both be considered to equal 0.

In the earlier publication, seven North American hunter–gatherer groups were examined: the Cahuilla, the Chimariko, the Modoc, the Chilcotin, the Chipewyan, the Montagnais, and the Kaska. The basic data concerning net primary production for each of these samples were derived from figures presented in Westlake (1963) and Kormondy (1969). These data were from selected ecosystems and were not necessarily representative of many of the geographic locations of the sample groups. In addition, it was necessary to make subjective evaluations of the extent of each of these particular vegetation types within the territory of each group. In order to correct this deficiency a second approximation method is presented below for estimating the net primary above-ground productivity which will not necessitate the use of the subjective evaluations presented above.

Holdridge (1967) has presented an excellent case for the value of water, in an available form, for the plant community. The crucial value required here is that for evapotranspiration (also referred to as actual evapotranspiration). This value is the sum of evaporation and transpiration. The importance of this for the present purpose is that Rosenzweig (1968) found that the net annual above-ground productivity of mature plant communities could be predicted quite accurately based only upon a knowledge of actual evapotranspiration. Rosenzweig (1968:67) defined actual evapotranspiration as "precipitation, minus runoff, minus percolation." This relationship can be expressed as follows:

$$\log_{10} NAAP = (1.66 \pm 0.27) \log_{10} AE - (1.66 \pm 0.07) \qquad (4)$$

where
$NAAP$ = the net annual above-ground productivity in gm/m^2; and
AE = the annual actual evapotranspiration in mm.

I have reproduced this relationship along with Rosenzweig's data points in Figure 1. Rosenzweig (1968:73) has stated that this close relationship is due "to the fact that AE measures the simultaneous availability of water and solar energy, the most important rate-limiting resources in photosynthesis."

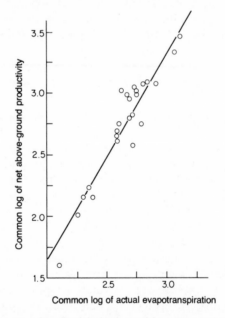

Figure 1.   Net above-ground productivity in grams of dry matter per square meter graphed against actual evapotranspiration in millimeters (after Rosenzweig 1968: Figure 1)

The value of Rosenzweig's formula for the present purpose is that one can now predict the net primary above-ground productivity precisely for specific geographic areas of one's own choosing and need not rely upon subjective assessments of the proportion of coverage of certain vegetation types and their productivities from a few selected geographic areas. Instead, to estimate $NAAP$ all one needs is the value of AE for the particular area under study. This value (AE) is easily obtained from the publications of Thornthwaite Associates (1962, 1963a, 1963b, 1963c,

1964a, 1964b, 1964c, 1965), in which AE values are presented for selected stations the world over.

Using the values of $NAAP$ arrived at by the above-mentioned method, the maximum population estimates arrived at earlier (Casteel 1972) for these seven North American Indian groups were recalculated. Table 1 presents the mean values of $P_{max(2)} \times$ area, both as derived earlier from the productivity estimates of Kormondy (1969) and Westlake (1963) and as determined from Rosenzweig's formula (1968). The resultant mean maximum population estimates were then compared in order to assess their correlation. They were found to be very highly correlated ($r = 0.99663$). This correlation is a significant at the $a = 0.01$ level ($z = 2.4412$). This is presented in graphic form in Figure 2. The estimates arrived at based upon Rosenzweig's formula are, on the average, about twice as high as the previous estimates.

Table 1. Estimated populations based upon two estimates of net productivity (mean values)

Group	Data from Kormondy (1969) and Westlake (1963)	Data from Rosenzweig (1968)
Cahuilla	27,162	11,846
Kaska	392,017	689,609
Chilcotin	55,029	69,009
Montagnais	3,348,149	8,446,435
Chipewyan	496,140	567,439
Chimariko	2,207	6,276
Modoc	22,803	79,222

Note: Population figures are those calculated as the maximum potential based upon total resources for each group. They represent maximum figures and should not be taken as estimates of the actual ethnographic population sizes.

Thus, knowing both the nature of the maximum population estimates arrived at based upon Rosenzweig's formula and their very high correlation with those obtained earlier, the use of Rosenzweig's estimates of $NAAP$ is recommended and they have been utilized in the examples which follow.

Next is required a sample of aboriginal groups in order to test the applicability of Malthus's thesis.

In order to attempt a quantitative estimate of the relationship between food energy potentially available and the actual size of a human population, a sample of all North American hunter–gatherer groups living at or above 60° north latitude was selected. These groups were taken from those listed in the Ethnographic Atlas (Murdock 1967). The following criteria were considered both necessary and sufficient for inclusion of a group in the sample: (1) subsistence must be based only upon hunting of land mammals, gathering, fishing (mainly freshwater), or some combina-

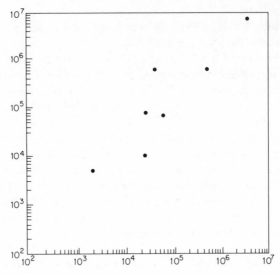

Figure 2. Mean population estimates based upon net productivity data from Westlake (1963) and Kormondy (1969) for the abscissa and Rosenzweig (1968) for the ordinate graphed as common logs

tion of these; (2) an estimate of the relative amount of time spent on each of these subsistence activities must be available; (3) estimates of each group's territorial boundaries must be available or calculable; and (4) independent ethnographic estimates of their population sizes must be available. Of all the groups available for study, only six met all the above requirements. These groups are presented in Table 2.

In the part of Malthus's work to be examined here it is assumed that the actual size of the human population (Y) is a direct function of the maximum amount of food available (carrying capacity) (X).

The concern here is, then, the examination of a deterministic model (Blalock 1964:15) of the form

$$X \rightarrow Y \tag{5}$$

where
X = the carrying capacity based solely upon the food or foods available to a human population relative to their intensity of exploitation; and
Y = the attained population size.

In order to examine the relationships under study and to test the hypothesized correlation between carrying capacity (here defined as food energy available relative to intensity of exploitation) and attained population size, a graphical method was chosen.

If the carrying capacity is plotted along the abscissa and the attained human population size plotted on the ordinate on an arithmetic system of

Table 2. Sample of North American hunter–gatherers

Group	Latitude and longitude	AE[a]	Area (square miles)	Fishing[b] index	Hunting	Gathering	Fishing	Mean[c] ethnographic population	Mean[d] ethnographic population	Mean[e] predicted population
Slave	61N 120W	243	68,827	5	50	10	40	938	400	523
Dogrib	63N 117W	225	93,681	5	30	20	50	990	895	890
Kutchin	66N 135W	255	210,134	1	40	10	50	1,021	1,021	841
Caribou Eskimo	63N 96W	258	91,962	5	50	10	40	600	500	699
Chipewyan	60N 105W	321	458,201	5	60	0	40	3,203	3,158	3,482
Nabesna	63N 141W	256	33,962	6	60	20	20	152[f]	152[f]	154

Source: Driver 1967; Thompson 1966; Hodge 1911; Swanton 1952; Murdock *et al.* 1962; Murdock 1963, 1964, 1967, 1969; Osgood 1936; Helm 1961; unless othewise indicated.

[a] Data from Thornthwaite Associates 1964a and 1964b.
[b] Data from Rostlund 1952; Map 45.
[c] Includes estimates of Mooney (1928) and Kroeber (1939).
[d] Does not include estimates of Mooney (1928) and Kroeber (1939).
[e] Based upon fish resources and fishing effort only.
[f] Only one estimate used.

coordinates, it is possible to show the attained human population size as a function of carrying capacity. This relationship may then be presented in the form of a linear equation of the form

$$Y = a_y + \beta X \tag{6}$$

where
Y = the human population size;
a_y = the Y intercept;
β = the slope of the line of regression; and
X = the carrying capacity.

This approach provides an economical way of examining the relationship between these two variables, for the value of β (beta) represents the percent of the carrying capacity at which the human population is established.

As an example, let it be assumed that the value of a_y is equal to 0. Likewise, let it be assumed that the value of β is equal to or less than 0.30 (Washburn 1968:84; Lee and DeVore 1968:11). The formula now becomes

$$Y = 0 + 0.30X \tag{7}$$

This relationship is presented in graphic form in Figure 3. The shaded area indicates all possible relationships meeting the above restrictions placed upon the value of β. If it may further be assumed that all values be perfectly correlated, then the value of ρ (rho) will be unity.

It is also possible to consider the case in which a single factor is assumed to be operative that will limit the size of the human population. Let it be

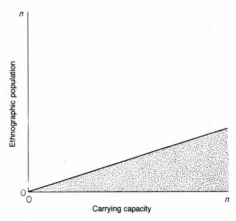

Figure 3.   Relationship between population size and carrying capacity assuming $a = 0$; $\beta \leq 0.030$; $\rho = 1$

further assumed that the human population be in perfect equilibrium with this factor, as in a population in which food supply is the limiting factor and population size is at the maximum permitted by this limiting factor. This may be considered as the extreme case of Malthus's model in which the operation of preventive checks upon the size of the human population is inoperative. If it may be assumed again that $a_y = 0$, then it can be seen that any change in the food supply will be matched in the system by a change of the same magnitude in the size of the human population. Here the value of β will be unity and the formula becomes

$$Y = 0 + 1X \tag{8}$$
$$\text{or}$$
$$Y = X \tag{9}$$

in which all characters are as previously defined. Assuming, again, that all values are perfectly correlated the value of ρ will be unity. This relationship is presented in Figure 4.

RESULTS

Turning now to the application of this method to the sample of six far-northern hunter–gatherer groups, it can be seen from examination of Table 3 that the relationship between the mean observed population values and the predicted values based upon all resources relative to their

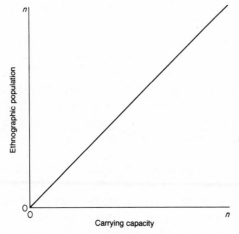

Figure 4.   Relationship between population size and carrying capacity assuming $a = 0$; $\beta = 1; \rho = 1$

intensity of exploitation (total) is fairly strong ($r > 0.87$). The value of β is 0.0042, which falls within the range given by Washburn (1968) and Lee and DeVore (1968), as shown in Figure 3. It is possible to partition the total available resources into the three major subsistence types (hunting, fishing, and gathering). The mean predicted population values based upon each of these alone relative to their intensity of exploitation may then be compared with the mean observed population sizes. Thus, an

Table 3. Observed mean human population as function of predicted mean human carrying capacity

Subsistence regime	r	z	B^a	A^b
Total	0.87677	1.9605	0.0042	−1.7537
Gathering only	−0.25415	−0.5683	−0.0013	1,497.9668
Hunting only	0.95746	2.1410	0.0046	551.5052
Fishing only	0.98741	2.2079	0.8177	266.3730

[a]   B=slope of Bartlett's "best-fit" line (Bartlett 1949).
[b]   A=Y-intercept of Bartlett's "best-fit" line.

attempt can be made at identifying any of these subsistence categories that might represent a factor limiting maximum population size. Examining gathering alone, it appears quite inconsequential. Looking at hunting, however, in concert with the percent of time spent in its prosecution, a very strong correlation with observed population sizes ($r > 0.95$) can be seen. Here the value of β is 0.0046 which, again, is well within the limits proposed by earlier investigators. A good case can be made for hunting being a controlling factor limiting population size. Along these same lines Lee (1968:42, Table 6) has shown that the groups in the area under consideration here do, indeed, spend most of their subsistence time engaged in hunting. There is, however, one subsistence activity left to examine — fishing.

Estimated mean population size based solely upon energy available from fishing relative to intensity of exploitation is very strongly correlated with the mean observed population sizes ($r > 0.98$). The value of β is greater than 0.8 and the relationship in general resembles that presented earlier in (8) and (9) and shown in Figure 4 for a population in equilibrium with and expanded to the maximum permitted by a limiting factor. Figure 5 presents the results of the present study based solely upon the fish resources.

The above results, presented in Table 3, are based upon population estimates from all sources available to the author. Lacking a sound reason for culling certain of these estimates, this seemed a wise approach. A couple of the population estimates (those of Kroeber 1939 and Mooney 1928) appear high. There seem to be some grounds for considering both these sources of estimates as being too high (Swanton in Mooney 1928;

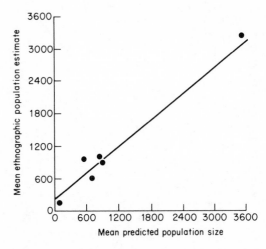

Figure 5. Relationship between mean ethnographic population and mean predicted population based upon energy available from fish resources relative to percent of time expended in procurement in five North American hunter–gatherer groups above 60° north latitude: $Y = 266.3730 + 0.8177 X; r = 0.98741$

Kroeber 1939:134). With this in mind, Table 4 was prepared in order to examine the effects caused by the removal of these high estimates upon the relationships under investigation.

Table 4. Observed mean human population as function of predicted mean human carrying capacity (without Mooney's and Kroeber's estimates)

Subsistence regime	r	z	B	A
Total	0.92204	2.0617	0.0048	−312.7039
Gathering only	−0.41797	−0.9346	−0.0017	1,490.9498
Hunting only	0.98091	2.1934	0.0053	327.5862
Fishing only	0.99182	2.2178	0.9225	23.2842

In general the same trends appear as were described above for the data in Table 3. The correlations become higher and the relationships more significant. The most striking change involves the relationship of fishing resources to population size. There appears to be a near perfect correlation ($r > 0.99$) and a value near unity for β, indicating a nearly one-to-one relationship between predicted and observed population sizes. This is a yet closer approximation to the earlier model (8) and (9) (see Figure 4) of a limiting factor. Figure 6 presents the results of this study regarding fish resources alone, eliminating Kroeber's and Mooney's estimates.

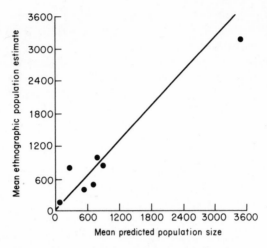

Figure 6.   Relationship between mean ethnographic population and mean predicted population based upon energy available from fish resources relative to percent of time expended in procurement in five North American hunter–gatherer groups above 60° north latitude: $Y = 23{,}2842 + 0.9225\ X; r = 0.99182$

COMPARISON WITH INDEPENDENT STUDIES

The view that the availability of fish resources might be of crucial seasonal importance to groups in this region gains some support from the personal records of early trappers and fur traders in this area. This independent data, referring not to Indian groups but to European groups operating in the same physical environment with roughly the same subsistence regimes, is enlightening.

The situation has been well summarized by McPhail and Lindsey (1970:3). I take the liberty of quoting them at length:

Aboriginal man in the north was sometimes heavily dependent on freshwater or anadromous fishes for food. . . .
Fishing success was often a matter of life or death to early explorers and fur traders in the north. Preble (1908) wrote "So important are whitefish as an article of diet that the sites of many, perhaps the majority, of the trading posts, as well as the wintering stations of a number of exploring expeditions, places which have become famous in Arctic literature, have been selected with a view to the local abundance of this fish." Entries in the journals of Samuel Hearne, Alexander Mackenzie, Warburton Pike, and Frank Russell describe parties going hungry because the gillnets were empty.

Commenting upon the utilization of but a single species indigenous to this area, *Coregonus artedii* (Lake Cisco), McPhail and Lindsey (1970:94) note that "in the lower Mackenzie and Great Bear Lake regions it is claimed that man and dogs can subsist all winter exclusively on this fish."

The pattern emerges of winter being an acutely lean season in this area and, concomitantly, supplies of fish (either stored or fresh) providing the major energy source during this crucial season.

This pattern is also present in the ethnographic literature. Murdock (1969:148), in a discussion concerning the relationship of subsistence to sedentariness, noted that "among the Northern Athapaskans, fishing is the single most productive source of food. . . ." Birket-Smith frequently noted that fish were an important item in the diet of the Caribou Eskimo. Concerning the seasonal importance of fish he states that "fishing is just as important in winter, when it forms the unfailing stand-by to the chance results of caribou hunting" (Birket-Smith 1929:117). Honigmann, in a study which reconstructed the nature of the food quest among the Slave Indians in the Fort Nelson area found that "from the data we can infer that in the Fort Nelson area, as elsewhere among the Northern Athapaskans, the local group lived together during the winter at some fish lake and subsisted principally on the fish they could obtain through the ice" (Honigmann 1946:40).

Also working among the Slave, Helm noted the pattern with regard to aboriginal conditions: "Informants' knowledge of the 'old days' suggests that the aboriginal pattern was to winter at a 'fish lake', thus assuring a food supply. At the 'fish lakes' there is almost always enough fish for human beings and their dogs" (Helm 1961:32). Campbell (1968:10) has described the process by which fish became crucial for survival among hunter–gatherers in northern Alaska and how this resource reflected itself in their settlement pattern:

Therefore, while the Tuluaqmiut were hunters, not fishermen, in those uncommon bad years when the game failed, the few trout lakes became crucially important to band survival. And even in usual or typical years, when outright starvation was not a threat, there were short periods when game was scarce, and when several species of fish, but most importantly lake trout were accordingly sought after. As a result, providing that fuel was locally available, and providing that big game in numbers could be intercepted from them, the trout lakes became headquarters or major encampment localitiess [sic] for the Tuluaqmiut.

In another study dealing with not only the Slave but also the Chipewyan, Dogrib, and Yellowknife in the region around Great Slave Lake, Mason found that:

Whitefish are almost as staple a food as caribou. . . . The fur posts are largely dependent on whitefish for their winter's supply of food and the forts are always established in the neighborhood of a good fishery. Certain sedentary natives living at or near the fur posts in permanent settlements also live almost entirely on whitefish and, even when traveling, the camp is generally pitched at a good spot so that the catch of fish may insure a good supply in event of failure in the chase. It may be questioned if fish do not play as important a role in the native economy as caribou (1946:18).

Leechman (1954:13), studying a Kutchin group, noted that fish were used "quite extensively as a food."

Of interest here also is Hickerson's reference (1965:59) to the "emphasis on fishing and storing of fish for winter use" among the Chippewa. Likewise, Birket-Smith noted (1930:18) that among the Chipewyan, "fishes are of very great importance to the population, fishing being an indispensable adjunct to caribou hunting" and (1930:26) that "after caribou hunting, fishing is undoubtedly the most important occupation." In a study regarding the relationship between caribou availability and population size among the Chipewyan, Thompson (1966:424) noted that:

Application of "Lebig's Law" implies that it would not be the caribou availability during the winter that actually limited the population, but the availability of the foodstuffs required for the survival of the human population at the worst time of the year — in this case, fish in the winter. . . . It would appear that a similar mode of attack concerned with fish and other major game or food resources might well be able to delineate within fairly narrow boundaries the actual aboriginal population size of the Chipewyan and possibly other Northern Athabascan groups as well.

The pattern presented in these studies is succinctly brought out by a translation of an Indian name for the whitefish from the eastern subarctic area. Richardson felt that the whitefish was next in importance to caribou as a food resource in the eastern Subarctic. He says the name for the whitefish translates as "caribou of the water" (Richardson 1851:51).

Examining worldwide population trends in prehistory, Braidwood and Reed (1957:25) present the same thesis outlined above: "the population of the primary hunting and collecting culture is not limited by the potential amount of food, but by man's ability to get it during the leanest season." Similar views have been presented by Netting (1971:11), Bartholemew and Birdsell (1953:488), and Burch (1972:360).

CONCLUSIONS

I feel obliged to conclude that the Malthusian thesis must be accepted on the basis of the results of the present investigation and within the frame of its samples. The significant correlation between observed mean population sizes and predicted mean population values based upon either hunting or fishing bears this out. Though it may be argued that correlation is not causation, within the framework of the present study it must be admitted that there are strong indications that such relationships do or did exist. This does not, however, invalidate other factors that could, and most likely often did, come into play prior to the ultimate check —

starvation. At the same time it is not unlikely that these preventive checks may have served to limit the maximum population to the level supportable during the leanest period. This would manifest itself in the same manner as observed with the correlation between fish resources and observed population size.

REFERENCES

BARTHOLEMEW, G., JR., J. B. BIRDSELL
  1953 Ecology   and   the   protohominids. *American   Anthropologist*
      55:481–498.
BARTLETT, M. S.
  1949 Fitting a straight line when both variables are subject to error. *Biometrics* 5:207–212.
BIRKET-SMITH, K.
  1929 The Caribou Eskimos. Report of the Fifth Thule Expedition 1921–24. *The Danish Expedition to Arctic North America in Charge of Knud Rasmussen* 5(1).
  1930 Contributions to Chipewyan ethnology. Report of the Fifth Thule Expedition 1921–1924. *The Danish Expedition to Arctic North America in Charge of Knud Rasmussen* 6(3):1–113.
BLALOCK, H. M., JR.
  1964 *Causal inferences in nonexperimental research.* Chapel Hill: University of North Carolina Press.
BOSERUP, E.
  1965 *The conditions of agricultural growth: the economics of agrarian change under population pressure.* Chicago: Aldine.
BRAIDWOOD, R. J., C. A. REED
  1957 The achievement and early consequences of food production. *Cold Springs Harbor Symposia on Quantitative Biology* 22:19–31.
BURCH, E. S., JR.
  1972 The caribou/wild reindeer as a human resource. *American Antiquity* 37:339–368.
CAMPBELL, J. M.
  1968 "Territoriality among ancient hunters: interpretations from ethnography and nature," in *Anthropological archaeology in the Americas.* Edited by B. J. Meggers, 1–21. Anthropological Society of Washington.
CASTEEL, R. W.
  1972 Two maximum population-density models for hunter–gatherers: a first approximation. *World Archaeology* 4(1):19–40.
DRIVER, H. E.
  1967 *Indians of North America.* Chicago: University of Chicago Press.
FLEW, A., *editor*
  1970 *Malthus. An essay on the principle of population.*
HELM, J.
  1961 *The Lynx Point people: the dynamics of a northern Athapaskan band.* National Museum of Canada Bulletin 176, Anthropological Series 53.
HICKERSON, H.
  1965 "The Virginia deer and intertribal buffer zones in the upper Mississippi valley," in *Man, culture, and animals.* Edited by A. Leeds and A. P. Vayda, 43–65. American Association for the Advancement of Science.

HODGE, F. W.
1911   *Handbook of American Indians north of Mexico.* Bureau of American Ethnology Bulletin 30, part one (A–M).
HOLDRIDGE, L. R.
1967   *Life zone ecology* (revised edition). Tropical Science Center.
HONIGMANN, J.
1946   Ethnography and acculturation of the Fort Nelson Slave. *Yale University Publications in Anthropology* 33:1–170.
KORMONDY, E. J.
1969   *Concepts of ecology.* Englewood Cliffs, N.J.: Prentice-Hall.
KROEBER, A. L.
1939   *Cultural and natural areas of native North America.* Sacramento: University of California Press.
LEE, R. B.
1968   "What hunters do for a living or, how to make out on scarce resources," in *Man the hunter.* Edited by R. B. Lee and I. De Vore, 30–48. Chicago: Aldine.
LEE, R. B., I. DE VORE
1968   "Problems in the study of hunters and gatherers," in *Man the hunter.* Edited by R. B. Lee and I. DeVore, 3–12. Chicago: Aldine.
LEECHMAN, D.
1954   *The Vanta Kutchin.* National Museum of Canada Bulletin 130, Anthropological Series 33.
MALTHUS, T. R.
1817   *An essay on the principle of population: or, a view of its past and present effects on human happiness; with an inquiry into our prospects respecting the future removal or mitigation of the evils which it occasions,* volume one (fifth edition). Murray.
1967   *Population: the first essay.* Ann Arbor, Mich.: Ann Arbor Paperbacks. (First edition 1798.)
1970   "A summary view of the principle of population," in *Malthus. An essay on the principle of population.* Edited by A. Flew, 217–272.
MASON, J. A.
1946   Notes on the Indians of the Great Slave Lake area. *Yale University Publications in Anthropology* 34:1–46.
McPHAIL, J. D., C. C. LINDSEY
1970   *Freshwater fishes of northwestern Canada and Alaska.* Fisheries Research Board of Canada Bulletin 173.
MOONEY, J.
1928   *The aboriginal population of America north of Mexico.* Smithsonian Miscellaneous Collections 80(7). Washington, D.C.
MURDOCK, G. P.
1963   Ethnographic atlas. *Ethnology* 2:541–548.
1964   Ethnographic atlas. *Ethnology* 3:107–116.
1967   The ethnographic atlas: a summary. *Ethnology* 6(2): 109–236.
1969   "Correlations of exploitative and settlement patterns," in *Contributions to anthropology: ecological essays.* Edited by D. Damas, 129–146. National Museum of Canada Bulletin 230, Anthropological Series 86.
MURDOCK, G. P., et al.
1962   Ethnographic atlas. *Ethnology* 1:113–134.
NETTING, R. McC.
1971   *The ecological approach in cultural study.* Reading, Mass.: Addison-Wesley.

OSGOOD, C.
1936 Contributions to the ethnography of the Kutchin. *Yale University Publications in Anthropology* 14.

RICHARDSON, SIR J.
1851 *Arctic searching expedition: a journal of a boat-voyage through Rupert's Land and the Arctic Sea, in search of the discovery ships under command of Sir John Franklin.* London: Longman, Brown, Green, and Longmans.

ROSENZWEIG, M. L.
1968 Net primary productivity of terrestrial communities: prediction from climatological data. *American Naturalist* 102:67–74.

ROSTLUND, E.
1952 *Freshwater fish and fishing in native North America.* University of California Publications in Geography 9. Sacramento: University of California Press.

SPOONER, B., *editor*
1972 *Population growth: anthropological implications.* Cambridge: Massachusetts Institute of Technology Press.

SWANTON, J. R.
1952 *The Indian tribes of North America.* Bureau of American Ethnology Bulletin 145.

THOMPSON, H. P.
1966 A technique using anthropological and biological data. *Current Anthropology* 7(4): 417–449.

THORNTHWAITE ASSOCIATES
1962 *Average climatic water balance data of the continents, Africa.* Laboratory of Climatology Publications in Climatology 15(2).
1963a *Average climatic water balance data of the continents, Asia (excluding U.S.S.R.).* Laboratory of Climatology Publications in Climatology 16(1).
1963b *Average climatic water balance data of the continents, U.S.S.R.* Laboratory of Climatology Publications in Climatology 16(2).
1963c *Average climatic water balance data of the continents, Australia, New Zealand, and Oceania.* Laboratory of Climatology Publications in Climatology 16(3).
1964a *Average climatic water balance data of the continents, Europe.* Laboratory of Climatology Publications in Climatology 17(1).
1964b *Average climatic water balance data of the continents, North America (excluding United States).* Laboratory of Climatology Publications in Climatology 17(2).
1964c *Average climatic water balance data of the continents, United States.* Laboratory of Climatology Publications in Climatology 17(3).
1965 *Average climatic water balance data of the continents, South America.* Laboratory of Climatology Publications in Climatology 18(2).

WASHBURN, S. L.
1968 "Discussions, part two," in *Man the hunter.* Edited by R. B. Lee and I. DeVore, 83–95. Chicago: Aldine.

WESTLAKE, D. F.
1963 Comparisons of plant productivity. *Biological Reviews of the Cambridge Philosophical Society* 38:385–425.

SECTION FOUR

Later Cultural Adaptations and Technological Studies

Introduction

There is a substantial literature on archaeological cultures in the United States dating to the last few thousand years. The selection of papers in this volume represents some of the kinds of trends in recent New World prehistory, particularly highlighting the new technological innovations in the last decade as applied to archaeological data.

The analysis of desiccated fecal materials in the arid areas of western North America, represented by the work reported by Fry, has given an important new dimension to our understanding of prehistoric dietary patterns. There is sufficient data for Fry to postulate two different dietary patterns for the Great Basin — a desertic pattern for the eastern sector, and a lacustrine pattern for the western section. Such analyses provide other data in addition to subsistence resources. Technology can be partially recovered; bits of charred basketry and grit from milling stones are found in some specimens and allow us to reconstruct technological methods of food processing. Study of parasites in the specimens reveals the presence of thorny-headed worms, pinworms, tapeworms, flukes, amoebas, and lice. In concert with the dietary patterns and the processing technology, indications of parasitic levels permit us to reconstruct general nutritional levels and general population vitality.

Adovasio's study of basketry from a wide variety of prehistoric environments on the continent has produced a model of development crosscutting culture areas and is representative of the kind of synthetic study which advances archaeology. The sequence of basketry techniques spans 10,000 years and is the best-controlled and most extensive sequence of perishable artifacts in the New World. The origins of twined and coiled basketry around 8000 B.C. are closely bound to the specialized food-preparation techniques developed in the western Great Basin. The shift to more intensive exploitation of seeds and other vegetal resources at this time saw the development of grinding or milling tools for processing the materials into a form more digestible for man, plus the development of basketry as specialized storage containers and as containers better suited to the parching of vegetal materials to prolong storage capabilities, a technology tied in with exploitation of a new food resource and with a new storage technology.

Much of the work in investigations of recent archaeological cultures is bound up with the analysis and ordering of ceramics to provide cultural units fixed in time and space with which to construct more sophisticated models. Peterson's paper on fiber-tempered ceramics indicates the possibility of an independent origin for North American ceramics. Rather than seeing this technological innovation as being borrowed from South America via Mesoamerica, Peterson argues that there is a zone of early ceramics, indicative of independent invention, along the Tennessee River and in parts of Georgia. These ceramics are seen as clearly indigenous, and, with a date of approximately 2000 B.C., they are certainly earlier than ceramics in northern Mesoamerica. This data supports a three-pronged model, rather than a simple single-center-of origin model, to explain the occurrence of ceramics in North America. In the far north, Eskimo ceramics are borrowed from Asia; in the southwest and in later cultures in the southeast, ceramic concepts enter the United States and later Canada from Mexico, ultimately being derived from earlier innovations in northwestern South America; and now we must look for an early independent center of ceramic innovation in the southeast prior to the introduction of ceramic concepts from Mexico.

The ceramic analysis represented by the contribution of Hurley is representative of the recent and continually more sophisticated attempts in archaeology to use multivariate analytical techniques to derive more rigorous typologies and more precise definitions. A shift from qualitative analysis to quantitative analysis is being emphasized by many scholars, who thus hope to apply more powerful statistical tools to archaeological data to develop more sophisticated reconstructions of lifeways.

Fowler's and Hall's papers are representative of the continued application of settlement-pattern analysis, with an eye toward developing a methodology more appropriate for sociological and demographic reconstructions. Thus archaeologists are now less concerned with description *per se*, and less concerned with chronological orderings and typologies, and more interested in developing techniques with which to reconstruct economic exchange patterns, social relationships, religious precepts, etc. The bulk of modern research appears to be along lines in this direction. Some would see this as a new school of thought, as "new archaeology," but it is clear that it is rather a shift in emphasis, being built upon more secure data bases.

Prehistoric Diet and Parasites in the Desert West of North America

G. F. FRY

In the context of this paper the Desert West includes the entire physiographic and cultural province known as the Great Basin, as well as an adjacent portion of the northern periphery of the greater American southwest.

Prehistoric dietary patterns are largely determined through analyses of macrofossils and pollen from archaeological sites. One type of archaeological macrofossil recovered in excavation of dry caves is desiccated fecal material, herein referred to as coprolites.

Coprolites are the remains of actual meals, and analysis of their contents is the most precise method available to the archaeologist for determination of ancient diets. These humble artifacts can be analyzed for undigested food remains, chemical content, and parasites. Techniques such as spectrophotometry and trace-element activation analysis promise additional information. Coprolites may yield information about diet, nutrition, resource utilization, ecological adaptation, disease and parasites, seasonality of site use, paleoclimate, aboriginal behavior, and culture change. Samples found in large numbers in stratified, well-controlled excavations are conducive to statistical analysis.

Coprolites are usually found only in dry caves but may occasionally be preserved in damp environments, such as bogs. The range of environments that can be studied by this method is thus limited. Human coprolites from the Great Basin contain a diverse mixture of food items including plant remains, bones, feathers, insect parts, and charcoal.

The methodology of coprolite analysis in the Great Basin is detailed in Heizer (1967), Fry (i.p.a, i.p.b), and Napton and Heizer (1970). The desiccated specimens are hydrated in 0.5 percent weight/volume solution of trisodium phosphate (Na_3PO_4), then wet-sifted through graded sieves, dried, separated, identified, and weighed. The history of archaeological coprolite analysis is reviewed by Heizer and Napton (1969), Napton and Heizer (1970), and Fry (i.p.b).

Large numbers of archaic coprolites have been analyzed from two sectors of the Great Basin: the eastern and western subareas. The eastern Great Basin includes most of the state of Utah north of the Colorado River, west of the Uintah Mountains, and south of the Raft River Mountains and a restricted adjacent portion of northeastern Nevada (Adovasio and Fry 1972). The western subarea of the Great Basin centers in the Humboldt/Carson Sink area of western Nevada. The Sierra Nevada Mountains form an effective western boundary, while other boundaries are poorly defined.

Coprolite analyses demonstrate that different patterns of prehistoric adaptation prevailed in the two sectors, resulting from ecological adjustment to different environments by Archaic peoples (Fry i.p.c). The desertic adaptation of the eastern sector was first postulated as the Desert culture (Jennings and Norbeck 1955; Jennings 1957), later Desert Archaic (Jennings 1964), and recently Western Archaic (Jennings 1968); the western adaptation is labeled the Limnosedentary pattern (Heizer 1967), or Lacustrine Subsistence pattern (Napton 1969).

DESERTIC ADAPTION

Archaic dietary data from the eastern Great Basin derive from coprolites from Danger Cave (Jennings 1957; Fry i.p.a, i.p.b) and Hogup Cave (Aikens 1970; Fry 1970, i.p.b), both of which are located in the northwestern corner of Utah. Danger Cave was occupied intermittently by Archaic populations from approximately 9000 B.C. until about A.D. 20, while Hogup Cave was periodically visited by Archaic people from about 6800 B.C. until about A.D. 400.

As described by Jennings (1964, 1968) the Desert or Western Archaic is a lifeway geared to seasonal exploitation of a wide range of natural resources by small sociopolitical units utilizing a specialized and efficient but simple technological complex. This complex includes the atlatl, basketry, cordage, milling stones, and special food preparation techniques directed toward small-seed utilization, e.g. the parching of seeds in coiled basketry trays, the milling of seeds, and the making of gruel or porridge.

Analysis of forty-six coprolites from Danger Cave and fifty specimens from Hogup Cave demonstrates that almost 95 percent of foods consumed were derived from desertic plants. However, it must be stressed that though coprolites from the eastern Great Basin indicate a desertic adaptation, it is likely that bog and mountain resources in this area were also utilized. The caves were occupied for just a few weeks in the fall, while bogs and relatively verdant mountains are within walking distance of both caves.

Chenopod seeds, primarily *Allenrolfea occidentalis* [pickleweed or burroweed], were the most common identified coprolite components at both caves; also common were tissues of *Opuntia* [prickly pear]. Nine other species of plants were recovered in minor amounts, as shown in Table 1.

Table 1. Comparison of Archaic coprolite components between caves (after Fry i.p.b)

Component	Danger Cave (n=46)	Hogup Cave (n=51)
Plant		
Atriplex confertifolia seed	8	3
Artemisia sp. fiber	–	3
Celtis occidentalis seed	–	3
chenopod seed	44	50
Chrysothamnus sp. seed	1	–
Compositae seed	2	–
Cornus stolonifera tissue	1	–
Gramineae seed	–	2
Lepidium montanum seed	–	1
Opuntia sp. tissues	7	30
Phlox sp. seed	1	–
Pinus sp. seed	2	–
Scirpus sp. seed	3	1
plant fiber	37	51
plant epidermis	43	46
plant stem	38	36
(?) seed	1	14
Nonplant		
antelope hair	32	37
bone	31	36
charcoal	45	51
grit	46	42
feathers	6	6
insect parts	15	9
sinew	18	1
reptile scale	–	1
(?) hair	42	46

Scirpus [bulrush] is the only wetland plant present, and since small bogs were located below both caves, this plant was an expected component. It occurred in small proportions in only four specimens, however, and was not a major food source.

Small seeds were parched in baskets and milled, hence the presence of charcoal and grit. Tiny rock crystals in grit are identical to crystals incorporated in milling stones from the caves, while numerous fragments of charred basketry parching trays (Adovasio 1970) were also recovered. Prickly pear cactus was prepared for consumption by burning off the spines. Tissues of this plant with spines burned off are common components of coprolites.

The environment at Hogup Cave is harsher than that at Danger Cave, where several ecological zones were available for exploitation (Jennings 1957; Fry i.p.b); this perhaps explains the presence of *Pinus*, *Phlox*, and *Cornus* at Danger Cave and their absence at Hogup Cave. Tiny fragments of bone, which I assume reflect meat-protein intake, were a common coprolite component at Danger Cave and Hogup Cave in Archaic times. Primary animal food sources were jackrabbit (*Lepus*) and pronghorn (*Antilocapra*). Pronghorn hair was a common coprolite component.

One Danger Cave coprolite was composed mainly of bark of *Cornus stolonifera* [red osier dogwood]. The only reported use for the plant bark is smoking it for a euphoric effect reputed to be similar to that of opium (Chamberlain 1911). The same effect could probably be achieved by eating the bark, since the psychoactive ingredient is probably an alkaloid.

Caloric value of uncooked *Allenrolfea* [burroweed] seed is 2.56 calories per gram (Fry i.p.b) or approximately 70 percent of the caloric value of uncooked whole-grain wheat, which is 3.70 calories per gram (Taylor and MacLeod 1949:204). This value and the highly varied nature of foods eaten indicate that major nutritional deficiencies were probably not experienced.

Eight Danger Cave coprolites and thirty-three Hogup Cave samples were also analyzed for pollen content (Kelso 1970). The dominant pollen types at both caves were cheno-ams (Chenopodiaceae–Amaranthaceae), just as the chenopod *Allenrolfea* is a major component of the deposits. Grass (Gramineae) pollen was significant at all levels at Danger Cave and after 2500 B.C. at Hogup Cave. Pollen types indicative of human agency in Danger Cave coprolites include *Sarcobatus* [greasewood], Rosaceae [rose family], *Polygonum* [knotweed], and *Ephedra* (Mormon tea).

Pollen types probably representative of human use in Hogup Cave coprolites include *Polygonum* [knotweed], *Artemisia* [sage], Compositeae (composite family), Cyperaceae (sedge family), Rosaceae (rose family), and *Pinus* [pine].

Chemical analysis of twenty-seven Hogup Cave coprolites indicates that excretion of nitrogen, calcium, and potassium was probably normal (Fry 1970a). Sodium excretion was abnormally high, probably due to high sodium intake as NaCl. Plants in the vicinity of Danger and Hogup caves are halophytic (salt-tolerant) and are salty to the taste. The water of Hogup spring, below the cave and a probable water source for inhabitants, is very salty — about 2,000 to 3,000 ppm. NaCl (Fry i.p.b). Nevertheless, it is doubtful that detrimental effects were suffered, since inhabitants had several millennia to adapt to high salt intake. In addition, a wide margin of safety existed, because I estimate maximum daily sodium intake to be seven grams, while thirty-five to forty grams per day can be ingested without detrimental effects (Shohl 1939:127).

Archaic coprolites from Hogup and Danger caves were conducive to computer analysis. Thirty coprolite-component variables were used in computer analysis by D. P. Adam, Department of Geochronology, University of Arizona. We wanted to ascertain if the diets between caves were different, if diets between time horizons, strata, and archaeological cultures were different, and how variables relate to each other and to diet. For comparison, coprolites were divided into early Archaic, about 9500–7000 B.C. (Danger Cave Levels I and II); middle Archaic, about 7000–3000 B.C. (Danger Cave Levels III and IV; Hogup Cave Strata 1–8); and late Archaic, about 3000 B.C.–A.D. 0 (Danger Cave Level V and Hogup Strata 9 and 10) (Fry and Adovasio 1970). Stepwise discriminant analysis (Dixon 1968) between age groups on raw percentages classed 71 percent of early Archaic coprolites together; 80 percent of middle Archaic coprolites were classed together. Only 53 percent of late Archaic coprolites were classed as late Archaic, probably an indication of culture change in late Archaic times. Stepwise discriminant analysis (Dixon 1968) between caves, on raw data, classed 89 percent of Danger Cave samples together and 95 percent of Hogup Cave specimens together. This demonstrates differences in microenvironments at the two caves that resulted in different patterns of resource utilization.

Archaic coprolites from the eastern Great Basin illustrate a food base that persisted virtually unchanged for about 10,000 years, until the influx of the formative stage Fremont and protohistoric Shoshoni peoples (Hogup Cave).

LACUSTRINE ARCHAIC ADAPTATION

The western or lacustrine adaptation is marked by a generally richer biota. This advantage is reflected in the abundance of coprolites. Literally thousands of coprolites have been recovered from Lovelock Cave as compared to hundreds from the eastern Basin. The most important archaeological site in this sector is Lovelock Cave (Loud and Harrington 1929). In addition, Roust (1967), Napton (1969), and Napton and Heizer (1970) report analysis of coprolites from Granite Point rock shelter, Baumhoff's rock shelter, Humboldt Cave in Humboldt Sink, and Hidden Cave in adjacent Carson Sink.

The Lacustrine Subsistence pattern as described by Napton (1969) includes intensive seasonal harvest of lacustrine food sources with extensive use of aquatic plants in manufacture of specialized artifacts for exploitation of lacustrine resources, such as reed boats, reed waterfowl decoys, reed mats, and string nets. Other traits include parching of seeds on mats and in coiled baskets and semisedentary occupation of lakeside villages of tule-thatched and brush-pit houses.

Components recovered from Lovelock Cave coprolites and listed in Table 2 include nineteen species of plants, twelve species of animals, seven of birds, three of fish, two of mollusks, and two of insects (Napton 1969:85). Here, at the terminus of the Humboldt River, the lacustrine adaptation reached its maximum expression. Although several biomes were exploited (Ambro 1967), at least 90 percent of foods consumed were obtained from wetland sources (Napton and Heizer 1970:107). The most important plant foods were seeds of bulrush (*Scirpus*), cattail (*Typha*), and wetland grasses — wild rye (*Elymus*) and witch grass (*Panicum*) (Napton and Heizer 1970:107). Other important dietary items were fish, primarily chub (*Gila bicolor*), ducks, and mudhens (Napton and Heizer 1970:107).

Table 2. Components of fifty Lovelock Cave coprolites (after Napton 1969)

Components	($n = 50$)
Plants	
Amaranthus sp. seed, pollen	2
Atriplex sp. seed	13
Chaenactus sp. seed	1
Distichlis stricta seed, fiber	11
Eleocharis of. *palustris* seed	2
Elymus triticoides seed, fiber	15
Equisetum sp. spores	1
Juncus sp. seed, fiber	1
Mentzelia gracilis seed	1
Panicum capillare seed	1
Phragmites communis fiber	2
Pinus monophylla seed	4
Rumex of. *utahensis* seed	2
Salsola of. *kali* pollen	1
Scirpus sp., achenes, tuber	1
Scirpus robustus, achenes, fiber	49
Sporobolus asperifolius seed	1
Stellaria sp. seed	3
Suaeda sp. seed, fiber	8
Typha latifolia seed, fiber	35
charcoal	22
pollen	4
roots	1
stem, leaves	45
tubers	6
twigs	3
Nonplant	
molluscs	
Gyraulus sp. shell	9
Stagnicola sp. shell	3
insects	
Anthrenus sp. body parts	18
Ptinus sp. body parts	8

Table 2. (*continued*)

Components	(*n*=50)
fish	
Catostomus tahoensis scales, bones	2
Gila bicolor scales, bones	2
Rhinichthys osculus robustus scales, bones	4
birds	
Anas sp. feathers, bones	1
Chen hyperborea feathers	1
Colymbus sp. feathers	2
Fulica americana feathers, bones	7
Nycticorax sp. feathers	1
Nyroca of. *valisineria* feathers	1
Pelecanus of. *erythrorhynchos* feathers	1
mammals	
Antilocapra americana hair	1
Bassaricus astutus nevadensis hair	3
Canis latrans hair	5
Citellus sp. hair	1
Eutamias sp. hair	1
Lepus of. *americanus* hair, bone	1
Odocoileus hemionus hair	3
Ovis canadensis hair	1
Peromyscus of. *maniculatus* hair	1
Sylvilagus sp. hair	1
Ursus americanus hair	1
Homo sapiens hair	13

The occupation of Lovelock Cave, marked by dependence on lacustrine-derived foods, began about 2000 B.C. and lasted as late as A.D. 1805 (Napton and Heizer 1970:109). It is probable, however, that the Lacustrine Subsistence pattern began much earlier (Napton 1969:48).

The biotic resources were apparently abundant enough to allow occupation of Lovelock Cave from late fall through early spring and to provide a reasonably well-balanced diet during the winter based on waterfowl and *Scirpus* seed (Napton and Heizer 1970:108). As in the eastern sector, a long stable dietary pattern is indicated here (Napton and Heizer 1970:109), although the much richer biota undoubtedly supported a larger population than that of the eastern Great Basin.

Seeds at Lovelock Cave were apparently parched and, as expected, charcoal is a regular coprolite component. Milling, however, was evidently not a regular treatment in preparation of seeds for consumption (Napton and Heizer 1970:107). Parched seeds were evidently eaten whole.

Pollen analysis of Lovelock Cave coprolites agrees with macrofossil analysis. Dominant pollen types are *Typha* [cattail] and Gramineae [grasses]. Of particular interest is a coprolite composed almost entirely of

Typha pollen that had a charred gray appearance, apparently the result of eating roasted pollen (Napton and Kelso 1969:22).

Analysis of coprolites from the western Great Basin substantiates the validity of the Lacustrine Subsistence pattern.

FORMATIVE-STAGE COPROLITES

Herein "formative" refers to more or less sedentary horticulturalists using one or more domesticated plant foods. In this context two major cultural manifestations have been studied through coprolite analysis.

Thirty Anasazi coprolites are from ten different sites now submerged under Lake Powell in the Glen Canyon. Three of the samples are from mummies, of which two were infants and one an adult.

Anasazi settlements in the Glen Canyon were derived from Mogollon areas further south about A.D. 300–400 according to Jennings (1966:68) and were present in the area until about A.D. 1300 (Jennings 1966:66). The Anasazi were foraging specialists who practiced horticulture of corn, beans, and squash but did not depend exclusively on these cultivars. They lived in temporary shelters or more permanent pit houses and built small storage granaries.

Thirty-two coprolites represent two variants of the Fremont culture, a distinctly Utah formative manifestation present in the state from about A.D. 400 to about A.D. 1300. The Fremont culture derives from a Desert Archaic base to which is added pottery, horticulture, pit houses, and small sedentary villages (Marwitt 1971). Marwitt defined five regional variants with different patterns of cultural–ecological adaptation.

Six coprolites derive from the Great Salt Lake Fremont occupation at Hogup Cave. This northern variant shared many affinities with Plains Indian groups to the north (Fry i.p.b). Sixteen coprolites from Clyde's Cavern in central Utah (Hall 1972) and ten samples from the Glen Canyon area (Fry 1970a) represent the San Rafael Fremont variant. This group was influenced by the Anasazi culture to the south but maintained its own distinctive culture.

In addition, three coprolites from Hogup Cave in northeastern Utah represent the historic Shoshoni or Numic speakers of Utah and Nevada (Fry i.p.b). These folk lived a life quite similar to that of the earlier Desert Archaic peoples with the addition of pottery, a notable exception. These samples are compared with the Great Salt Lake Fremont coprolites from Hogup Cave in Table 3.

Fremont and Shoshoni occupants of Hogup Cave were apparently also occasional visitors for a few weeks in the fall like the earlier Archaic peoples. The influx of these peoples at Hogup Cave reflects only slight changes (as reflected in percentage weights of components) in subsis-

Table 3. Comparison of Fremont and Shoshoni coprolite component occurrences, Hogup Cave (after Fry i.p.b)

Component	Fremont ($n=6$)	Shoshoni ($n=3$)
Plant		
Atriplex confertifolia seed	2	1
Artemisia sp. fiber	–	2
Celtis occidentalis seed	1	–
chenopod seed	5	2
composite disc flowers	–	1
Gramineae seed	3	2
Opuntia sp. tissues	5	2
Poa sp. seeds	–	1
Zea mays seed	1	–
Plant fiber	6	1
Plant epidermis	4	2
Plant stem	5	3
(?) seed	2	–
Nonplant		
antelope hair	5	3
bone	3	3
charcoal	6	3
grit	6	3
eggshell	1	1
feathers	2	1
insect parts	2	3
sinew	2	2
(?) hair	6	3

tence from the earlier Archaic. The changes include a slightly decreased use of chenopod seed and prickly pear cactus with increased use of grass seed as food. Also, Fremont coprolites have a lower average percentage weight bone content, which reflects an increase in the use of bison as a food source; this is also reflected by analysis of faunal remains from the cave deposits. One Fremont sample contained large amounts of probable intestine, and another contained large amounts of finely chopped plant fiber and stem that is undoubtedly herbivore browse. Thus Great Salt Lake Fremont people apparently ate viscera and stomach contents of large herbivores.

The coprolite components from Clyde's Cavern, Utah (San Rafael Fremont) are seen in Table 4. A wide variety of resources were utilized, especially seeds, which were roasted and milled before being eaten (Hall 1972). According to Hall's analysis, corn formed only part of a composite diet of seeds and nonseed plant material and did not become a staple until late in the occupation. Game animals were apparently an unsubstantial part of the prehistoric diet.

Seeds of *Sporobolus* [dropseed] and *Elymus* [wild rye], both of which are grasses, were apparently milled but not parched. Cheno-am

Table 4. Coprolite components from Clyde's Cavern, San Rafael Fremont (after Hall 1972)

Component	(n = 16)
Cheno-am seed	7
Compositae seed	6
Elymus sp. seed	2
Lepidium sp. seed	1
Pinus edulis seed	1
Scirpus sp. seed	1
Sporobolus sp. seed	12
Zea mays seed, tissue	7
Nonseed plant	9
Bone	3
Charcoal	10
Grit	16
Hair	3
Insect parts	–
Antelope hair	3
Debris	15

(chenopod-amaranth) seeds and *Oryzopsis* sp. [Indian rice grass] seeds were parched and milled. *Pinus edulis* [pinion pine] seed and *Scirpus* sp. [bulrush] seed have not been major food resources at any sites investigated via coprolite analysis in the eastern Great Basin to date. *Zea mays* [corn] was occasionally eaten off the cob but was more commonly shucked and ground.

The occurrence of components of Glen Canyon coprolites are compared in Table 5. The two groups (Anasazi and San Rafael Fremont) are quite similar in having a variable content. Twenty-four plant taxa were identified in addition to nonspecific plant categories and nonplant materials. Fremont coprolites contained sixteen taxa, seven of which were not found in Anasazi samples. These include *Yucca* pod, *Artemisia* [sage] fiber, *Juniperus* [juniper] fiber, *Phaseolus* [bean], *Equisetum* [horsetail] stems, conifer bark, and *Amelanchier* [serviceberry] seed. Anasazi coprolites include eighteen taxa, of which nine were not found in Fremont samples. These include seeds of *Celtis* [hackberry], *Gossypium* [cotton], *Cleome* [beeweed], *Cryptantha* [catseye], *Ephedra* [Mormon tea], and *Oryzopsis* [Indian rice grass], *Pinus* [pine] bark along with resin, *Polygonum* [knotweed] seed, and *Portulaca* [purselane] seed. Plants common to both Fremont and Anasazi coprolites include seeds of *Amaranthus* [amaranth], chenopods of several varieties, composites, and *Cucurbita* [squash pumpkin], Gramineae [grasses], *Lepidium* [peppergrass], *Zea* [corn] *Scirpus* [bulrush] and *Opuntia* [prickly pear] tissues. The Gramineae [grasses] represent at least six unidentified taxa. The most important food source was evidently *Cucurbita*, followed by *Zea* and *Opuntia*. *Cucurbita* seed and tissues were a major component in both

Table 5.   Comparison of Glen Canyon coprolite components (after Fry i.p.b)

Component	Anasazi (n=30)	Fremont (n=10)
Plant		
Amaranthus seed	10	6
Amelanchier seed	–	2
Artemisia fiber	–	1
Celtis seed	5	–
Chenopod seed	16	5
Cleome seed	5	–
Compositae seed	8	3
conifer bark	–	1
Cryptantha seed	1	–
Cucurbita seed, tissues	20	9
Ephedra seed	1	–
Equisetum stem	–	1
Gossypium seed	9	–
Gramineae seed	14	4
Juniperus fiber	–	1
Lepidium seed	5	1
Opuntia seed, tissues	16	6
Oryzopsis seed	5	–
Phaseolus seed	–	1
Pinus seed	1	–
Pinus resin	2	–
Polygonum seed	1	–
Portulaca seed	2	–
Scirpus seed	1	1
Yucca pod	–	2
Zea mays seed	18	3
plant fiber	28	9
plant epidermis	24	10
plant stem	13	5
(?) seed	17	9
Nonplant		
bone	15	5
charcoal	25	8
grit	29	9
feather	6	1
(?) hair	24	8
antelope hair	2	–
insect	7	3
reptile scale	1	1
sinew	1	–
Debris	30	10

Fremont and Anasazi coprolites. *Zea* was of greater importance in Anasazi coprolites than in Fremont samples. *Opuntia* tissues were present in about one-half of both Fremont and Anasazi coprolites. *Opuntia* pods were prepared for eating by burning off the spines. *Gossypium* [cotton] seed was used for food among the Anasazi. *Phaseolus* [bean] seed was apparently not a major food source for the Fremont or the

Anasazi unless *Phaseolus* fragments are destroyed by the digestive processes (E. O. Callen, personal communication).

PARASITES

Parasite analysis of Archaic coprolites from the eastern Great Basin showed that 15 percent of Danger Cave specimens and 3 percent of Hogup Cave samples contained eggs of *Acanthocephala* [thorny-headed worm], probably of the species *Moniliformis Clarki* (Moore *et al*: 1969; Fry 1970a). These could represent false parasitism by ingestion of adult worms with eggs in the bodies of rodents, or true parasitism by ingestion of the larval stages in the bodies of insects. If true parasitism, there were lethal potentialities for victims. The worm burrows into the intestinal wall with its proboscis, often causing death by perforation.

Five Archaic coprolites contained eggs of the human pinworm *Enterobius vermicularis* (Fry and Moore 1969). Pinworm infection is species-specific for man. Essentially benign, it probably had little effect on health. Specimens from Danger Cave Level II (ca. 8000 B.C.) represent the oldest demonstrated human parasite infection in the world.

One specimen from Danger Cave and five (3 percent) from Hogup Cave contained tapeworm eggs of the superfamily Taenioidea (Faust and Russel 1964:517). Species cannot be determined for these eggs, and thus life cycle and effect on human health remain unknown.

A louse nit attached to a human hair was found in a coprolite from Danger Cave Level V (ca. A.D. 20) and may be indicative of prehistoric grooming behavior. In addition, lice are primary disease vectors.

Parasite analysis of western Great Basin coprolites from Lovelock Cave yielded one example of Charcot-Leyden crystals, indicative of intestinal amoebiasis or dysentery (Heizer 1967:11). A single egg of an unidentified fasciolid trematode [fluke] is reported from one sample (Dunn and Watkins 1970:178). Several free-living or plant parasite rhabditoid nematode larvae are also reported (Dunn and Watkins 1970:178), as are fourteen Sarcoptiform mites (Radovsky 1970). A louse was also recovered from one sample (Napton 1969:32); as mentioned earlier, lice are vectors for numerous diseases. With the exception of amoebiasis, no detrimental effects on health are apparent from these findings.

Although parasite analysis of Great Salt Lake Fremont coprolites was negative, probably due to the small sample size ($n=6$), some formative-stage coprolites were positive for parasite ova.

San Rafael Fremont coprolites from Clyde's Cavern were positive for *Enterobius vermicularis* in one instance and for an unidentified species of

Acanthocephala in two instances (Hall 1972). A third sample has been identified as possibly *Strongyloides stercoralis* [threadworm], but for the present this identification is extremely tentative.

The Glen Canyon coprolites were positive for parasite eggs in three samples (Fry 1970a). A single Anasazi coprolite contained eggs of Acanthocephala, problably of the species *Moniliformis clarki*. One Anasazi sample and one San Rafael Fremont coprolite were positive for eggs of the tapeworm superfamily Taenioidea.

SUMMARY AND CONCLUSIONS

Coprolite analysis of Archaic coprolites demonstrates the validity of the concepts of desertic adaptation in eastern Great Basin and lacustrine adaptation in the western Great Basin. Local biota obviously dictated the structure of diets in each of these areas during aboriginal occupation.

Analysis of formative coprolites derived from Great Salt Lake Fremont peoples solidifies the viewpoint that northern Fremont peoples had more affinities with Plains aboriginals than more southerly Fremont peoples. These affinities include a lesser reliance on plant domesticates as food sources and a greater reliance on the gathering of wild plant foods and on hunting.

San Rafael Fremont peoples apparently had greater reliance on the gathering of wild plant foods than on hunting. Domesticated corn, beans, and squash were used, with squash having greatest importance. Most meals were primarily combinations of wild plant resources with domesticates as dietary supplements. Anasazi people in the Glen Canyon, although relying on domesticates more heavily than did Fremont folk, also depended largely on wild plant resources for subsistence.

Archaic populations in the eastern Great Basin were infected with human pinworm as early as 8000 B.C., as well as with tapeworm and lice. In addition, they may have been parasitized by the potentially dangerous thorny-headed worm.

Western Great Basin Archaic peoples were apparently occasionally parasitized by amoebas, flukes, and lice.

Formative peoples of the San Rafael Fremont culture were parasitized by the pinworm and the tapeworm, and possibly by the thorny-headed worm and the threadworm. Glen Canyon Anasazi peoples were occasionally infected with tapeworm and possibly with thorny-headed worm.

In sum, coprolite analysis in the Desert West has demonstrated strong ecological influence in prehistoric adaptation to the several different local ecosystems of every aboriginal culture studied to date.

REFERENCES

ADOVASIO, J. M.
1970   The origin, development and distribution of western Archaic textiles. *Tebiwa* 13(2):1–40.

ADOVASIO, J. M., G. F. FRY
1972   "An equilibrium model for culture change in the Great Basin," in *Great Basin cultural ecology* 67–71. Desert Research Institute Publications in the Social Sciences 8. Reno, Nevada.

AIKENS, C. M.
1970   *Hogup Cave.* University of Utah Anthropological Papers 93.

AMBRO, R. D.
1967   Dietary–technological–ecological aspects of Lovelock Cave coprolites. *University of California Archeological Survey Reports* 70:34–47. Berkeley.

CHAMBERLAIN, R. V.
1911   "Ethnobotany of the Gosiute," in *Memoirs of the American Anthropological Association*, volume three, part five.

DIXON, W. J.
1968   BMD 07M — stepwise discriminant analysis. *University of California Publications in Automatic Computation* 2. Berkeley.

DUNN, F. L., R. WATKINS
1970   Parasitological examinations of prehistoric human coprolites from Lovelock Cave, Nevada. *Contributions of the University of California Archaeological Research Facility* 10:176–185.

FAUST, E. C., P. F. RUSSELL
1964   *Clinical parasitology*, seventh edition. Philadelphia: Lea and Febiger.

FRY, G. F.
i.p.a   "Prehistoric diet at Danger Cave, Utah: as determined by the analysis of coprolites." University of Utah Anthropological Papers.
i.p.b   "Prehistoric human ecology in Utah: based on the analysis of coprolites." University of Utah Anthropological Papers.
1970   "Preliminary analysis of the Hogup Cave coprolites," in *Hogup Cave*. By C. M. Aikens, appendix 3. University of Utah Anthropological Papers 93.
i.p.c   "Prehistoric diet," in *The handbook of North American Indians*, volume ten: *Great Basin*. Edited by W. D'Azevedo.

FRY, G. F., J. M. ADOVASIO
1970   Population differentiation in Hogup and Danger caves, two Archaic sites in the eastern Great Basin. *Nevada State Museum Anthropological Papers* 15.

FRY, G. F., J. G. MOORE
1969   Enterobius vermicularis: 10,000-year-old human infection. *Science* 166:1,620.

HALL, H. J.
1972   "Diet and disease at Clyde's Cavern, Utah: as revealed via paleoscatology," Unpublished M.A. thesis, University of Utah.

HEIZER, R. F.
1967   Analysis of human coprolites from a dry Nevada cave. *University of California Archaeological Survey Reports* 70. Berkeley.

HEIZER, R. F., L. K. NAPTON
1969   Biological and cultural evidence from prehistoric human coprolites. *Science* 165:563–568.

JENNINGS, J. D.
  1957 *Danger Cave.* University of Utah Anthropological Papers 27.
  1964 "The Desert West," in *Prehistoric man in the New World.* Edited by
        J. D. Jennings and E. Norbeck, 149–174. Chicago: University of
        Chicago Press.
  1966 *Glen Canyon: a summary.* University of Utah Anthropological Papers
        81.
  1968 *Prehistory of North America.* New York: McGraw-Hill.
JENNINGS, J. D., E. NORBECK
  1955 Great Basin prehistory: a review. *American Antiquity* 21(1):1–11.
KELSO, G. K.
  1970 "Hogup Cave, Utah: comparative pollen analysis of human coprolites
        and cave fill," in *Hogup Cave.* By C. M. Aikens, appendix four. Univer-
        sity of Utah Anthropological Papers 93.
LOUD, L. L., M. R. HARRINGTON
  1929 Lovelock Cave. *University of California Publications in American
        Archaeology and Ethnology* 25:1–183.
MARWITT, J. P.
  1971 *Median Village and Fremont culture regional variation.* University of
        Utah Anthropological Papers 95.
MOORE, J. G., G. F. FRY, E. ENGLERT, JR.
  1969 Thorny-headed worm infection in North American prehistoric man.
        Science 163:1,324–1,325.
NAPTON, L. K.
  1969 The Lacustrine Subsistence pattern in the Desert West. *Kroeber
        Anthropological Society Special Publications* 2:28–97.
NAPTON, L. K., R. F. HEIZER
  1970 Analysis of human coprolites from archaeological contexts,with
        primary reference to Lovelock Cave, Nevada. *University of California
        Contributions of the Archaeological Research Facility* 10:87–129.
NAPTON, L. K., G. KELSO
  1969 Preliminary palynological analysis of Lovelock Cave coprolites.
        Kroeber Anthropological Society Special Publications 2:19–27.
RADOVSKY, F. J.
  1970 Mites associated with coprolites and mummified human remains in
        Nevada. *University of California Contributions of the Archaeological
        Research Facility* 10:186–190.
ROUST, N. L.
  1967 Preliminary examination of prehistoric human coprolites from four
        western Nevada caves. *University of California Archaeological Survey
        Reports* 70:49–88.
SHOHL, A. T.
  1939 *Mineral metabolism.* New York: Reinhold.
TAYLOR, C. M., G. MacLEOD
  1949 *Rose's laboratory handbook for dietetics,* fifth edition. New York:
        Macmillan.

Prehistoric Basketry of Western North America and Mexico

J. M. ADOVASIO

In the present context, "basketry" refers to coiled, twined, and plaited containers, regardless of flexibility, as well as to matting of all types. "Western North America" herein refers to the continental United States west of the Mississippi River and includes the country of Mexico from the Rio Grande to the Yucatan Peninsula.

Within much of the area defined above, the production of basketry is one of the oldest technical activities known in the archaeological record. Although basketry of one sort or another (probably twined) may have been manufactured during the Paleo-Indian or Big Game Hunter stage, its first documented appearance seems intimately related to the crystallization of the cultural stage or adaptive strategy known variously as the Desert culture (Jennings 1953, 1957), the Desert Archaic, or, more recently, the Western Archaic (Adovasio 1970a). Basketry is, in fact, usually cited as one of the "twin hallmarks" of the Archaic stage (the other being the milling stone) in western North America (Jennings 1957, and others).

Analytical and descriptive studies of prehistoric basketry from western North America are numerous (see Adovasio 1970a, 1970b, i.p.a, i.p.b for references) but are usually limited to sections of site reports in which the coverage ranges from extensive to practically nil. Until quite recently, no serious effort had been made to compare large quantities of prehistoric basketry for a number of reasons. Among them were the lack of standardized descriptive terminology used in the analysis of perishables, the wide dispersal of collections, and the general lack of chronological controls over some of the collections.

About ten years ago, this writer, working with extensive and well-dated basketry collections from the eastern Great Basin, devised a standardized terminology for basketry descriptions that seemed to facilitate large-scale comparisons. Subsequently, with generous funding from a number of organizations and individuals, it was possible to examine firsthand, and to apply this descriptive format to, some 30,000 examples of basketry from many parts of the western United States and Mexico. In addition, where warranted, numerous radiocarbon dates were run either on the specimens themselves or on directly associated materials to provide a measure of temporal control on the data under study. The preliminary results of this research are presented below by region, followed by a general discussion of all areas for which firm developmental sequences are now available. The final report on this data is now in preparation and some of the details presented below may be modified, particularly as regards aspects of the chronology. For those unfamiliar with basketry terminology, I have included a partial glossary in the Appendix at the end of this paper.

GREAT BASIN

Few areas of North America have yielded more or better-preserved prehistoric basketry remains than the Great Basin of the western United States. The relative abundance of dry caves and rock shelters from almost all sections of this physiographic and cultural area have provided, through controlled excavations, a series of textiles spanning 10,000 years of occupation. This is not only the longest but perhaps the best-controlled textile sequence in the world, thanks to the great number of radiocarbon dates available for both the perishables themselves and directly associated materials.

Prehistoric Regional Centers

As a result of the recent comparative studies noted above, it has been possible to establish the existence of three regional, prehistoric, basketry manufacturing centers within the Great Basin. These are labeled simply the northern, the western, and the eastern Basin centers, although occasionally their limits extend out of the physiographic limits of the Great Basin proper. Each has its own special characteristics and developmental sequence, and each manifests varying degrees of relationship to the others in time and through time. Taken as a unit, these three centers exhibit a variety of basic relationships to other prehistoric basketry centers in the western United States and northern Mexico and may conceivably be viewed as the ultimate sources or stimuli of much of the early textile production in western North America.

The Northern Basin Center

The northern Basin center is located in south-central Oregon and includes adjacent portions of northern California and northwestern Nevada. Principal basketry-bearing sites from this area include Roaring Springs Cave, Catlow Cave number 1, Fort Rock Cave, the Paisley Five Mile Point Caves, the Warner Valley Caves, Guano Valley Cave, Massacre Lake Cave, the Tule Lake Caves, and Antelope Overhang (Adovasio 1970a).

Within this center some thirteen different basketry techniques are known, including seven twining variations and six coiling methods. However, the vast majority of recovered perishables are twined and have been produced by one of three basic methods: close simple twining (plain two-element), z-twist weft; close diagonal twining (twill twining), z-twist weft; or open simple twining, z-twist weft. Decorative techniques are common and include overlay and false embroidery in a variety of designs. Coiling is present but very scarce, and few generalities may be made about it beyond stating that there appears to be a definite preference for split stitches on the nonwork surface, for right-to-left work direction, and for multiple-rod foundations. Decoration appears to be limited in both occurrence and complexity. Plaiting, both checker and twill, is totally lacking from this center.

Because there are fewer dates from this center than from the other two, it is somewhat more difficult to reconstruct the developmental sequence in terms of basketry manufacturing. It would appear, however, that the earliest technique is close simple twining with a z-twist weft and that this technique without evidence of decorative embellishment is certainly in use by 7000 B.C. Various elaborations in twining occur by 5000 B.C., including the appearance of diagonal or twill twining, but coiling is totally absent until relatively late and probably does not appear in the northern Basin center until well after 2000 B.C.

The earliest coiling in the northern Basin center closely resembles both contemporary and earlier material from the western Basin and probably represents an introduction from that area. However, even after coiling appears, twining techniques still predominate and continue to do so into historical periods.

The Western Basin Center

This center encompasses much of west-central Nevada as well as immediately contiguous portions of California. Principal sites from this area include Lovelock Cave, Humboldt Cave, Leonard Rock Shelter, Horse Cave, Fishbone Cave, Stick Cave, Chimney Cave, Guano Cave, Crypt

Cave, Cowbone Cave, Ocala Cave, and the Falcon Hill Caves (Adovasio 1970a).

Sixteen basketry techniques are represented in the western Basin center. Of these, seven are coiling variations, eight are twining, and one is a peculiar form of plaiting known in the literature as Lovelock wickerware. The favored twining techniques include open and close simple twining, z-twist weft; and close simple twining, s-twist weft. The remaining twining techniques are of little consequence. As in the northern Basin center, a variety of decorative techniques are practiced, particularly in later periods. The seven coiling techniques — two basic multiple-rod foundation types, three rod-bunched, and two rod-and-welt — constitute the great majority of coiled baskets recovered from this area. Again, as in the northern Basin, split stitches predominate with noninterlocking and interlocking types rarely evidenced. Work direction strongly tends toward right-to-left, though the reverse technique is known. Various decorative techniques are employed in coiling, including the well-known use of feathers in the production of certain types of bowls.

Interestingly, the most common basketry technique represented in western Basin sites is plaiting in the form of Lovelock wickerware, though the initial appearance and subsequent popularity of this type is relatively late when compared to that of other basketry variations. Fortunately, there is a large number of radiocarbon dates from the western Basin, so a much more complete picture of the development of this center is possible. For the sake of clarity, this development is presented below in stages.

Stage I: 8000–4500 B.C. Twining predominates in the complex; the earliest types include both open and close simple twining, z-twist weft, followed by close simple twining, s-twist weft. There is no coiling, nor is there any Lovelock wickerware. Diagonal twining is present by 5000 B.C. and can be viewed as a direct elaboration of the simple twining forms already cited.

Stage II: 4500–2000 B.C. Coiling in the form of multiple-rod varieties appears and gradually gains popularity. Twining types steadily decline in frequency. No Lovelock wickerware is present.

Stage III: 2000–1000 B.C. Coiling continues to increase in popularity while twining decreases, though no twining types disappear entirely. I suggest that Lovelock wickerware may appear at this time, though Grosscup (1960) assigns it to transitional Lovelock about 1000 B.C. to 1 B.C.

Stage IV: 1000 B.C.–A.D. 1000 or later. Twining, though present, is insignificant. Coiling of the three rod-bunched varieties is still common, as is Lovelock wickerware, but the latter, as Grosscup points out (1960), might be declining after A.D. 1.

The Eastern Basin Center

The eastern Basin center spans the state of Utah north of the Colorado River and adjacent portions of western Wyoming, southern Nevada, southern Idaho, and northwestern Colorado. Among the important sites are Danger Cave, Hogup Cave, the Promontory Caves, Evans Mound, Paragonah, Caldwell Village, Median Village, Old Woman, the Fremont River area, Antelope Cave, and Sand Dune Cave in Utah; Yampa Canyon and the Uncompahre Plateau in Colorado; Little Lost River Cave, Pence Duerig Cave, and Jack Knife Cave in Idaho; Spring Creek Cave and Daugherty Cave in Wyoming; Etna Cave and 26 LN402 in Nevada (Adovasio 1970a).

The eastern Basin center is represented by nineteen basic techniques, the largest number of any center. Eight of these are twining variations, while the remainder are coiling types. Plaiting in any form is absent.

Three twining variations — close simple twining, s-twist weft; open diagonal twining, z-twist weft; and open simple twining, z-twist weft — are important in the eastern Basin, while the remaining five are but seldom utilized. Of the large number of coiling techniques known, single-rod types and variants are by far the most popular, with multiple-rod types clearly secondary. Split stitches on the nonwork surface predominate, as does right-to-left work direction. Interlocking and noninterlocking stitch types do occur, and the former are rather common in early periods. Decoration of any sort on any type of eastern Basin textile is exceptionally rare and very few examples are known.

As in the western Basin center, a large number of radiocarbon dates exist, upon which a detailed developmental sequence may be postulated.

Stage I: 8000–6500 B.C. Twining dominates the eastern Basin center. No coiling is present. The principal techniques present are close simple twining, s-twist weft; open diagonal twining, z-twist weft; and open simple twining, z-twist weft. As in the case of the other centers, I suspect that the earliest twining is of the simple or plain variety, while the diagonal types appeared somewhat later.

Stage II: 6500–4500 B.C. Coiling appears in small amounts near the beginning of this stage. It appears to be confined to what is now the state of Utah. The earliest coiling is close coiling on a one-rod foundation with an interlocking stitch and is used almost exclusively for the production of parching trays. By the end of this stage, coiling has reached a percentage parity with twining, though twining clearly dominates the early part of this period.

Stage III: 4500–2000 B.C. Coiling dominates the complex, while twining is clearly on the decline. One-rod and one-rod variants, particularly one-rod-and-bundle, are the most popular coiling foundations, though multiple-rod types are also present. Both the one-rod variants and the multiple-rod variants may be viewed as simple progressive elaborations on the basic one-rod technique.

Stage IV: 2000 B.C.–A.D. 1200. One-rod-and-bundle foundation coiling dominates the entire eastern Basin center, though one-rod and other one-rod variants as well as multiple-rod coiling are present to some degree. Twining is still represented, though clearly in limited numbers. Toward the latter half of this stage, basic eastern Basin coiling techniques appear in southern Nevada, southern Idaho, and northwestern Colorado, as well as in portions of Wyoming.

Comparison of the Centers

A comparison of the three Great Basin centers indicates that basketry manufacturing in each extends back to the ninth millennium B.C. In each center, the earliest techniques are twining, to the exclusion of all others, and in one of the centers, the northern Basin, twining will dominate the area into historic times. Early coiling, however, is clearly restricted to the eastern Basin and appears there some 2,000 years earlier than in any other center. This innovation appears to be a functional necessity in a lifeway predicated around small-seed processing through parching, a use for which twining is ill suited. After two millennia of evolutionary changes, coiling ultimately diffuses to the western Basin center and from there to the northern Basin. Single-rod variants of coiling dominate the eastern Basin from 4500 B.C. until historic times; while in the western Basin, multiple-rod coiling and Lovelock wickerware are the dominant types after 45000 B.C.

There is a marked trend toward regional specialization and technical divergence in each of the complexes through time, though at no period is evidence for mutual influence entirely lacking. Finally, it appears that throughout the evolution of these three centers the western and northern Basin were more closely related than either was to the eastern Basin, the only major exception to this being the period during which coiling spread out of the east to the other two areas.

MEXICO AND SOUTHWEST TEXAS

Within this vast area, which includes all of trans-Pecos Texas and most of Mexico as far south as the Yucatan Peninsula, a reasonably large quantity of perishables has been recovered. The number of examples differs drastically from region to region. This differential recovery is, of course, directly proportional to the amount of archaeological research within these regions as well as to factors of preservation. Excellent chronological controls exist in some portions of this area, while in others temporal placement of basketry remains is tenuous at best.

Two major centers, or more accurately two centers and a satellite center, can be recognized at present within the area under discussion. These are the central Mexican highlands and northern Mexico, with a directly derived and closely related complex in trans-Pecos Texas.

Northern Mexico

While this region includes the modern states of Sonora, Chihuahua, Coahuila, Nuevo Leon, Tamaulipas, and Baja California, only two of these districts have yielded prehistoric basketry in significant amounts and under good chronological controls. These are Coahuila and Tamaulipas.

The basketry sequence from Coahuila is perhaps the longest and most complete of any area outside the Great Basin of the United States, and its evolution may, with caution, be viewed as generally reflective of developments in the arid deserts of northern Mexico. The sequence presented below is based principally on materials recovered by W. W. Taylor (1948, 1966) from a series of rock shelters and caves in the Cuatro Cienegas Basin of north-central Coahuila. Fortunately, a large number of radiocarbon dates are available on the basketry from these sites and on directly associated materials. A detailed account of the prehistoric basketry of Coahuila is currently in preparation.

Stage I: 7500–4000 B.C. Twining, plaiting, and coiling are represented, though coiling is very rare and is restricted to single-rod types. The earliest coiling type present is whole-rod with a split stitch on the non-work surface. This is soon followed by the appearance of other whole- and half-rod variations. Twining includes both simple and diagonal varieties with the former predominant, while simple plaiting is outnumbered by twill plaiting. Significantly, all the early coiling is in the form of parching trays.

Stage II: 4000–2000 B.C. Nine varieties of coiling are being produced, including six single-rod variants and three bundle-foundation types. Bundle-foundation coiling appears at the beginning of this stage in small numbers and does not appear to be a local invention. Throughout this and the following stage, single-rod types are considerably more popular than bundle-foundation varieties. Twining diminishes considerably in popularity, though it continues to be present in the form of bags and mats. Twill plaiting continues to predominate over simple plaiting. At the end of this stage whole-rod coiling varieties abruptly disappear and only half-rod types remain, along with the bundle-foundation types. In this, as in all stages, split stitches on either the nonwork surface or both sides predominate.

Stage III: 2000 B.C.–A.D. 500. Twining regains favor, at least in comparison to the preceding period, while the amounts of twill and simple plaiting are now equal. Coiling, which is extremely common, is of twelve different types, including five bundle varieties and seven single-rod types. Simple geometric decorations appear toward the end of this stage on the coiled pieces. Bundle-foundation coiling begins to outnumber single-rod types in various parts of this region.

Stage IV: A.D. 500–contact. Elaborate twilled and plaited mats are common, as are decorated coiled baskets with either a bundle or a single-rod foundation. Twining is present but scarce. In some areas only bundle-foundation coiling is being produced, while in others single-rod types continue to be made.

The basketry sequence from Tamaulipas is considerably less precise than that from Coahuila. It is based on rather less material (most very fragmentary) and considerably fewer dates. Again twined, plaited, and coiled materials are known, though the great variety of coiled types represented in Coahuila would appear to be lacking in this region.

It is not possible, at present, to summarize basketry developments in Tamaulipas in terms of stages, but the following observations can be made.

Twining in the form of rigid baskets, soft bags, and matting is present in the Sierra Madre of Tamaulipas by 7000 B.C. Also present are plaited mats, both simple and twilled. By 5000 B.C., if not earlier, coiled basketry appears in the Sierra de Tamaulipas constructed on a one-rod foundation. Coiling is very shortly thereafter reported in other areas of Tamaulipas and includes both bundle and single-rod varieties. As in Coahuila the bundle-foundation coiling does not seem to be a local innovation. From 4000 B.C. to late precontact times, twilled matting remains highly developed and includes many elaborate decorated varieties. Coiling is likewise present and includes decorated forms, while twining is a very minor component of the basketry assemblage.

Southwest Texas

The arid reaches of southwestern or trans-Pecos Texas have yielded literally thousands of basketry fragments spanning almost 9,000 years of occupation. These include twined, coiled, and plaited materials, in most respects highly similar to materials from northern Coahuila. The degree of affinity is so great as to suggest that the trans-Pecos basketry materials are in fact directly derived from essentially north-Mexican basketry industries. There are affinities to other areas as noted below, as well as certain other differences between the Texas materials and northern-Mexican basketry, but these do not, for the moment, overshadow the basic relationship of these two complexes. The general evolution of the trans-Pecos basketry center parallels that already described for Coahuila but with a time lag in some instances of several hundred years for the introduction of specific types. A summary of developments in the area is presented below.

Stage I: 7500–4000 B.C. Twining, coiling, and plaiting are represented but all are relatively scarce. Twining is the earliest technique represented, while coiling appears sometime between 7000 and 6000 B.C. The first occurrence of plaiting is difficult to establish with precision. The earliest coiling is of the single-rod type with stitches split on the nonwork surface. Again, all early coiled specimens are portions of parching trays. By the end of this stage, bundle-foundation coiling with predominantly split stitches on the nonwork surface or on both sides is established in this area. There appears to be quite well-defined subregional specialization in coiling, with single-rod types dominant in certain drainages and bundle types in others. Twining remains relatively minor throughout this period.

Stage II: 4000–1000 B.C. Plaiting in the form of mats becomes extremely common, as does bundle-foundation coiling, though single-rod types are still produced. Split stitches continue to predominate in most parts of this area, though interlocking types are also known. The plaited mats, both simple and twilled, are very elaborate by the end of this period. Twined items continue to be produced in minor quantities.

Stage III: 1000 B.C.–A.D. 1000. Bundle-foundation coiling is the dominant coiling variety, while single-rod types are exceedingly rare. Plaiting, especially of the twilled variety, is very plentiful and is occasionally decorated with geometric designs. Some Puebloid items appear in the extreme western tip of trans-Pecos Texas at this time, including the highly diagnostic two-rod-and-bundle coiled ware.

Stage IV: A.D. 1000–contact. Plaiting continues but the elaborate forms noted in the last stage diminish in frequency, then disappear entirely. Coiling is exclusively bundle-foundation in most areas, though Puebloid influences are still notable along the New Mexico boundary.

Central Mexico

The highlands of central Mexico have produced a basketry sequence rather different from that in northern Mexico. Basketry developments in this area are reconstructed principally on the extensive perishable remains from the Tehuacan Valley.

The principal types of textiles recovered from the Tehuacan Valley include both coiled and twilled basketry. No twining was found. A considerable amount of loom-woven material was also recovered from the later phases, but this is beyond the scope of the present study.

As MacNeish *et al.* (1967) point out, the dominant kind of basketry present in the Tehuacan Valley is coiling. Apparently, a sequence exists in which close coiling on a bundle foundation with noninterlocking stitches is the earliest form of basketry in the complex. This type is succeeded by close coiling on a bundle foundation with split stitches, a style that retains its popularity throughout the remainder of the sequence. MacNeish assigns close-coiled, bundle-foundation basketry with a predominantly noninterlocking stitch to the El Riego phase, dated between 6500 and 4800 B.C., and coiled-bundle foundation with split stitches to the succeeding phases, which begin at 4800 B.C. and extend into protohistoric times. Twilling in the form of mats or bags is also known from the Santa Maria phase, beginning about 900 B.C., and lasts well into historic times.

On the basis of the perishables recovered from the Tehuacan Valley, MacNeish postulates that the evolution of basketry in Mexico is very different from the sequences known in the Great Basin and the southwest. The total lack of early twining is cited as "proof" that coiling is the first form of basketry present. Further, he suggests that close coiling on a bundle foundation might have developed first in the central Mexican highlands and subsequently spread north. Since twilling and simple plaiting are apparently earlier in northern Mexico, he feels these types may have been spreading south (and north into Texas and the southwest) at the same time bundle-foundation coiling was diffusing northward.

This writer feels that certain of MacNeish's interpretations are open to serious question. While there appears to be little doubt that bundle-foundation coiling is earlier in central Mexico than in the north, it is highly doubtful that this is the earliest basketry technique known in this area. Sites in the central highlands with perishables ascribable to periods before 6500 B.C. are totally unknown at present, but there is a distinct possibility that should such sites be found they will contain twining and perhaps single-rod coiling. This, at least, is the situation in northern Mexico and in every other area in which a long basketry sequence exists. While it may be that coiling was independently invented in the central Mexican highlands without any twining antecedents, such a prospect seems highly unlikely.

This writer does feel that bundle-foundation coiling, whatever its antecedents (if any), did spread north into Tamaulipas and Coahuila and ultimately into trans-Pecos Texas and the greater southwest. Likewise it would appear that plaiting of the simple and twilled types is Mexican in origin and also spread north out of Mexico. This conclusion is based principally on the total lack of early plaiting (with the exception of the anomalous Lovelock wickerware) and bundle-foundation coiling in North America north of Mexico and trans-Pecos Texas before 4000 B.C.

THE AMERICAN SOUTHWEST

Within the context of this discussion, the geographical boundaries of the southwest are essentially those set forth by Reed (1964). He describes the southwest as encompassing all the territory lying between Durango, Colorado, in the north and Durango, Mexico, in the south. On the west and east its boundaries are Las Vegas, Nevada, and Las Vegas, New Mexico, respectively. This includes most of the states of New Mexico and Arizona as well as portions of northern Mexico, southern Colorado, southern Utah, and extreme southern Nevada.

Within this fairly restricted area, three major and more or less contemporary cultural traditions arose; the Mogollon, the Anasazi, and the Hohokam. Each dominated a particular area of the southwest and each was, to varying degrees, influenced by its neighbors. Furthermore, all three traditions are assumed to have evolved from a Western Archaic base through stimulus from Mexico.

Prior to 1959, no basketry of an antiquity comparable to that already discussed from the Great Basin was known in the southwest. However, archaeological researches on the Rainbow Plateau area of southern Utah and northern Arizona have revealed an early pre-Basketmaker II occupation (Lindsay *et al.* 1968). This occupation, now called the Desha complex, is dated about 5500–6000 B.C. and contains the earliest basketry in the southwestern area as defined here. As these Desha complex materials were directly followed by basketry of distinctly Basketmaker II type, they have considerable importance in clarifying the history of basketry developments in the southwest.

From the Desha level at Sand Dune Cave, as well as the mixed Desha–Basketmaker II level immediately above. Lindsay recovered some eighteen pieces of closely coiled one-rod-foundation basketry with an interlocking stitch. In all particulars, this basketry is identical to the earliest one-rod coiling from northern Utah, and it is my hypothesis that it diffused southward from the Utah area. In addition to the distinctly eastern-Basin-derived one-rod coiling, the Desha and mixed Desha–Basketmaker II levels also contained the typical southwestern technique of two-rod-and-bundle coiling with a noninterlocking or split stitch. As this technique has no early occurrence north of the Colorado River, it appears to be a local and early elaboration on the basic one-rod technique. As is well known, once this technique arose, it became the standard coiling technique for much of the southwest (Morris and Burgh 1941). Within both the Desha and mixed Desha–Basketmaker II levels were also recovered closely twined bags with stitch slant down to the right on a flexible warp. This is perhaps further corroboration of a Great Basin origin for early southwestern basketry, as this technique is common in the northern Basin and western Nevada from 8000 B.C. Like two-rod-and-bundle coiling, it also becomes a standard southwest technique by Basketmaker II.

In summary, the Desha materials seem clearly to be of eastern Basin origin and, moreover, seem to provide the base of both twining and coiling upon which subsequent southwestern basketry traditions were built. Here it should be noted with some emphasis that once basic Great Basin twining and coiling were established in the southwest, local variations arose that show little resemblance to contemporaneous Basin materials. Moreover, as will be shown below, later exchanges between the Great Basin and the southwest, at least in terms of basketry developments, are slight.

Rather than attempt to list in detail subsequent developments in the three major southwestern traditions, I shall discuss the representative materials from each area that provide general indications of later developments. Some of the earliest basketry in the Mogollon area was recovered from Tularosa and Cordova caves (Martin *et al.* 1952). These materials included coiled, twilled, and twined pieces, as well as over-one–under-one woven cloth. The predominant coiling technique is two-rod-and-bundle with noninterlocking or split stitches; and based on examination of the specimens, it is virtually indistinguishable from similarly made coiling from Desha and mixed Desha–Basketmaker II layers at Sand Dune Cave. Other coiling techniques are bundle-with-rod-core, bundle-foundation, and half-rod-and-bundle — none of which ever attained much popularity. Twilling and twining are present, though twining is relatively rare and twilling never common until the later phases (Martin *et al.* 1952). As has been noted elsewhere, twilling may represent a diffusion into the southwest from Mexico.

Recent discoveries of basketry from Fresnal Shelter in New Mexico that may be ascribable to the second millennium B.C. contain distinctly Mogollon elements as well as basketry that is decidedly north-Mexican in character. These latter materials include simple plaiting and bundle-foundation coiling and may represent the earliest evidence of the diffusion of Mexican basketry into the southwest (excluding trans-Pecos Texas). Most importantly, these early Mexican-derived perishables were associated with primitive maize and other domesticates.

In the Hohokam area the earliest basketry is from Ventana Cave (Haury 1950). The dating on these pieces probably falls in the vicinity of A.D. 800–1400; so they are, relatively speaking, quite recent. Nonetheless, I believe them to be indicative of basic Hohokam developments. As was the case in the Mogollon area, twining, though present, appears to be of little consequence, while coiling is extremely common. There is also a little twilling. However the basic coiling techniques differ somewhat from those of the Mogollon area and tend to include more varieties known from the eastern Basin. At Ventana, as in the Basin, the most popular techniques are one-rod variants, but the techniques (with one exception) are not similar to one-rod Basin varieties. These include bundle-foundation coiling, bundle-with-rod-core, and one-rod coiling. This last is quite similar to the one-rod coiling from the eastern Basin and, more importantly, to the one-rod coiling from Sand Dune Cave, whence it may be derived. Other coiling techniques present include one-rod-and-bundle, one-rod-and-welt, two-rod-vertical, two-rod-and-bundle, two-rod-and-welt, and three-rod-bunched. All these last, with the exception of two-rod-and-bundle, are uncommon.

The Ventana materials indicate that, in the Hohokam area, one-rod varieties that may have emerged from basic one-rod interlocking-stitch coiling remained popular throughout the sequence despite the elaboration of other techniques. Once again it should be noted that the presence of bundle-foundation coiling and twilling may indicate diffusion from areas of Mexico.

From the Basketmaker–Anasazi area, a large number of twined and coiled materials have been recovered and described by Kidder and Guernsey (1919), Guernsey and Kidder (1921), Morris (1919), Morris and Burgh (1941), and others. In this general area, twining reaches a high level of sophistication during Basketmaker II times, but afterward steadily declines with the rise in popularity of coiling. Coiling reaches its highest degree of elaboration in the Anasazi area and includes many close-coiled varieties. The earliest and most well developed spaced or open coiling also originates here and enjoys considerable popularity. Throughout this sequence, close-coiled two-rod-and-bundle foundation with a noninterlocking or split stitch is the predominant kind of coiling present and must have attained its popularity very early, as indicated by its notable presence in the mixed Basketmaker–Desha levels at Sand Dune Cave. Some twilling and bundle-foundation coiling is present, though rather late, and could mark the northern limits of the diffusion of these techniques from Mexico, at least in this period.

From the above summaries, it becomes apparent that each area developed its own regional textile techniques. Moreover, it is also clear that all these areas shared a large number of techniques — specifically two-rod-and-bundle coiling, bundle-foundation coiling, and twilling — although the popularity of each technique is variable from area to area.

The relationship of later southwest textiles to developments in the Basin remains to be discussed. Evidently no standard southwestern techniques ever appeared in significant numbers in the Basin at contemporaneous periods and vice versa. As a result, no recognized basketry-complex boundaries are as well defined as those which exist between the Fremont area and the northern borders of the southwest. This does not mean that single techniques are not shared or that distinctly southwestern varieties do not appear in the eastern Basin. In fact, spaced coiling or open coiling with an intricate stitch occurs sporadically and quite late in areas as far removed from the southwest as Wyoming (Frison 1965, 1968), Idaho (Gruhn 1961), and Utah (Jennings 1957; Adovasio 1970b). As there is no history of development of this technique in the Basin, these pieces are presumed to represent tradeware and, as such, could be indicative of the limits of exchange between the southwest and areas further north. Similarly, one or two pieces of bundle-foundation as well as bundle-with-rod-core coiling have been found in Utah. These are also presumed to be intrusions from the southwest.

CALIFORNIA

In terms of basketry developments and available evidence, California is certainly a marginal area. Early materials assigned to periods contemporary with the initial stages of the Archaic Basin complexes are almost totally lacking, while later materials tend to range from A.D. 1100 to historical times. As Rozaire (1957) points out, "The confinement of the textile materials to the relatively short 700 year time span does not permit the tracing of local cultures or movements of techniques." Nonetheless, I believe a few general statements may be made regarding the California area.

Basketry remains from California tend to suggest that twining diffused there early, probably from southern Oregon. The twining that is present is already well developed and suggests either a long antecedent development or continued contact with southern Oregon and western Nevada. Twining in California retains its popularity throughout most of the known sequence, and broad parallels may be drawn with the Oregon area, since the most popular techniques include close simple twining, stitch slanted down to the right; and open simple twining, stitch slanted down to the right. Both of these techniques are well known in the northern Basin. Coiling is clearly not an indigenous development and appears quite late, being introduced in already developed form from western Nevada. As is well known, coiling in California reached a high level of sophistication, but this occurred only in late protohistoric and historical times.

As a conclusion for the California area, I feel a brief discussion of the basketry from Coville Rock Shelter in Inyo County (Meighan 1953) is in order. Both twined and coiled basketry were recovered by Meighan, and the variety of techniques is highly indicative of contacts between southern California, the southwest, and western Nevada.

The techniques present at Coville Rock Shelter include close simple twining, stitch slanted down to the left; close simple twining, stitch slanted down to the right; open simple twining, stitch slanted down to the left; and open simple twining, stitch slanted down to the right. (In open simple twining, the right stitch slant is predominant.) This assemblage is consistent with twining assemblages from elsewhere in the California area as well as those from western Nevada.

Of greater importance in the present context is the presence of thirty specimens of three-rod-bunched coiling with predominantly split stitches, which is a major characteristic of the western Nevada area. This tends to substantiate the direct diffusion and subsequent elaboration of western Nevada techniques in at least the southern California area, as no earlier coiling has been found there. A second coiling technique is also represented and, for the moment, constitutes the westernmost distribution of its type now known. The technique is two-rod-and-bundle coiling; its heartland is the southwest and its presence in California could indicate limited southwest influences on California developments. However, the two-rod-and-bundle specimens could be tradeware.

In the absence of more data it is impossible to reconstruct further the development of California basketry. It appears that developments in California are influenced by at least two areas, southern Oregon and western Nevada, and conceivably by the southwest, as indicated by the Coville Rock Shelter materials.

THE PLAINS

In the context of this discussion, "the Plains" refers to a broad geographical region extending from the borders of the eastern woodlands to the Rocky Mountains. On the north it extends into the western provinces of Canada, while in the south it includes portions of Texas and New Mexico. Within this vast area, basketry remains are quite rare, being relatively common only in the northwestern Plains, and thus do not give a full picture of all the techniques presumed to have existed there. Nonetheless, on the basis of available remains, several inferences may be made.

Twining is a relative rarity on the Plains and no early evidence of it is known. Plaiting is very rare, while coiling has been reported from such widely disparate areas as the Texas panhandle, the eastern front of the Rockies, and various sites in Wyoming, Kansas, and Nebraska.

The earliest basketry from anywhere on the Plains is from Level 30 at Mummy Cave in the state of Wyoming. The technique represented is close coiling on a one-rod-and-welt foundation with a basically noninterlocking stitch, and the associated date is 2470 B.C. More coiled basketry was recovered from Level 36, with a date of A.D. 720. In all instances, the basketry from this cave closely resembles the basketry of the eastern sector of the Great Basin, as do all the basketry remains from other sites in the northwestern Plains and Colorado's mountain front. This strongly suggests a direct dispersal into these areas of a fully developed basketry technology from the Great Basin.

The basketry from the Texas panhandle, and from other sites on the central and southern Plains, has strong affinities to developments in the southwest and trans-Pecos Texas, and these materials are in general much later than the basketry from the northwest.

All the sparse data from the Plains suggests that there is no Plains basketry complex or complexes in the sense of indigenous groups of techniques that evolved in and are subsequently characteristic of various areas in the Plains. Rather it would seem that basketry, as noted above, diffused onto the Plains at a relatively late date from neighboring areas in which it was highly developed and possessed a great antiquity. The functional necessity for basketry on the Plains may have been mitigated by the availability of other types of containers, particularly those made from animal hide.

DISCUSSION AND CONCLUSIONS

From the foregoing and admittedly brief summaries, it may be concluded that the manufacture of basketry is well established in many parts of western North America and Mexico by 8000–7000 B.C. Notable exceptions would appear to be California and the Great Plains. In the former case, the available data is simply incomplete, while in the latter, the craft seems to have been introduced at a fairly late date, though this is far from certain.

Despite some contradictory data from Mexico, the earliest technique in all areas in which long sequences are available would appear to be twining, which may also be part and parcel of the Paleo-Indian craft milieu as well. This conclusion seems particularly plausible in light of recent discoveries in highland South America that exclusively indicate the presence of twining in that area by 8600 B.C. (Adovasio and Lynch 1973). The origin of twining is itself somewhat enigmatic, but it may be simply an outgrowth of weaving techniques used in the manufacture of nets or fish traps. This idea is somewhat reinforced by the prehistoric distribution of twining in North America. Both prehistorically and historically, the densest distribution of twined basketry is coastal, while coiling tends to be an interior phenomenon.

Though twining seems to be widespread by 8000 B.C. and is even further dispersed in the succeeding two millennia, the prehistoric incidence of the earliest coiling is quite restricted. Specifically, coiling would appear to have developed in a narrow belt or corridor extending from northern Utah through Arizona and down into arid northern Mexico. Invariably the earliest coiled basketry takes the form of parching trays made on a one-rod foundation (either whole or half). The stitch is usually interlocking north of the Rio Grande and split on the nonwork surface in northern Mexico. This brings us to the problem of determining how many times the process of coiling was invented. Originally this writer was of the opinion that the earliest coiling was exclusively an eastern Great Basin innovation, which only later spread south, west, and east. While this interpretation is still tenable, it is also possible that coiling was invented repeatedly in a number of areas along the corridor just described by peoples whose lifeways were predicated around small-seed processing.

Here it may be inserted that split stitches on the nonwork surface of a coiled basket are technically intermediate forms between interlocking stitches on the one hand and noninterlocking forms on the other. Noninterlocking stitches are definitely the latest of the three types to appear archaeologically, and there is strong evidence that interlocking types are the first. If this thesis continues to be supported by radiocarbon dates, then the early north-Mexican coiling (with split stitches on the nonwork surface) may indeed be derived from forms farther north (whose stitches are interlocking). Likewise, the early bundle-foundation coiling from the central Mexican highlands may be a local copy of single-rod types introduced from the north, in which the rod has been exchanged for a fiber bundle.

Whether invented once or repeatedly, the origins of coiling seem to be inextricably bound to the specialized food-preparation techniques used by desert-dwelling Archaic populations. Seed parching necessitates proper parching trays, and these trays *cannot* be very successfully made by twining or plaiting techniques because of structural factors that render the surface of such containers susceptible to burning and ultimate disintegration. In close coiling, with the stitches tightly packed, such a possibility is quite limited, because the surface allows a more even distribution of heat without temperature buildup at any one point (Adovasio 1970a:22).

Another factor readily apparent from the archaeological record is that coiling never appears in an area, save in the case of diffusion, without prior presence of a developed twining technology. It may be that coiling is the result of the elementary process of turning simple twining "sideways" and using one "warp" of indefinite length sewed back on itself, rather than multiple warps of fixed lengths.

Whatever the origin, once developed within the interior deserts, coiling spreads rapidly to most parts of the western United States and Mexico and, once established, tends to become highly regionalized with a distinctive "local flavor."

Certain summary comments may be made about basic affinities of the centers discussed above. In earliest times, that is, 8000–6000 B.C., the technical connections between the northern Great Basin and the western Great Basin are highly developed, while early eastern Great Basin basketry is only generally similar to complexes elsewhere. Should there prove to be early twining in California, its probable affinities should lie with the northern and/or western Great Basin. The principal connections of the eastern Great Basin lie to the south and east, that is, with the earliest developments in the southwest and with much later developments in the Plains.

As noted, the basketry of the southwest, while it may, and probably does, derive much of its stimulus from the Great Basin, shares few later developments with that area. There are, however, clear ties between basketry developments in the southwest and those in Mexico. The diffusion of bundle-foundation coiling, twilling, and simple plaiting out of Mexico into the southwest seems to be well established, and it may well prove that these introductions occur at the same time as the diffusion of maize, beans, and squash. Likewise the connections between the basketry of trans-Pecos Texas and that of northern Mexico are clear-cut and of long duration.

The scarce basketry of the Plains has firm ties to the eastern Great Basin on the northwest and possible connections to the southwest and trans-Pecos Texas in the central and southern reaches of this cultural province.

While many details could be added to the general picture presented here, any major substantive additions by this writer would be premature at best and foolhardy at worst.

APPENDIX: GLOSSARY

This glossary is not complete and is not intended as a guide to basketry analysis. Its sole purpose is to acquaint the reader with terms used in this paper. Portions of this glossary are adapted from Morris and Burgh (1941), and Cressman (1942). A complete glossary explicitly designed for basketry analysis is forthcoming in a subsequent article.

Bunched Foundation. A coiling foundation composed of two or more elements placed side by side or in triangular arrangement so that the basket wall has a double thickness of elements in each coil. In the present study such foundations are also referred to as multiple-rod variants and include two-rod-and-welt, three-rod-bunched, and two-rod-and-bundle. The difference between two-rod-and-welt and three-rod-bunched is slight. In both, the foundation elements are arranged in a triangle, but in three-rod-bunched the top or apex is split by the stitch, while in two rod-and-welt the top element is flat and is not split.

Bundle. A flexible foundation element of plant material used alone or in combination with rods in coiled basketry. It may consist of loose fibers, a mass of stems or twigs, or a single fibrous leaf. Its function is to engage the stitches by which one coil is fastened to another as well as to provide a framework for the coil itself.

When properly made (i.e. with the stitches closely packed) and particularly when used with a single split rod, this foundation is watertight.

Close Coiling. A type of coiled basketry in which the stitches are closely packed together. In such basketry, the stitches may be interlocking, noninterlocking, or split.

Coil. The structural unit of coiled basketry. It consists of a foundation enclosed by a sheath formed by successive stitches.

Coiled Basketry. A class of basketry fabrics manufactured by sewing stationary, horizontal foundation elements with vertical moving stitches.

Diagonal Twining. A variety of twined textiles in which pairs of warps are utilized instead of single warps between each weft stitch. Moreover, each succeeding weft row engages alternate warps of each pair, producing a diagonal effect. This technique is also called "twilled twining," though Cressman (1942) reserves "twilled twining" for reference to diagonal twining only on flexible warps. The stitch slant for diagonal twining may be right or left as in simple twining. Also, the weft rows may be closely spaced or spaced at intervals. If the weft rows are widely spaced, it is called open diagonal twining; if they are closely spaced, it is called close diagonal twining.

Direction of Work. The direction in which a stitch is sewn along the foundation in making coiled basketry. Work direction may be to the right or to the left and is generally consistent for a given culture.

Foundation. That part of a single coil enclosed by the stitches. It may consist of one element or many elements. See also Bunched Foundation, Stacked Foundation, Bundle, Rod-in-Bundle, and Rod.

Interlocking Stitch. A stitch which passes diagonally through the top or a stitch immediately below. In so doing it may pierce the foundation element or completely encircle it.

Intricate Stitch. A type of stitch used only in open or spaced coiling. It is produced by a manipulation of the sewing element so that it engages adjacent foundation units one or more times and is wrapped in a false knot around its standing portion to accomplish the spacing between the coils. Many types of intricate stitches were known in the prehistoric southwest (Morris and Burgh 1941), though outside this area their occurrence is sporadic.

Lovelock Wickerware. A named type of plaited basketry common in the western Nevada area. The warps consist of peeled whole twigs that are rigid, while the wefts are made of two thin flexible elements. The relationship of the wefts is variable; they may be directly superimposed over one another, overlap each other, or be separated completely. The plaiting is of the simple variety with the wefts passing over and under one warp at a time.

Multiple-Stitch-and-Wrap Coiling. A variety of open coiling that employs a wrapping stitch that successively encircles a single foundation coil before engaging the next coil.

Noninterlocking Stitch. A stitch that engages the foundation element below without passing through another stitch. It may completely encircle the underlying foundation or pierce it.

Nonwork Surface. The surface of a coiled basket upon which the sewing awl emerges. Also called reverse surface. See also Work Surface.

Open Coiling. A class of coiled basketry in which the stitches are not closely packed together. Three types of stitches may be used in such basketry: interlocking stitches, intricate stitches, and multiple-stitch-and-wrap.

Plaited Basketry. A class of basket fabrics that are woven instead of sewn. In simple plaiting and twill plaiting the weaving elements are flexible strips of uniform width and lenghth. In wicker plaiting, flexible wefts are interlaced upon rigid warps. See also Lovelock Wickerware, Simple Plaiting, and Twilling.

Rod. A rigid or semirigid foundation element used in coiled basketry either alone or in combination with other rods, bundles, or welts. It may be used split or unsplit, though both varieties are herein generally referred to as one rod.

Rod-in-Bundle. A foundation used in coiled basketry wherein a fiber bundle surrounds a single rod.

Simple Plaiting. A variety of plaited basketry in which the weaving elements pass over each other in single intervals.

Simple Twining. A variety of twined textiles in which single warps are utilized between weft stitches. Each succeeding weft row engages the same warps. The stitch slant may be to the right or the left and the weft rows may be closely spaced or spaced at intervals. If the weft rows are closely spaced, it is called close simple twining; if widely spaced, it is called open simple twining.

Split Stitch. A stitch that is split open to receive a stitch from the coil immediately above it. Three types of split stitches are known: those split on the nonwork surface, those split on the work surface, and those split on both sides.

Stacked Foundation. An arrangement of foundation elements in a coil, one above the other, like logs in a cabin wall. Such foundations include one-rod-and-welt, two-rod vertical, and one-rod-and-bundle. In this paper, stacked-foundation coiling types are generally referred to as single-rod variants, as opposed to multiple-rod variants, which are bunched-foundation types.

Stitch Slant. A term used to denote the pitch or lean of the wefts in twined textiles. The stitch slant may be to the right or the left.

Twilling. A variety of plaited textiles in which the weaving elements pass over each other in intervals of two or more.

Twining. A class of basket fabrics manufactured by sewing stationary vertical elements called warps with horizontal moving elements called wefts.

Warp. The stationary vertical element in twined basketry. It may be flexible or rigid, and it is this element that is engaged by the movable weft.

Weft. The moving horizontal element in twined basketry. It engages the warps and may be closely spaced or widely spaced.

Welt. An element used in coiled foundations in conjunction with one or more rods. The welt is generally a small flattened twig which is stacked vertically on a single rod or used in a triangular arrangement with two or more rods. When it is used in a triangular arrangement with two rods, the welt is rarely split.

REFERENCES

ADOVASIO, J. M.
1970a The origin, development and distribution of Western Archaic textiles. *Tebiwa* 13(2):1–40.
1970b "Textiles," in *Hogup Cave*. By C. M. Aikens, 133–153. University of Utah Anthropological Papers 93.
i.p.a "Prehistoric Great Basin textiles," in *The handbook of North American Indians,* volume ten, *Great Basin*. Edited by W. D'Azevedo.
i.p.b "Basketry and netting in North America," in *The handbook of North American Indians,* volume eleven, *Technology and visual arts*. Edited by W. C. Sturtevant.
ADOVASIO, J. M., THOMAS LYNCH
1973 Prehistoric textiles and cordage from Guitarrero Cave, Peru. *American Antiquity* 38(1):84–90.
CRESSMAN, LUTHER S.
1942 *Archaeological researches in the northern Great Basin*. Carnegie Institution of Washington Publication 538. Washington, D.C.
FRISON, GEORGE
1965 Spring Creek Cave. *American Antiquity* 31:81–94.
1968 Daugherty Cave. *Plains Anthropologist* 13:253–295.
GROSSCUP, GORDON L.
1960 *The culture history of Lovelock Cave, Nevada*. Reports of the University of California Archaeological Survey 52. Berkeley: University of California Press.
GRUHN, RUTH
1961 A collection of artifacts from Pence-Duerig Cave in south central Idaho. *Tebiwa* 4:1–23.
GUERNSEY, S. J., A. V. KIDDER
1921 Basketmaker caves of northeastern Arizona. *Papers of the Peabody Museum of American Archaeology and Ethnology* 8 (2).
HAURY, EMIL W.
1950 *The stratigraphy and archaeology of Ventana Cave, Arizona*. Albuquerque: University of New Mexico and University of Arizona Presses.
HUSTED, WILFRED M.
1969 *Bighorn Canyon archaeology*. Smithsonian Institution River Basin Surveys 12. Washington, D.C.
JENNINGS, JESSE D.
1953 Danger Cave: a progress summary. *El Palacio* 60:179–213.
1957 *Danger Cave*. University of Utah Anthropological Papers 27.
KIDDER, A. V., S. J. GUERNSEY
1919 *Archaeological explorations in northeastern Arizona*. Bureau of American Ethnology Bulletin 65.
LINDSAY, ALEXANDER J., JR., J. RICHARD AMBLER, MARY ANNE STEIN, P. HOBLER
1968 Survey and excavations north and east of Navaho Mountain 1959–1962. *Bulletin of the Museum of Northern Arizona* 45.
MacNEISH, RICHARD S., ANTOINETTE NELKEN-TERNER, IRMGARD W. JOHNSON
1967 *The prehistory of the Tehuacan Valley,* volume two: *Non-ceramic artifacts*. Austin and London: University of Texas Press.

MARTIN, PAUL S., JOHN B. RINALDO, ELAINE BLUHM, *et al.*
1952   Mogollon cultural continuity and change. *Fieldiana: Anthropology* 40:1–528.

MEIGHAN, CLEMENT W.
1953   The Coville Rock Shelter, Inyo County, California. *Anthropological Records* 12:171–223.

MORRIS, E. H.
1919   "Preliminary account of the antiquities of the region between the Mancos and La Plata rivers in southwestern Colorado," in *Bureau of American Ethnology, thirty-third annual report*.

MORRIS, E. H., R. F. BURGH
1941   *Anasazi basketry, Basketmaker II through Pueblo III*. Carnegie Institution of Washington Publication 533. Washington, D.C.

REED, ERIK K.
1964   "The greater southwest," in *Prehistoric man in the New World*. Edited by Jesse D. Jennings and Edward Norbeck, 175–192. Chicago: University of Chicago Press.

ROZAIRE, CHARLES E.
1957   "Twined weaving and western North American prehistory." Unpublished Ph.D. dissertation, U.C.L.A.

TAYLOR, WALTER W.
1948   A study of archaeology. *American Anthropologist*, Memoir 69.
1966   "Archaic cultures adjacent to the northeastern frontiers of Mesoamerica," in *Handbook of Middle American Indians*, volume 4. Series editor, Robert Wauchope, 59–94. Edited by Gordon F. Ekholm and Gordon R. Willey, Austin: University of Texas Press.

The Introduction, Use, and Technology of Fiber-Tempered Pottery in the Southeastern United States

DREXEL A. PETERSON, JR.

Two topics in American archaeology have received increasing attention in the last few years. James Ford (1966, 1969) provoked much comment on long-distance contacts and migrations in his discussions of the "American Formative." By his inclusion of fiber-tempered pottery in North and South America he intersected another area of concern. Elizabeth Weaver (1963) also provoked comment with her suggestion that fiber-tempering in the American southeast was not tempering at all. Subsequent studies by this author and by Jeffrey Brain (1971), as well as by Donald Crusoe (1971), Crusoe and De Pratter (1972), and David Dye (1972), have continued to emphasize the technical as well as the cultural aspects of fiber-tempering in the southeastern United States. The "context, origins, and significance" of fiber-tempering were also the topic of a symposium at the 1969 meeting of the American Anthropological Association (Bullen and Stoltman, editors, 1972).

With all this work and still more that remains to be mentioned, it would seem that the phenomenon of fiber-tempered pottery in the Americas and its cultural significance should be clear, and for some areas and topics it is. But some of the apparent conflicts involving relationships or the proposed mechanisms for dispersal of the ideas, as well as some details of occurrence, remain to be worked out. Certainly the technical qualities of fiber-tempered pottery need to be stressed to understand clearly why this cultural phenomenon was practiced or accepted over such a wide space and time.

Fiber-tempered pottery occurs both north and south of the Caribbean. Well-reported occurrences of these ceramics include Puerto Hormiga and surrounding coastal and inland sites (Reichel-Dolmatoff 1965, 1972); Florida (Bullen 1972, and several earlier reports summarized therein); Georgia–South Carolina (Waring 1968; Stoltman 1972); the

Tennessee Valley of northern Alabama and western Tennessee (Webb 1939; Haag 1942; Dye 1972); and, in smaller numbers of sherds and sites, the Gulf coastal plain from Mobile to the Mississippi River (Ford and Webb 1956: 105; summary information in Ford 1969: 177, 181).

James Ford argued in 1966, even before the summary publication of proposed Formative contacts in 1969, that the complexes of fiber-tempered pottery found in the American southeast, as indicated in Map 1, were derived from various pottery styles of South America including, of course, Puerto Hormiga. Ford concluded that,

> . . . the compared complexes seem to follow one another in the proper order and to be coeval. Direct derivation of the two groups of Southeastern ceramics from Ecuador is not to be inferred, for they incorporate certain features that existed at early dates in northern Colombia [Puerto Hormiga] and in Mesoamerica . . . (1966:796).

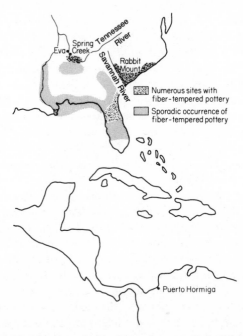

Map 1.   Fiber-tempered pottery sites in the southeastern United States and Colombia

The mechanism for the derivation was concluded to be colonial settlements after long-distance voyages.

It is not my desire here to argue about the theories or methods that Ford or anyone else has used to organize the evidence in order to suggest contact between the fiber-tempered ceramic users of Colombia and those of the southeast. What I will present is evidence to show that fiber-tempered pottery is a nondisruptive and positive trait addition to existing cultures in the southeast and not the symptom of wide-ranging movements of people. Stoltman, in his prefacing remarks to the AAA Symposium (1972), has summarized this antimigration approach after stating that "the possibility of culture contact cannot be dismissed out of hand":

That this culture contact came in the form of colonizing ventures as Ford (1966:782) has suggested seems unlikely in light of the current evidence. Both Bullen and Stoltman emphasize [1972] . . . that in Florida and along the Georgia–South Carolina coast fiber-tempered pottery appears as a non-disruptive additive to a cultural inventory whose local roots are far deeper than the pottery itself. If actual movements of populations were involved, . . . one would expect to find an assemblage of demonstrably intrusive traits indicative of a site-unit intrusion. . . . In the absence of such evidence, however, fiber-tempered pottery has more the appearance of a trait-unit intrusion in the Southeast if, in fact, it is intrusive at all and not an independent invention (1972:iii-iv).

There are two new developments which add to the unlikelihood of site-unit intrusions coming into the southeast and which, I think, point more toward the local development of fiber-tempered pottery in this region of the United States. The first is the evidence assembled by David Dye for the nature of the occurrence of fiber-tempered pottery in the Tennessee Valley and presented to the Twenty-ninth Southeastern Archaeological Conference in 1972; the second contribution, presented to the same conference, concerns the suitability of the South Carolina–Georgia littoral for shellfish-gathering subsistence in the third millennium B.C., as reported by Donald Crusoe and Chester De Pratter.

The material reported on by Dye concerns the most inland occurrence of fiber-tempering in the southeast as established first by Webb (1939) and Haag (1942) for the Wheeler and Pickwick dam basins in Alabama. This distribution has recently been expanded into Tennessee below Pickwick Dam for some thirty miles by the research of this author, Mr. Dye, and others from Memphis State University (see Map 1). At first glance, the common inland occurrence of fiber-tempered pottery would not seem relevant to the argument of South-to-North American contact. It could easily be said, and it has been said, that the fiber-tempered ceramics of the Tennessee Valley are later and were introduced from the coast (Ford 1966:783; Ripley Bullen, personal communication).

But Dye's argument follows quite a different tack. The case is made that for the Tennessee Valley, as for coastal Florida or Georgia–South Carolina, the introduction of ceramics with fiber-tempering is nondisruptive. These ceramics are limited to only the most southerly portion of the looping course of the Tennessee, and this portion is best described ecologically as an extension of the coastal plain. Fiber-tempering then occurs in the Tennessee Valley only where an adaptation similar to that of the coastal-plain river valleys could be practiced. In other words, even for the most "land-locked" occurrence of fiber-tempered ceramics in the United States, this cultural element, wherever it first originated, did not appear suddenly or disruptively as if the influences were anything more than gradual diffusion.

This argument for general cultural continuity between the coastal plain and the Tennessee Valley in its southern reaches assumes even more importance in light of the ideas presented by Crusoe and De Pratter in 1972. It is their contention that the coast along the Sea Island portion of Georgia and south Carolina was not suitable for shellfish-oriented subsistence at the time that fiber-tempering first appears in either North or South America. From a study of the adjustments of the sea level during the last several thousand years, they state that the marshes along the coast would not have supported major colonies of shellfish before 2200 B.C. at any time during the last several millennia. This reconstruction of the coastline includes the opinion that no currently submerged sites or shellfish beds can be postulated for that segment of the coast.

Crusoe contends that the immediate coast of Georgia and South Carolina could not have participated in the development of shellfish-oriented subsistence, and the often-associated fiber-tempered ceramics, if shell middens and fiber-tempered pottery occur anywhere before 2200 B.C. in the southeast, and he notes that both traits can be found earlier in the southeast. The earliest fiber-tempered ceramics currently dated in the area appear about 2500 B.C. from the Savannah River valley in Stoltman's excavations at Rabbit Mount (Stoltman 1966). Shell middens have clearly been dated earlier in the Eva site along the Tennessee River. Stratum IV Bottom at Eva with a heavy shell concentration has yielded a radiocarbon date of 5200 B.C. ± 500 (Lewis and Lewis 1961:13) (clouding the certainty of such an early date may be the mixture indicated for this stratum from an analysis of the tabular data supplied by Lewis and Lewis 1961:Table 6). Among other sites to suggest a temporal priority for shell middens along the Tennessee or other inland rivers is the Spring Creek site currently being excavated by the author. The deepest zone yet excavated has yielded a date of 2645 B.C. ± 210. This site has two dense shell middens exposed by the erosive action of the Tennessee River up to three meters below this current limit of excavation.

It is Crusoe's argument that fiber-tempering and shellfish-oriented subsistence occurred first inland and moved from there to the coast. There is no occurrence of sites old enough along the Georgia or South Carolina coasts to be the intrusive colonies Ford would have expected, nor could there have been. There are also no sites early enough in Florida (pre-2000 B.C.) although there is the possibility that sufficiently old sites are now covered by the Atlantic or the Caribbean (Bullen 1972:24).

Current evidence best supports an inland priority for fiber-tempered ceramics and shell-midden production. The position that the Tennessee

Valley fiber-tempered ceramics need be later in time for stylistic or other reasons should now be reexamined. There are no unquestioned age determinations for fiber-tempered pottery in the Tennessee Valley, only suggested cross-dates to the coastal sequences (e.g. Griffin 1972). However unlikely it may be that fiber-tempering originated in the southeast with the shell-midden depositors of the Tennessee Valley, this logical extension of Dye's argument cannot be discounted out of hand.

The southern loop of the Tennessee River contains an environment as well as cultures that can be best viewed as extensions of those found along the coastal-plain rivers (Dye 1972). Archaeological evidence suggests that the immediate littoral of Georgia and South Carolina (Crusoe and De Pratter 1972) and probably Florida cannot have temporal priority over the inland portion of the coastal plain for fiber-tempering and shellfish subsistence. Therefore, it could be that fiber-tempered ceramics and all associated traits, including shellfish subsistence, began in the southeast in the Tennessee Valley just as plausibly as in other valleys of the coastal plain proper. Certainly this extreme seems far more likely today than an intrusion of peoples from South or Central America. The possibility of a trait intrusion from the south is not rejected but made less likely when the inland areas must be considered to have the earliest fiber-tempered pottery in the United States southeast.

Arguing against a connection, no matter how tenuous, between Puerto Hormiga and the southeast also creates some problems. Stoltman has summarized the arguments for such a connection in aspects other than the ceramics: the shellfish subsistence and midden deposition, the overlap in dates, the winds and currents prevailing in the proper direction (south to north), specific ring-shaped middens, and shell hammers (Bullen and Stoltman, editors, 1972:iii). Discounting the site-unit intrusion, of course, does not discount the trait-unit intrusion, so these similarities can suggest "that the probability of contact is indeed high enough to warrant serious further investigation" (Bullen and Stoltman, editors, 1972:iii). The stumbling block presented by this paper and those cited here is getting the fiber-tempering from anywhere in South or Central America to the earliest currently known southeastern occurrence in inland South Carolina. Perhaps more work will reverse this inland priority and make it easier to accept again a diffusion of fiber-tempered ceramics and other traits from the south continuously along the littoral or even by accidental or planned voyages.

Instead of ending on this negative note, I would like to continue by making a more positive statement about the occurrence of fiber-tempered pottery in the southeast, at Puerto Hormiga, or anywhere else for that matter. The early nature of fiber-tempered pottery wherever it occurs in the world has been briefly summarized by Bullen (1972:22) for Alaska, the Malay Peninsula, Japan, Colombia, the southeastern United

States, the Hebrides Islands, and even northern Khuzistan. Following from the early nature of such pottery is the idea that fiber-tempered pottery is primitive, poor, or at least "often indicative of an early technological level" (Reichel-Dolmatoff 1972:4).

I cannot argue with this statement of Reichel-Dolmatoff, but there are more positive reasons for the actual use of fiber-tempering on an admittedly early time level. I have previously presented these favorable attributes of fiber-tempering in specific reference to the palmetto fibers used in the southeast (Peterson 1971). Earlier work had established the identity of the tempering fibers as unquestionably palmetto (Brain and Peterson 1971).

This positive argument for the use of palmetto fibers is valid, I think, for the southeast and probably for the other areas of the world in which similar cultural conditions occurred and in which plants like palmetto also occurred. Certainly, the area around Puerto Hormiga abounds in palms and related plants that yield the proper fibers, but I also recognize that more than one kind of fiber was used there, which complicates this argument (Reichel-Dolmatoff 1965:20–22). The many other areas of the world in which other vegetal or animal fibers were used may not easily fit this argument. I would suggest, however, that technological studies on the availability and suitability of the possible tempers in each of these regions would support my conclusions based on palmetto fibers.

The argument boils down to the following: given a semisedentary subsistence economy with easily available vegetal fibers and a positive need for leakproof containers, fiber-tempered ceramics are as good as or better than any others that could be produced at an "early technological level." If the ceramics are good and the need is there, the invention of fiber-tempering in many areas of the world should not be surprising. I should also point out that, even if contacts and diffusion can be shown to connect certain of the centers of fiber-tempering, such as Colombia and the southeastern United States, this argument still helps explain the situation. If the ceramics are good and the need is there, the adoption of fiber-tempering in many areas of the world should not be surprising.

Preceding the specific argument for the adoption of palmetto-fiber-tempering in the southeast, pottery is known in general to provide a substantial and versatile but also fragile container.

Therefore, I must invoke the idea of a necessary sedentary pre-adaptation to the use of ceramics. Nomadic wandering bands are not notorious potters. . . .

In the Southeast, clearly a semi-to-completely sedentary pre-adaptation did exist, and with it comes palmetto-tempered pottery. . . . It occurs in areas where the pre-adaptation was seasonal or year-round shellfishing. Palmetto-tempered pottery does not occur away from areas where shellfishing was very important. The minute valleys, the Piedmont, and the Appalachians all lack shell middens and fiber-tempered pottery. But if you go only a few miles to large valleys or to the moderate feeder streams, you find shell middens and fiber-tempered pottery. Of course, such pottery also occurs at sites without shell middens and in small river valleys where shellfishing would be marginal or impossible, . . . but I would suggest seasonality of occupation as one possible solution (Peterson 1971:6–7).

In addition, Brain and I have argued (1971), that the occurrence of palmetto itself in the southeast limited the occurrence of fiber-tempered pottery, excluding some areas that do have shell middens. Extending Dye's argument involving the ecological and cultural extensions into the Tennessee Valley should further clarify the many cultural factors allied with shellfish utilization that may have helped to limit the range of fiber-tempered pottery in the southeast.

The reason that some groups did not or could not adopt palmetto-tempered or any fiber-tempered ceramics is beyond the scope of this paper. Some groups, however, in the southeast did; and the carrying, storing alive, and cooking of shellfish would all benefit from the use of any ceramics. Baskets are ill-suited, especially for the last two jobs:

To keep shellfish alive longer, they can be stored in cool water; and a pottery container out of the sun would fill the bill better than anything else before refrigeration. The evaporation through the relatively porous walls would keep the water cooler than anything else but would keep the water in! (Peterson 1971:7).

The specific use of palmetto fibers in the southeast is also reinforced by the localization of settlements for shellfishing. "Even with pottery to keep them alive, who needs day-old transported shellfish?" (Peterson 1971:8). Clearly shell middens in the southeast occur along streams that did support shellfish colonies. Living along such streams also put the people in close proximity to the wet environments favored by palmetto. Palmetto fibers were easily available, and they must now be shown to have technical advantages over other potential and easily available tempers.

Palmetto fibers are available year-round and require virtually no preparation or equipment to gather. The drying leaves peeling back from the plant's head yield fibers in big handfuls without cutting.

Palmetto fibers mix easily and evenly into wet clay. They do not stiffen the clay, create weak planes in the vessel wall as cut leaves would, or even jab and scratch the hands of the potter (Peterson 1971:9–10).

The prime advantage of palmetto fibers, however, is their effectiveness as tempering agents during the drying and firing process. First appearances suggest that the characteristic holes left in the fabric by the charring and firing-out of the fibrous material would weaken the vessel walls. There are, however, six positive results of such tempering and porosity that more than balance out possible negative aspects:

1. The fineness of palmetto fibers precludes the concentration of explosive and destructive gas pockets in the wall, unlike heavier vegetal materials.

2. Before firing, the channels of palmetto fibers help to even out the drying process and act as a good aplastic by differentially contracting with the ceramic fabric to alleviate stresses.

3. The palmetto tempering fibers have a linear, interlocking distribution, and their porosity can channel out through their protrusions to the surface any expansive gases produced in the firing. Carbonaceous clays or lack of complete drying within the thick vessel walls found in early southeastern pottery would contribute various gases in firing that such tempering can handle.

4. The burning-out of the fibers conducts heat to the thick center of the walls, evening out the quick and primitive firing.

5. Southeastern fiber-tempered pottery is not coiled but made by sandwiching the tempering fibers between wet clay slabs. This practice concentrates most of the tempering to the core, where the aplastic is most needed. Some fibers, by their ease of manipulation, then reach the surface and "aerate" the core in drying and firing.

6. With the slab or patchwork method of vessel construction, the interlocking of the sheets of fibers from one slab with another could help to bind the seams together.

Each of these six points has been examined experimentally with the production of test sherds or briquettes. In most cases the advantages noted involve the linear, channelized nature of palmetto fibers achieving what particulate solid tempers could not with thick walls or mediocre clays. The greater efficiency of palmetto fibers over most other vegetal fibers stems from the fiber's fineness, the ease of working, and the lack of potential explosive gas pockets being formed in the firing process.

Palmetto tempering then is not particularly primitive, marginal, or desperate; in the southeast it was convenient, easy, and successful. There are other fibers and other areas of the world to consider, and these specific arguments may not be valid for Alaska, northern Khuzistan, or even Colombia. But the suggestion of the high efficiency of fiber-tempering in the southeast points out that we may be dealing not with an unusual but with a useful trait. This trait should be studied for its technological contributions and should not be reduced to a mere index of time or cultural contact.

REFERENCES

BRAIN, JEFFREY, DREXEL PETERSON
   1971   Palmetto tempered pottery. *Southeastern Archaeological Conference Bulletin* 13:70–76. Morgantown, West Virginia.
BULLEN, RIPLEY P.
   1972   "The Orange period of peninsular Florida," in *Fiber-tempered pottery in the southeastern United States and northern Colombia: its origins,*

context, and significance. Edited by Ripley Bullen and James Stoltman, 9–33. Florida Anthropological Society Publications 6, part 2. Fort Lauderdale: The Florida Anthropologist.

BULLEN, RIPLEY P., JAMES STOLTMAN editors
1972 *Fiber-tempered pottery in the southeastern United States and northern Colombia: its origins, context, and significance.* Florida Anthropological Society Publications 6, part 2. Fort Lauderdale: The Florida Anthropologist.

CRUSOE, DONALD
1971 The missing half: the analysis of the ceramic fabric. *Southeastern Archaeological Conference Bulletin* 13:109–114. Morgantown, West Virginia.

CRUSOE, DONALD, CHESTER DE PRATTER
1972 "A new look at the Georgia coastal shell mound Archaic." Paper presented at the Twenty-ninth Southeastern Archaeological Conference, October 13, Morgantown, West Virginia.

DYE, DAVID
1972 "The distribution of the Wheeler series in the Tennessee River Valley." Paper presented at the Twenty-ninth Southeastern Archaeological Conference, October 13, Morgantown, West Virginia.

FORD, JAMES
1966 Early Formative cultures in Georgia and Florida. *American Antiquity* 31(6):781–799.
1969 *A comparison of Formative cultures in the Americas.* Smithsonian Contributions to Anthropology 11. Washington, D.C.

FORD, JAMES, CLARENCE H. WEBB
1956 Poverty Point, a late Archaic site in Louisiana. *American Museum of Natural History, Anthropological Papers* 46(1).

GRIFFIN, JOHN W.
1972 "Fiber-tempered pottery in the Tennessee Valley," in *Fiber-tempered pottery in the southeastern United States and northern Colombia: its origins, context, and significance.* Edited by Ripley Bullen and James Stoltman, 34–36. Florida Anthropological Society Publications 6, part 2. Fort Lauderdale: The Florida Anthropologist.

HAAG, WILLIAM G.
1942 "A description of the Pickwick pottery," in *An archaeological survey of the Pickwick Basin in adjacent portions of the states of Alabama, Mississippi, and Tennessee.* Edited by W. S. Webb and D. L. DeJarnette, 511–526. Bureau of American Ethnology Bulletin 129. Washington, D.C.

LEWIS, THOMAS M. N., MADELINE KNEBERG LEWIS
1961 *Eva: an Archaic site.* University of Tennessee Studies in Archaeology. Knoxville.

PETERSON, DREXEL A.
1971 "The cultural excuses for fiber-tempered pottery." Paper presented at the Twenty-eighth Southeastern Archaeological Conference, November 13, Macon, Georgia.

REICHEL-DOLMATOFF, GERARDO
1965 *Excavaciones arqueologicas en Puerto Hormiga.* Antropologia 2. Bogota: Ediciones de la Universidad de los Andes.
1972 "The cultural context of early fiber-tempered pottery in northern Colombia," in *Fiber-tempered pottery in the southeastern United States and northern Colombia: its origins, context, and significance.* Edited by

Ripley Bullen and James Stoltman, 1–8. Florida Anthropological Society Publications 6, part 2. Fort Lauderdale: The Florida Anthropologist.

STOLTMAN, JAMES
1966   New radiocarbon dates for southeastern fiber-tempered pottery. *American Antiquity* 31(6):872–874.
1972   "The late Archaic in the Savannah River region," in *Fiber-tempered pottery in the southeastern United States and northern Colombia: its origins, context, and significance.* Edited by Ripley Bullen and James Stoltman, 37–62. Florida Anthropological Society Publications 6, part 2. Fort Lauderdale: The Florida Anthropologist.

WARING, ANTONIO J., JR.
1968   *The Waring papers: the collected works of Antonio J. Waring, Jr.* Edited by Stephen Williams. Papers of the Peabody Museum of Archaeology and Ethnology 58. Cambridge, Massachusetts.

WEAVER, ELIZABETH
1963   Technological analysis of prehistoric lower Mississippi ceramic materials: a preliminary report. *American Antiquity* 29(1):49–56.

WEBB, WILLIAM S.
1939   *An archaeological survey of Wheeler Basin on the Tennessee River in northern Alabama.* Bureau of American Ethnology Bulletin 122. Washington, D.C.

Coding and Cluster Analysis of Wisconsin Ceramics

WILLIAM M. HURLEY

The most difficult task confronting an archaeologist today is resolving which form of analytical methodology he will use to assure that his artifact categories, reconstructions, associations, and sequences are as accurate as possible. During the first third of this century, most New World archaeologists described specimens as being representative or unique without quantifying or qualifying the site assemblage. During the late 1930's and 1940's, large quantities of data were being synthesized via mode and attribute analyses or through typological methods, and these techniques were being offered as the key to our understanding prehistoric culture patterning (Krieger 1944; Rouse 1939). During the past twenty years, archaeological theses or dissertations included several pages or a chapter restating or reconfirming one or both or even combinations of these approaches as the means of ordering material-culture items. With the advent of dam, pipeline, and highway salvage programs the former techniques of site sampling (generally related to limited budgets) yielded to larger excavations that increased the number of recovered artifacts. Hundreds of diagnostic artifacts gave way to the thousands of specimens needing washing, cataloguing, and marking prior to the protracted laboratory time needed to describe and deal with the greater variety of artifacts. During the second third of this century, the ordering and categorization of artifacts into recognizable formally named types became the archaeologist's methodological core from which cultural reconstruction, relative chronologies, trade patterns, and prehistoric market places were described. Sequences became more complex, and the temporal and spatial connections between cultural manifestations increased in degree and detail.

The temporal aspects of sites were not generally controlled except in those areas in which tree-ring (dendro-chronological) dating techniques could be applied. The McKern or Midwest taxonomic method ordered prehistoric culture manifestations according to a relative ranking system in the absence of reliable methods of dating such phenomena. Such methodological constructs were greatly dependent upon establishing the existence of related classes of artifacts, which were ordered and ranked according to an ever-expanding range and variation of attributes, which were then used to describe the category or the proposed types. Subsequent controls placed on a type, such as quantification and qualification of micro- and macroattributes, provenience associations, spatial ranges, and temporal ordering according to chronometric determinatives, aided in the establishment of local and regional sequences, cultural chronologies, and prehistoric culture areas. The plethora of formal artifact types and subvarieties has now reached a point at which the archaeologist has difficulty controlling all the data from a subcontinental area. With the increase of the number of artifact types, such as the ceramic types, the archaeologists have grouped many types together under a more inclusive hierarchical heading called the ware group (Madison ware, which includes Madison Plain and Madison Cord Impressed type), associated more ceramic types with a prehistoric culture, or rejected the technique of naming subvarieties and shifted into attribute analysis for category groupings.

In the latter technique a type is generally not given a formal designation but is ordered into a particular category with the diagnostic attributes (color, decoration, shape, size) listed and quantified with the totals of the percentages recorded. This method sets one category off from another while demonstrating shared common or specific attributes.

There are numerous archaeological reports in which attribute analyses have formed the major research method. As one researcher has stated:

The advantage of attribute analysis lies in its reduction of the data to their simplest denominator thereby allowing ready comparison with later data. It also permits the individual testing of attributes to determine their relative worth as time and space indicators. The disadvantage of the technique lies in the overwhelming mass of descriptive data involved which inhibits communication, especially to those not directly involved in the specific problems . . . (Wright 1967:3).

Krieger has stated that,

. . . the purpose of a type in archaeology must be to provide an organizational tool which will enable the investigator to group specimens into bodies which have *demonstrable historical meaning in terms of behaviour patterns* . . . and thus serve as tools for the retracing of cultural developments and interactions (1944:272).

The final classification of various types is ". . . a process of discovery of combinations of attributes favoured by the makers of the artifacts, not an arbitrary procedure of the classifier" (Spaulding 1953:305). The question of type versus attribute analysis is not the view that attributes do not form types but that the researcher feels that the information is not complete enough to permit the step from meticulous attribute comparison to formally proposing a type (Wright 1967:3). Baerreis (1968:145) has advocated that both techniques can be combined when he started that:

Typology is a powerful and indeed an essential research tool of sound archaeological and anthropological investigation ... While it is evident that many types ... could be improved, archaeologists are caught in a dilemma in that in order to attain comparability with published data, older but inadequate types are often retained. Perhaps we should be more willing to restudy earlier collections to update inadequate descriptions though this is a difficult decision when so much recent work is entirely undescribed.

In an earlier report on the Effigy Mound tradition (Hurley 1970), the ceramic artifacts were examined according to their diagnostic attributes, grouped into types and categories, and examined according to their internal spatial and temporal relationships. The typological methods were limited to only quantity and percentage, and they may have failed to give convincing support to the conclusions drawn. In order to test those conclusions, it is necessary to amplify the quantitative data according to procedures which should clarify the original interpretations. It is hoped that subjecting my own typological data to impersonal statistical techniques will improve inadequate and rudely presented relationships. Finally, there are many statistical techniques currently being used by archaeologists, e.g. chi-square, "t" tests, coefficients of similarity, or association analysis (Loy 1968; Whallon 1972). I will not attempt to review or assess the procedures utilized by others, as there are numerous papers, with statistical proof, demonstrating the procedures and the results. One technique that has been considered as being too laborious for normal typing purposes is the principal component method (Rao 1964). It is this procedure, plus others, which will be used to clarify the full range of the artifact associations.

During the original analysis, various rude codes were attempted to order the wide range of attributes present on collared ceramics. One guide used was the code devised for the analysis of the Aztalan Collared and Point Sauble Collared ceramics (Baerreis and Freeman 1958). However, the time expended seemed inordinate for a sample of fewer than twenty specimens. With continued examination of the decorative techniques or cord and fabric impressions or incising versus trailing (Hurley 1970), it became apparent that the discontinuous attributes of decoration and location of decoration seemed to be the major criteria used to define Effigy Mound pottery types. Prehistoric decisions seemed to have been made according to predetermined cultural patterns when the location and type of decoration were being considered by the artisan. Decorative attributes seemed to be shared by several types, and stylistic analyses were ultimately envisioned. The listing of microattribute analysis (cord twist and not just the presence of cord impressions) increased the descriptive detail given to individual or related specimens so that the typological method seemed to revert to descriptions of single specimens.

Further complications in the ceramic analyses arose when it was realized that a pottery type lasted for several hundred to over a thousand years while still recognizable as a number of an established type. Changes must have taken place through time and space although they were generally not noticed when a type was used or viewed within a temporal reconstruction. For example, site Y dating at A.D. 900 with type 1 may be compared to site Z, which also had type 1 specimens, which were undated but in reality belonged to a period of A.D. 400 to A.D. 500. The attribute changes of one type and their effects on related types may not have been immediately synchronic either at a site or even within the prehistoric culture area.

A selective analytical code was devised which included provenience data, radiocarbon date, proposed type, and decoration information. The code was not an exhaustive descriptive code, as the variables of site, time, space, and decoration appeared to be the maximum detail that I could hope to control with the limited means then at my disposal. The code covered two cards and consisted of the following:

Card A
Columns

1–4	New reference number
5	Card designation
6–8	Site number
9–16	Horizontal grid location
17–18	Level
19–21	Specific artifact number
22	Soil horizon (mound, submound, nonmound)
23–34	Mound number
25	Type of mound (five types): effigy, conical, linear, oval, natural
26–27	Feature number
28–29	Burial number
30–35	Radiocarbon date
36–37	Ceramic type
38	Rim or body sherd
39	House number
40	House level

Card B

Columns

1–4 New reference number

5 Card designation

6–7 Location of decoration (first of series): twelve possible locations

8 Type of decoration (first location): nine possible types

9–10 Type of fabric (one maximum — first location): nineteen possible types

11–12 Type of cord (first location – first of three possible): eighty-three possible types

13–72 (Continued combination of decorative, location, and type of decoration)

All the rim sherds and decorated body sherds (258) from the Bigelow site (47–Pt–29) were coded (excluding pieces from a single vessel, which were counted as one specimen), as listed in Table 1. Advice was then sought from Norman Wagner of Waterloo Lutheran University. His

Table 1. Frequency of rims and associated body sherds from 47–Pt–29

	Rim sherds		Body sherds		Combined rims and body		Estimated no. of vessels	
	no.	%	no.	%	no.	%	no.	%
Madison Cord Impressed	13	7.9	1,053	83.4	1,066	74.8	12	8.3
Madison Fabric Impressed	7	4.2	22	1.7	29	2.0	23	16.0
Madison Folded Lip	1	0.6			1	0.07	1	0.6
Madison Plain	103	63.1	168	13.3	271	19.0	74	51.7
Madison Punctated	6	3.6	4	0.3	10	0.7	8	5.5
Leland Cord Marked	6	3.6	13	1.3	19	1.3	10	6.9
Aztalan Collared	11	6.7			11	0.7	10	6.9
Hahn Cord Impressed	1	0.6			1	0.07	1	0.6
Point Sauble Collared	2	1.2			2	0.1	2	1.3
Unclassified A	1	0.6	2	0.1	3	0.2	1	0.6
Unclassified B	1	0.6			1	0.07	1	0.6
Unclassified C	11	6.7			11	0.7	?	
Madison Ware Total	150	92.0	1,260	99.84	1,410	98.94	141	98.60
Total	163	99.4	1,262	100.10	1,425	99.99	143	99.00

preliminary report on computer studies of Ontario Iroquois ceramics (1971a, 1971b) indicated that he had begun to evaluate critically the merits and limitations of coding ceramics. We agreed that an equal size sample would be coded from the second site, Sanders (47–Wp–26), shown in Table 2, even though the Bigelow sample represented the total diagnostic ceramics. The Bigelow sample was then printed out according to specimen number, card number, location of decoration, type of deco-

Table 2. Frequency of rims and associated body sherds from 47–Wp–26

	Rim sherds		Body sherds		Combined rims and body		Estimated no. of vessels	
	no.	%	no.	%	no.	%	no.	%
Sister Creeks Pt.	2	0.2	6	0.4	8	0.3	6	0.5
Rocker Stamped			1	0.07	1	0.04	1	0.09
Shorewood C. R.	3	0.3	1	0.07	4	0.1	3	0.3
Dane Incised	40	3.9	250	17.6	290	11.8	185	16.9
Dane Incised variant f.1.	18	1.8	30	2.1	48	2.0	40	3.7
Madison Cord Impressed	67	6.6	126	8.7	193	7.9	96	8.8
Madison Fabric Impressed	31	3.0	77	5.4	108	4.4	86	7.9
Madison Folded Lip	32	3.1			32	1.3	20	1.8
Madison Plain	645	63.4	142	10.0	787	32.1	462	42.3
Madison Plain variant Pt.	9	0.9			9	0.4	5	0.4
Madison Plain variant jar	16	1.6			16	0.6	12	1.0
Madison Punctated	24	2.4	250	17.6	274	11.2	60	5.5
Leland Cord Marked	48	4.7	131	9.2	179	7.3	36	3.3
Aztalan Collared	11	1.0	1	0.07	12	0.5	11	1.0
Hahn Cord Impressed	1	0.09			1	0.04	1	0.09
Point Sauble Collared	15	1.5	168	11.8	183	7.5	13	1.2
Heins Creek C.S.	7	0.7	30	2.1	37	1.5	20	1.8
Grand River Trailed	6	0.6	14	0.9	20	0.8	10	0.9
Grand River Plain	42	4.1	1	0.07	43	1.7	25	2.2
Grand River body sherds			203	14.3	203	8.3	0	0
Total	1,017		1,421		2,448		1,092	

ration, type of fabric, and type of cord. Histograms of location and type of decoration were then plotted, and only location of decoration, type of decoration, type of cord, location of second decoration, and type of decoration at second location were significant in their numerical distributions. These five variables with their frequency counts are presented in Figure 1.

These variables were then subjected to a principal component analysis, whose role in research is the simplification of data relationships by reducing the number of variables.

When a large number of measurements are available, it is natural to enquire whether they could be replaced by a fewer number of the measurements or of their functions, *without loss of much information*, for convenience in the analysis and in the interpretation of data. Principal components, which are linear functions of the measurements ... provide a reduction of the data without much loss of *information we are seeking from the data* (Rao 1964:329).

Principal component analysis is somewhat similar to factor analysis as the "... former is the first step of factor analysis but the aim of each approach is quite different" (Wagner 1971b:18). To paraphrase Clarke (1968:563–564), a principal component analysis commences with a

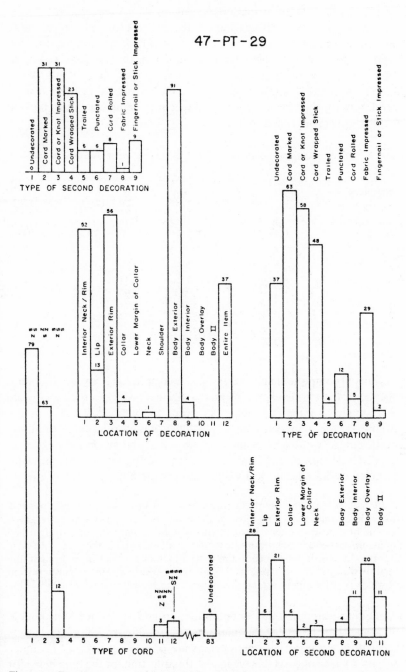

Figure 1. Frequency counts of five variables of decorations in specimens from 47–Pt–29

complete table of intercorrelations among the data, expressed as a matrix
of correlation coefficients varying in value from -1 to $+1$, according to
the degree of correlation between the variables concerned. This variation
in value is measured by the variance or square of the standard deviations
of the variables in the matrix. A principal component table of intercorrelations among the Bigelow specimens was plotted according to a matrix of
correlation coefficients in a numerical specimen sequence, and a portion
of this run is reproduced in Table 3.

Table 3. Principal component analysis of 47–Pt–29: 258 specimens, five variables of
decoration

Eigenvalues				
1.71176	1.25183	0.92378	0.79860	0.31402
Cumulative percentage of eigenvalues				
0.34235	0.59272	0.77747	0.93719	0.99999

Item	X	Y	K	L
233	0.75698	0.88867	103	100
183	0.71892	1.81962	104	77
45	0.70979	0.65378	104	105
46	0.70979	0.65378	104	105
47	0.70979	0.65378	104	105
231	3.36161	0.46448	202	132

Principal component analysis assumes a correlation between the values
of some of the variables, the common variance, which is then expressed
by a smaller number of factors in order to summarize the common
variance of the many variables. To achieve this correlation, a similarity
coefficient, a coefficient of linear correlation (the symbol is r) is computed. To do this, pairs of units such as measurements, counts, or ratios
are given definite numerical values and compared.

. . . the coefficient r is essentially an indicator of how close the best possible
straight line comes to passing through all the points then shown in a scattergram.
A value of r close to plus 1 means that the points almost lie on a straight line
sloping up to the right, while an r close to minus 1 means that the points are close
to a straight line sloping down to the right. In either case, a simple straight-line
equation will enable one to predict the value of one variable quite accurately from
knowledge of the other variables' value in a specific case (Cowgill 1968:371).

Wagner has stated that this is contentious ground ". . . since some people
will argue that the use of the linear coefficient of correlation (r) distorts
the picture, since not all relationships are of a linear nature" (Wagner
1971b:18). He suggests that we ignore this question for the time being for
". . . what we are after is a reduction in the number of variables . . . without any loss of information" (1971b:18).

The procedures outlined by Wagner (1971b:18) were then utilized to reduce the number of variables. "By calculating the eigenvalues and eigenvectors . . . of a matrix of correlation [Table 3] we arrive at a new set of variables which are linear combinations of the original variables and which are independent from one another." Table 3 shows that the first eigenvalue accounts for 34 percent of the total variance, while the second brings the total to 59 percent. This means that the two new values, which are uncorrelated with one another, can account for 59 percent of the variance. If we were to consider the third, we would have 77 percent. However, it must be remembered that these new variables are combinations of the original attribute classes.

Each of the 258 specimens had the individual attributes multiplied with each respective member of the eigenvectors, arriving at a ranked value, which is known as the inner product. The results of this run were achieved by taking the first two eigenvalues and plotting them according to two vectors. Clarke (1968:670) defines a vector as "a compound entity, having a definite number of components." Eigenvalues (λ_1 and λ_2) are also called latent roots or characteristic roots. Eigenvalues are quantities analogous to variances, and they measure variability along the major and minor axes respectively. The results were then plotted by reducing the three vectors to two vectors, illustrated in the scattergram of Figure 2. A third dimension could be added to this scattergram by using a vertical scale or different-sized dots.

Much of the rationale behind principal component analysis is a direct outgrowth of numerical taxonomy, and Clarke (1968: chapter 12) gives an excellent synthesis of this approach. He makes several important observations considering it as a useful analytical tool for archaeologists. Numerical taxonomy has the capacity,

. . . for a more objective definition of our conceptual and actual archaeological entities . . . [gives us] the ability to determine and express the degree to which different entities are similar or dissimilar using an explicit and repeatable procedure . . . [and allows for the entities] to be ranked relative to one another in a hierarchy of increasing structural complexity . . . (1968:518–519).

There is repeatability and objectivity allowing for the ascertaining of groups by giving equal weight to all traits utilized, which are then placed in a sorted matrix (Table 3). They are then clustered according to two or three dimensions, which produces clusters ". . . closely approaching our prevailing constellation of mind-models of archaeological relationships" (1968:543). However, these relationships are taxonomical and not typological.

Clarke argues that archaeological taxonomy should be "natural" in an empirical sense and one which allows the most propositions to be made about its constituent entities or the taxonomy with the best predictive

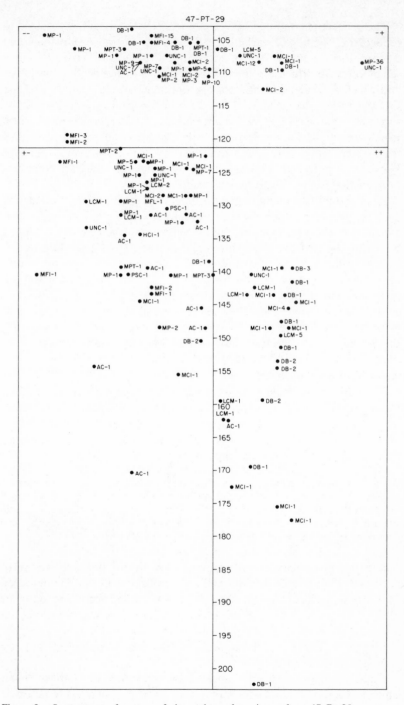

Figure 2. Scattergram of vectors of eigenvalues of specimens from 47–Pt–29

capacity. As most archaeological entities are structured and can be ordered or clustered, they can then be ranked in a hierarchy of propositions. Typology he maintains, embraces the sequential ordering of data on a seriation basis (time and space), which can be measured and expressed within limits (1968:517–519). The degree of similarity between the Bigelow ceramic specimens has been arranged into a matrix rearranged (Table 3) and then clustered according to positive and negative status (Figure 2). It must be emphasized that the traits considered are discontinuous "subjective" ones of decoration and location instead of continuous "objective" ones of length, width, or thickness. Cowgill has pointed out that one can calculate a correlation coefficient for variables that can be measured *or counted* (1968:371). The decoration traits are considered here to be exceedingly important attributes that will yield as correct results as those that are measured.

The groups and relative distances between the ceramic specimens from the Bigelow site are indicated by the type abbreviation (MP = Madison Plain) and the number of specimens at each location. Table 3 and Figure 2 show the item, the two vectors (X and Y), their minus or plus values plotted to five places and arranged according to minus/minus, minus/plus, plus/minus and plus/plus in the four quadrants according to vertical position (lines 103 to 202 under K), and the horizontal position, if on the same line, under column L. In some instances, specimens from widely differing areas of the site are considered so similar that they are plotted to one location, e.g. the thirty-six Madison Plain on line 108 (Figure 2), or they are tightly grouped together as are the Madison Ware specimens in the scattergram. Those specimens that clustered together, as those between lines 103 and 115, 118 and 135, and 137 and 165, could be treated as three separate entities until all specimens are incorporated into one tight cluster, but Cowgill (1968:370) has argued that pieces are then forced together even if they are not related in any meaningful way. Clarke cautions us that:

It cannot be emphasized too strongly that these factors, like all the summarizing statistical relationships, including correlation coefficients, [represent] statistical relationships which may not be simply interpreted as archaeological relationships. The groups of artifact-types or attributes constituting the factors will be related in a statistical association—the exact archaeological relationships responsible for this statistical relationship may well be very subtle and complex (1968:563).

The same procedures were used in the principal component analysis of the Sanders material, except instead of every rim sherd we used every sixth specimen for equality of comparison and the same five variables were examined both in histograph form, shown in Figure 3, and in a sorted correlation coefficient, ranked as given in Table 4 and then clustered into a scattergram, shown in Figure 4. Table 4 shows that the first eigenvalue accounts for 36 percent of the total variance, the second for 62 percent, and the third for a total of 80 percent. The first two eigenvalues were again plotted according to two vectors, and each location has had the pottery type (or category) plus frequency added (Figure 4).

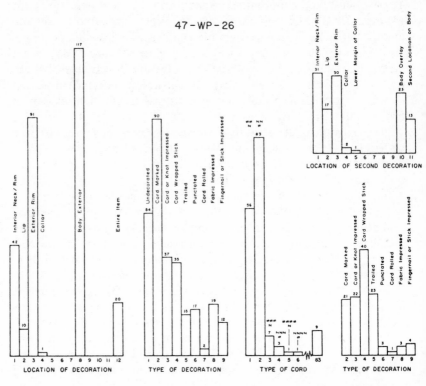

Figure 3.   Histograph of five variables of decoration in specimens from 47–Wp–26

Table 4.   Principal component analysis of 47–Wp–26: 281 specimens, five variables of decoration

Eigenvalues				
1.82619	1.28757	0.92426	0.68274	0.27921
Cumulative percentage of eigenvalues				
0.36524	0.62275	0.80760	0.94415	0.99999

The samples from 47–Pt–29 and 47–Wp–26, which totaled 539 specimens, were then combined and subjected to a final principal component analysis. Table 5 shows that the first eigenvalue accounts for 35 percent of

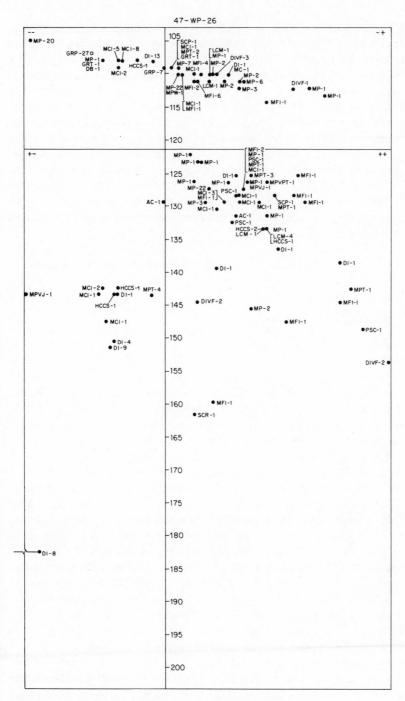

Figure 4. Scattergram of sorted correlation coefficient from Table 4

the total variance, while the second brings the total to 60 percent. The results of Table 5 were then plotted according to two vectors, illustrated in the scattergram of Figure 5; this scattergram is somewhat different from those of Figures 2 and 4 in that more specimens in tighter clusters occur above the 115 line and between the 115 and the 135 line. The specimens from both 47–Pt–29 and 47–Wp–26 are also reclustered between the 135 and the 160 line. One cannot simply read these clusters from top to bottom as less decoration in few locations with fewer cord or fabric impressions (top); more decorations in more locations with more cord or fabric impressions (middle); and most decoration in most locations with most cord or fabric impressions (bottom). The configurations of these five variables do not add up in this manner, as we now have two vectors, which are two new configurations, which are more than the sum of the five variables.

Table 5. Principal component analysis of 47–Pt–29 and 47–Wp–26: 539 specimens

Eigenvalues				
1.76051	1.25270	0.88956	0.79830	0.29890
Cumulative percentage of eigenvalues				
0.35210	0.60264	0.78055	0.94021	0.99999

In order to measure the dispersion or variation in which these five ceramic variables were classified, the data were subjected to a multivariate analysis of variance program. Multivariate analysis deals with the simultaneous variation of two or more variables, and in this instance, a number of variables (five) have been measured for two samples.

Table 6 is the output from this program, and two measurements have taken place. First, the program measures the total variance *within* each group and between several groups. Second, it measures the extent to which each annotation class (e.g. color versus yellow, which is an attribute) contributes to the separation of the two groups. Discussion of this program and its use to archaeology will be found in a manuscript in preparation by Wagner, as well as clarification concerning F-ratio's. For our purposes we will look at the ETA square column. If the ETA square were close to 0.1, it would indicate that the variables were not related. The farther away from 0.1, the more related they are, or the less useful for distinguishing one from the other. Variables 3 and 5 are not good, variables 1 and 2 are closely related, whereas variable 4 is the highest. In general, the program suggests that the two sites are similar.

The degree of site similarity can be seen in Table 7, where the two groups are again compared; and if one centroid is positive and the other negative, we can see that the degree of difference in a multiple group discriminant analysis program is indicated as 0.008, or, again, that the

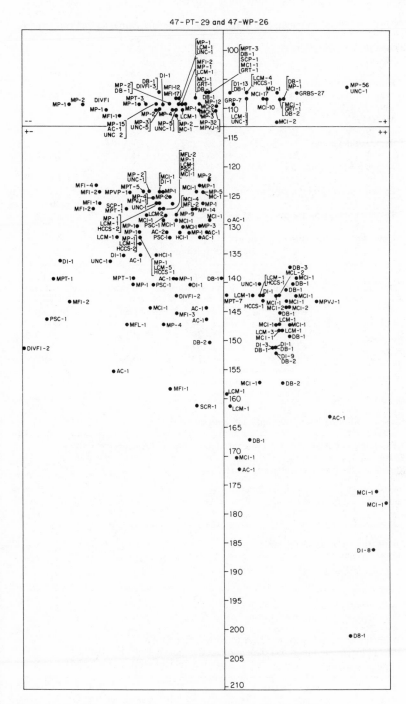

Figure 5.   Scattergram of sorted correlation coefficient from Table 5

Table 6. Multivariate analysis of variance analysis for five variables and two groups

47–Pt–29 (258 specimens)
Means

5.72	3.51	3.18	2.35	1.67

Standard deviations

3.81	2.15	12.49	3.71	2.30

47–Wp–26 (281 specimens)
Means

5.39	3.33	3.60	1.93	1.67

Standard deviations

3.34	2.29	14.50	3.41	2.23

Means for total sample

5.55	3.42	3.40	2.13	1.67

Pooled-samples standard deviations

3.57	2.22	13.58	3.56	2.26

Test for equality of dispersions, $M = 32.332$
$$F = 2.134$$
Univariate F-ratios with one and two
degrees of freedom $= 537$

Variable	Among means square	Within means square	F-ratio	ETA square
1	14.60	12.77	1.14	0.0021
2	4.39	4.94	0.89	0.0017
3	24.50	184.39	0.13	0.0002
4	24.58	12.67	1.94	0.0036
5	0.00	5.12	0.00	0.0000

Table 7. Multiple group discriminant analysis

Wilks Lamda $= 0.9911$ generalized correlation ratio, ETA square $= 0.0089$
F-ratio for H2, overall discrimination $= 0.95$
Chi-square tests with successive roots removed

Roots removed	(ETA) canonical R	(ETA square) R squared	Eigenvalue	Chi-square	N.D.F.	Lamda	Percent trace
0	0.094	0.009	0.009	5.0	5.0	0.99	100.00

Factor pattern for discriminant functions
Test 1 $= 0.488$
  2 $= 0.430$
  3 $= 0.166$
  4 $= 0.635$
  5 $= 0.012$
Communalities for one discriminant factor

1 = 0.238	2 = 0.185	3 = 0.028	4 = 0.403	5 = 0.000

Percentage of trace R accounted for by each root 1.17086
Centroid for group one in one-dimensional discriminant space 1 = 0.098
Centroid for group two in one-dimensional discriminant space 1 = −0.090

sites are similar. The results of these three forms of analysis were based on only five multistate continuous variables. Two-state or alternative variables (continuous or discontinuous) might yield similar or dissimilar results. In order to evaluate properly the full range of ceramic attributes, a class and attribute list for ceramic analysis (Wagner 1972a, 1972b) has been devised, and both late Woodland and Oneota specimens (4,000) have been coded according to this more exhaustive system. The results of this research will be available soon. Until that time it would seem desirable that we all begin to move in the direction of more accurate measuring of the degree of ceramic or site associations so that we might be more precise in the conclusions drawn from archaeological data and more accurately assess and evaluate culture contact, culture change, acculturation, or assimilation.

REFERENCES

BAERREIS, DAVID A.
   1968   Review of *Hopewell and Woodland site archaeology in Illinois. The Wisconsin Archaeologist* 49(3):138–146.
BAERREIS, DAVID A., JOAN E. FREEMAN
   1958   Late Woodland pottery in Wisconsin as seen from Aztalan. *The Wisconsin Archaelogist* 39(1):35–61.
CLARKE, DAVID L.
   1968   *Analytical archaeology.* London: Methuen.
COWGILL, GEORGE L.
   1968   Archaeological applications of factor, cluster, and proximity analyses. *American Antiquity* 33(3):367–375.
HURLEY, WILLIAM M.
   1970   "The Wisconsin Effigy Mound tradition." Unpublished Ph.D. thesis, University of Wisconsin, Madison.
KRIEGER, ALEX
   1944   The typological concept. *American Antiquity* 9(3):271–288.
LOY, JAMES D.
   1968   "A comparative style analysis of Havana series pottery from two Illinois Valley sites," in *Hopewell and Woodland site archaeology in Illinois.* Bulletin 6, Illinois Archaeological Survey. Urbana: University of Illinois Press.
RAO, C. RADHAKRISHNU
   1964   The use and interpretation of principal component analysis in applied research. *Sankhya: the Indian Journal of Statistics*, series A:329–358.
ROUSE, IRVING
   1939   *Prehistory in Haiti: a study in method.* Taplinger Human Relations Area. (Reprinted 1964.)
SPAULDING, ALBERT C.
   1953   Statistical techniques for the discovery of artifact types. *American Antiquity* 18(4):305–313.
WAGNER, NORMAN E.
   1971a   *Computer studies of Ontario Iroquois.* Waterloo, Ontario: Waterloo Lutheran University Press.

1971b *Coding and clustering pottery by computer.* Waterloo, Ontario: Waterloo Lutheran University Press.

WHALLON, ROBERT
1972   A new approach to pottery typology. *American Antiquity* 37(1):13–33.

WRIGHT, J. V.
1967   *The Laurel tradition and the middle Woodland period.* National Museum of Canada Bulletin 217.

The Temple Town Community: Cahokia and Amalucan Compared

MELVIN L. FOWLER

It is a common weakness among archaeologists to use the term *village* interchangeably with the term *site*, that is, locality where archaeological materials are found. This usage overlooks the sociological implications which terms such as "village" or "town" can have. The sociological implications of terminology are, in fact, quite important and need to be well developed.

For the concept of village, I prefer a combination of two definitions extant in the literature. Haury (1962:118), first of all, has provided the following explanation:

I see [villages] . . . as distinct from the earlier long occupied camps . . . whether in caves or in the open, because of formalized architecture perhaps a closer clustering of houses, usually the presence of a larger apparently non-domestic structure, and a greater complexity of the material possessions. . . . The house pits . . . reflect a solidity of construction and an investment of labor that would arise only from need for prolonged residence.

Haury has stressed the physical aspects, such as clustering of houses, a specialized structure, and the relative permanence of occupation. On the other hand, Mumford (1961:18) adds a social dimension to the definition when he states:

Everywhere, the village is a small cluster of families, from half a dozen to three score perhaps, each with its own hearth, its own household gods, its own shrine, its own burial plot within the house or in some common burial ground . . . [E]ach family follows the same way of life and participates in the same labors.

Mumford's stress is on the commonality of life in a village and the lack of specialization.

Other dimensions to the definition of "village" would depend upon the context in which it is found. It is possible for villages of the type outlined above to be at the peak of sociopolitical organization and territorial dominance in an area, or for such villages to be satellites to larger, more complex communities. In the latter case, a village may be a specialized craft center participating in the great tradition of the larger centers. In the former context, the village represents a point of sociopolitical development made possible by agriculture or some other stable food supply.

An even more distressing misapplication of the term "village" is when it is applied to large and complex archaeological sites. These are sites that show evidence of functionally distinct precincts within their boundaries, a large hinterland which they seem to dominate, and related and smaller satellite communities. One of the details that puts these larger communities apart from their satellites is a central precinct set aside for religious and political purposes and manifested in specialized architecture. Among other characteristics, there is probably craft specialization within the community so that segments of the population are participating in only part of the total life, as compared to the commonality Mumford specified for the village. There may also be centers and mechanisms for redistribution of goods and services, both for the community itself and for the hinterland. For these types of communities I prefer the term "town." Such towns could have arisen as a manifestation of the growing need for social and political control of increasing populations resulting from effective agricultural subsistence. Agriculture is not necessary for village life but it is a prerequisite for town life and its sociological implications.

In North America, archaeological sites that can be classed as towns are found in three different cultural settings. In one context, they are found as satellites to urban centers. This will not be discussed in this paper. In a second context, towns, especially in central Mexico, can be found preceding the period when urbanism appears as a facet of developing territorial control. In this context are sites of the late Preclassic or Formative period. Braidwood and Willey (1962:350 ff.) refer to these as "temple centers" and a "kind of incipience to urbanization" which is present in the New World but which is not clear from the archaeological record of the Old World. Willey (1960) in another article used the term "temple town" to refer to this type of development. I accept this term and will use it henceforth in this paper, attributing to it the characteristics I have briefly outlined above.

The third context for such towns in North America is in areas peripheral to nuclear America, where they appear as the pinnacle of the sociopolitical development. This appears to be especially true of the Mississippi Valley and southeastern areas of the United States. In this area the chroniclers of the De Soto expeditions described many such communities and their hinterlands. These men were conscious of moving from one political province to another and of going to each principal town. They met merchants who were traveling from community to community with goods to trade. They marveled at the towns with their walls and moats, dug to bring water from the river around the town. They saw the mounds upon which the temples and the houses of the notables were constructed. Archaeological research has confirmed much of what was reported by these men.

In a move to contribute to our understanding of urbanism and its development, this article presents an examination of two archaeological sites, comparing them in terms of the concept of the temple town outlined above. One of these communities is the Cahokia site near East St. Louis, Illinois, which has long been known as the largest, and perhaps the earliest, of this type of site in eastern North America. The other site is Amalucan, near the city of Puebla in the central highlands of Mexico. This site is of the middle to late Preclassic period. More detailed descriptions of these sites will follow. The main purposes of this comparison can be stated as follows:

1. Can superficially similar sites such as Amalucan in Mexico and Cahokia in Illinois be meaningfully compared?

2. In what ways, if any, is it illuminating to consider these two communities to be "temple towns"?

3. Does such a grouping elucidate the concept of "temple town," bound it, and specify more clearly the area of its possible usefulness? A subsidiary question is

4. What is the effect of cultural–historical (for example, marginality) and ecological (dry highland versus humid lowland) factors on the nature of communities which have been provisionally called "temple towns"?

The following comparison will not provide definitive answers to these questions since the kinds of data available are not yet sufficiently inclusive. The comparison will, however, yield suggestions and a programmatic definition of goals for developing research.

CAHOKIA

The first site to be considered in this comparison is Cahokia, near East St. Louis, Illinois. The central feature of this locality is a large terraced mound covering sixteen acres and rising to a height of over one hundred feet above the surrounding valley floor. Grouped around this large mound in a series of avenues and plazas are over eighty other mounds of varying sizes and shapes.

This group of mounds and related occupation areas covers an area of about fifteen square kilometers (about five square miles). The total area thought to have been utilized is bounded in two ways. First, there are outlying mounds suggestive of limits to the major site area. At least two of these mounds, Rattlesnake and Powell, were of essentially the same shape, a long rectangular mound with a ridgelike top. There are no other mounds of this shape within the limits we have suggested. These are two mounds of the southernmost and westernmost areas included within the site limits. At roughly corresponding points on the north and east are other mounds.

A second factor suggesting limits to the site are certain lines which appear on old aerial photographs suggestive of palisade and ditch lines surrounding the area. One of these lines has been tested and proven to be such a palisade. These lines converge at points on the main north–south axis of the site.

Within these limits are several areas of apparent functional difference. There are materials now coming out of the ground that suggest that the main mound and the mounds immediately around it were walled off from other parts of the town, thus setting them apart. This is doubly interesting, if further excavation confirms it, since the big mound is the only mound with four terraces; it is thus possible that it represents a structure of special importance not only for the town itself but for the surrounding areas. At one time there was a conical eminence on the third terrace of this mound. This is suggestive in light of the data we have on the Natchez that the Sun or major leader of a Natchez territory would ascend an eminence near his house every morning to greet the sun at dawn. Perhaps the big mound and its enclosed compound represent the residence and precinct of the chief political leader of the area.

Other functional areas are suggested by the different shapes of mounds within the site area. There is only one other multiple-stage or terraced mound and that is just west of the big mound, outside the proposed enclosed compound. Besides these, there are several rectangular and square flat-topped mounds that are obviously platforms. Another form of mound is a conical and round-topped type. There is some suggestion that these may be burial mounds, although this possibility has not been thoroughly investigated. A study is currently underway classifying the types of mounds at the Cahokia site in order to determine the distribution of the types and the possible functional significance of the differing types and their distributions.

Besides the mound types mentioned above, recent excavations have demonstrated that there are other functional areas within the site. Some of these excavations have shown the residential areas to be quite intense with rebuilding of houses on the same locality several different times. In some cases these houses are well aligned with each other and form sections with streetlike areas between the houses. Other areas have yielded data on what were probably plazas and ceremonial and communal structures. In some cases residential areas were built over what had earlier been public plazas.

Of particular interest is one area where a large circle of posts had been placed in the ground. This circle of evenly spaced posts had at its center another large post. Dr. Warren Wittry (1964), who excavated this structure, has carried out studies indicating that this circle of posts called Woodhenge by him, may well have been an observatory for noting both the rising and setting of the sun and moon to determine critical days for measuring the year. In line with this kind of data suggesting a concern for things astronomical is the fact that the site seems to be aligned on an axis about three degrees east of true north. The main axes of the site, the big mound, and the other larger mounds seem to follow this alignment. Currently a precise map of the entire site is being made that will give us data enabling a more precise definition of this orientation.

The question of craft specialization within Cahokia has not been studied as yet. At the present time, surface distribution studies of materials are being undertaken by investigators from two institutions. It is to be hoped that these studies will give us data on this and other problems. There is some suggestion of such specialized areas in the finding of artifacts called microdrills in a rather limited area of the site. Gregory Perino suggests that these might have been used to drill shells in the process of bead manufacture, implying that this was a craft-specialized area.

Petrographic thin-section studies of ceramics from the Cahokia site and surrounding area have been carried out in the past several years. Suggestions from these studies are that there were several local areas of pottery manufacture using clays locally available. Perhaps more detailed studies of this type will make it possible to trace an interchange of such local ceramic wares.

That Cahokia participated in a larger interchange of goods not only with the surrounding area but with other regions as well is an accepted but poorly documented hypothesis. Certain exotic materials such as galena and conch shells suggest this. That trade routes were established and goods interchanged in the southeastern United States as early as 3000 B.C. has recently been demonstrated.

How the goods were distributed within Cahokia is another unanswered question. A structure very suggestive of a market area was excavated about 250 meters west of the big mound. This apparently was a large square enclosure of upright log construction. Spaced at regular intervals along the walls of this enclosure were circular rooms opening toward the center of the area. Only the size and shape of this structure suggest a market, since no data exist to confirm this idea. Another such enclosure is indicated on the early aerial photographs of the site about 500 meters to the east of the big mound.

Several other sites exist in the area surrounding Cahokia, suggesting a series of smaller towns, villages, and farmsteads related to the larger center. Among these are Pulcher about ten miles to the south and Mitchell about seven miles to the north. Although these sites are rather large in themselves, none is as large and complex as Cahokia and none has terraced mounds. It is my hypothesis that these are satellite communities dominated by the larger town.

It may well be that there was a well-defined political territory immediately controlled by Cahokia. In this territory there were probably two distinct ethnic groups, as is suggested by ceramic and other data. These ethnic groups lived at the same time within the confines of Cahokia and in separated communities outside as well.

Cahokia exerted an influence over a much larger area, in fact most of the Mississippi Valley, but this is a problem beyond that which we have chosen to discuss.

As a final note on this discussion of Cahokia, some mention should be made of the time of its occupation. Radiocarbon dates suggest that human habitation of the site area began as early as A.D. 800 and continued until at least A.D. 1500. However, it is my opinion that it reached its peak and functioned as a temple town between about A.D. 900 and A.D. 1200. After that time, it was a different type of community and had a qualitatively different relationship to the surrounding area.

AMALUCAN

The description of the Amalucan site will be much shorter, since much less archaeological research has been conducted at that site. Some investigations were carried out by Linné (1942), Noguera (1940), and Krieger and Sanders (1951).

Amalucan is the name of a large *hacienda* located just to the east of the city of Puebla south of the volcanic peak of Malinche. Most of the archaeological site is now in the *ejido* lands of the village of Chachapa. The natural features dominating the landscape in this immediate area are two conical hills rising abruptly from the valley floor. The largest of these, Cerro Amalucan, has a large mound group and plaza area on its peak, and the slopes of the hill were terraced. The smaller hill, Amaluquillo, was apparently not utilized.

The main cultural feature of the site is a large mound group to the east of Cerro Amalucan. This group is made up of one large multiple-stage mound, a long rectangular platform mound, and some smaller mounds forming a plaza area. Besides this main group there are several smaller groups of mounds.

Since the whole valley floor seems to have been occupied in Preclassic times, it is difficult to delimit the site. Using data such as continuity of surface distribution and natural features such as *barrancas*, I estimate that the site covers an area of ten square kilometers (three square miles). The surface material scattered over this area is uniformly middle to late Preclassic.

Similar late Preclassic sites literally surround Amalucan. To the east is a site at Chachapa. To the north is a site of similar nature and mound types near Parecio. To the south is the site of Totimehuacan recently excavated by Dr. Bodo Spranz of the Freiburg Ethnographic Museum. In terms of site distribution and density, one might say that one of the major features of the distribution of archaeological sites in the Puebla Valley is that some 90 percent of them are Preclassic. The settlement pattern of that period seems to have been a series of towns and their supporting lands almost cheek by jowl with each other. This pattern of settlement seems to have changed in Classic times with the domination of Cholula over this entire area.

Returning to the site of Amalucan itself, there seem to have been functionally distinct areas within the site. The major precinct seems to have been that of the main mound group and plaza. Only one mound at the site is multiple-stage, suggesting some special function for it. This mound is nearly identical in shape to Mound 1 of Totimehuacan (Spranz 1966), including a similar depression on one side of the upper terrace, which Spranz found at Totimehuacan to be a room that had been filled in.

Excavations in three different areas of the site have suggested other specialized areas. One of these excavations was carried out in the wall of a *barranca* to the south of the main pyramid group. Refuse pits and possibly house floors were noted in this *barranca*. Excavation demonstrated that there had been a series of refuse pits here and that there were several levels of occupation. Nearby were large, flat-bottomed pits suggesting houses. Since these types of features were not found in other excavated sections of the site, it is suggested that this was an area of habitation throughout the history of the site.

Another specialized area was discovered through the study of aerial photographs. On the photos, a straight dark line was noted extending in a northeasterly direction from the central part of the large mound of the major group to an old stream channel. Further study of the photo indicated that there were similar lines nearly perpendicular to the first at regularly spaced intervals. A trench was put across the main line of this series. The excavations demonstrated that these lines were the remains of an ancient series of canals. These canals were utilized over a long period and, as they silted in, were reexcavated to clear the channel. This happened on at least five different occasions. Finally it appears that the canals were filled in and the ground leveled, probably in preparation for the building of the big pyramid. Indications are that these lines continue under the main pyramid. Thus there is evidence not only of a water distribution system but of a changed function for this section of Amalucan through time.

There is no evidence as yet to suggest the actual use to which the canals were put. One good possibility of course is irrigation. Another possibility is that they were used to distribute water to the residents of the town.

In the northwestern portion of the site, at the foot of Cerro Amalucan, are other markings on the aerial photos showing the same dark discoloration of the soil. These have not yet been investigated by excavation but undoubtedly represent a major aboriginal feature of the site.

The time when Amalucan was occupied can be defined by three lines of evidence. One is that the bulk of material found on the surface and in the excavations to date is Preclassic. The one exception to this is the southeastern portion of the site, where some Classic material has been found. By far the most common form of figurine found to date is one similar to Vaillant's type E-2. This suggests a Zacatenco–Ticomán affiliation for the site.

In the stratigraphy of the site, there is a dark, black zone found in all excavations that caps all other strata below. This was found over the canal area as well as over the area of refuse pits. It appears that this is an old humus line, which apparently represents a time when the site was abandoned. The material below this line is all Preclassic. This suggests that before Classic times the site was completely abandoned and not utilized intensively again until colonial times.

The third line of evidence is a radiocarbon date from Totimehuacan Mound 2 (Spranz, personal communication). While appraisal of this date must await Dr. Spranz's detailed analysis, it suggests an age of ca. 100–300 B.C. for some of the activity of that group.

CONCLUSION

Superficially, both Amalucan and Cahokia seem to have been the same *type* of community. Both contained a central precinct that probably represents a center of social, religious, and political control. Both had other public works of community importance. There is some evidence of craft specialization at Cahokia, but this type of data has not yet been collected at Amalucan. Both seem to be involved in a relationship with their own hinterlands and with a broader network. In this aspect, there appear to be differences in their individual relationships with the total settlement pattern. Amalucan seems to have participated in a more densely settled area with other similar communities close at hand. Cahokia was a larger community but with a much less densely settled hinterland and with more space between communities. These conclusions are speculative, since very little study or thought has been given to this type of problem. In neither of the communities are we able to make estimates of population, since sufficient control over occupation unit data has not been achieved. In both cases, however, we would surmise that population was in the order of thousands rather than hundreds.

Further studies need to be made in order to define accurately "temple town" communities and to compare or contrast these two adequately. These types of studies need to take lines suggested by Schaedel (1969), Mann (1969), and Longacre (1969). Particularly important to arriving at the kinds of data needed for such studies and conclusions is an application of the methods outlined in Crawford's *Archaeology in the field* (1953). Attention in this type of approach should be given to delineation of site area, collection of distributional data from the surface, definition of specific features on the basis of aerial photos, distribution data, and excavation, and a reconstruction of the history of the site area. From this should develop a description of the community through time, with special emphasis on functional divisions within the community and on population growth. Developed along with this would be a concern for understanding the setting, both cultural and ecological, in which the community is found. Interpretation of the above types of data will be of necessity based upon ethnographic data on communities of types comparable to that thought to be represented by the archaeological sites being investigated.

When these studies have been carried out, we will be able to go somewhat beyond the hypotheses and descriptions presented above.

REFERENCES

BRAIDWOOD, ROBERT J., GORDON R. WILLEY, *editors*
  1962 *Courses toward urban life.* Viking Fund Publications in Anthropology 32. Chicago: Aldine.
CRAWFORD, O. G. S.
  1953 *Archaeology in the field.* London: Phoenix House.
HAURY, EMIL W.
  1962 "The greater American southwest," in *Courses toward urban life.* Edited by Robert J. Braidwood and Gordon R. Willey, 106–131. Chicago: Aldine.
KRIEGER, ALEX, WILLIAM SANDERS
  1951 "Map of Amalucan," in *Anales de INAH,* volume four: 1923–1953, *Estados de Nayarit, Nuevo León, Oaxaca, Puebla, etc.* Varios, Sección 8. Mexico City: Instituto Nacional de Antropología e Historia.
LINNÉ, S.
  1942 *Mexican highland cultures: archaeological researches at Teotihuacán, Calpulalpan and Chalchicomula in 1934–1935.* Ethnographical Museum Publications 7. Sweden.

LONGACRE, WILLIAM A.
1969 "Urbanization in pre-Columbian America," in *The urbanization process in America from its origins to the present day.* Edited by R. P. Schaedel and J. E. Hardoy, 15–32. Buenos Aires: Instituto Torcuato Di Tella.

MANN, LAWRENCE
1969 "Activity density–intensity analysis: a research framework of ancient settlements and modern cities," in *The urbanization process in America from its origins to the present day.* Edited by R. P. Schaedel and J. E. Hardoy, 159–170. Buenos Aires: Instituto Torcuato Di Tella.

MASON, RONALD J., GREGORY PERINO
1961 Microblades at Cahokia, Illinois. *American Antiquity* 26(4):553–557.

MUMFORD, LEWIS
1961 *The city in history.* New York: Harcourt Brace Jovanovich.

NOGUERA, E.
1940 "Excavations at Tehuacan," in *The Maya and their neighbors*, 306–319.

SCHAEDEL, RICHARD P.
1969 "On the definition of civilization, urban, city and town in prehistoric America," in *The urbanization process in America from its origins to the present day.* Edited by R. P. Schaedel and J. E. Hardoy, 5–13. Buenos Aires: Instituto Torcuato Di Tella.

SPRANZ, BODO
1966 *Las Piramides de Totimehuacan*, volume one. Puebla: Instituto Poblano de Antropologiá e Historia.

WILLEY, GORDON R.
1960 New World prehistory. *Science* 131(3,393):73–86. (Reprinted in *Annual Report of the Smithsonian Institution*, 1960.)

WITTRY, WARREN L.
1964 An American Woodhenge. *Cranbrook Institute of Science News Letter* 33(9):102–107. Bloomfield Hills, Michigan.

An Interpretation of the Two-Climax Model of Illinois Prehistory

ROBERT L. HALL

In the late summer of 1673, over three hundred years ago, a party of Frenchmen led by Louis Jolliet and the Jesuit father Jacques Marquette passed through a prairie wilderness called Chicago while returning to Canada from a voyage of discovery by birchbark canoe upon the Mississippi River. They had ventured south to within several days' travel of the Gulf of Mexico and of Indians in contact with the Spanish. They concluded their journey at this point for fear of capture in Spanish territory and returned to report their discovery of new tribes, new lands, and new waterways including the Mississippi, the Missouri, the Ohio, and other rivers draining an area we know today to comprise a million and a half square miles of the heart of America. Of the valley of the Illinois, Marquette records for history that ". . . we have seen nothing like this river that we enter, as regards its fertility of soil, its prairies and woods, its cattle [bison], elk, deer, wildcats, bustards [turkeys], swans, ducks, parroquets, and even beaver."[1] History confirms the accuracy of Marquette's rhetoric in describing the richness of the area he helped to open for exploration and settlement, but history came to Illinois too late to record the highest achievements of the native inhabitants of Illinois. There are living in Chicago today more Indians than Jolliet and Marquette probably saw in their entire period of travel within the valley of the Mississippi, but at best a handful of these modern Indians can count ancestors among the Kaskaskia, the Peoria, the Michigamea, or the other Illinois tribes that Jolliet and Marquette visited in 1673. This group of related tribes, which gave Illinois its name, almost passed from existence within a century and a

[1] "Nous n'avons rien vue de semblable a cette rivière où nous entrons pour la bonté de terres, des prairies, de bois, des boeufs, des cerfs, des chevreux, des chatz sauvage, des outardes, des cygnes, des canards, des perroquetz, et mesmes des castors" (Thwaites 1896–1901, volume 59: 161–162).

half of Marquette's time and was replaced in its lands by other tribes — the Potawatomi, the Ottawa, the Kickapoo, the Sauk, and the Fox — just as the Illinois themselves had probably replaced earlier tribes in the Illinois Valley not many centuries before the arrival of the French.

When Hernando De Soto's expedition explored the southeastern U.S. and the lower Mississippi Valley in A.D. 1540–1542 for Spain, they found populous nations of Indians with an advanced culture that can only be described as civilization aborning, a civilization in process of birth. This nascent civilization, too, had all but disappeared by the end of the following century. Introduced diseases account in great part for the depopulation and cultural decline in the lower Mississippi Valley in the years between De Soto's entrada and French contacts of the late seventeenth century. Disease alone is insufficient to account for a similar and parallel cultural decline experienced in the upper Mississippi Valley during the centuries just preceding the Jolliet–Marquette expedition of 1673, and there are no grounds for believing disease was a factor in an even earlier cultural decline experienced in the same area a millennium before Columbus's time.

The upper Mississippi Valley saw two major periods of culture climax, to which the names Hopewell and Mississippi have been applied in the literature of prehistory. Both had major expressions along the route of the expedition. Had Jolliet and Marquette passed through the greater St. Louis area in the reign of Louis IX (A.D. 1226–1270) rather than during the reign of their sovereign Louis XIV (A.D. 1643–1715), they could have returned to report the largest native American community north of Mexico, a domain to which the term "state" may well apply, with its center at the prehistoric town archaeologists today call Cahokia, a town urban in proportions whose buried ruins cover almost six square miles (fifteen square kilometers) of Mississippi River bottomland (Fowler 1969). Here some 100 earthen mounds rose above the valley plain, most of them once platforms of truncated pyramid shape surmounted in their day by temples of vertical pole construction with gabled, thatched roofs. The largest of these temple platforms, known as Monks Mound, covered an area at its base 1,037 by 790 feet (314 by 239 meters) in extent and rose to a height of 100 feet (30 meters) above ground level (Reed et al. 1968; Reed 1969), with a terraced summit spacious enough to accommodate a structure the size of the Parthenon in Athens.

Had a Jolliet or a Marquette passed this way in the century of Louis IX, Louis the Saint, he might well have been escorted to an audience with a priest–chief who probably styled himself the "Sun" in the manner of Natchez leaders met by later French travelers farther to the south. From the top of the man-made mountain supporting the medicine lodge of the Sun such a visitor could have seen clearly the palisaded and bastioned most-sacred inner precinct of Cahokia and then, beyond this, residential zones, other temple precincts and pyramid mounds, ceremonial plazas, and ritual areas extending in all directions until they were lost in the haze.

The city of St. Louis, Missouri, to the west, has been known for years as the Mound City because of the Mississippian temple-mound center found there when the city was established by French settlers in 1764. These mounds have all been destroyed by nineteenth-century urban construction, just as the numerous mounds of the temple-mound center at East St. Louis were destroyed within the present century. If these mounds could be investigated today the exact relationships of these outlying prehistoric sites to the Cahokia site might be known. As it is, the archaeological record is nearly as silent for them as the historical record. No Jolliet or Marquette passed through the area of St. Louis the city in the age of its patron St. Louis the king, and the Great Sun who presided at Cahokia in the time of Louis IX, the king–saint, left no heir to greet the French in the time of Louis XIV, known himself as *le Roi Soleil*, the Sun–King.

THE CONCEPT OF CLIMAX

"Culture climax" was a concept introduced by Alfred L. Kroeber at the conclusion of his *Cultural and natural areas of native North America* (1939:222–228) to draw together certain geographical and "historical" aspects of culture. By "history" Kroeber was not limiting himself, of course, to the written record of events of the past but was referring to culture seen in a time perspective, culture seen as the end product of processes operating through time. He saw climax as a focus of cultural intensity within a culture area, a point of culmination in space and time of the interaction of diffusion and innovation leading to an elaboration and richness of culture content in both quantity and organization.

The term "climax" is relative, in that a level of culture that might be climactic for an area of low culture intensity might be subclimactic for an area of higher culture intensity. In Kroeber's usage a climax is also obviously not something meant to coincide with an entire culture area or to represent it as a whole but to represent the highest level of development within it. He lists, for example, the many traits that the Natchez and neighboring tribes of the lower Mississippi Valley share with other tribes of the southeastern United States as a culture area, but he places the southeastern climax in the restricted area of the Natchez and their immediate neighbors, where European observers documented ritual human sacrifice within the context of a uniquely patterned stratified social structure topped by a supreme or "Sun" class. Kroeber comments, "There is about this Natchez system something of the quality of a remnant . . ." (1939:62) and archaeology confirms that it is probably a survival of practices more widespread in earlier times.

Prehistorians who now use the term "climax" have available to them culture history with a greater time depth than Kroeber had available in 1939. Kroeber, in fact, actually completed his manuscript in 1931, but publication was delayed by the economic depression of the time. Ironically, the same depression that delayed the appearance of his book led to many of the large-scale archaeological projects that underlie much of our present knowledge of U.S. prehistory. In the total context of North American prehistory north of Mesoamerica, Jesse D. Jennings identifies three culture climaxes (1968:182–183). One of these is located in the southwest of the United States and adjacent northwestern Mexico, where Jennings sees a crescendo of cultural intensity beginning faintly about 400 B.C. and peaking between A.D. 400 and 1700, with a maximum areal extent reached by about A.D. 1100. The earliest of the remaining two climaxes he calls the Adena–Hopewell and places between 800 B.C. and about A.D. 600 in the Mississippi and Ohio valleys, followed by a Mississippian climax in the southeast "at its apogee by perhaps A.D. 1400 to 1500" and disappearing by A.D. 1700.

Jennings's usage of "climax" can be considered broad, in that the period of culmination of cultural intensity is merged with the period however many centuries long of cultural development that lead up to that culmination as well as the period of descent and decline. The time limits for his Adena–Hopewell climax nearly coincide with those of the Burial Mound I and Burial Mound II periods of James A. Ford and Gordon R. Willey (1941) as set forth more recently in a revised chronology by Willey (1966). These limits bracket almost the entire period of origin of the practice of mortuary mound construction from a base in the late Archaic period, in addition to several centuries of what in the Ohio and upper Mississippi valleys is referred to as the "post-Hopewellian decline."

Like Jennings, James B. Griffin sees two culture climaxes in the prehistory of the eastern U.S., but in defining them more narrowly Griffin follows Kroeber's usage more closely. Griffin recognizes the origin of the patterns he terms "Mississippian" in the years A.D. 700 to 900 but does not see a climax reached until about A.D. 1200 to 1500 (Griffin 1967: 189–190). Similarly Griffin restricts the Hopewellian climax to a period of about 200 B.C. to A.D. 400, observing at the same time that some classic expressions of Hopewell style or custom do not appear until about 100 B.C. and are in decline by A.D. 300 (1967:177, 183–187).

Griffin's two-climax model of eastern U.S. prehistory is the one most suitable to Illinois. In Illinois as in the upper Mississippi Valley generally there was a pronounced period of apparent decline of cultural intensity falling within the early part of the "Late Woodland" period with the Hopewellian climax confined to an earlier "Middle Woodland" period of

200 B.C. to A.D. 400 (Griffin 1967:183, 186–187). This period of decline between the Hopewellian and Mississippian climaxes coincides fairly closely in time with the Dark Ages in Europe between A.D. 476 and 1000. The Dark Ages were a period of transition and cultural reorganization between the fall of the Roman Empire in western Europe and the emergence of mediaeval European civilization. For western Europe this amounts to a two-climax model, but the Roman Empire fell only in the west. The Byzantine or eastern half of the Roman Empire flourished and preserved a reservoir of European classical learning, much of which was ultimately returned to western Europe indirectly through Islam via Moorish Spain. Similarly the Hopewellian climax began in Illinois and the Ohio Valley, spread into adjoining areas, and ultimately from the Canadian border to the Gulf of Mexico; and while collapsing in the north of its origin still survived in the Gulf states of the south, where it contributed to a sustained climax of restricted area that overlapped in time with the later Mississippian climax spreading out from the central Mississippi Valley (cf. Griffin 1967:187; Sears 1964:270–273). In this particular sense there was no complete Hopewellian decline, and the application of a two-climax model to the whole eastern U.S. minimizes or obscures the importance of the Deep South at a time when it was actually an important reservoir of tradition. Clearly, what is "climax" and what is "anticlimax" is relative. If European contact had been established along the Gulf coast or in the lower Mississippi Valley in A.D. 400 to 700, the cultures described then could well have met Kroeber's criterion for subareal climax. When I speak therefore of a two-climax model of Illinois prehistory or of upper Mississippi Valley prehistory, I am acknowledging that I am using a northern perspective.

Terms of reference may differ if we are speaking of a Woodland climax in the Illinois area alone, the Ohio area alone, or the eastern woodlands of North America generally. In the Ohio Valley the cultural development called Adena began earlier than Hopewell and with Hopewell forms a logical unit when considering the climaxing of the Woodland cultural tradition in that area. Both Adena and Hopewell are characterized by impressively monumental mound burial and earthwork enclosures. James B. Griffin and others with a more northern perspective use the names "Early Woodland" and "Middle Woodland" for the periods in which Adena and Hopewell, respectively, are the most prominent developments, with the rubric "Late Woodland" reserved for the period of transition leading to the emergence of the Mississippi pattern or Mississippian tradition of the succeeding period. Gordon R. Willey prefers the terms Burial Mound I in places in which early Woodland might be applied by others and Burial Mound II for both middle Woodland and much of late Woodland.

Nothing that can be called Adena as a culture or phase or in level of development at an equivalent time is found in Illinois, although individual traits of early Woodland flintwork, ceramics, etc., may be similar in the two areas. The designation "Adena–Hopewell climax" is thus meaningful in Illinois only as it relates Illinois to events broadly in the northeastern United States or to prehistory in the eastern United States, generally with the qualification that it represents a northern perspective. For Illinois the Adena–Hopewell climax is simply a Hopewellian climax.

THE CONCEPT OF HOPEWELL

Joseph R. Caldwell neatly summarizes a dimension of the problem of Hopewellian identity when he says (1964:136) that the prehistoric Hopewellian situation has been called ". . . a civilization, a culture, a complex, a phase, a regional expression of a phase, a period, a style, a cultural climax, migrations of a ruling class, a technological revolution, a social revolution and an in-place development out of previous antecedents." Mostly simply, "Hopewell" is a name that came to be applied in the early twentieth century to certain archaeological remains in the north-central United States that had a high archaeological visibility and that were dramatically different from anything left by Indians of the generations found by early explorers or later settlers in the same area. The Hopewell remains included enormous burial mounds, geometric earthworks, and a variety of artistically crafted objects often found with status burials — stone pipes of animal form on a platformlike base, panpipes and earspools suggesting South American and Middle American contacts, cutouts of sheet mica, copper axes, fired clay figurines, necklaces of river-pearl beads, fine ceramics and flintwork, and many other manufactures. The use of exotic materials from sources scattered over thousands of miles suggested a vast trade network.

Because the Hopewellian remains excavated had been originally confined largely to burial mounds, with scant attention to village or camp sites, these remains were often thought to represent a burial complex or mortuary cult. With increasing knowledge of habitation sites it became obvious that Hopewellian art was more than the material expression of a mortuary cult. Stuart Struever expresses the more likely purpose of Hopewellian "mortuary objects" when he recommends that it is,

. . . better to conceive of them as status-specific objects which functioned in various ritual and social contexts within community life. Eventually all or a portion were removed from this milieu and deposited as personal belongings or contributed goods with the dead, reaffirming the status of the deceased (1964:88).

This is a simple but very important point, since it forces our attention away from a sink of Hopewellian energy to the social system in which the buried individuals functioned in life and to the role of the artifacts themselves in possibly symbolizing the status of these individuals. We cannot explain the emergence of the elaborate Hopewellian mortuary complex nor its disappearance without such information. "The burial ceremonialism was not a special exotic cult but a climactic expression of a central theme of their way of life" (Griffin 1967:184). I disagree especially with the view that the aim of Hopewellian interarea exchange was "the production of ceremonial objects primarily intended for deposition with the dead" (Prufer 1965:132).

To satisfy many problems of description and taxonomy it has also recently come to be useful to think of Hopewell as an episode of social interaction that for several centuries linked several regional cultural traditions of the middle Woodland period — in the north-central states the Havana, Pike, Crab Orchard, and Scioto traditions (Caldwell 1964; Prufer 1964b; Struever 1964, 1968a). The concept of a "Hopewellian interaction sphere" accounts for the exchange of ideas and materials between widely scattered and distinct peoples without resorting necessarily to migration or conquest, acknowledging that the smaller, regional traditions were distinct in their local antecedents yet shared elements of a greater tradition at one time and at one level of their organization. Caldwell saw in Hopewell the elements of a "Great Tradition" in Robert Redfield's sense of the term. "Interaction spheres and Great Traditions serve as mechanisms for keeping little traditions in communication over significant periods of time" (Caldwell 1964:143).

I think the emphasis, however, can only be on recognizing elements entering into the mechanism of communication per se rather than on seeking the organization of the content of any Hopewellian Great Tradition. While it would be impossible to reconstruct the detailed philosophical content and organization of any preliterate tradition long dead, it takes only a little imagination even after two millennia to suggest the nature of some of the common understandings that may have permitted the Hopewellian interaction to operate. One of these understandings almost has to be the sacredness of tobacco, *Nicotiana rustica*. In historic times *Nicotiana rustica* was used so widely in eastern North America in such uncountable ways for sanctifying and validating transactions between Indians as individuals or groups and between Indians and the supernatural that great time depth is indicated. This and the prominence of smoking pipes in Hopewellian culture indicate to me that the Indians participating in the Hopewellian interaction accepted the holiness of tobacco or at least of smoking in solemnizing the affairs of men and nature. Pipes predate the Hopewellian interaction by many centuries in the United States, but it is uncertain whether they were used specifically for smoking tobacco or for any other of many smoking materials. I nevertheless feel that by Hopewellian times tobacco itself was important.

Other elements that could have been involved in the interaction mechanism were the use of fictions of kinship and the inviolability or sacredness of certain occasions or precincts for purposes of interpersonal and intertribal exchange, elements for which there are historical examples, and possibly also the use of honorific weapons of special manufacture to validate peaceful intergroup relations. Other elements may also possibly be inferred from the use of raptorial-bird designs when thought is turned to the problem, and perhaps from the Hopewellian use of panpipes. The archaeological record must be examined in a broad ethnographic perspective.

James B. Griffin has expressed his doubt that "Hopewellian social or political organization was as advanced as that of the early historic Iroquois or of the Delaware and Shawnee" (1964:241). He tells us the "... Adena–Hopewell continuum represents the gradual shift from societies on a level that may be similar to northern Chippewa to ones approaching the southern Central and Coastal Algonkians of the historic period" (1964:241–242). With this I would have no serious argument. While the ultimate sources of some Hopewellian contacts may be far-flung, one need not seek sociopolitical models to explain Hopewellian society that would be foreign to the northeastern Woodlands. It remains to draw together the particular combination of events that may have mobilized the energy of Hopewellian societies to produce the material remains that set Hopewell aside from the historically known Indian societies of the same area.

THE HOPEWELLIAN ECONOMIC BASE

Caution must be taken when conceptualizing the settlement pattern, the economic base, and other aspects of Hopewellian "society." If Hopewell is viewed as an interaction phenomenon, a Great Tradition, or an exchange system relating smaller regional traditions, then many differences may be expected from the effect of local conditions and local traditions. Olaf Prufer sees the settlement system of Ohio Hopewell to involve individual farmsteads scattered through the alluvial valleys of the Scioto and other rivers of the Ohio Valley (1964b, 1965). Stuart Struever (1964) has detailed a system for Illinois Valley Hopewell centering not on scattered farmsteads but on base settlements of 2.5 to 8 acres located on talus slopes at the bases of bluffs bordering the Illinois River and at points where small tributary valleys open into the valley proper of the Illinois.

The association of Hopewell sites with major river systems has been apparent to many archaeologists. Subareal associations of particular

Hopewell phases with environments of special character have also been identified. In Illinois the Crab-Orchard–Hopewell phase occupies the dissected hill country with its oak–hickory forests in the extreme southern part of the state (Struever 1964:90–92, 1968a:158). The Havana–Hopewell phase occurs within the Havana tradition, whose distribution coincides well with the eastward extension of prairie grasslands into Illinois known as the Prairie Peninsula. One archaeologist has described the adaptation of Havana peoples to the prairie in three words, "They avoided it," which may be close to the truth for the prairie itself but minimizes one important role of the prairie presence. The prairie/forest transition zone did provide browse for white-tailed deer and furnished hazelnuts and a variety of berries, which in turn supported bear and other wild life of value to Havana peoples. This transition zone was in many ways more useful than either prairie or climax forest considered separately. James A. Brown reviews the human ecology of the Prairie Peninsula at length in his dissertation (1965: chapter 4 and passim). In particular he examines the Prairie Peninsula as an area of social interaction in Woodland, Mississippian, and historic times. Its value as a unit of study will become obvious.

Except for their bison in the seventeenth and eighteenth centuries and elk to some extent throughout the whole time in which we are interested, the prairie grasslands themselves could not be profitably exploited by aboriginal technology and were something of a *containing force* for Indians adapted to the shrubby margins of the prairie and to the forested river valleys fingering out into the prairie. Forays might be made into the prairie, but the economic adaptation of Woodland Indians in Illinois was more akin to that described by Joseph Caldwell's conception of primary forest efficiency, representing a cultural adaptation based upon "increasingly successful adjustment to the eastern forest environment" (1958: vii).

During the middle Woodland period, the upland forest in its turn was itself something of a containing force relative to the natural abundance of resources of the alluvial valley of the Illinois River, especially in its central and lower reaches, and even to parts of lesser rivers such as the Sangamon and the Kaskaskia. Struever has, in fact, coined the term "intensive harvest collecting" to denote an adaptation in the Illinois Valley centering on exploitation of selected, high-yielding native food resources of the valley and its margins (1968b:305–308). From its great bend near Hennepin to its mouth at the Mississippi River the Illinois is characterized by a gentle gradient and a broad alluvial valley containing numerous sandy ridges interspersed with permanent and seasonal lakes refilled by seasonal floods not only with water but also with populations of fish from the main stream. In both Woodland and later Mississippi times major habitation sites were located to take advantage of the renewable resources of the overflow lakes, which could be completely fished out yet which would be replenished annually by nature. Major categories of resources utilized in intensive harvest collecting as originally conceived were certain species of fish; migratory water fowl, themselves attracted to the rivers and lakes in spring and fall; white-tailed deer in the valley plain and uplands at various seasons; nuts and acorns, particularly the hickory nut; and the seeds of plants such as *Iva* [sumpweed or marsh elder], *Polygonum* [smartweed] and *Chenopodium* [goosefoot or lamb's quarters](Struever 1968b:305). Compared even to the resources of the prairie/forest margins, the abundance of the Illinois Valley made it an Eden, and we recall Marquette's observations on the natural wealth of this portion of his route in 1673. I see the resources of the Prairie Peninsula in Illinois for prehistoric man as graded outward from the riverine locations into the prairie/forest margins and then into the tall-grasslands of the prairie itself. For Indians with preferential access to the valley proper the outlying areas were tantamount in an increasing degree to boundaries circumscribing this Eden, much as desert circumscribes the valley of the Nile in Africa or the Fertile Crescent in southwestern Asia. This did not prevent communication throughout the prairie area, however, as Brown demonstrates (1965).

Among the native plant foods of the Illinois Valley were some whose propagation was apparently being encouraged by aborigines in Illinois beginning in middle Woodland times and even earlier in Ohio and Kentucky. *Iva* and *Chenopodium*, while native, were part of a grouping of plants comprising what has been called, at least, an "eastern agricultural complex" representing a proposed hearth of New World plant domestication distinct from that of tropical nuclear America (Fowler 1971a; Gilmore 1931; Jones 1936; Yarnell 1964, 1969, 1972. The place of these native foods in Illinois Valley archaeology has been examined in great detail (Struever 1962, 1964, 1968a, 1968b; Struever and Vickery 1973). Struever relates the appearance of some of this complex in the Illinois Valley to the hypothesized innovation of a technologically simple form of plant cultivation that takes advantage of the adaptation of these plants to open or disturbed habitats. For this he suggests the name "mud-flat horticulture" (Struever 1964).

Thinking on the economic base that supported the Hopewellian climax ranges between two apparent extremes, Gordon R. Willey expresses one polar view when he writes:

I firmly believe that the growing of crops was more than a casual adjunct of Woodland economy and that economically significant maize farming was introduced into the Eastern Woodlands from Mesoamerica during the Burial Mound I Period or shortly after 1000 B.C. The huge earthwork constructions of some of the cultures of the Burial Mound I Period, together with their ceremonial and mortuary elaborations are in my opinion insupportable on the kind of a subsistence base that one can envision for the environment with only hunting, fishing, food-collecting, and incipient agricultural techniques (1966:268).

A contrasting opinion, identified with Joseph R. Caldwell, is developed along with Caldwell's concept of primary forest efficiency in his *Trend and tradition in the prehistory of the eastern United States:*

Archeologists have been too willing to interpret the ability to construct large mounds and earthworks as representing an economic surplus which could only be derived from food production on an extensive scale. This need not have been the case. There is no evidence that the Hopewellians made any more use of cultivated plants than of natural supplies or that they considered such plants as more than a supplementary source of food. . . . This is not to say Adena or Ohio and Illinois Hopewell cannot be regarded as cultural climaxes; but they were climaxes, it appears, in a hunting–gathering stage with planting still subsidiary, and each was followed by a decline from its former level (1958:viii).

As extreme as these views seem, they really represent just different appraisals of the economic role of cultigens and tropical cultigens in particular within early and middle Woodland (Burial Mound I and Burial Mound II) times. There was little basis for quantifying these judgments at the time and not much more even now. Caldwell was asking us to examine the potential of wild plant and animal foods for supporting a cultural climax. Willey saw more than coincidence in the climaxing of Woodland culture at a time when archaeological evidence of tropical cultigens was beginning to appear in the archaeological record in the eastern United States. At issue is the manner in which the abundance of nature, an introduced Mesoamerican agricultural complex, an incipient native eastern U.S. agricultural complex, and any other factors interact and relate to the Hopewellian climax. The ultimate resolution of this issue seems now to lie partly in the recognition of the demographic factor in the evolution and devolution of societies, in the utilization of more sophisticated ways of rallying ecological data to archaeological problems, and perhaps in learning more of primitive methods of rallying economic production to societal ends.

The most useful and continuous record of paleoenvironmental information bearing on the foregoing is that emerging from the lower Illinois Valley archaeological program initiated by Stuart Struever in 1959, a record I have already drawn upon. At the Koster site there is great stability from 5000 to 2000 B.C., with scant evidence for the use of small-seed foods or for any increasing interest in the utilization of nuts other than hickory through this time. Other nuts were nevertheless available and assumed some importance elsewhere in the valley, where the record is available, by middle Woodland times, as did small seeds. Asch, Ford, and Asch propose,

. . . that for a small population dependent on wild foods, concentration on hickory nuts is more efficient than concentration on some other kinds of nuts or seeds or on a more balanced combination, the term "efficient" being used in Boserup's sense of per capita labor inputs. If this is true, then the difference between Archaic and Woodland subsistence patterns does not represent an increment of evolutionary advance, i.e. a progressively better solution to the subsistence problem. Rather if Woodland populations were larger, they would have required more food, and thus they might have been forced to collect a greater range of plant foods even though greater per capita labor input would be required (Asch *et al.* 1972:29).

Archaic-period Indians were undoubtedly long aware of a great variety of food resources they chose not to make use of because they could more economically restrict their collecting to a narrower range of foods. Consequently, as Asch, Ford, and Asch see it from the point of view of leisure time, the trend was toward less leisure time per capita rather than more. Increasing technological efficiency in confronting the environment would not in this sense release more of every individual's time for nonsubsistence activities and might actually have been a response to need. Thus for reasons of population stress Indians in the lower Illinois Valley were motivated to use a broader resource base at greater labor cost to themselves within middle Woodland times and experienced a cultural climax at a time when leisure time was diminishing. If this is the case, then the mere availability of time would not be the real key to societal evolution and the innovation of a more labor-efficient economic base might under the right circumstances even open a route away from climax. A "progressively better solution to the subsistence problem" might lead to societal devolution. We can also consider basically nondietary explanations for plant cultivation in the presence of adequate or abundant natural foods.

A cost/benefits type of analysis may be useful for interpreting the presence of tropical cultigens in the eastern United States in early times. Squash of the species *Cucurbita pepo* was apparently cultivated early for use as containers, though apparently also for its seeds as in Mexico. For the early use as containers there is both linguistic and archaeological evidence (Munson 1973; Yarnell 1969; Cutler in Yarnell 1969). The words for "squash" and "container" are cognate through an important part of the Algonkian language family with great time depth indicated.

The flesh of the early gourdlike thick-shelled varieties of this species was probably thin (Cutler in Yarnell 1969). We cannot therefore properly understand the cultivation of this tropical cultigen by comparing it only with other available foods on a labor cost/nutritional value basis if the better comparison may be against the alternatives for use as containers and the relative labor cost of producing baskets, net bags, pottery bowls, etc. Cultivation of cucurbits for this purpose should have been comparatively labor-efficient. This would help to explain the willingness of early Woodland Indians to plant squash of limited food value.

For years the problem was debated of the presence of maize in middle Woodland times. There is now no seriously considered reason for doubting the presence of maize then. With new evidence from three recently excavated sites in Ohio and Kentucky reopening the arguments for maize late in *early* Woodland contexts, it has become a problem of learning just how extensively and with what significance maize was present in the early and middle Woodland horizons (cf. Struever and Vickery 1973 and *infra*). Three lines of inquiry — ethnographic, archaeological, and linguistic — converge to suggest that originally maize could have been grown, in the north at least, only as a food in its green state, not as grain matured and harvested for storage and consumption through the winter and spring and on until the next harvest.

In Salts Cave, Kentucky, Richard Yarnell found no evidence of the presence of aboriginal maize in cave passages nor in desiccated feces recovered for ethnobotanical analysis from a series covering the entire early Woodland period, even though abundant evidence was present for the economic importance of sunflower, *Iva*, and *Chenopodium*, all domesticated or encouraged native seed plants (Watson and Yarnell 1966; Yarnell 1969). Seeds of these native species were believed to have been harvested in quantities that permitted storage and consumption through the year. If maize was eaten then, it was a minor element of diet or one so restricted in season that it did not appear among any of 100 fecal samples. Only 23 of 100 feces examined contained squash or gourd seeds or both, compared with 90 containing sunflower, 87 containing marsh elder, 87 containing *Chenopodium*, and 78 containing hickory-nut shell. Squash seeds comprised only 3.3 percent of the material analyzed, compared with 23 percent for sunflower, 18 percent for marsh elder, 21 percent for *Chenopodium*, and 17 percent for hickory-nut shell. Twenty-nine field lots of squash and gourd shells were collected and analyzed to represent ten vessels of squash shell and twenty-five gourds. Hugh Cutler describes the squash as "about midway between the edible squashes and the ornamental yellow-flowered gourds" (in Yarnell 1969:51). It would be hard to quantify the actual importance of squash meat as a food because the meat leaves few clues for macroscopic examination. Squash and pumpkin were often cut and dried in historic times in the eastern United States and stored for later use. John Witthoft has also called to our attention that:

One of the recurrent features of the maize complex of the Eastern Woodlands is the correlation of a major ritual with the *ripening* of corn. Such green corn ceremonies were generally more important than planting or harvest rituals. . . . Such rituals appear to be specific to the Eastern Woodlands . . . and to differ significantly from any aspects of southwestern or Mexican ceremonialism (1949:82; emphasis added).

Witthoft interprets this to relate green-corn ceremonialism with eastern Woodlands rites relating to the first seasonal use of major animals and to a basic substratum of hunting ceremonialism. On the other hand Patrick J. Munson argues convincingly that on linguistic grounds maize may have been utilized in the northeast first as sweet corn, eaten seasonally in its green state. He summarizes his findings in the form of the hypothesis that:

Maize was being grown by Algonquian speakers at a time when Central-Eastern Algonquian formed a geographical unit (although this is *not* to imply necessarily that this unit was comprised of a single dialect: i.e. proto-Algonquian), and at this time the term for "maize" included both the stem "raw" and the root "grain," implying I would think that it was being used primarily in its immature state: i.e. as "sweet corn" (this, incidentally, might have very important implications in regard to the extreme paucity of remains of maize in Middle Woodland sites; only a relatively small amount of seed corn need be stored) (1973:118).

This makes sense on botanical grounds because for a variety of reasons the earliest varieties of maize grown in the north were necessarily ill-adapted to the shorter frost-free growing season and shorter summer-night photoperiod of these northern latitudes, which did not permit subtropically adapted maize to mature early enough to provide consistently or reliably either a dry, storeable mature grain crop or seed for the following year. We may consider then that for centuries maize could have been a luxury food in the north, grown as a seasonal treat or for ceremonial use but not as an economic staple. The presence of maize in late early Woodland contexts, the possibility suggested by finds in Ohio and Kentucky, *need not*, therefore, indicate the presence of a Mesoamerican cultigen that was a *precondition* for the Adena–Hopewell developments of that area. If the effort was made to grow maize for use mainly as a food in its green state, such seed being allowed to mature as the season permitted to provide seed to perpetuate the practice, then maize would actually in a sense have been a luxury *supported by* a mixed economy of hunting, gathering, and incipient food production and not have been much of a contribution to it. This may not have been the case in the south with its longer growing season, where maize could have matured and dried in the ear and been stored centuries earlier than in the north.

I see one alternative explanation for the coddling of an exotic plant in the north for centuries until finally a variety was isolated and propagated that was adapted to northern latitudes, an explanation which may be valid beginning locally in the middle Woodland period. From the Iroquois country to the Plains in historic times there was knowledge of preparation of green corn for use as a storeable staple. Parker mentions the technique for the Iroquois (1910:75–76). Wilson details the process for the Hidatsa (1917:39–41). Will and Hyde tell us much of the practice in the Missouri Valley from the Pawnee northward (1917:116–123). It would be hard to judge how important green-corn processing of this sort may have been in prehistory, but green-corn use should have been relatively more important before the availability of corn adapted to shorter growing seasons and short summer nights.

To prepare immature corn for storage the ears were either first boiled in kettles and then shelled and dried, as among the Hidatsa, or roasted over hot embers in the husk, as among the Arikara, and then processed like the boiled corn. A shell was used to remove the kernels, which were then spread over a blanket or skin to dry in the sun. The corn could then be stored and later used in much the same manner as fresh green corn. Information varies as to the proportion of the crop prepared in this way, but a reasonable figure from an Indian source indicates that in the upper Missouri Valley a quarter or a little less was used for feasting and for preparation of dried green corn for winter use. The balance of the crop was allowed to mature for drying on the cob in the field (Will and Hyde 1917:116).

Will and Hyde tell us (1917:118–119) that, according to John Dunbar,

. . . the Pawnees returned from their summer hunt about September 1, and at once began to roast and dry corn that was in the milk. From morning to night the women and children were in the patches, gathering fuel, making fires, picking, roasting, and drying corn. This was called the roasting-ear time. "In one direction squaws are coming in staggering under immense burdens of wood and leading lines of ponies equally heavily loaded. In another the store of wood is already provided, the fires brightly burning, in them corn roasting, and near by other corn drying, while children passing busily to and fro are bringing loads of corn from the patch. The atmosphere is saturated with the pleasant odor of the roasting and drying corn" (Dunbar 1880:277 in Will and Hyde).

The corn preferred for green-corn use was apparently the softer, more starchy flour variety rather than the harder flint variety used for hominy (cf. Parker 1910; Will and Hyde 1917:286). Among the Iroquois the cooking and drying of the green corn was consummated in the single act of "parching." For green parching, flour corn ears were roasted over coals until brown and then pounded into a meal that could be stored longer than corn matured and dried in the field and could then be eaten dry or reconstituted with water and cooked as a pudding (Parker 1910). Parker quotes Lewis Henry Morgan as saying, "The Iroquois were accustomed to bury their surplus corn and also their charred green corn in caches, in which the former would preserve uninjured through the year, and the latter for a much longer period," and then adds, "The Iroquois have not abandoned this custom even now. Among the more primitive the custom of burying parched corn and other vegetables is still [1910] in vogue" (Parker 1910).

For the Illinois tribe of the late seventeenth century there is an exceptionally detailed description of green and mature corn preparation attributed to the Sieur Deliette, nephew of Henri Tonti, a lieutenant and successor of the Sieur de La Salle at Fort St. Louis on Starved Rock:

To return to the occupations of the women, at the end of July they begin to mix or dry the corn. They make two kinds. That which they roast gives them more trouble than that which they boil, for they have to make large griddles and exercise particular care to turn the ears from time to time to prevent their burning too much on one side, and afterwards they have to shell off the kernels. They therefore make very little of this kind. The kind which they boil they gather just as tender as the corn for roasting, and with shells, which they find more convenient than knives, they cut all the kernels, throwing away the cobs, until they have about the quantity they wish to cook for the day. They never keep any for the next day because of the excessive care needed to prevent it from turning sour. After this, as soon as it has boiled for a few minutes, they spread it on reed mats, which they also make in the same manner as those that serve for their cabins. The drying process usually takes two days. *They make a great store of this kind.*

As regards the large ears which are ripe at the end of August, after they have gathered it they husk the ears and spread them on mats. In the evening they gather them into a heap and cover them well; when the sun has risen they spread them again, and they keep this up for a week: then they thresh it with big sticks six or seven feet long, in a place which they surround with matting to prevent the flying kernels from getting lost (Pease and Werner 1934:434–344; emphasis added).

Green corn utilized in the manner described would have been a valuable carbohydrate supplement to a diet balanced with vitamin- and protein-rich foods from other sources. It would also have provided a light-weight energy food for traveling, but by itself it would have been nutritionally inferior, say, to hominy prepared from dried, mature, flint corn hulled with the aid of lye from wood ashes. Aside from the naturally higher protein content of flint corn, there were advantages to be gained in the processing itself. Katz, Hediger, and Valleroy (1973) have surveyed the food-preparation practices of forty-three societies making minor or major use of corn in their diets and found that all societies with a major dietary dependence on corn also used either lime or wood ashes in preparing corn for consumption. As it turns out, dilute hot alkali treatment enhances the relative nutritional quality of corn in a manner that tends to counteract some of the natural deficiencies of untreated corn. The authors survey the literature to show that corn is especially deficient in the essential amino acids lysine and tryptophane and in niacin, an essential B-complex vitamin necessary for carbohydrate metabolism.

The amino acid and vitamin deficiencies of corn can be made up with a diet supplemented with beans, fish, or meat. Beans are rich in lysine and tryptophane, the latter a precursor of niacin from which niacin may be formed in the body. Beans were not available in the northern United States in Hopewellian times. Their presence is not demonstrated in the Mississippi Valley until well into the Mississippi period, and their appearance when it occurs seems to be tied to the westward diffusion of eight-rowed, eastern complex corn from the Iroquois country and lower Great Lakes area (Chmurny 1973:137–138; Munson 1973:111, 118–119, 129–130). Because beans did not originate in Iroquoia, they must have gotten there by a route for which there is no archaeologically visible trace, and Munson suggests that it could have been through the Gulf area and thence northward through the eastern states (1973:130).

Considering the known importance of corn, beans, and squash in the southeast in historic times, there is a surprisingly disproportional scarcity of evidence for these foods in the southern archaeological record. It must be there but is archaeologically invisible, so to speak. For the much earlier Hopewellian period site of "Fort Center" in southern Florida, William Sears sought the assistance of pollen science to demonstrate the presence of corn. Pollen grains of maize were found adhering to the pigment on a wooden carving preserved by immersion and also in soil samples. This is relevant because the aboriginal inhabitants of the site had burned great quantities of river-mussel shells to produce lime, much of which was found hardened into a cement and archaeologically quite conspicuous:

With corn present on the site, we can identify it as a part, almost certainly the major part, of the economic base. Since the lime is explicable only in terms of an economic process, and is used commonly elsewhere in the preparation of corn, the very large quantities of it suggest preparation of a great deal of corn (Sears 1971:328–329).

It is reasonable to assume that corn was economically important in the south before it was in the north, because it would have had a longer time to adapt to the latitude. It would also be reasonable to expect that corn might have been processed in a manner similar to that practiced in Mesoamerica, where limestone, and locally shell, was burned to produce lime for this purpose (cf. Katz *et al.* 1973; Linton 1924). Corn may at first have been eaten or parched in its green state in the north and only later grown for hominy as corn fully adapted to northern latitudes became available and as the technology of processing corn with wood ashes was developed, accepted, or adapted from previous experience. So long as parched green corn or green corn-on-the-cob were the only manners of corn use in the north, and especially in the absence of beans, any strong shift away from hunting and fishing toward greater dependence upon corn farming would have been unwise from both an economic and a nutritional point of view.

Little is known for sure of the antiquity of ash processing of corn in the eastern United States, but we must allow for the possibility that ash processing is older than corn itself and not derived by analogy from the use of burnt limestone in processing corn in Mesoamerica or possibly in the southeast at an early time. The powdery nature of ashes made them useful as an insulator which permitted foods baked in them to bake without burning. "Ash cakes" were so baked. Ashes of various organic materials from hickory bark to deer bones were used as salt substitutes in foods in the eastern U.S. (c.f. Swanton 1946:268, 270, 274, 303–304; Wilson 1917:53–54). It would be a small step from dry-parching corn in ashes or using ash for seasoning to recognizing the special properties of unleached wood ash for hulling corn. A pioneer description of the making of hominy grits helps to explain the use of ashes in processing corn:

The corn is first parboiled in water; then drained and well dried. When it is perfectly dry, it is then roasted on a plate made for that purpose, ashes being mixed with it, to prevent it from burning; and it is kept continually stirred, that it may take only the red colour which is wanted. When it has got that colour, the ashes are removed, it is well rubbed, and then put into a mortar with the ashes of dried stalks of kidney-beans, and a little water; it is then beat gently, which quickly breaks the husk, and turns the whole into meal. This meal, after being pounded, is dried in the sun; and, after this last operation, it may be carried anywhere, and will keep 6 months, if care be taken from time to time to expose it to the sun. When wanted for consumption, it is mixed in a vessel two-thirds water with one-third meal, and in a few minutes the mixture swells greatly in bulk, and is fit to eat. It is a very nourishing food, and is an excellent provision for travellers, and those who go to any distance to trade (Imlay 1797).

Ralph Linton as far back as 1924 suggested that the use of wood ashes for hulling corn in the eastern United States may have been a survival of an old method of processing grains and that the corn complex in the eastern United States was perhaps superimposed upon an older pre-agricultural food complex. His remarks proved prophetic in two respects. The postulated or so-called "eastern agricultural complex" based on native weedy plants conforms nicely to Linton's recognition of the possibility that "eastern tribes had developed at least the beginnings of agriculture," citing in particular the planting of various small grains in the southeast. Linton also recognized the possible significance of the Iroquois practice of boiling acorns in lye to remove the tannic acid:

As these wild foods must have been known and used long before the introduction of maize, it seems probable that the use of wood ashes was developed in connection with them and later applied to the new staple (Linton 1924:348).

Linton could not have known when he wrote that archaeology within a decade would provide a picture of the prehistoric use of acorns processed in ash among the preagricultural Archaic Indians of the Lamoka phase in New York State at 3400 to 3000 B.C. (solar calendar):

Fire beds, as defined at the only site of their occurrence, Lamoka Lake (Ritchie, 1932, pp. 86–87), were massive ash accumulations ranging in length from about twenty to fifty-five feet, up to ten feet in breadth, and three feet in thickness. . . . Charcoal granules had a profuse distribution throughout the ash, and burned acorn-hull fragments were a common inclusion, but animal bones and artifacts were virtually absent. It was believed that these features had accumulated gradually as the result of long-continued fires for drying and smoking fish and game, suspended in strips from pole scaffolds. To this surmise may be added the roasting of acorns to rid them of tannic acid, as suggested by the abundance of hull particles found throughout (Ritchie 1965:60).

If this pattern can be projected into later years, it would not be surprising if the ash processing of foods had survived in the New York Iroquois country and perhaps elsewhere and had contributed to the technological elaboration of the maize complex when maize appeared. The Indians responsible for the refuse accumulations at the Lamoka Lake site left bones behind representing an estimated 285,000 pounds of deer, elk, and bear meat and five tons of bird and small mammal meat, so we can guess that the Lamoka Indians balanced their acorn consumption with high-quality protein foods (Ritchie 1965:55–56). Acorn meal contains about five percent protein or roughly half that of corn (Heizer and Whipple 1971:305).

For the Havana–Hopewell and Pike–Hopewell phases in the Illinois Valley the adaptation was apparently oriented around hunting and floodplain-lake protein sources, with nut and seed gathering and possibly cucurbit cultivation providing needed energy foods, with a bonus of about 12 percent protein in hickory nuts (Asch *et al.* 1972:11, for nutritional value of nuts). For Scioto–Hopewell in Ohio the adaptation could have been oriented more strongly toward hunting supplemented by curcurbit and corn cultivation employing a swidden or "slash-and-burn" technique, an "extensive" form of cultivation suggested by its more dispersed settlement pattern. The destruction of pecan and hickory groves in the alluvial Illinois Valley in the course of swidden agriculture would have been unthinkably uneconomic for the Indians; the loss of the nut resources available for the gathering would not have been balanced out by the products of primitive agriculture at greater effort. In Ohio the lack of equally bountiful floodplain resources may have led to a balance of hunting and cultivation closer to the pattern I suggest for the late Woodland period in Illinois beyond the Illinois Valley, yet not to intensive cultivation as followed in Illinois during the early Mississippi period. When intensive cultivation became necessary in Illinois in the Mississippi period to sustain major population aggregates, these large Mississippian towns were situated adjacent to river bottoms, overflow lakes, and sloughs, upon which the Indians had depended greatly in middle Woodland times for high-protein foods. When beans became available in

Illinois later in the Mississippi period, these locations apparently lost some of their importance.

The importance of floodplain-lake resources in the Woodland economy in the Illinois Valley can be assessed from estimates of meat foods represented by bones recovered in excavations at the Apple Creek site, Greene County, Illinois. In the middle Woodland period during the Pike–Hopewell Phase, archaeological refuse represents the consumption of some 217 pounds of fish and mussel and 1,169 pounds of mammal meat, compared with 1,708 pounds of fish and mussel and 658 pounds of mammal meat during the early late Woodland White Hall phase (Parmalee *et al.* 1972:55–56). The amount of mammal meat represented by Pike–Hopewell deposits is biased somewhat by the presence of a single elk representing 350 pounds of consumable meat. The fish species represented are interpreted to indicate the importance of an overflow lake and slough as against a river source for the fish (Parmalee *et al.* 1972:21) The dramatic increase in importance of fish as a protein source in the early late Woodland period could be a reflection of the wetter climate that Struever and Vickery (1973) suggest for that time. Parmalee, Paloumpis, and Wilson point to the advantages of high water levels for restocking the floodplain lakes, especially during the spring spawning season when the lakes would be connected with the river, and to the disadvantages of low water levels for reducing food supply, stranding fish, and causing unhatched eggs to dry out (Parmalee *et al.* 1972:19–20). This would not indicate whether summer rainfall was greater, however. Only winter snows and spring rainfall might have been heavier.

From all the foregoing one may gather that the Hopewellian economic base is possibly as varied as the geographic differences between the regions to which the Hopewellian interaction extended. It would be an oversimplification to say that the Hopewellian climax was made possible by the introduction of tropical cultigens from Mesoamerica or that it was exclusively based on a hunting, fishing, gathering economy. It is more reasonable to look to the regional differences of geography and economy for the regional differences of Hopewellian expressions. The settlement pattern of Hopewell in Ohio, in the Illinois Valley, and in intermediate and outlying areas must reflect local differences in subsistence patterns. The natural abundance of native wild foods in the Illinois Valley probably contributed a conservatism to the adaptation there which was not shared in Ohio, for example. Locally the underlying subsistence habits and skills persisting even from the Archaic period may have contributed directly to the successes and differences of the Hopewellian and post-Hopewellian adaptations as they developed.

THE NORTHERN ADAPTATION OF MAIZE

Ironically enough, the very richness of the ethnographic record of maize use in the eastern United States has probably helped to obscure our knowledge of maize in the archaeological past. Ethnographic analogy is an approach ordinarily used to illuminate views of prehistory, but some images of the ethnographic present may not be appropriate for projection back into time. European explorers and settlers found maize cultivation in the eastern United States everywhere that maize cultivation was possible, but the ethnographic and historical records provide only clues to the nature of maize agriculture in the region that now constitutes America's "corn belt" at a time when maize was newly introduced and not yet fully adapted to northern latitudes.

The earliest evidence for maize points to an origin in highland Mesoamerica, a tropical zone that includes southern Mexico and Guatemala. The diffusion of maize as a cultigen northward into the United States required a succession of adaptations to varied conditions of altitude, amount and pattern of rainfall, soil, daily and seasonal temperature range, and latitudinal variations in the length of the day during the growing season. Of these, the factor receiving most attention from archaeologists in the northern United States is the growing season, expressed as the mean number of frost-free days in the locations of their interest. Anthropologists are certainly aware of the photoperiodic response of maize to latitudinal variation in the lengths of days and nights (cf. Munson 1963:21; Yarnell 1964:149), but some of the research implications for prehistory of photoperiodism in maize have not been explicitly stated.

As with many familiar plants, the time for flowering in maize may be cued or signaled by the length of the night, a factor that varies from latitude to latitude for any given day of the year. Photoperiodic responses are so sensitive that even twilight before sunrise and after sunset must be entered into the calculations (Chang 1968:70). Because of its tropical origins maize is basically a short-day/long-night plant which may have gone through thousands of generations of selection to develop strains that would mature in the short summer nights of the northern United States and southern Canada. Seed from a tropically adapted strain of maize transported directly to the United States may not flower until late September, much too late to mature within the limits of the growing season (Jenkins 1941:315). This behavior is taken advantage of when southern varieties of maize are purposely grown in the north to produce green silage for cattle feed, because until flowering begins plant growth is concentrated in the leaves and stems. A reverse effect may be achieved when maize adapted to northern latitudes is grown farther to the south. One writer quantifies these effects for modern blends by stating, "In general it may be said that as we go north or south of a given latitude a variety becomes one day later or earlier for each 10 miles of travel, the altitude remaining the same" (Hunt 1904; Jenkins 1941).

Photoperiodism explains why a single strain of seed sown over a period of weeks in the spring may produce plants that all flower and mature simultaneously. This situation causes problems in the scheduling of farm activities for modern corn farmers, especially for those producing sweet corn, which is at its best for only a few days and which must be pulled and canned the same day. It could have led to problems of scheduling for prehistoric Indians as well.

After about A.D. 1100–1300 the preferred and dominant varieties of prehistoric maize grown in the eastern United States belonged to a race comparable to the "northern flint" race of historical times, a race adapted to the short summer nights and short growing season at the northern limits of maize agriculture in North America. Northern flint varieties are early maturing and therefore shorter in the stalk than more southern races. Adapted to summer nights as short as six and a half hours from twilight to twilight, these varieties found nights of sufficient length anywhere in the south to enable them to flower in spring or fall as well and to be planted more than once in the same year, because they matured in two to three months from planting. The hard flinty endosperm of the kernels also made these strains more resistant to insect damage in the ear and in storage. The archaeological corn with morphological characteristics comparable to northern flint is referred to as "eastern complex."

In July of 1673 Father Jacques Marquette recorded of the Arkansa village he was then visiting, "they have an abundance of Indian corn, which they sow at all seasons. We saw at the same time some that was ripe, some other that had only sprouted, and some again in the Milk, so that they sow it three times a year" (Thwaites 1896–1901).[2] For the Natchez lying just below the Arkansa in the lower Mississippi Valley, Le Page Du Pratz has described a seasonal cycle with a harvest of the "little corn" in May and one of the "great corn" in September (1758, in Swanton 1946:260–261). J. Gravier places the harvest of the "little corn" in June and the main harvest at the end of November (Swanton 1946).

A rapid spread of eastern complex maize southward in the Mississippian period was probably facilitated by the nature of its photoperiodic adaptation, which found no barrier to southward diffusion. Northern flint and flour varieties today have effectively lost the photoperiodic response of their distant southern ancestors. Galinat and Gunnerson (1963) saw northern flint deriving from the southwestern United States out of a blend of the "Chapalote" and "Harinoso de Ocho" races of maize

---

[2] ". . . ils ont le blé d'inde en abondance, qu'ils sement en toutes saisons, nous vismes en mesme temps qui estoient en maturité. D'autre qui ne foisoit que pousser, et l'autre qui estoict en Laict, de sorte qu'ils sement trois l'an" (Thwaites 1896–1901).

together with the wild grass teosinte. This hypothesis suited the data at the time because it presumed the arrival of Harinoso de Ocho in the southwestern United States out of northwest Mexico about A.D. 700, and there was no reason at the time to look for an earlier ancestor for the historical period eight-row corn in the eastern United States known as northern flint. It has become clear since 1963 that we must look back much farther into time than A.D. 700 for the ancestry of the eastern complex.

In 1963 Olaf H. Prufer excavated the McGraw site in southern Ohio, where carbonized corn remains were found in a dated late Hopewellian context; this helped to confirm some suspicions about the antiquity of corn in the eastern United States. Hugh C. Cutler saw the McGraw site corn as "considerably advanced over the twelve- or fourteen-rowed, small-cobbed, flint or pop corn one would expect to find as the oldest corn," which to Cutler, "suggests that agriculture in Ohio had been practiced for at least several hundred years before this site was occupied," and together with other evidence indicates, "that in many areas agriculture may have been earlier or more advanced than archaeologists suspected" (Cutler 1965). Cutler then saw in the McGraw corn evidence of the early presence or formation of characteristics which would become accentuated in northern flint as that type achieved its historically known form. Six McGraw-site radiocarbon dates on charcoal range from A.D. 140 to 481, with an additional date on bone at 230 B.C. ± 80 (Prufer 1965:105).

Subsequently even older carbon-dated evidence for maize was found at the Jasper Newman site located in the central Kaskaskia valley in Illinois at 39.5° north latitude. Nine measurable charred corncobs were excavated from a middle Woodland pit associated only with Havana tradition ceramics. A wood charcoal date from the same level of this feature dated to 80 B.C. ± 140 (M-1790; Crane and Griffin 1968:81; Cutler and Blake 1973:27; Gardner 1969:34). Another middle Woodland pit with associated Havana ceramics from the same site dated to 50 B.C. ± 140 (M-1789; Crane and Griffin 1968:81). Cutler then said of this Hopewell corn,

... the first kinds [of corn] to reach Illinois apparently were small hard flints and popcorns with 12 to 14 rows of grains. ... These early corns have been called Tropical Flints and were similar to the Mexican and Southwest races called Chapalote and Reventador. ... Only nine of the corn cob fragments from the oldest feature (Feature 33, Middle Woodland) of the Jasper Newman site could be measured. Four of these fell within the area where we usually find older kinds of corn and, in addition, had slightly softer and less-thickened cobs. Five fell within the area of the Northern Flints. ... The diversity of corn in Middle Woodland at this site, even when measured by only the nine fragments excavated, is such that one must conclude either a well-developed agriculture preceded this period in this region or was brought into the area from areas near enough so that the corn types readily adapted themselves to the length of day and other environmental factors of central Illinois (Cutler and Blake 1969b).

Several comprehensive reviews are available of maize occurrences in middle Woodland contexts in Illinois and the eastern United States (Cutler and Blake 1973; Munson 1973; Struever and Vickery 1973; Vickery 1970; Yarnell 1964). One of these includes as well a summary of recent early Woodland maize finds (Struever and Vickery 1973) with references to a carbonized ear still in the husk of a ten-row tropical flint corn from an Adena mound in Athens County, Ohio (Murphy 1971; Cutler and Blake 1973:56); two charred cob fragments from the Hornung site in Jefferson County, Kentucky; and carbonized maize grains from two features of the Leimbach site near Lake Erie in Lorain County, Ohio. A date of 280 B.C. ± 140 (M-2049) was determined for the Adena mound. Dates of 520 B.C. ± 310 (OWU-185), 510 B.C. ± 260 (OWU-250), and A.D. 15 ± 240 (OWU-251) were reported for the early Woodland component in which the maize was found at the Leimbach site. The early Woodland position of corn from the Williams site in Georgia (Morse and Morse 1960:88) was discounted and a charred wood date of A.D. 1480 ± 75 (M-1107) from the feature containing the corn cited (Crane and Griffin 1963).

In seeking the origin of Mississippian period eastern complex ("northern flint") corn, we obviously cannot begin with a maize variety already adapted to mature in 60 to 70 days within the limits of a variable and unpredictable frost-free growing season of 90 to 100 days. We can begin by assuming the availability of corn physiologically adapted to mature within perhaps a 180- to 200-day growing season. There is also increasing reason from finds already made to believe that the morphological characteristics of northern flint and flour corns could have been latent within the genetic variability of middle Woodland corn in the eastern United States and within early corn in the American southwest (cf. Cutler 1965; Cutler and Blake 1973:5; Richard I. Ford, personal communication). Hopewell corn was predominantly of twelve- and fourteen-row varieties closely resembling southwestern types grouped as the "Hohokam–Basketmaker" or "Basketmaker/Pima–Papago" complex (Carter and Anderson 1945; Jones 1949:245–246) and referred to by Cutler also as tropical flint. Within the Carter and Anderson terminology northern flint varieties are described as the "eastern complex" because of their distribution, which was general through the eastern United States in historical and late prehistoric times.

The parallels of latitude from 30° to 35° north bracket southern Arizona and New Mexico, central Texas, southern Arkansas, most of Louisiana, all of Mississippi, Alabama, Georgia, and South Carolina, and northern Florida. Maize growing in these latitudes never has more than

15.5 hours of photoeffective light during any day of the year. The frost-free growing season available from Louisiana to Georgia is seldom less than about 215 days, lasting for seven months from March 31 or earlier to October 31 or later (U.S. Department of Agriculture 1941:744–746 *et passim*). Days are longest and nights shortest at the time of the summer solstice. At this time a site at 40° north latitude can expect nights 0.6 hour shorter than at the more southern latitude of Memphis, Tennessee (approximately 35° north). This means, in effect, that in central Illinois at 40° north latitude one must wait thirty-three days or until about July 24 to have nights as long as those beginning June 21 near Memphis, 340 miles to the south. At 40° north latitude one must wait twenty-nine days or until about August 12 for the arrival of nights as long as those beginning July 14 at 35° north latitude. The tasseling and silking of a subtropically adapted maize moving northward in the Mississippi Valley would thus be pushed farther and farther toward the limit of the growing season determined by the fall frosts. In this situation the absolute length of the growing season cannot be considered aside from the initiation of flowering programmed by the phytochemistry of the variety and triggered by a period of exposure to nights of the minimum length.

A corn plant whose seed is not fully developed before the autumn frosts cannot reproduce itself. We have considered earlier the incentive to prehistoric Indians in a temperate climate for encouraging a Mesoamerican cultigen until through centuries of selection it eventually adapted itself to a new habitat. Another approach would be to examine the implications of an observation by Richard A. Yarnell that sites in the northeastern United States producing archaeological evidence of cultigens are predominantly located in zones whose mean annual frost-free period is above the latitudinal average (Yarnell 1964:135–140, 150). The Great Lakes and major river valleys have an ameliorating effect on climate, well known to modern occupants of the area whose livelihood is affected by the nature of the growing season. Peach and cherry orchards are commercially reliable in extreme southwestern Michigan, where an extension of the Illinois Valley Havana tradition was found in Hopewellian times. A frost-free growing season averaging up to 160 days extends like a finger up the Mississippi Valley into eastern Minnesota at a latitude of 45° north, where it is twenty to forty days longer than the seasons in nearby counties elsewhere in Minnesota and adjacent Wisconsin (U.S. Department of Agriculture 1941:746; Yarnell 1964:127). The growing season in the Buffalo, Rochester, and Finger Lakes area of western New York State at 43° north latitude is between 160 and 180 days because of the warming effect of lakes Erie and Ontario, a season several weeks longer than the latitudinal average. Here today are the fruit-growing and wine industries of that state. Even smaller pockets of favorable microclimate exist within these favored regions such that a bluff-top location may be free of frost for several days to a week or more longer than an adjacent hollow or lower-lying area into which the denser cold air of a still evening will flow by gravity, filling it like an icy pool (Fagerlund *et al.* 1970:178–179; Franklin 1955:67–68, Plate 3; Gibson 1973). Under these conditions it would theoretically have been possible for maize to move northward within extensions and enclaves of longer growing season where natural selection toward a northern photoperiodic adaptation could take place

To adapt to shorter summer nights, subtropical maize must have been protected within temperate latitudes long enough for selection to be accomplished. It is difficult to account in any other way for the presence of corn at the Leimbach site in extreme northern Ohio in early Woodland times at the latitude of Cleveland except for the peculiarity that Lake Erie's presence modifies the climate of its southern shores to an extent that provides a growing season there of 180 to 200 frost-free days, a season comparable to that around the early Woodland Hornung site near Louisville, Kentucky, where early Woodland corn was also reported. The number of frost-free days available for corn actually diminishes as one moves south from Lake Erie into southern Ohio and almost to the Ohio River itself. A climatic warming could easily have permitted maize to move into favored locations in the lower Great Lakes, where it could have remained as a relict species or a northern outlier even after a subsequent cooling trend.

Yarnell's climatic observations are especially relevant to thinking by Patrick J. Munson over the last decade on the relationship between maize in Ohio Hopewell and the origins of the northern flint complex (Munson 1963, 1973, and personal communication). Manifestations of Ohio Hopewell extend from the Ohio Valley northward into western New York and adjacent Ontario, Canada, where Hopewellian elements are added to a Woodland cultural tradition with continuity from pre-Hopewellian into historical times and an ethnic identity as Iroquois. The Hopewellian corn at the McGraw site in southern Ohio includes a cob intermediate between corn of an earlier generalized Basketmaker or tropical flint appearance and the later northern flint. Archaeological evidence is coming to support the later movement of eight-row eastern complex corn throughout the eastern United States to its historically recorded distribution *from the north and from the east* rather than from the south and west (cf. Cutler 1958:40 Cutler and Blake 1973: *passim*). Combining archaeological and linguistic evidence Munson summarizes the situation with the statement that:

The archaeological–botanical record shows that, subsequent to the introduction of the early, rather primitive, many-rowed "Basketmaker" race of maize, an eight-rowed variety appeared which was much like the modern Northern Flint (a race extremely well-adapted to a northern climate and quite productive), and this race seems to be earliest (*ca.* A.D. 900) in a "pure" form in the New York state region among prehistoric peoples who were very probably proto-Iroquois (1973:118).

From his linguistic data Munson draws the relevant implication that,

. . . the first Central Algonquian speakers to obtain the greatly superior Northern Flint variety of maize, as well as beans, were the Ojibwa–Ottawa–Potawatomi (peoples living just to the west of the Iroquoian speakers), and these two items then diffused *east to west* through the other Central Algonquian groups (1973:129).

The near-absence of direct evidence of maize in post-Hopewellian sites until about A.D. 900 to 1000 cannot indicate the absence of maize in fact but more likely the failure of archaeologists to be as concerned with the small and uninteresting post-Hopewellian campsites of the northern states as with the more obvious and spectacular expressions of the Hopewellian climax. I will add to this that the apparent atomization of Woodland society in post-Hopewellian times may have directly contributed to the appearance and selecting-out of those growing characteristics of northern flint and flour corns that enabled them to adapt to latitudes as far north as the Gulf of St. Lawrence and Gaspé Peninsula in Canada. I see the multiplication of small isolated plots of corn as a situation likely to intensify genetic drift effects and to permit inbreeding analogous to the artificial self-pollination used by corn geneticists to create pure-breeding lines of corn representing all the latent variability of a strain under investigation. Male and female organs of maize are widely separated and pollination is accomplished by the wind. Pollination in a large field of maize is a virtual orgy of crossbreeding, which can, potentially, result in the 400 seeds of a single ear being fathered by pollen from 400 different plants. The dispersing of corn cultivation into hundreds of tiny plots through thousands of square miles of wilderness is the nearest approximation outside the experimental field station to artificial self-pollination that would bring out variation for selection by nature or by man. Within this northern milieu the early maturing characteristics of maize found in the Mississippi period may have segregated and survived associated with the eight-row trait for reasons perhaps some day explainable from an examination of the high-altitude adaptation of other eight-row corn in South and Middle America (cf. Galinat 1965:355).

A satisfactory explanation of the development of northern flint and flour corns must begin earlier than the late Woodland period, however. The morphological characteristics of eastern complex ears and kernels appear *before* the late Woodland period both in Ohio and in Illinois, earlier in fact in Illinois if we go by radiocarbon dates. It is easy to see how early maturing characteristics might be selected out during the late Woodland period if the climate at the time were cooler and more moist, as Griffin, Vickery, and Struever suggest (Griffin 1960; Vickery 1970; Struever and Vickery 1973). Both northern flint and flour corns mature early but northern flint in particular can germinate reliably in the cooler, moist soils of late northern springs where other varieties fail. This characteristic relates mainly to the retention of the flinty quality of all primitive races and varieties of corn with their horny endosperm. Both flint corns and popcorns fall in this broad category. It is much less obvious how eastern complex corn could have developed during the middle Woodland period or earlier in the context of the sub-Atlantic climatic episode of 940 B.C. to A.D. 260 if this period in the area of the historical Prairie Peninsula were warmer and drier than the late Woodland period. Corn with the archaeological characteristics of northern flint was present at the Jasper Newman site in central Illinois at 80 B.C. This would seem to argue either against an *in situ* or "in place" development of northern flint in the northeastern United States and in favor of diffusion from the southwest or to argue for a colder, more moist climate in middle Woodland times. Perhaps we should look at the total plant. Many archaeologists have excavated kernels and cobs of prehistoric corn. A few can claim to have seen caches of corn. None in the northeast, at least, has yet claimed to have excavated a grown stalk with ears attached.

Eastern complex corn was grown in the Missouri Valley by the Mandan Indians of North Dakota and their neighbors at the same lattitude as Quebec and by the Assiniboine Indians of Canada and Montana at about the latitude of the Gaspé Peninsula at the mouth of the St. Lawrence. It differed in the stalk greatly from corn raised even by the Pawnee in the central Plains at the latitude of Illinois:

The corn raised by the Indians of the Missouri Valley varies from the Pawnee corn, some six to ten feet high, to the corn obtained in late years by the Assiniboins of Montana from the Mandans and by the Assiniboins of Canada from the Sisseton Sioux, which has been acclimated by them and which seldom attains a height of over two feet. From the Pawnee corn in the south we get a regular gradation as we ascend the river, the size of the plants and ears decreasing and the length of the season required to mature the crop diminishing (Will and Hyde 1917:69).

From Mandan Indian corn of this northern stock the Will seed company had developed a variety called Will's Dakota White Flint, described as having eight to twelve rows of kernels, ears six to ten inches long, gently tapering, stalks twenty-eight to forty-eight inches high "according to season," ears born four to ten inches above the ground, and fine leaves (Will and Hyde 1917:27, 31). White settlers disliked this corn because it matured so early that the ears appeared to sprout from the ground; it could not be picked by machine and hand picking was a back-breaking chore. The corn was bushy but short and fine-leaved. Little energy was expended in vegetative growth to produce leaves and stalks. As it turns out these are precisely some of the qualities which produce drought resistance in corn — early flowering to reduce vegetative growth and the combination of low total leaf area with a narrow leaf characteristic (Jenkins 1941:312–314). Less moisture is lost through transpiration, so the moisture requirements of the plant are less than would be the case, say, of Pawnee corn ten feet high.

[Early flints] will stand more hardship in the way of droughts, poor cultivation, frosts, etc. than any other kind. They have been the highest yielders of grain, as a group, of all the varieties tested in the Montana on dry land. They are the earliest matured, withstanding hail well, and make a crop even in a very dry year (Atkinson and Wilson 1915 in Will and Hyde 1917).

[Northern Missouri corn] is extremely hardy, not only adapting itself to varying amounts of moisture and producing some crop under drought conditions, but resistant also to the unseasonable frosts which are apt to occur in the home region. It will sprout in spring weather that would rot most varieties of corn, and once sprouted it grows very rapidly. Its period from planting to maturity is about sixty days in a favorable year, and rarely are more than seventy days required (Will and Hyde 1917:72).

It would appear that the early maturing characteristics of northern flint could have at least started their development quite easily under conditions of scant summer rain on sandy and silty soils in the Prairie Peninsula, even without the need of early fall frosts to select against later-maturing corn. Under these circumstances the corn with northern flint characteristics at the Jasper Newman site in Illinois at 80 B.C. could even have been preadapted to some extent to the shorter growing season of the late Woodland period that followed, granting for argument that the late Woodland period was cooler and more moist. We should not assume a fixed equation between morphological characteristics of the ear and the plant, however. Hugh Cutler and Leonard Blake tell us, "Occasional 8-rowed ears are frequently borne on the upper parts of many-eared corn plants because upper ears tend to have fewer rows of grains. Similarly, when adverse growing conditions result in smaller plants, there is an increase in the number of 8-rowed ears" (Cutler and Blake 1969a:134). Eastern complex corn for some reason apparently did not continue its evolution in Illinois or the Mississippi Valley but in the east and far northeast (Cutler 1965; Munson 1973).

Early Mississippi corn and Woodland corn of the Mississippi period in Illinois had twelve to fourteen, even sixteen rows of kernels (Cutler and Blake 1969b). It is hard to balance natural selection against cultural preference, local climate and microclimate against zonal climate, and opportunistic finds of corn against systematic searching for corn in lesser-known archaeological areas and times. Going back even further into the past, additional factors may have to be considered. We cannot assume economic corn production from the beginning, which in the north may even have been some part of the early Woodland period. One may have to begin calculating the improbability of recovering archaeological corn from the deposits of a time in the past when perhaps, as in the historical present, tobacco, sacred rattle gourds, and sacred corn were cultivated only in small remote plots where the power and value of these plants would not be destroyed by the ritually contaminating presence of women (cf. Le Page Du Pratz 1972:321; Radin 1970:68; Will and Hyde 1917:278).

THE CHALLENGE OF ABUNDANCE AND THE DECLINE OF ILLINOIS HOPEWELL

Before radiocarbon dating expanded the chronological frame of reference of Midwestern archaeology there was little awareness of the interval called the post-Hopewellian decline. The periods of Hopewell and Mississippi were believed to be contiguous in time and their climaxes separated by a few centuries at most (cf. Martin *et al.* 1947:290, 293–294) with some examples of continuity between (cf. Griffin 1949:46–47). In a sense the discovery of post-Hopewellian decline is a product of the atomic age. An explanation for the decline is not so evident. There was little satisfaction in the idea that the Hopewellians had just "reached a level beyond which they found it impossible to go" and succumbed to "cultural fatigue" (Griffin 1952:361), yet it was almost a decade before there were any better explanations to offer. The explanations that finally came during the early 1960's represented almost the full range of possible explanations, and though none is inherently unlikely some would be harder to demonstrate than others. Disease and plague were possibilities for which there was no apparent evidence. The evidence for external conflict and warfare in Ohio Hopewell was summarized by Prufer (1961, 1964a:66–70, 1964b:100–102, 1965:135). Wray and MacNeish considered internal conflict (1961:67) as well as the influence of new technology on both subsistence and warfare:

One additional change which may have been very important was the introduction of the bow and arrow and the decline of the spear and atlatl as the chief weapons. This not only changed the kind of projectile points which were most useful but probably also switched the hunting habits which were still important to these people. It may be that the use of the bow and arrow made available new sources of food and new methods of warfare which helped to break up the old order (Wray and MacNeish 1961:67–68).

James B. Griffin considered the adverse effect of a cooling climate on Hopewellian agriculture (1960) and Charles E. Cleland the adverse effect of improved Hopewellian agriculture on the Hopewellian reciprocal trade network (1966:29, 94–95). The latter two of these explanations for the Hopewellian decline are in obvious conflict in several ways that I find fascinating. Griffin's hypothesis required the demonstration of a worsening climate toward the end of the middle Woodland period, but the hypothesis also assumes (1) that Hopewellians were dependent in an important way on an agriculture and (2) that a pattern of failure of agricultural products would contribute to the decline of the Hopewellian pattern. Cleland conceived a different situation:

The presence of an abundant and storeable food resource produced a social and technological milieu suitable for a new focal adaptation. Presumably, the *arrival of corn*, sometime late within the Middle Woodland Period, provided the catalyst for this new adaptation. . . . Concentration on one subsistence activity [corn] negated the necessity of social control over widely scattered resources, and as a result, intragroup contact was reduced to a minimum. Neutral or even competitive relationships replaced the once thriving reciprocal trade networks of earlier times. No doubt, the so-called "Hopewellian decline" which was characterized by such features as a cessation in the flow of exotic burial goods and raw materials and a breakdown in the communication of stylistic design motifs was the result of newly established focal agricultural economics (1966:94–95; emphasis added).

If we follow Cleland's line of reasoning a climatic change *beneficial* to agriculture could presumably have led to the dissolution of the Hopewellian interaction sphere, the same effect Griffin sees for a climatic change harmful to agriculture. At first thought Cleland's argument seems to oppose all logic. It opposes in particular an idea of the relationship of food production and agricultural surpluses to societal evolution that several generations of archaeologists learned in their first courses from the writings of V. Gordon Childe and others with the same views (cf. Childe 1936, 1942, 1951, 1958). It agrees beautifully, however, with an example I have used for some years in lectures to illustrate a fallacy of the Childean premise when unqualified. The negative effect on Hopewell which Cleland sees for the appearance of the new resource, corn, is essentially the same as the phenomenon I refer to as the "shmoo effect."

The shmoo is a cute mythical animal known to readers of the newspaper comic strip "L'il Abner" by the American cartoonist Al Capp. This loveable little creature is a friend of humanity, for whom it lays eggs, provides milk (already in the bottle), butter, and cheese (both domestic and imported). When broiled it tastes like steak; when fried it tastes like chicken. Its hide can be sliced thick to provide leather or thin to provide cloth and the eyes used for buttons. The shmoo requires no food and multiplies instantly at will. In sum, the shmoo symbolizes inexhaustible abundance. The "shmoo effect," however, is the devolution of societal organization in the face of this abundance. Food industries close because they are unneeded. Transportation systems similarly collapse wherever the shmoo migrates because any human becomes self-sufficient with a pair of shmoos. Servants leave the services of their masters and businesses lose their clientele as the reasons for their interdependence vanish. When finally government shmooicide squads exterminate all shmoos to restore the previous order, L'il Abner philosophizes, "Ef only folks stopped a-fightin', and a-grabbin' — they'd reelize thet *this* shmoo — the earth — got plenty o' ev'rything — fo' ev'rybody!" (Capp 1948:77).

The dilemma produced by Griffin's and Cleland's contrasting views of the effect of dependable agriculture in Hopewell is compounded by the additional conflict between views on the nature of the climate in middle and late Woodland times. Griffin (1960) interprets the record of historical climatology to indicate a warm period between 200 B.C. and A.D. 200 correlating well with the Hopewellian climax, followed by a cooling from A.D. 200 to 700. Working with similar clues, David A. Baerreis and Reid A. Bryson (1965a) have proposed a sequence of climatic episodes, one of which, the sub-Atlantic, is characterized by a "more severe" climate lasting between about 600–500 B.C. and A.D. 300–400. This is followed by a warmer "Scandic" episode from A.D. 300–400 to A.D. 800–900 and a "neo-Atlantic" episode terminating A.D. 1200, which everyone seems to agree was a definitely warm or warmer time with a pattern of rainfall that saw the expansion of farming settlements northward in the American southwest and westward into the Plains and, in the east, the emergence of the Mississippian culture tradition, providing the second climax in our two-climax model of Illinois prehistory.

Cleland resolves the problem by phrasing it in a manner that should be capable of testing in the field, so far as site distributions can provide an answer:

If, as Griffin implies, Hopewellian peoples were agriculturalists who expanded northward during the Hopewellian warm phase and were later thwarted in their effort to produce corn in the face of cooler weather, we would expect to find both a southward retraction and a decrease in the density of Middle Woodland sites within this period. If, as it has been suggested, the reverse is true, then we must follow the suggestion of Baerreis and Bryson that the climate of the late Hopewell period was becoming warmer and therefore more favorable to the production of food (1966:30).

Kent D. Vickery (1970) has written in support of Griffin's position in the matter of both climatic shifts and their effect, basing his argument largely on pollen profiles and what they imply for climate in the Midwest. I choose not to enter the controversy on climate directly, because I think that argument is pointless if there is no resolution first of the relation of food production to the Hopewellian interaction. If only a climatic argument were involved, it would seem to be supported by the failure of Hopewell to decline in the south (cf. Griffin 1960:32). I see the more fundamental problem of assumptions underlying the relation of food production to the Hopewellian climax.

Cleland has phrased the economic adaptation of Hopewellians at the time of their climax as "diffuse," diffuse in the sense of having a generalized adaptation, depending upon specialized skills but skills many in number, involving many technologies employed to utilize a variety of resources. This recalls the idea of primary forest efficiency (Caldwell 1958). The shift Cleland sees late in middle Woodland times is toward a "focal" adaptation involving concentration of attention on one or few resources. The Hopewellian interaction is viewed as something of an exchange network required to integrate the varied resources of a region maximally within a single diffuse societal economy. I will call this a synchronic view of utilizing resources. A diachronic view is provided by Paul Diener (1968). Diener attacks the problem of Hopewellian integration from the point of view of resources utilization and fluctuation over a period of time, a matter especially important for a society unable to pack its baggage and move as necessity or opportunity demands. Thinking in particular of the Hopewellian interaction, Diener observes that:

The importance of exotic items may be traced to the delayed nature of the resource exchanges postulated here. . . . rank societies are not highly specialized, and during periods of resource sufficiency there is no immediate reason to trade. It is during such periods that inter-societal ties would tend to break. The value of ritual exchange goods is that they mediate such periods maintaining social contacts which may become crucial during periods of famine (1968:8).

The mediating effect of ceremonial exchange that Diener sees is akin to the principle involved in the "giveaways" of horse nomads like the Teton Dakota, who were unable to accumulate or store wealth and effectively hedged against the future by giving away their temporary wealth, in a sense making an investment in "good will."

The idea that intersocietal and intrasocietal ties can loosen during extended periods of abundance is essentially a statement of the shmoo effect. The principle can be observed in a variety of historical situations. The Black Death in late fourteenth-century Europe saw a population depletion of as much as 40 percent by the end of that century for many European nations (Russell 1948:40–50; Peterson 1961:365). With the land base fixed this amounted to a per capita increase of up to 67 percent in the amount of land available to survivors. The resulting labor shortage and surplus of land helped to accelerate some trends that had already been taking Europe out of the age of feudalism. Feudalism involved a set of obligations between landowners and their tenants. In England the plague amplified the trend toward substituting monetary wages or rent for labor service owed to the lord. On manors where the landowner would not make concessions to his serfs, the serfs had the option because of the labor shortage of the time to seek another master, who in turn was often more than willing to accept them on their own terms (Ziegler 1969:chapter 15).

Feudalism had grown in Europe during the Middle Ages under given circumstances that could not be transmitted to the New World. France attempted to establish its seigniorial system in New France but the nature of Canada, the Great Lakes, and the Mississippi Valley waterways prevented this:

It was physically impossible for anything like the feudalism of France to exist in this French colony, and the reason is really quite simple. A basic competition of the Old World was turned upside down in the New World. Here it was a competition between seigniors for tenants, whereas there it was between peasants for land owned by seigniors. This inversion emptied feudalism of its substance, leaving only a hollow shell. North American conditions of life emancipated the French peasants who migrated to the St. Lawrence, where they cleared and occupied only a narrow ribbon of land running along the banks of the great river and its tributaries. With liberty forever beckoning to them through the trees of the forest just behind their cottages, and up the water that flowed past their doors, how could they be ridden by feudal lords? If anyone found life in the colony too cramping, nothing — not even his wedded wife — could hold him from running away into the woods to live a wilder life with the Indians, among whom he could always find, if he wished, a wife à la mode (Burt 1965:61).

Fort St. Louis at Starved Rock on the upper Illinois River was for nine years the seat of a fur-trading operation begun by René Robert, Sieur de La Salle (1643–1687). The ambitions of the founder are obvious in the seigniorial grants around Starved Rock made by La Salle to his faithful followers, phrased with references to "rights of dovecote, of wine press, of fortifications, and of low justice," to churches, mills, hunting and fishing rights, quarries, and trade, to navigation, roads, planted fields, and pastures, in return for expressions of fealty and homage to the seignior and seigniorial rents and privileges (cf. Pease and Werner 1934:19–36, 42–44). Fort St. Louis had been established near the village of the Kaskaskia–Illinois Indians that Jolliet and Father Marquette had visited in 1673 on their return trip from the lower Mississippi Valley. Encouraged by the French presence, this village came to number in the thousands. When finally the distance to firewood became too great and the advantage of the fort on Starved Rock too dubious, the Illinois just resolved to move their village to Lake Peoria and the French were obliged to follow. There was nothing in nature and no one in New France to stop them. Fort St. Louis, originally named after La Salle's sovereign lord, the sun-king Louis XIV, was then reestablished in 1691–1692 at Peoria and came to be better known as *Fort Pimitoui* after the Indian name of the location, which means Fat Lake (Lac à la Graisse), "so called on account of the abundance of game there" (DeGannes 1934:326–327; Pease and Werner 1934:277). *Sic transit gloria mundi.*

The examples I have given of the negative effects of abundance on societal relationships should recall for Americanists the writings of the Wisconsin historian Frederick Jackson Turner (1861–1932). Turner will always be identified with the "frontier hypothesis" in American history (cf. 1893; 1947) and for our purposes can be associated with the idea of societal devolution in the presence of an advancing frontier and societal reevolution with the passing of the frontier situation. "The frontier to Turner was not merely a borderland between unsettled and settled lands; it was an accessible area in which a low man–land ratio and abundant natural resources provided an unusual opportunity for the individual to better himself" (Billington 1967:19).

. . . in the long run the effective force behind the American democracy was the presence of the practically free land into which men might escape from oppression or inequalities which burdened them in the older settlements. This possibility compelled the coastwise States to liberalize the franchise; and it prevented the formation of a dominant class, whether based on property, or custom (Turner 1910, 1947:274).

The West . . . is a form of society, rather than an area. It is the term applied to the region whose social conditions result from the application of older institutions and ideas to the transforming influences of free land. By this application, a new environment is suddenly entered, freedom of opportunity is opened, the cake of custom is broken, and new activities, new lines of growth, new institutions and new ideals are brought into existence. The wilderness disappears, the "West" proper passes on to a new frontier, and in the former area, a new society has emerged from its contact with the backwoods. Gradually this society loses its primitive conditions and assimilates itself to the type of older social conditions of the East; but it bears within it enduring and distinguishing survivals of its frontier experience (Turner 1896, 1947:205).

Demographically oriented anthropologists should see that Turner's frontier hypothesis is essentially an inverse statement of Robert L. Carneiro's thinking on the role of *circumscription* in the advancement of systems of cultivation and in the creation of the state. Albert C. Spaulding introduced me to Carneiro's ideas in about 1966 at a meeting at which he announced to Joseph Caldwell and myself, "I know now why Hopewell failed to become a civilization. There was nothing to *contain* it. It fizzled like a firecracker with the paper wrapping torn." He need have said no more. There was a clear picture of the eastern woodlands as a frontier for Indian and European colonist alike. The late Woodland period that followed the Hopewellian decline in the north did not seem to be a time necessarily of depopulation — more a time of population redistribution. Writing in 1966, Melvin L. Fowler observes:

Following the Hopewellian Interaction there seems to have been a cultural decline in the area. This decline took place in the sense that all areas were no longer tied together by the tomb-burial cult, its attendant ceremonialism, and the common fine goods associated with this practice. There seems to have been a return to regionalism in that the local ceremic traditions continued on. That this decline took place also in settlement size, population, and other facets of culture is sometimes implied but little data bearing on this is known. As a matter of fact, there may have been a population increase in this period over the Hopewellian Interaction. There is some evidence that corn can be associated with those post Hopewellian or Late Woodland settlements throughout the entire area (Fowler 1971b:398).

The late Woodland period was a period of innovation in several ways that had been obscured by the short time scale available for eastern U.S. archaeology before radiocarbon dating and by the taxonomic approach to eastern archaeology. The bow and arrow were believed to have been present in the Mississippi period, as they indeed were. The atlatl and throwing spear were believed to have composed the principal missile system in middle Woodland times and earlier, as they probably did. The idea that too often must have come across, however, was that the presence of small triangular flint projectile points of "Mississippi type" indicated contact with or influence from Indians of the Mississippi culture. Stemmed and notched points of small size could be interpreted as an example of the translation of the larger Woodland atlatl "dart" (spear) points into the smaller size suitable for the arrow, a shift of dimensions within the older pattern. With radiocarbon-dated finds and newly excavated information it did not take long to realize that the bow and arrow were present in the late Woodland period and antedated the Mississippian emergence in the Illinois area at least. We recall again Wray and MacNeish's speculation on the meaning of the shift to the bow and arrow with a corresponding decline in popularity of the atlatl and spear: "It may be that the use of the bow and arrow made available new sources of food and new methods of warfare which helped to break up the old order" (1961:68). The unanswered question would be whether the bow and arrow were simply a superior weapon system for the situation in which Illinois Indians found themselves in post-Hopewellian times or whether the bow and arrow actually helped to *produce* that situation.

Cleland saw the beginning of effective corn agriculture as a possible explanation for the Hopewellian decline. Wray and MacNeish saw the bow and arrow in a possibly similar role. Spaulding saw the forward progress of Hopewell prevented by the lack of a containing or circumscribing force for reasons Carneiro's hypotheses explain. How might these ideas be related? I much earlier described the Illinois prairie as a boundary circumscribing the wooded valleys of the Illinois and its tributaries and the climax forest as a boundary circumscribing the alluvial valleys with lakes, marshes, and varied resources. The climax development of Hopewell in Illinois was confined to locations in which *intensive harvest collecting* and *mud-flat horticulture* were possible, as described by Stuart Struever for the Illinois Valley. These locations had a very restricted distribution, as he has emphasized. Any combination of subsistence activities that would permit the permanent occupation of outlying areas would in effect create a vast frontier and would in a stroke improve the per capita ratio of available resources. At the same time it would relax the need for economic exchange between groups with differential access to previously scarce resources in the manner discussed by Cleland and diminish the need for ceremonial exchange either for the reasons given by Diener or for the purpose of stabilizing intergroup relations. Compare the situation with examples provided by Carneiro:

Those regions where a notable intensification of agriculture followed an increase of population are distinguished by an important characteristic: *They are regions where the area of cultivable land was distinctly circumscribed.* Areas of distinctly circumscribed arable land are, typically, narrow valleys, sharply confined and delimited by mountains or deserts. It is in such areas that most of the early advances in agriculture, and in other aspects of culture, took place.

It is a curious and significant fact that these advances were not made in areas of broad and uninterrupted expanses of arable land, regardless of their degree of fertility. The forested plain of northern Europe, the Russian steppes, the Eastern Woodlands and the Prairies of the United States, today the most important area of cultivation in the world, initially lagged far behind the narrow river valleys and littorals in their agricultural development. The reason for this relative backwardness becomes evident in the light of our theory: With extensive and unbroken agricultural land at hand, population increase was followed by the dispersion of peoples. With serious pressure on the carrying capacity of the land thus avoided, the ecological impetus required to turn extensive into intensive cultivation would have been absent (1961:60).

The idea of resource concentration and circumscription can be applied to the origins of civilization and to political development as easily as to the origins of intensive forms of food production. Carneiro makes a point especially pertinent to our argument when he calls attention to the narrow watered valleys of the Peruvian coast bounded by desert (1970:737) and quotes E. P. Lanning on early developments on the Peruvian coast, which were, to the best of his knowledge, "the only case in which so many of the characteristics of civilization have been found without a basically agricultural foundation" (Lanning 1967:59). Caldwell had stated a similar kind of view when he regarded the Hopewellian climax as a climax in a "basically hunting–gathering stage with planting still subsidiary" (1958:viii). A primitive form of food production has since been shown to have been a factor in the Hopewellian adaptation, but in Illinois at least there is more evidence for encouragement of wild and near-wild native eastern species — *Iva, Chenopodium, Polygonum*, and the like — than of cultigens of tropical origin. Mud-flat horticulture may have been either a response to population growth or a precondition for it. In either case it would not have been possible to expand this form of cultivation beyond the areas to which it was naturally suited. That middle Woodland populations expanded beyond the watered valleys there now seems no doubt. We may also assume that this expansion required some technological readaptation.

In a survey report on a major tributary valley of the lower Illinois, Kenneth B. Farnsworth combines reporting and interpretation in an insightful analysis with a direct bearing on all the foregoing. Farnsworth found no evidence of early Woodland occupation in the Macoupin Valley nor of early middle Woodland material. He did find evidence of middle Woodland settlements of a later time, estimated at A.D. 100 to 400, as well as evidence of a trend toward the moving of settlements from the bottoms to the bluff crests (1973:26–27).

Since backwater-lake fish populations and migratory waterfowl served as fundamental subsistence resources for Illinois Valley Middle Woodland peoples, we should expect that if breakaway groups entered Macoupin Valley, forsaking basic aquatic resources previously available to them, significant restructuring of subsistence and interrelated social subsystems of culture would be forced. . . .

The precise nature of Middle Woodland subsistence readaptation upon loss of fishing and wildfowl resources and the significance of observed differences between the Illinois and Macoupin valley settlements must remain highly conjectural until excavations have been conducted at Macoupin Valley Middle Woodland sites. . . .

In making such a move, these individuals lost fundamental fish and wildfowl resources for which other foods had to be substituted. *Only one subsistence item known to them could offer comparable productive potential: corn* (Farnsworth 1973:27–28).

Farnsworth sees the shift to bluff-top locations as an indication of a mobile slash-and-burn subsistence pattern, possibly on an isolated-farmstead basis. He sees also the implications of this new pattern for the breakdown of the Hopewellian interaction in the manner indicated by Cleland (Farnsworth 1973:28–29; Cleland 1966:95). I would add to Farnsworth's interpretation a point I think important. The milieu he describes seems to be exactly that in which the bow and arrow would provide an adaptation superior to the spear. It is the ambush weapon *par excellence*, ideally suited for lone hunters and to the shrubby prairie/forest transition at the periphery of the wooded valleys.

If as many personal academic fortunes were thought to depend upon finding arrowheads in early contexts as upon finding corn, we would possibly already have answers to many problems in Midwestern prehistory. Corn with early late Woodland associations has not been found, possibly because sites of this period may be scattered and small single family camps are difficult to recognize and expensive to confirm. Or, if the climate of the time was colder, as Griffin believes, the corn may just not be there, or it may be only on sites farther south. Arrowheads *do* occur with early associations, however, dated both by radiocarbon and by their associations.

The earliest dated find of an arrowhead in Illinois was made by Patrick J. Munson at the Scovill site. Scovill is a terminal middle Woodland site near the Spoon River about eight miles from its mouth in the central Illinois Valley. Scovill is a pure component of the Weaver phase of the Havana tradition. Of 1,000 sherds even from surface collections at the site only two were not Weaverware and these two were Baehr Brushed, a late middle Woodland type. Five of six projectile points found in excavated pits were spear points of the type Steuben Expanding Stemmed. The sixth was a small arrowpoint compared to the type Koster Corner-Notched (Munson *et al.* 1971:411; Perino 1963). A single date of A.D. 450 ± 120 (M-1685) was obtained from a sample of wood charcoal from the site, but this date agrees well with the expected dating. Koster-type arrow points have been dated to A.D. 650 ± 120 (M-1357) in Koster Mound 2 at the type site for this projectile point type in the lower Illinois Valley. The date in this particular mound is believed to be too early and the sample itself is of charred human bone (Crane and Griffin 1966:264). Such material can produce anomalous results.

Other early dates for the appearance of arrowpoints in the Illinois area are A.D. 600 ± 110 for the type of Klunk Side-Notched (Crane and Griffin 1964:6; Perino 1966) from Calhoun County and A.D. 490 ± 150 for Mound 6 of the Beloit Group just north of the Illinois–Wisconsin state line. A small unnotched triangular projectile point was found in Mound 4 of this group (Bastian 1958:164; Crane and Griffin 1961:111). Radiocarbon dates are subject to question. What is important is that arrowpoints have been found in contexts that belong to a terminal phase of the Havana tradition (Scovill) and to before the time of the late Woodland "Bluff" culture (Klunk).

Without convincing data on climate, site distributions, and cultural adaptations in the middle Woodland and late Woodland periods, we cannot demonstrate that a worsening climate did not contribute to the Hopewellian decline in the way Griffin suggests. What I have suggested in the foregoing is that conditions and adaptations favorable to the spread of corn agriculture through Illinois and not tied to the restricted environmental requirements of mud-flat horticulture could also have contributed to the Hopewellian decline. The bow and arrow could have assisted in this readaptation by improving the technological access to alternative protein resources. One may ask why, if my model of the Hopewellian decline is correct, does the definitely warm neo-Atlantic climatic episode of A.D. 800–900 to A.D. 1200 correspond to the period of the societal reorganization along highly structured lines? Precisely, I would say, for the same reason that gave rise to the Hopewellian climax. The population density of Illinois rose during the late Woodland period to a point at which there was competition for preferential access to resources within even the new and broader resource base, and that resource base may then have been severely restricted. This is the story of the Mississippian emergence in Illinois and the story of climax and decline at Cahokia.

THE CHALLENGE OF STRESS AND THE CAHOKIA CLIMAX

Just as the Hopewellian adaptation had been tied to a riverine resource area of limited availability, so also the late Woodland adaptation in Illinois had its bounds. The limit of cultivation for prehistoric man in Illinois was the prairie, as it was for the French, for the English, and for the early American settlers who succeeded them. Pioneering farmers avoided the tall-grass prairie and first settled the southern Illinois hill country, which provided timber for construction and a thin sod easily broken for cultivation. The deep, black prairie soil required new technology for plowing because of its thick sod, as well as a costly investment in ditching or tiling to drain. Early travelers from the French onward comment on the flooding of the prairie by spring and fall rains that found no outlet on the level plain. The prairie contained the broadest expanse of rich soil on the American continent, except perhaps for the desert soils of the west, which required even more investment in irrigation and water management to utilize.

When we first become aware in time of an obvious late Woodland presence in Illinois, the sites were frequently located on timbered tracts, often on bluffs overlooking streams. The names given cultures and sites are often clues to their adaptation. In Wisconsin there are sites of the upper Mississippi tradition with names like Carcajou Point, Lasley's Point, Crabapple Point, Point Sable — names indicating a lacustrine adaptation. In Illinois there is the Jersey Bluff culture, "Bottoms Bluff" Woodland, the Bluff aspect, all describing late Woodland units.

Sites on timbered bluff locations offer several advantages. There is the advantage of water drainage because of both the contour of the land and the nature of the soils. Upland sites near the Mississippi and Illinois rivers are usually on light loess soils. Loess is an aeolian soil of silt-sized particles that drains quickly. This is especially useful for the cultivation of cucurbits — squash and pumpkin — which can rot on heavier soils in wet seasons. It would also be an advantage for corn. In cold, wet springs corn seed can rot before it germinates. Such a situation in nature would select for corn with the characteristics of northern flint, whose hard endosperm resists these effects. Struever and Vickery (1973) have seen in early late Woodland times reason for believing that a wetter climate existed in the lower

Illinois Valley. Resettlement from the bottoms to the bluffs could provide a reason why the cultivation of maize and cucurbits could have advanced in the early late Woodland period despite the cooling that Griffin sees in the record of historical climatology for that time. Bluff locations provide the advantage of cold-air drainage, which extends the growing season in both spring and fall by providing a microclimate slightly warmer than valley bottoms lacking major water bodies. This phenomenon did not escape the attention of the Hidatsa Indians of North Dakota. We learn from Gilbert Wilson's informant, Buffalo-bird woman, that:

The fields that lay on the west side of our village got frosted more easily than those on the east side. Indeed, our west-side gardens suffered a good deal from frost.

The reason was that the ground along the Missouri was lower on the west side of the village; and fields that lay on lower ground, we knew, were more likely to get frosted than those on higher ground. *Gardens on the higher grounds east of the village were seldom touched by frost* (Wilson 1917:115; emphasis added).

If Hopewellian cultivators had been forced to move southward by a more severe climate, the corn photoperiodically acclimated to any given latitude in Illinois would have been even more successfully adapted to a more southern location. A week's advantage in growing season would have been obtained by using in the lower Illinois Valley corn acclimated to the central Illinois Valley or by using seed from the latter area in the American Bottoms south of Cahokia. In any case the dispersing of many small plots through Illinois, if this is the correct interpretation, would accelerate the rate at which seed characteristics better adapted to Illinois could segregate and be selected by differential survival.

The deep shade of the closed forest cover prevents both the appearance of undergrowth and the formation of a sod deeper than an inch or two. The soil can be exposed to sunlight by girdling, cutting the living bark and permitting the trees to die. The dead trees themselves provide firewood in great quantity for years, and former plantings abandoned to regrowth provide berries for bear and other wild life and browse for deer, and effectually create within the climax forest the kind of shrubby environment that was maximally useful to man and beast beyond the valley itself when food production involved only mud-flat horticulture. The thin sod of the forest required nothing more than a digging stick for planting, and for a long time new forest was abundantly available for clearing when regrowth eventually hindered productivity or required excessive labor.

There is no record of the prehistoric Indians' attitude toward the beasts his cultivated fields attracted. In historic times, however, wild animals were a usually undesired byproduct of food production. One pioneer in Ohio reminisced, half-seriously:

The crops were generally divided pretty equally between the wild animals and the landlord. . . . At times [gray squirrels] became so numerous and destructive to crops that they were more feared than is the rabbit in California or grasshopper in Kansas. For many years, settlers were obliged to guard their fields when planted with corn, or droves of foraging bands would dig up the hills and eat the growing grains; when the crops matured, they were still more destructive (Jones 1898:26, 166–167; cf. Utter 1942:147–148).

[The rabbit] loves civilization and prefers the grassy fields, standing corn and sunny hillsides to the wilds of the forests, and is always as ready to care for the waste apples in the orchard as he is to bark around the young trees (Jones 1898:172).

To the Indian some attention of wild animals to the crops would be beneficial if he could take advantage of the situation to kill or snare them.

One evening while hunting . . . I counted more than fifty deer in a herd, but I could not get within shooting distance. Later in the season, when our cabbages in the garden were nearly full grown, they were almost all eaten up one night by a lot of deer which had jumped the fence, within a hundred feet of our dwelling, and regaled themselves at our expense (Rodolf 1900:353).

The creation by slash-and-burn cultivation of garden plots scattered through the forest would in time lead to many openings whose young, low vegetation and resources would essentially duplicate the conditions at the prairie/forest border, which was bountiful in game and wild plant foods. I assume that this was a factor that grew in importance. Lysle R. Pietsch notes that white-tailed deer populations undergo a population increase in the early stages of forest clearance, when forest edges would be at a maximum, although they diminish when deforestation is complete (Pietsch 1954:54). Slash-and-burn cultivation through the Illinois woodlands could thus have been reinforced by the opening of climax forest and the increased supply of deer and other natural foods. This would be an example of the operation of the "second cybernetics" of Magoroh Maruyama (1963). Kent V. Flannery, who has applied a systems analysis to human adaptation in Mesoamerica, explains the first cybernetics as involving the study of "negative feedback" processes to promote equilibrium and resist deviations from stable situations. "The second cybernetics is the study of 'positive feedback' processes which amplify deviations, causing systems to expand and eventually reach stability at higher levels" (Flannery 1968; 1972:223). The secondary benefits to be derived from opening the Illinois woodlands to cultivation could initially have provided just such a positive-feedback effect needed to assist the shift to upland food production from mud-flat horticulture. Farnsworth sees continued population increase through middle Woodland times in the Illinois Valley as the "initial kick" that could have started the shift away from dependency upon river and lake resources (1973:28). I see the initial consequences of opening the woodlands in the manner described above as one of the positive-feedback mechanisms Farnsworth then suggests would be needed to reinforce the direction of this change ". . . until a new level of cultural integration based on agricultural production is reached" (1973:28).

The agricultural methods American pioneers in Illinois used to initiate their holdings in the woodlands were essentially based upon those used in Ohio, Kentucky, and other states of their origin, and ultimately largely upon the methods and crops of the Indians. An important difference was that the long-range objective of the white man was to clear the land for permanent fields and pastures. This entailed the removal of the trees and roots that would obstruct plows. The first plantings might be done with a digging stick between girdled trees, but in time the methods changed toward more intensive forms of cultivation and other tools. Land was cheap but homesteads were circumscribed by the holdings of others. The hardwood trees killed by girdling could be left to decay.

In that part of the country where the oak — mostly white oak — prevailed, the land was all cleared by the process of "deadening": that is, the small stuff was grubbed out by the roots; that too large to grub, and less than a foot in diameter, was cut down and burned on the spot; and the larger trees were girdled by chopping them round with an axe, cutting through the bark and sap-wood (which killed them so that they put forth no leaves, or if in leaf, withered), and left standing. . . . From that time forward there was a constant dropping from the deadened trees, first of leaves, twigs and bark, then of the larger limbs, and lastly the trunk, which would fall in any way the wind or its weight threw it (Howells 1963:115–116).

These dead trees would not all disappear from a field in less than fifteen or twenty years. Our place had been cleared about ten or twelve years, and the dead trees were just in the condition to cover the fields each winter most plentifully. . . . It was a common thing for the fire to get into the dead trees in the spring time where it would burn for several days and nights together. . . . The dry, half-rotten bark and sap-wood of the old trees was like tinder, and if a spark lodged in them it would set the tree in a blaze which would creep up to the top and along the branches, and the wind would blow it to other trees, the fences, forests and everywhere (Howells 1963:116–117).

Arthur C. Parker says for the Iroquois that fields with standing dead trees were not regarded as safe after the first year and that efforts were made to burn the trees down. "In the Seneca invocations to the Creator at the midwinter thanksgiving is a prayer that the dead branches may not fall upon the children in the fields" (Parker 1910:21–22).

The system of slash-and-burn cultivation that could have been initially practiced with the least effort in Illinois is that called "forest-fallow" in Ester Boserup's classification of systems of land use (1965:15). Forest-fallowing requires the making of clearings in the forest, which are actually planted for a year or two and then allowed to return to forest. Boserup's classification is based upon the length of time a field is cultivated within any base period chosen. Forest-fallowing may see two years of sowing and planting and twenty or twenty-five years of abandonment. "Bush-fallowing" sees anywhere from one or two to eight years of annual cropping followed by six to eight years of fallowing. In bush-fallowing the fields return to brush and small trees but not to forest. "Slash-and-burn" agriculture subsumes both forest-fallowing and bush-fallowing. In "short-fallow" cultivation only grasses have time to invade the field in a fallow period of a year or two. "Annual cropping" and "multiple crop-ping" are almost self-explanatory.

The classification progresses from the least intensive form of cultiva-tion, forest-fallowing, to the most intensive, multicropping, in which the same field is made to produce several crops in a single year. Forest-fallowing is the system most efficient from the point of view of per capita effort and the most logical to expect when the forest resources are available. Boserup shows that tribes practicing forest-fallowing resist shifting to more labor-intensive systems so long as forest is available (1965:31, 44–48). The shift to more intensive systems is usually forced upon them under natural conditions by competition for suitable forest or, more recently, by government restrictions. Warfare is an alternative at this as at other times when a choice must be made and when there is nowhere to migrate.

The same squeeze in available arable land that led to the development of more intensive farming in certain areas of the world, gave rise to another important cultural phenomenon as well: competition between one tribe and another over land. In areas like the Amazon basin, where cultivable land is abundant and population relatively sparse, competition over land is not well marked. But in the areas of the world that begin to experience a shortage of agricultural resources, desire for land emerges as a predominant cause of war (Carneiro 1961:60).

Fortified living sites must be a response to pressures that are compel-ling because they require a great original investment in labor, mainten-ance, and renewal, and usually a more intensive system of cultivation. In Illinois they are identified with the emergence of middle Mississippi cultures and with a return to the major river valleys. The Mississippian emergence proceeded faster in some areas than in others. Near the great Cahokia site west of Collinsville the period of heaviest occupation was the so-called Fairmount phase of A.D. 900–1050. At this time most other parts of Illinois were still at a late-Woodland stage of development. There is no confusing of defensive walls with ceremonial enclosures in the Mississippi period because the walls were constructed with projecting towers or "bastions." Placed at short intervals along the wall, bastions gave a tactical advantage to defenders attacking parties scaling the walls. The central part of the Cahokia site, that part including the great Monks Mound, was enclosed by a sequence of bastioned palisades beginning around A.D. 1100 (Anderson 1969). It is assumed that other bastioned walls formed a perimeter defense, but in a site almost six square miles in extent and occupied for centuries it is difficult to define boundaries of occupational areas by excavation. Smaller sites, like the Kincaid site near the Ohio River and the Aztalan site in Wisconsin, have defensive walls that can be distinguished even without excavation.

Lewis H. Larson (1972) has drawn together some key points relating to fortified villages in the southeast. He notes that there is a high correlation between the location of Mississippian sites and the occurrences of sandy and silt loam soils, and that these are the only soil areas

... that can be intensively and extensively cultivated in the Southeast with hoe techniques. Further, these are areas of soil which, because they occur proximate to rivers, have moisture, a critical consideration in view of the very localized and low southeastern rainfall during the important plant growth period in July. These are also areas that, again because they are adjacent to rivers, are subject to periodic overflow with the resultant renewing of soil fertility (Larson 1972).

Especially pertinent is the point that the lighter soils needed for hoe cultivation were severely restricted in quantity and location. The soil type on which the great Etowah site was located in Georgia made up only 2,496 acres or eight-tenths of 1 percent of the total surface soils of the entire county. Larson suggests that the objective of warfare in the southeast was strategic, involving the destruction of towns controlling valuable bottomlands and the dispossessing of the inhabitants of their territory by death or dispersal. He sees evidence of expanding populations in the rebuilding and expanding of town walls. I will add to Larson's line of reasoning the suggestion that the failure of this pattern of defense to continue into the time of Marquette and Jolliet's expedition (1673) or into the period of the later French observers like Le Page Du Pratz was because of the release of this demographic pressure on severely circum-scribed resources.

The heavily defended southeastern towns seen by Hernando DeSoto's party in A.D. 1540–1542, often surrounded by moats and very numerous, were only memories by Marquette's time. The depopulation was prob-ably accomplished by diseases introduced by Europeans, although the Indians accounted for the disaster in their own way. History records the following story of the event told to Le Page Du Pratz by the Great Sun of the Natchez tribe:

Our nation was formerly very numerous and very powerful; it extended more than twelve days' journey from east to west, and more than fifteen from south to north. We reckoned then 500 Suns, and you may judge by that what was the number of the nobles, of the people of rank, and the common people.

Now in times past it happened, that one of the two guardians, who were upon duty in the temple, left it on some business, and the other fell asleep, and suffered the fire to go out. When he awakened and saw that he had incurred the penalty of death, he went and got some profane fire, as tho' he had been going to light his pipe, and with that he renewed the eternal fire. His transgression was by that means concealed; but a dreadful mortality immediately ensued, and raged for four years, during which many Suns and an infinite number of the people died.

The guardian at length sickened, and found himself dying, upon which he sent for the Great Sun, and confessed the heinous crime he had been guilty of. The old men were immediately assembled, and by their advice, fire being snatched from the other temple, and brought into this, the mortality quickly ceased (Le Page Du Pratz 1972:316).

European disease cannot account for the depopulation of the Cahokia site. The climactic period of Cahokia development for community structures, though not apparently of population, was possibly in the Moorehead phase, A.D. 1150 to 1250, and the site as a whole was in decline through the following three centuries and abandoned about A.D. 1500 at the end of the Sand Prairie phase (see Fowler and Hall 1972 for Cahokia phases). Both the Mississippian emergence in Illinois and the rise of the Cahokia site in importance coincide with the neo-Atlantic climatic episode after A.D. 900, a time when increased summer rainfall in the Great Plains saw the westward extension of corn farming (Baerreis and Bryson 1965a; Bryson and Wendland 1967). Exactly what the rainfall pattern was like in the Cahokia area is not known.

It could be argued that the increasing warmth of the period permitted a longer frost-free growing season and this, a more successful agriculture, and this, sedentary life and complex society. I have argued that a cooler, moist climate at the beginning of the late Woodland period could also have led to a more successful agriculture in Illinois but then subsequently to a *decline* from complex society. Part of the argument hinges on what the climate was really like in the early late Woodland period, since there is disagreement. Another important part of my argument depends upon the assumption that there was indeed extensive corn or at least cucurbit cultivation in Illinois at the time, and there is no evidence for corn at all. There is uncontested evidence of cucurbit cultivation. A test of my position might be found in the examination of the neoboreal of about A.D. 1550 to 1880 (Baerreis and Bryson 1965b).

Also called Little Ice Age, the neoboreal is well documented from historical records in Europe (cf. Ladurie 1971). The colder, wetter summers of this period have been seen as possibly contributing to the decline of prehistoric agriculture in the Midwest on the eve of European contact (Baerreis and Bryson 1965a; Bryson and Wendland 1967:296). Certainly Cahokia is abandoned after A.D. 1550, as were all middle Mississippi temple towns of the Illinois Valley and possibly elsewhere in Illinois except in the extreme south. Kincaid at the extreme southern tip of the state may have retained something of a major community organization into the seventeenth century. By this time the dominant corn in Illinois is northern flint, however, a corn adapted to shorter growing seasons and to germination in cold, moist soil. Northern flint or the eight-row eastern complex corn appears at Cahokia well before the neoboreal, starting at least by A.D. 1200. It would be contrary to expectations if agriculture deteriorated with the onset of a climate to which this corn had a superior adaptation. As I see it, agriculture during the neoboreal could have become more efficient of labor and extended over a broader land base. This would contrast with middle Mississippi agriculture, which was more intensive, requiring a shorter fallow cycle.

In the area of Rock Island, Illinois, around A.D. 1820 an estimated 5,000 Sauk and Fox Indians were producing annually 7,000 to 8,000 bushels of corn in addition to pumpkins, beans, and melons on "upwards of 300" acres of land under cultivation (Blair 1911–1912: vol. 2, pp. 148–151). Judging by the corn being raised in the same area by the Sauk in the period of A.D. 1790–1810, these fields must have been planted predominantly with eastern complex corn — 86 percent eight-rowed and 12 percent ten-rowed (Cutler and Blake 1973:17). In addition to these cultivated vegetable foods, the Sauk and the Fox drew from a tremendous larder of animal foods exploited during their summer and winter hunts for food and furs. To judge from the number of skins and furs provided by the Sauk and the Fox to traders during the season, including the winter, of 1819–1820, the Sauk and the Fox had available for consumption, if they actually chose to consume it all, some 3,240,140 pounds of edible meat plus 286,800 pounds of deer tallow, bird meat represented by a ton and a half of feathers, and honey represented by a half-ton of beeswax. An annual kill of this magnitude, including 28,680 deer, 13,440 raccoons, and 12,900 muskrats, would not have been maintained except for the incentive of the fur trade. Even so, the agricultural produce alone suggests an economy technologically adequate for subsistence needs with sufficient surplus to permit about a thousand bushels of corn to be sold annually to traders and others (Blair 1911–1912: vol. 2, p. 151). More archaeological corn (1,300 cobs) was recovered from a single Rock Island County Sauk village of the time A.D. 1790–1810 than has been found in all other archaeological excavations of all periods in the entire state of Illinois, including the Cahokia site (587 cobs for Cahokia; Cutler and Blake 1973:17–27). It is difficult under these circumstances to think of the subsistence adaptation of Illinois Indians in the historic period as representing a step backward from what it had been during the Mississippian climax. Indian agriculture of the historic period might more properly be considered the adaptation upon which a *third*, post-Mississippian aboriginal climax would have soon been built in Illinois and the Mississippi Valley, just as the late Woodland adaptation of the period of the post-Hopewellian decline provided the background from which the Mississippian pattern emerged.

Taking a clue from Larson's analysis of southeastern U.S. site distributions, I would guess that the bottomland locations that Mississippians preferred were also important partly because of their higher water tables. In the southeast the sandier, siltier soils were scarce and located mainly in alluvial valleys, where they were also well-watered and renewed by flooding. In Illinois the lighter soils were widespread because they included loess-covered uplands in addition to sandy and silty ridges in the bottoms, an important point. Perhaps a special attraction of the American Bottom and a clue to Cahokia's importance was its control of one of the largest expanses of better watered, less droughty bottomland in the upper Mississippi Valley. Any unfavorably dry summer rain pattern after A.D. 900 would have made agriculture unreliable on the well-drained loess hills and bluffs in Illinois and accentuated a competition for land that must have grown through the late Woodland period. This would partly account for the increasing need for fortifications.

The so-called Bluff Woodland Indians found the American Bottoms increasingly attractive after A.D. 900. They formed a recognizable group at Cahokia through the Fairmount phase (A.D. 900–1050) until they lost their taxonomic identity as "Woodland" and came to be called "Mississippian." There is disagreement over whether the first Mississippians at Cahokia appeared from farther south as fully developed Mississippians or merely became Mississippians by acculturation. There is more general agreement that around A.D. 1050 some Cahokia Mississippians moved into the Illinois Valley and established the Spoon River variant of the Cahokian Mississippian tradition. This movement is generally attributed to population pressure, and I would agree. I differ in seeing the population pressure as arising from the growing need for scarce bottomland for agriculture, perhaps because of drier conditions, or perhaps because of the protein resources of floodplain lakes if hunting was becoming less productive and more competitive. The latter situation would have provided some of the "positive feedback" needed to strengthen the switch to intensive cultivation and establish the middle Mississippi pattern of adaptation (see discussion above of the "second cybernetics"). I see population not only increasing during Mississippian times but also being compressed. As the resource base became restricted, as populations became circumscribed in aggregates within the valley bottoms, social structure also adapted along lines suggested by Carneiro.

I have presented a picture so far that can be dismissed as largely conjectural. What I have been doing is to examine the assumptions behind some archaeological interpretations to date and to try to show how some alternative assumptions can account equally well or even better for events in prehistory. I am using essentially the same field data. I am trying to make a more meaningful interpretation. If I am right my model should make equal sense or at least suggest fresh lines of inquiry.

Consider the role of demographic stress in providing a milieu in which state organization can arise.

The Pacific climatic episode that began A.D. 1160–1200 was believed to have been especially droughty in the central Plains, with the Prairie Peninsula extending even farther east from Cahokia and southern Wisconsin and making cultivation more difficult (Baerreis and Bryson 1965a; Bryson *et al.* 1970). In the Plains area, Indian agriculturalists in Nebraska and Iowa were forced to move or readapt because of insufficient summer rain, while the agricultural potential of the Texas and Oklahoma panhandle region benefited from newly increased summer rainfall. The demonstration of these climatic and social effects has been pursued by David A. Baerreis and Reid A. Bryson and their colleagues in a series of projects and papers over most of a decade (Baerreis and Bryson 1965a, 1965b, 1966; Bryson and Wendland 1967; Henning, editor, 1968, 1969; Bryson *et al.* 1970). The Cahokia site is located on one of the largest expanses of watered alluvial bottomland in the northern Mississippi Valley. In a period of dramatically warmer and drier summer weather in Illinois one might expect that the Cahokia area and similar oases like the Illinois Valley would be under special pressure. Summer rainfall in southern Illinois had probably diminished to between 25 and 50 percent below normal (Bryson *et al.* 1970: Figure 8). It is probably no coincidence that the climactic Moorehead phase at Cahokia had been assigned to the years A.D. 1150–1250.

During the Moorehead phase, Cahokia became the center of an intensified network of interaction extending from western Iowa eastward to the Wabash and north to Wisconsin and Minnesota. This must in part have been ceremonial, perhaps along lines of the later calumet dance recorded by Marquette for the Peoria and serving to stabilize tense intertribal relations in a time of stress. Like the calumet ritual, however, it was probably also economic. The Cahokia interaction is largely confined to the Prairie Peninsula, the specific area of stress, and actually began during the Cahokia Fairmount phase (A.D. 900–1050).

Watered bottomland must have become a prize elsewhere in the Prairie Peninsula in Illinois as well. While the Eveland site, the type site of the Eveland phase (A.D. 1050–1200), was a village located at the base of a bluff, the Larson site, type site of the Larson phase (A.D. 1200–1300) was fortified on a nearby bluff. Lawrence A. Conrad and Alan D. Harn (1972) feel that the Larson phase was a climactic phase of the Spoon River tradition in the Illinois Valley. It was followed by the Dickson phase of A.D. 1300–1350 with smaller populations (population aggregates?) and a trait list described as largely "negative," relative to the Larson phase, for example.

The period of climax in the Spoon River tradition corresponds fairly well with the period of climax at Cahokia. The periods of decline correspond as well, and both these cultural events correspond with the onset (A.D. 1160–1200) of the Pacific episode (A.D. 1200–1500) and the partial return to more humid conditions around A.D. 1450. In the Illinois Valley the Crable phase of A.D. 1350 to about A.D. 1450 marks both the appearance of intensive contact between Indians of the Spoon River tradition and those of the Oneota tradition to the north and west and the end of the Spoon River tradition. It is not clear from the archaeological record whether the inhabitants of the Crable site simply fell victim to expanding populations of newcomers operating from the base, perhaps, of a superior adaptation, or whether the carriers of the Spoon River tradition merely found it possible and desirable sometime in the early fifteenth century to emerge from behind their walls as the relative advantage of their locations for agriculture and fishing diminished. It is hard to look at the ridge-top location and tightly clustered houses of the Crable site and not see it as a fortified town. Nevertheless, when the Illinois Valley first appears on the pages of written history, the pattern of temples, plazas, and dwellings walled for defense on a height overlooking a floodplain lake has vanished. When the lily banner of Louis XIV first casts its shadow over the destiny of the Indian inhabitants of Illinois, the valley of this name was occupied by tribes of the Illinois Confederacy. Writing on the depopulation of the Illinois Indians, Emily J. Blasingham tells us that the Illinois never adapted a pattern of tightly nucleated villages built for defense:

It should . . . be noted that throughout the 17th and 18th centuries the Illinois persisted in their old village pattern of widely spaced houses, and never constructed compact, fortified villages. When danger threatened they relied on fortifications erected by the French, taking refuge in French forts and abandoning their homes, fields, and all their personal possessions to the raiders. We know that this occurred at least twice, at two widely spaced intervals, in 1684 and in 1752 (1956:395).

The village of the Illinois at Starved Rock before 1680 consisted of mat-covered lodges scattered through almost two square miles of bottomland along about 2.7 miles of the Illinois River (Brown 1961:11). An occupation of this character and houses of this type can be the despair of archaeologists to excavate and interpret. Six or more villages of the Illinois existed for several decades of the seventeenth and eighteenth centuries on or near Lake Peoria, yet none has been either located or excavated, much less identified. Does a situation such as this account for the cultural hiatus in the Spoon River local sequence for the ten generations preceding the arrival of the French? If so, were the Illinois the descendents of the Spoon River people, as some would say (Wray and Smith 1943, 1944)? Or, were the Illinois part of the reason for the disappearance of temple towns from the Illinois Valley?

Or, did the Illinois merely fill a power vacuum left by the departure of others?

The period of climatic and demographic stress in the Cahokia area and the Illinois Valley also corresponds with the time when eight-row eastern complex corn seems to appear more commonly among the older late Woodland corn varieties at Cahokia and when beans begin to appear in the archaeological records (Chmurny 1973:135). Hugh Cutler and Leonard Blake (1969a) have noted that adverse growing conditions can produce smaller plants and that these plants may have an increased number of eight-rowed ears. They continue:

Eight-rowed ears were not abundant until very late periods of Cahokia. Corn from a cache on the south terrace of Monks Mound . . . is nearly identical to the Northern Flint corn grown in historic times by the Fox Indians at Tama, Iowa. The cobs are as large as those of modern corn and are the extremes for Cahokia, although occasional cobs from other locations reach this size. The cache apparently is a selected lot. In general, Cahokia corn is more conservative and more southern in its characters than corn from other sites in the region (Cutler and Blake 1969a:134).

The failure to find more corn with northern flint characteristics at Cahokia must be partly correlated with the falling-off of the occupation itself. Considering the great number of radiocarbon dates at Cahokia for the period of A.D. 1000 to 1200, for example, there are precious few radiocarbon dates even in the 1300's (Hall 1966), and even some of the later ones that do exist are anomalously late because of isotopic fractionation and belong more than two centuries earlier (Hall 1967a; 1967b; Bender 1968). The appearance of some of the eight-rowed corn at Cahokia must originate from the growth processes Cutler and Blake describe, which would be accentuated during a time of climatic stress.

Some eight-row corn may also be there in part because it has an adaptation which would give it an advantage over the older tropical flint or Basketmaker corn. The same adaptation that made the northern flint race suitable to northern latitudes had incidentally made it more resistant to dry weather. Through the late Woodland period, selection had been toward early maturing characteristics in the far northeast. This produced a short plant that spent little energy on vegetative growth before flowering. It is precisely this characteristic that is sometimes even artificially induced in some corn today to adapt it to conditions of deficient summer rainfall and sandy soil in South Carolina and neighboring states. Such corn has a lower total leaf area and loses less moisture through transpiration (Jenkins 1941:312–314).

I think it could be significant that the Cahokia climax, which peaked with the onset of a time of hydraulic stress, does not appear to have continued long into the Sand Prairie phase (A.D. 1250–1500). Some

Cahokians may have simply moved elsewhere. Early in the phase the Kincaid site was established in southern Illinois on the Ohio River, where summer rainfall patterns may have been less affected by the onset of the Pacific episode, as they may also have been in the lower Wabash Valley, southern Indiana, and other places (Bryson *et al.* 1970: Figure 8, for rainfall pattern). What I think is more significant is that with a return to more humid conditions beginning around A.D. 1450 and definitely after A.D. 1550 there was no return to climax. The climax seems to be associated with stress. With corn increasingly better adapted both to hot, dry summers and to short, cool, moist summers, there was less premium on moist bottomland or locations with mild climates, and with beans available there would have been less need for floodplain-lake protein resources. About A.D. 1300 the Oneota culture began to spread southward and westward across the Prairie Peninsula from a Minnesota–Wisconsin lake-and-river habitat and also south into Illinois. Late in the Sand Prairie phase at Cahokia, a ceremonial plaza has reverted to residential use. By the end of the phase Cahokia is abandoned except possibly for an occasional Oneota camp.

As Cutler and Blake tell us, corn cannot be rapidly moved from low latitudes to high latitudes because of the nature of its photoperiodic adaptation (Cutler and Blake 1969a:135). It can, nevertheless, be moved rapidly east or west along the same latitude and also easily from north to south. This may someday help to explain the rapid spread of Oneota culture after A.D. 1300. The common association of beans with eight-row corn when it becomes popular in the prairie states suggests to me that these crops were moving as a complex and probably from the north and east as Munson suggests (1973).

Meanwhile, the records of history were neglectful of the Cahokia site. One of the few early written descriptions of Cahokia comes from the field book of a deputy surveyor named Messinger adjusting the township boundary line that today serves in part as the Madison–St. Clair county line. Working from the "caving banks" of the Mississippi River opposite St. Louis, Messinger arrived on January 9th, 1808, at a section corner close to where State Route 111 and U.S. Route 40 now cross. He first notes "two large Mounds Bearing N.E. in the Edge of a large Prairie." One of these can only be the large Powell Mound at the western limit of the Cahokia site. He then goes on to describe:

Twenty four or more of those mounds in Sight at one View — one whose Base is nearly 6 Acres by estimation — & 100 Feet in Height — Others of Various sizes from 6, to forty feet in height, & Various form — some round, some oblong or Rect. angled Parallelograms and others irregular — *All Covered with Simtoms of ancient Ruins* — Soil first Rate (Messinger 1808; emphasis added).

Whatever the circumstances that had induced Cahokians to invest the effort to maintain a ceremonial center covering six square miles, they had passed. The occupation of the Cahokia area had dropped after A.D. 1500 to a level it had not seen since the Patrick phase of about A.D. 600 to 800. I see the decline of the large Mississippian temple towns in the American Bottom and Illinois Valley through the 1400's as due in great part to processes similar to those which I see operating during the much earlier Hopewellian decline. New subsistence adaptations perhaps combined with or permitted by altered environmental factors again balanced out the special advantages of certain favored but areally limited floodplain locations for habitation. Populations again dispersed into smaller aggregates with weaker internal controls, less external pressure to maintain strong central authority, fewer economic reasons for exchange networks, and fewer sociopolitical needs for ceremonial interaction through the Cahokia hinterland.

Cahokia may have become the seat of the most powerful political body north of Mexico. The scores of human sacrifices in mass graves excavated at Cahokia by Melvin L. Fowler and his associates imply powerful central authority. The monumental construction indicates the temporal power or spiritual influence to command labor and resources. The circumstances that saw the rise and climax of Cahokia then apparently passed. A few centuries later the canoe carrying Jolliet and Marquette glided almost within sight of Cahokia's greatest temple. They saw no Indian.

REFERENCES

ANDERSON, JAMES P.
  1969 "A Cahokia palisade sequence," in *Explorations into Cahokia archaeology*. Edited by Melvin L. Fowler, 89–99. Illinois Archaeological Survey Bulletin 7. Urbana: University of Illinois.
ASCH, NANCY B., R. I. FORD, D. L. ASCH
  1972 *Paleoethnobotany of the Koster site: the Archaic horizons*. Illinois State Museum Reports of Investigations 24. Springfield, Ill.
BAERREIS, DAVID A., REID A. BRYSON
  1965a Climatic episodes and the dating of the Mississippian cultures. *Wisconsin Archeologist* 46 (4):203–220.
  1965b Historical climatology and the southern Plains: a preliminary statement. *Bulletin of the Oklahoma Anthropological Society* 13:69–75.
  1966 Dating the Panhandle Aspect cultures. *Bulletin of the Oklahoma Anthropological Society* 14:105–115.
BASTIAN, TYLER
  1958 The Beloit College mound group (Ro 15) — a preliminary report. *Wisconsin Archeologist* 39 (3):155–173.
BENDER, MARGARET M.
  1968 Mass spectrometric studies of carbon-13 variations in corn and other grasses. *Radiocarbon* 10 (2):468–472.

BILLINGTON, RAY A.
1967 "The American frontier," in *Beyond the frontier*. Edited by Paul Bohannan and Fred Plog, 3–24. Garden City, N.Y.: Natural History Press.

BLAIR, EMMA H.
1911–1912 *The Indian tribes of the upper Mississippi Valley and the region of the Great Lakes*, two volumes. Cleveland: Arthur Clark.

BLASINGHAM, EMILY J.
1956 The depopulation of the Illinois Indians. *Ethnohistory* 3 (3):193–224; 3 (4):361–412.

BOSERUP, ESTER
1965 *The conditions of agricultural growth: the economics of agrarian change under population pressure.* Chicago: Aldine.

BROWN, JAMES A.
1961 *The Zimmerman site.* Illinois State Museum Reports of Investigations 9. Springfield, Ill.
1965 "The Prairie Peninsula: an interaction area in the eastern United States." Unpublished Ph.D. dissertation, Department of Anthropology, University of Chicago.

BRYSON, REID A., DAVID A. BAERREIS, WAYNE M. WENDLAND
1970 "The character of late-glacial and post-glacial climatic changes," in *Pleistocene and recent environments of the central Great Plains.* Department of Geology, University of Kansas Special Publication 3. Manhattan, Kans.

BRYSON, REID A., W. M. WENDLAND
1967 "Tentative climatic pattern for some late glacial and postglacial episodes in central North America," in *Life, land and water: proceedings of the 1966 conference on environmental studies of the glacial Lake Agassiz region.* Edited by W. J. Mayer-Oakes, 271–298.

BURT, A. L.
1965 "If Turner had looked at Canada, Australia, and New Zealand when he wrote about the West," in *The frontier in perspective.* Edited by Walker D. Wyman and Clifton B. Kroeber, 59–78. Madison: University of Wisconsin Press.

CALDWELL, JOSEPH R.
1958 *Trend and tradition in the prehistory of the eastern United States.* American Anthropological Association Memoir 88.
1964 "Interaction spheres in prehistory," in *Hopewellian studies.* Edited by Joseph R. Caldwell and Robert L. Hall, 133–143. Illinois State Museum Scientific Papers, volume 12. Springfield, Ill.

CAPP, AL
1948 *Life and times of the shmoo.* New York: Simon and Schuster.

CARNEIRO, ROBERT L.
1961 "Slash-and-burn cultivation among the Kuikuru and its implications for cultural development in the Amazon Basin," in *The evolution of horticultural systems in native South America, causes and consequences.* Edited by J. Wilbert, 47–68. Caracas, Venezuela: Sociedad de Ciencias Naturales La Salle.
1970 A theory of the origin of the state. *Science* 169:733–738.

CARTER, GEORGE F., EDGAR ANDERSON
1945 A preliminary survey of maize in the southwestern United States. *Annals of the Missouri Botanical Garden* 32:297–322.

CHANG, JEN-HU
1968   *Climate and agriculture: an ecological survey.* Chicago: Aldine.
CHILDE, V. GORDON
1936   *Man makes himself.* London: Watts.
1942   *What happened in history.* Harmondsworth and New York: Penguin.
1951   *Social evolution.* London: Watts.
1958   *The prehistory of European society.* Harmondsworth: Penguin.
CHMURNY, WILLIAM W.
1973   "The ecology of the middle Mississippian occupation of the American Bottom." Unpublished Ph.D. dissertation, Department of Anthropology, University of Illinois.
CLELAND, CHARLES E.
1966   *The prehistoric animal ecology and ethnozoology of the upper Great Lakes region.* University of Michigan Museum of Anthropology Anthropological Papers 29. Ann Arbor, Mich.
CONRAD, LAWRENCE A., ALAN D. HARN
1972   "The Spoon River culture in the central Illinois River valley." Mimeographed.
CRANE, H. R., JAMES B. GRIFFIN
1961   University of Michigan radiocarbon dates VI. *Radiocarbon* 3:105–125.
1963   University of Michigan radiocarbon dates VIII. *Radiocarbon* 5:228–253.
1964   University of Michigan radiocarbon dates IX. *Radiocarbon* 6:1–24.
1966   University of Michigan radiocarbon dates XI. *Radiocarbon* 8:256–285.
1968   University of Michigan radiocarbon dates XII. *Radiocarbon* 10:61–114.
CUTLER, HUGH C.
1958   Corn cob from shelter, Van Buren County, Arkansas. *Missouri Archaeological Society Newsletter* 119:4.
1965   "Cultivated plants," in *The McGraw site: a study in Hopewellian dynamics.* Edited by Olaf H. Prufer, 107–112. Scientific Publications of the Cleveland Museum of Natural History, n.s. volume 4 (1).
CUTLER, HUGH C., LEONARD W. BLAKE
1969a "Corn from Cahokia sites," in *Explorations into Cahokia archaeology.* Edited by Melvin L. Fowler, 122–136. Illinois Archaeological Survey Bulletin 7. Urbana: University of Illinois.
1969b "Plant materials from the Jasper Neuman site, Ks-4, Moultrie County, Illinois," in "The Havana cultural tradition occupation in the upper Kaskaskia River valley, Illinois." By William M. Gardner, 228–237. Unpublished Ph.D. dissertation, Department of Anthropology, University of Illinois.
1973   *Plants from archeological sites east of the Rockies.* St. Louis: Missouri Botanical Garden.
CUTLER, HUGH C., THOMAS W. WHITAKER
1961   History and distribution of the cultivated cucurbits in the Americas. *American Antiquity* 26 (4):469–485.
DE GANNES, DELIETTE
1934   "Memoir of De Gannes concerning the Illinois country," in *The French foundations 1680–1693.* Edited by Theodore C. Pease and Raymond C. Werner, 302–395. Collections of the Illinois State Historical Library, volume 23. Springfield, Ill.

DIENER, PAUL
1968 "The demographic dilemma of food-producing 'revolutions': Hopewell." Paper presented at the Annual Meeting of the Central States Anthropological Society.

DUNBAR, JOHN B.
1880 The Pawnee Indians: their history and ethnology. *Magazine of American History* 4 (4): 241–281.

FAGERLUND, E., B. KLEMAN, L. SELLIN, H. SVENSSON
1970 Physical studies of nature by thermal mapping. *Lund Studies in Geography*, series A: *Physical Geography* 47:169–180.

FARNSWORTH, KENNETH B.
1973 *An archaeological survey of the Macoupin Valley.* Illinois State Museum Reports of Investigations 26. Springfield, Ill.

FEHRENBACHER, J. B., G. O. WALKER, H. L. WASCHER
1967 *Soils of Illinois.* University of Illinois College of Agriculture Agricultural Experiment Station Bulletin 725. Urbana, Ill.

FLANNERY, KENT V.
1968 "Archeological systems theory and early Mesoamerica," in *Anthropological archeology in the Americas.* Edited by Betty J. Meggers, 67–87. Washington, D.C.: Anthropological Society of Washington.
1972 "Archaeological systems theory and early Mesoamerica," in *Contemporary archaeology.* Edited by Mark P. Leone, 222–234. Carbondale: Southern Illinois University Press.

FORD, JAMES A., GORDON R. WILLEY
1941 An interpretation of the prehistory of the eastern United States. *American Anthropologist* 43 (3):325–363.

FOWLER, MELVIN L.
1969 "The Cahokia site," in *Explorations into Cahokia archaeology.* Edited by Melvin L. Fowler, 1–30. Illinois Archaeological Survey Bulletin 7. Urbana: University of Illinois.
1971a "The origin of plant cultivation in the central Mississippi Valley: a hypothesis," in *Prehistoric agriculture.* Edited by Stuart Struever, 122–128. Garden City, N.Y.: Natural History Press.
1971b "Agriculture and village settlement in the North American east: the central Mississippi Valley area, a case history," in *Prehistoric agriculture.* Edited by Stuart Struever, 391–403. Garden City, N.Y.: Natural History Press.

FOWLER, MELVIN L., ROBERT L. HALL
1972 *Archaeological phases at Cahokia.* Illinois State Museum Research Series, Papers in Anthropology 1. Springfield: Illinois State Museum.

FRANKLIN, T. BEDFORD
1955 *Climates in miniature: a study of microclimate and environment.* New York: Philosophical Library.

GALINAT, WALTON C.
1965 The evolution of corn and culture in North America. *Economic Botany* 19 (4):350–357.

GALINAT, W. C., J. H. GUNNERSON
1963 Spread of eight-rowed maize from the prehistoric southwest. *Botanical Museum Leaflets, Harvard University* 20 (5):117–160.

GARDNER, WILLIAM M.
1969 "The Havana cultural tradition occupation in the upper Kaskaskia

River valley, Illinois." Unpublished Ph.D. dissertation, Department of Anthropology, University of Illinois.

GIBSON, ROBERT O.
1973   "Monache Meadows and cold air drainage — a hypothesis." Paper presented at the Thirty-Eighth Annual Meeting of the Society for American Archaeology, San Francisco.

GILMORE, MELVIN R.
1931   Vegetal remains of the Ozark bluff-dwellers culture. *Papers of the Michigan Academy of Science, Arts, and Letters* 14:83–102.

GRIFFIN, JAMES B.
1949   "The Cahokia ceramic complexes," in *Proceedings of the Fifth Plains Conference for Archeology*. Assembled by John L. Champe, 44–58. Notebook 1, Laboratory of Anthropology, University of Nebraska.
1952   "Culture periods in eastern United States archeology," in *Archeology of the eastern United States*. Edited by James B. Griffin, 352–364. Chicago: University of Chicago Press.
1960   Climatic change: a contributory cause of the growth and decline of northern Hopewellian culture. *Wisconsin Archeologist* 41 (2):21–33.
1961   Some correlations of climatic and cultural change in eastern North American prehistory. *Annals of the New York Academy of Science* 95 (1):710–717.
1964   "The northeast woodland area," in *Prehistoric man in the New World*. Edited by Jesse D. Jennings and Edward Norbeck, 223–258. Chicago: University of Chicago Press.
1967   Eastern North American archaeology: a summary. *Science* 156 (3,772):175–191.

HALL, ROBERT L.
1966   "Cahokia chronology." Paper presented at the Annual Meeting of the Central States Anthropological Society, St. Louis.
1967a   "More about corn, Cahokia and carbon-14." Report prepared for the Cahokia Field Conference, Collinsville, Ill.
1967b   Those late corn dates: isotopic fractionation as a source of error in carbon-14 dates. *Michigan Archaeologist* 13 (4):171–180.
1973   "Mud-flat horticulture: a 'fossil' technology surviving among the 18th-century Natchez." Unpublished manuscript.

HEIZER, ROBERT F., M. A. WHIPPLE, *editors*
1971   *The California Indians*. Berkeley: University of California Press.

HENNING, DALE R., *editor*
1968   Climatic change and the Mill Creek culture of Iowa, Part I. *Journal of the Iowa Archeological Society* 15.
1969   Climatic change and the Mill Creek culture of Iowa, Part II. *Journal of the Iowa Archeological Society* 16.

HOWELLS, WILLIAM COOPER
1963   *Recollections of life in Ohio from 1813–1840* (a facsimile reproduction of a work originally published in 1895). Gainesville: Scholars' Facsimiles and Reprints.

HUNT, THOMAS F.
1904   *The cereals in America*. New York.

IMLAY, GILBERT
1797   *A topographical description of the western territory of North America*. London. (Reprinted in 1968 by Johnson Reprint Corp., N.Y.)

JENKINS, MERLE
  1941   "Influence of climate and weather on the growth of corn," in *Climate and man, yearbook of agriculture*, 308–320. U.S. Department of Agriculture. Washington, D.C.: U.S. Government Printing Office.
JENNINGS, JESSE D.
  1968   *Prehistory of North America.* New York: McGraw-Hill.
JONES, N. E.
  1898   *The squirrel hunters of Ohio, glimpses of pioneer life.* Cincinnati: Robert Clarke.
JONES, VOLNEY H.
  1936   "The vegetal remains of the Newt Kash Hollow shelter," in *Rock shelters in Menifee County, Kentucky.* Edited by W. S. Webb and W. D. Funkhouser, 147–167. University of Kentucky Reports in Anthropology and Archaeology 3 (4).
  1949   "Maize from the Davis site: its nature and interpretation," in *The George C. Davis site, Cherokee County, Texas.* By H. Perry Newell and Alex D. Krieger, 241–249. Memoirs of the Society for American Archaeology 5.
KATZ, S. H., M. L. HEDIGER, L. A. VALLEROY
  1973   "Anthropological and nutritional significance of traditional maize processing techniques in the New World." Paper prepared for the IXth International Congress of Anthropological and Ethnological Sciences, Chicago.
KROEBER, ALFRED L.
  1939   *Cultural and natural areas of native North America.* University of California Publications in American Archaeology and Ethnology 38. Berkeley.
LADURIE, EMMANUEL LE ROY
  1971   *Times of feast, times of famine.* Garden City, N.Y.: Doubleday. (Originally published in 1967 as *Histoire du climat depuis l'an mil.*)
LANNING, E. P.
  1967   *Peru before the Incas.* Englewood Cliffs, N.J.: Prentice-Hall.
LARSON, LEWIS H., JR.
  1972   Functional consideration of warfare in the southeast during the Mississippi period. *American Antiquity* 37 (3):383–392.
LE PAGE DU PRATZ, ANTOINE SIMON
  1758   *Histoire de la Louisiane*, three volumes. Paris.
  1972   *The history of Louisiana and of the western parts of Virginia and Carolina* (reprint based on the London edition of 1774). Baton Rouge: Claitor's Publishing Division.
LINTON, RALPH
  1924   The significance of certain traits in North American maize culture. *American Anthropologist*, n.s. 26:345–349.
MARTIN, PAUL S., GEORGE I. QUIMBY, JR., DONALD COLLIER
  1947   *Indians before Columbus.* Chicago: University of Chicago Press.
MARUYAMA, MAGOROH
  1963   The second cybernetics: deviation-amplifying mutual causal processes. *American Scientist* 51:164–179.
MESSINGER,–.
  1808   "Field notes for south edge of town 9 north, range 3 west of third principal meridian, dated Saturday, January 9th," in *Illinois land records, original field notes*, volume 12:76. Springfield: Illinois State Archives.

MORSE, DAN, PHYLLIS MORSE
  1960 A preliminary report on 9-Go-507, the Williams site, Gordon County, Georgia. *Florida Anthropologist* 13 (4):81–99.
MUNSON, PATRICK J.
  1963 "The origin and evolution of maize agriculture in the eastern United States." Unpublished manuscript.
  1973 "The origins and antiquity of maize–beans–squash agriculture in eastern North America: some linguistic implications," in *Variation in anthropology*. Edited by Donald W. Lathrap and Jody Douglas, 107–135. Urbana: Illinois Archaeological Survey.
MUNSON, PATRICK J., PAUL W. PARMALEE, RICHARD A. YARNELL
  1971 Subsistence ecology of Scovill, a terminal middle Woodland village. *American Antiquity* 36 (4):410–431.
MURPHY, JAMES L.
  1971 Maize from an Adena mound in Athens County, Ohio. *Science* 171:897–898.
PARKER, ARTHUR C.
  1910 *Iroquois uses of maize and other food plants.* New York State Museum Bulletin 144. Albany. (Reprinted in 1968 by Syracuse University Press in *Parker on the Iroquois*, edited with an introduction by William N. Fenton.)
PARMALEE, PAUL W., ANDREAS A. PALOUMPIS, NANCY WILSON
  1972 *Animals utilized by Woodland peoples occupying the Apple Creek site, Illinois.* Illinois State Museum Reports of Investigations 23. Springfield, Ill.
PEASE, THEODORE C., RAYMOND C. WERNER, *editors*
  1934 *The French foundations 1680–1693.* Collections of the Illinois State Historical Library 23. Springfield: Illinois State Historical Library.
PERINO, GREGORY
  1963 Tentative classification of two projectile points and one knife from west central Illinois. *Central States Archaeological Journal* 10 (3):99–100.
  1966 "Three late Woodland projectile point types from Illinois." Descriptions prepared for distribution at the Twenty-Fourth Plains Conference, Lincoln, Nebraska.
  1973 "The Koster mounds, Greene County, Illinois," in *Late Woodland site archaeology in Illinois I: investigations in south-central Illinois*. Edited by James A. Brown. Illinois Archaeological Survey Bulletin 9. Urbana, Ill.
PETERSON, WILLIAM
  1961 *Population.* New York: Macmillan.
PIETSCH, LYSLE R.
  1954 *White-tailed deer populations in Illinois.* Biological Notes 34. Urbana: Illinois Natural History Survey.
PRUFER, OLAF H.
  1961 "The Hopewell complex of Ohio." Unpublished Ph.D. dissertation, Anthropology Department, Harvard University.
  1964a The Hopewell cult. *Scientific American* 211 (6):90–102.
  1964b "The Hopewell complex of Ohio," in *Hopewellian studies*. Edited by Joseph R. Caldwell and Robert L. Hall, 35–83. Illinois State Museum Scientific Papers 12. Springfield.
  1965 *The McGraw site: a study in Hopewellian dynamics.* Scientific Publications of the Cleveland Museum of Natural History, n.s. 4(1). Cleveland.

RADIN, PAUL
1970   *The Winnebago tribe.* Lincoln: University of Nebraska Press.
REED, NELSON A.
1969   "Monks and other Mississippian mounds," in *Explorations into Cahokia archaeology.* Edited by Melvin L. Fowler, 31–42. Illinois Archaeological Survey Bulletin 7. Urbana: University of Illinois.
REED, NELSON A., JOHN W. BENNETT, JAMES W. PORTER
1968   Solid core drilling of Monks mound: technique and findings. *American Antiquity* 33 (2):137–148.
RITCHIE, WILLIAM A.
1932   *The Lamoka Lake site, the type station of the Archaic Algonkin period in New York.* Researches and Transactions of the New York State Archaeological Association, volume 7 (4). Rochester, N.Y.
1965   *The archaeology of New York State.* Garden City, N.Y.: Natural History Press.
RODOLF, THEODORE
1900   "Pioneering in the Wisconsin lead region," in *Wisconsin historical collections,* volume 15. Edited by Reuben G. Thwaites, 338–389. Madison: State Historical Society of Wisconsin.
RUSSELL, J. C.
1948   *British medieval population.* Albuquerque: University of New Mexico Press.
SEARS, WILLIAM H.
1964   "The southeastern United States," in *Prehistoric man in the New World.* Edited by Jesse D. Jennings and Edward Norbeck, 259–287. Chicago: University of Chicago Press.
1971   Food production and village life in prehistoric southeastern United States. *Archaeology* 24 (4):322–329.
STRUEVER, STUART
1962   Implications of vegetal remains from an Illinois Hopewell site. *American Antiquity* 27:584–587.
1964   "The Hopewell interaction sphere in riverine–western Great Lakes culture history," in *Hopewellian studies.* Edited by Joseph R. Caldwell and Robert L. Hall, 85–106. Illinois State Museum Scientific Papers 12. Springfield, Ill.
1968a   "A reexamination of Hopewell in eastern North America." Unpublished Ph. D. dissertation, Department of Anthropology, University of Chicago.
1968b   "Woodland subsistence-settlement systems in the lower Illinois valley," in *New perspectives in archeology.* Edited by Sally R. Binford and Lewis R. Binford, 285–312. Chicago: Aldine.
STRUEVER, STUART, KENT D. VICKERY
1973   The beginning of cultivation in the midwest–riverine area of the United States. *American Anthropologist* 75(5):1197–1220.
SWANTON, JOHN R.
1946   *The Indians of the southeastern United States.* U.S. Bureau of American Ethnology Bulletin 137. Washington, D.C.: U.S. Government Printing Office.
THWAITES, REUBEN G., *editor*
1896–1901 *The Jesuit relations and allied documents: travels and explorations of the Jesuit missionaries in New France, 1610–1791,* seventy-three volumes. Cleveland: Burrows Brothers.

TRANSEAU, EDGAR N.
1935   The prairie peninsula. *Ecology* 16:423–437.

TURNER, FREDERICK JACKSON
1893   "The significance of the frontier in American history," in *Report of the American Historical Association*, 199–227.
1896   The problem of the West. *Atlantic Monthly* 78:289–297.
1910   "Pioneer ideals and the state university." Commencement address at the University of Indiana. (Reprinted 1947 in *The frontier in American history*, by Frederick Jackson Turner, 269–289.
1947   *The frontier in American history.* New York: Holt, Rinehart and Winston.

TURNER, LEWIS M.
1931   "Ecological studies in the lower Illinois River valley." Unpublished Ph.D. dissertation, University of Chicago.

U.S. DEPARTMENT OF AGRICULTURE
1941   *Climate and man, yearbook of agriculture.* Washington, D.C.: U.S. Government Printing Office.

U.S. NAVAL OBSERVATORY
1970   *The nautical almanac for the year 1972.* Washington, D.C.: U.S. Government Printing Office.

UTTER, WILLIAM T.
1942   *The frontier state 1803–1825*, volume two of *The history of the state of Ohio.* Edited by Carl Wittke. Columbus: Ohio State Archaeological and Historical Society.

VICKERY, KENT D.
1970   Evidence supporting the theory of climatic change and the decline of Hopewell. *Wisconsin Archeologist* 51 (2):57–76.

WATSON, PATTY JO, RICHARD A. YARNELL
1966   Archaeological and paleoethnobotanical investigations in Salts Cave, Mammoth Cave National Park, Kentucky. *American Antiquity* 31 (6):842–849.

WEDEL, WALDO R.
1941   Environment and native subsistence economies in the central Great Plains. *Smithsonian Miscellaneous Collections* 101 (3):1–29. (Reprinted by the Bobbs-Merrill Company as A-233 of the reprint series in the social sciences.)

WILL, GEORGE F., GEORGE E. HYDE
1917   *Corn among the Indians of the upper Missouri.* Little histories of North American Indians 5. Cedar Rapids, Iowa: Torch Press.

WILLEY, GORDON R.
1966   *An introduction to American archaeology*, volume one: *North and Middle America.* Englewood Cliffs, N.J.: Prentice-Hall.

WILSON, GILBERT L.
1917   *Agriculture of the Hidatsa Indian: an Indian interpretation.* University of Minnesota Studies in the Social Sciences 9. Minneapolis.

WITTHOFT, JOHN
1949   *Green corn ceremonialism in the eastern woodlands.* Occasional Contributions from the Museum of Anthropology of the University of Michigan 13. Ann Arbor.

WITTRY, WARREN L., JOSEPH O. VOGEL
1962   "Illinois State Museum projects," in *First annual report: American Bottoms archaeology, July 1, 1961–June 30, 1962.* Edited by Melvin L. Fowler, 15–30. Urbana: Illinois Archaeological Survey.

WRAY, DONALD E., RICHARD S. MacNEISH
    1961   "The Hopewellian and Weaver occupations of the Weaver site, Fulton County, Illinois." Illinois State Museum Scientific Papers 7 (2). Springfield.
WRAY, DONALD, HALE SMITH
    1943   The Illinois Confederacy and middle Mississippian culture in Illinois. *Transactions of the Illinois Academy of Science* 36 (2):82–86.
    1944   An hypothesis for the identification of the Illinois Confederacy with the middle Mississippi culture in Illinois. *American Antiquity* 10 (1):23–27.
YARNELL, RICHARD A.
    1963a   Comments on Struever's discussion of an "Eastern Agricultural complex." *American Antiquity* 28 (4):547–548.
    1963b   Reciprocity in cultural ecology. *Economic Botany* 17 (4):333–336.
    1964   *Aboriginal relationships between culture and plant life in the upper Great Lakes region.* University of Michigan Museum of Anthropology Anthropological Papers 23. Ann Arbor.
    1969   "Contents of human paleofeces," in *Prehistory of Salts Cave.* By Patty Jo Watson, 41–54. Illinois State Museum Reports of Investigations 16. Springfield.
    1972   *Iva annua* var. *macrocarpa*: extinct American cultigen? *American Anthropologist* 74:335–340.
ZIEGLER, PHILIP
    1969   *The Black Death.* New York: John Day.

Biographical Notes

Z. A. ABRAMOVA. No biographical data available.

ROBERT E. ACKERMAN is Professor of Anthropology at Washington State University, Pullman. He received his Ph.D from the University of Pennsylvania in 1961. His areas of specialization are archaeology and ethnology of Arctic and sub-Arctic North America and Siberia.

J. M. ADOVASIO is Associate Professor and Director of the Archaeological Research Program at the University of Pittsburgh. He received his Ph.D from the University of Utah in 1970. His areas of specialization are prehistory, archaelogical theory and method and primitive technology, particularly in North America, Mesoamerica, and the Near East.

GEORGE J. ARMELAGOS is Professor of Anthropology at the University of Massachusetts, Amherst. He received his Ph.D from the University of Colorado in 1968. His areas of special interest are physical anthropology, sketal biology, and demography, particularly in the Mediterranean and Africa.

DAVID L. BROWMAN is Associate Professor of Anthropology at Washington University, St. Louis. He received his Ph.D from Harvard University in 1970. His major research interests are general New World prehistory, but particularly Andean archaeology and ethnohistory.

JANE E. BUIKSTRA is Associate Professor of Anthropology at Northwestern University, Evanston, Illinois. She received her Ph.D from the University of Chicago in 1972. Her areas of specialization are osteology, paleopathology, primate paleontology, and mortuary site archaeology.

GEORGE F. CARTER is Professor in the Department of Geography, Texas A. and M. University. He studied at the University of California, Berkeley. His major areas of interest are the antiquity of man in America, the origins of agriculture (particularly in the western hemisphere), and the evidence concerning pre-Columbian contacts with America by sea.

RICHARD W. CASTEEL is Associate Professor of Anthropology at Simon Fraser University, Burnaby, Canada. He received his Ph.D from the University of California, Davis in 1972. His areas of specialization are zooarchaeology and North American prehistory.

A. McFADYEN CLARK is Athapaskan ethnologist at the National Museum of Man (Canadian Ethnology Service), Ottawa. She received her M.A. from George Washington University in 1966. Her areas of specialization are ethnology and culture history of northern North America and among the northwestern Eskimos.

DONALD W. CLARK is a staff member of the Archaeological Survey of Canada. National Museum of Man, Ottawa. He received his Ph.D. from the University of Wisconsin in 1968. His areas of special interest are archaeology and ethnohistory of the Western Boreal Forest and Alaska.

DON W. DRAGOO studied at Indiana University and the University of New Mexico. He was until recently Curator of Anthropology at the Carnegie Museum of Natural History, Pittsburgh. He has worked extensively on the prehistory of North America and Old World prehistoric contacts. He has done fieldwork and research in the U.S., Canada, Arabia, Australia, Japan, and many other areas. He is the author of the book *Mounds for the dead* and numerous monographs and articles.

MARY F. ERICKSEN is a Lecturer at the George Washington University Medical Center. She received her Ph.D. from George Washington University in 1973. Her area of special interest is osteology.

MELVIN L. FOWLER is Professor of Anthropology at the University of Wisconsin, Milwaukee. He received his Ph.D. from the University of Chicago in 1959. His areas of specialization are cultural anthropology, archaeology, urbanization and social development, particularly in the Mississippi Valley and Mexico.

G. F. FRY is Associate Professor of Anthropology at Youngstown State University. He received his Ph.D. from the University of Utah in 1970. He is especially interested in physical anthropology, human evolution, paleopathology, primate ethology, archaeology, paleoecology, particularly of North America and the Mediterranean.

ROBERT L. HALL is Professor of Anthropology at the University of Illinois, Chicago Circle. He received his Ph.D. from the University of Wisconsin in 1960. His special interests are cognitive archaeology and chronological methods in the eastern United States.

WILLIAM M. HURLEY is Associate Professor of Anthropology at the University of Toronto. He received his Ph.D. from the University of Wisconsin in 1970. His areas of specialization are archaeology of North America, Japan, and Early Jomon; prehistoric cordage and fabrics, and archaeological method and theory.

DONALD L. JOHNSON is Associate Professor in the Department of Geography, University of Illinois, Urbana.

JOHN LALLO is Assistant Professor of Anthropology at both Youngstown State University and Cleveland State University. He received his Ph.D. from the University of Massachusetts in 1973. His special interests are in paleopathology, epidemology, cultural ecology, and urban anthropology, particularly in North America.

JU. A. MOCHANOV. No biographical data available.

DREXEL A. PETERSON JR. is Associate Professor of Anthropology at Memphis State University and Assistant Professor at the State University of New York, Albany. He received his Ph.D. from Harvard University in 1971. His areas of specialization are archaeology, anthropological theory, and physical anthropology, in North and South America.

BRUCE E. RAEMSCH. No biographical data available.

B. O. K. REEVES is Associate Professor of Archaeology at the University of Calgary, Canada. He received his Ph.D. from the University of Calgary in 1970. His areas of specialization are archaeology, geology, paleoenvironment, and the Quaternary, in the Plains and Western montane areas of North America.

JEROME CARL ROSE is Assistant Professor of Anthropology at the University of Arkansas, Fayetteville. He received his Ph.D. from the University of Massachusetts in 1973. His special interests are in physical anthropology, dental anthropology, osteology, and paleoepidemiology.

RUTH D. SIMPSON is County Archaeologist and Curator of Anthropology at the San Bernardino County Museum, California. Her areas of specialization are Pleistocene archaeology, lithic typology, and rock art, particularly in North America. Her publications include "The Calico Mountains archaeological project", "An archaeological survey of Troy Lake, San Bernardino County" and "Tule Springs, Nevada, with other evidences of Pleistocene Man in North America".

RONALD A. STAGG. No biographical data available.

WILLIAM W. VERNON. No biographical data available.

FREDERICK HADLEIGH WEST. No biographical data available.

Index of Names

Index of Subjects

Scovill site, 439
Seneca culture, 291, 443
Shellfish-oriented subsistence, and fiber-tempered pottery, 366–367, 368–369
Shoop site, 76
Short-fallow cultivation, 444
Site, as a term in archaeology, 391
Slash-and-burn cultivation, 419, 442, 443–444
Slave Indians, 315
Smithsonian Institution, Physical Anthropology Division of the National Museum of Natural History, 239n, 242
Spoon River tradition, and Cahokia, 449–450
Squash, cultivated for containers, 412–413
Starved Rock, Fort St. Louis, 416, 434–435, 450
Stutz Bluff shelter site, 74
Sumnaghi: culture, 128–129; site, 122
Sun, leader of the Natchez, 394, 402, 403, 445–446
Susquehanna River, 43–44, 46, 63
Swidden agriculture, 419, 442, 443–444
Synergistic effect of infectious disease and malnutrition, 204

Taber Child, 5
Taber site, 95
Tangle Lakes site, 166, 167
Temple town, as a term in archaeology, 393, 399
Temple town community, the: Cahokia and Amalucan compared, 391–400; culture climax and, 402–403; Mississippian, decline, 453
Tennessee Valley, fiber-tempered pottery in the, 364, 365, 366, 367
Teton Dakota Indians, 433
Time-specific life table, 214
Timlin site, 43–66; dating, 63–66; log interpretation of a core, 54; soil investigations, 47–53; tools, study of, 46–47, 62–66
Ting-ts'un site, 121, 127, 133–134
Tlingit culture, 189
Tobacco, wide use in eastern North America, 407–408
Totimehuacan site (Mexico), 397, 398
Trail Creek caves, 168
Tree-ring: chronology of climate, 105–106; dating techniques, 373
Trimmed cores, Asiatic-American contacts, 69–81; Australian parallels, 78, 79

Tuktu site, 164
Tula (Mexico) site, 43, 50–66
Tule Springs site, 72–73, 119
Twenty-Ninth Southeastern Archaeological Conference, 1972, 365
Two-climax model of Illinois prehistory, 401–462; and James Griffin, 404, 405

U.S.S.R. Academy of Sciences, Siberian Section, 122
Ulalinki site, 121
Upper Paleolithic, sites in Alaska, 170–171
Upper Pleistocene, migrations, 119–121, 129
Ust-Bilir II site, 123, 125
Ust-Dyuktai I site, 123, 124, 126
Ust-Kansk Cave, 121, 134
Ust-Mil II site, 122, 125, 126

Valsequillo area (Mexico), 72
Village, as a term in archaeology, 391–392
Vorontosovo transgression, 120, 121, 128

Washington State University, 189
Washington, University of, Computer Center, 301n
Weanling diarrhea, from the interaction of disease and malnutrition, 204
Weathered soil, Timlin site, chemical analysis, 48–49
Wells Creek site, 74, 75–76, 77
West Creek site. *See* Timlin site
Wild animals and food production, prehistoric and historic, 441–442
Will seed company, and Dakota White Flint, 428–429
Williamson site, 75
Wisconsin and pre-Wisconsin stone industries, 41–67
Wisconsin ceramics, coding and cluster analysis, 373–390
Wisconsin glacial period, 10, 28, 29, 31–32, 33; and migrations, 120, 121; ceramics, 373–390; stone industries, 41–67, 190
Wood ash, in the preparation of corn, 416–419
Woodhenge, 395

Yager Museum, 41n
Yakutia, first site of prehistoric man discovered, 122
Yermo Formation, 9, 10, 19